Explorer Crete

Christopher Somerville

Publishing

Front cover
Top: *Ayios Nikolaos harbour at sunset* (K Paterson); Centre (left to right): (a) *fresco, Ayia Paraskevi* (K Paterson); (b) *seafood platter* (K Paterson); (c) *geraniums* (P Enticknap); (d) *tending vines* (K Paterson); (e) *Falasarna beach* (P Enticknap);
Back cover
Left: *Mosque of the Janissaries* (P Enticknap); Right: *view across valley from Vathiepetro* (K Paterson)

All pictures from AA World Travel Library

Opposite: *Hrissoskalítissas Monastery*

Written by Christopher Somerville
Updated by Lindsay Bennett
Original photography by Ken Patterson

Reprinted 2008. All information verified and updated
First published 1995
Edited, designed and produced by AA Publishing
Maps © Automobile Association Developments Limited 1995, 1998, 2001

A CIP catalogue record for this book is available from the British Library.

ISBN: 978-0-7495-5565-8

Published by AA Publishing (a trading name of Automobile Association Developments Limited, whose registered office is Fanum House, Basing View, Basingstoke, Hampshire RG21 4EA. Registered number 1878835).

Titles in the Explorer series…
Australia • Boston & New England • Britain • Brittany
California • Canada • Caribbean • China • Costa Rica
Crete • Cuba • Cyprus • Egypt • Florence & Tuscany
Florida • France • Germany • Greek Islands • Hawaii
India • Ireland • Italy • Japan • London • Mallorca
Mexico • New York • New Zealand • Paris • Portugal
Provence • Rome • San Francisco • Scotland • South Africa
Spain • Thailand • Tunisia • Turkey • Venice • Vietnam

Find out more about AA Publishing and the wide range of services the AA provides by visiting our website at www.theAA.com/travel

A03259

How to use this book

ORGANISATION

Crete Is, Crete Was
Discusses aspects of life and culture in contemporary Crete and explores significant periods in its history

A to Z
Breaks down the island into regional chapters, and covers places to visit, including walks and drives. Within this section fall the Focus On articles, which consider a variety of subjects in greater detail

Travel Facts
Contains the strictly practical information that is vital for a successful trip

Hotels and Restaurants
Lists recommended establishments throughout Crete, giving a brief summary of their attractions

KEY TO ADMISSION CHARGES
Standard admission charges are categorised in this book as follows:
Inexpensive less than €3,
Moderate €3–€5
Expensive more than €5

ABOUT THE RATINGS
Most places described in this book have been given a separate rating. These are as follows:

▶▶▶ **Do not miss**

▶▶ **Highly recommended**

▶ **Worth seeing**

MAP REFERENCES
To help you locate a particular place on a map, every main entry in this book is given a map reference, such as 176B3. The first number (176) indicates the page on which the map can be found; the letter (B) and the second number (3) pinpoint the square of the map in which the main entry is located. The map on the inside front cover is referred to as IFC

SPELLINGS
So far as possible, placenames are spelt according to the BGN/PCGN Romanisation System for Greek, designed for English-language speakers, i.e., Knosós and Irakleío, for example, rather than Knossós and Heráclion

Contents

How to use this book 4

Contents pages 5–7

My Crete 8

CRETE IS 9–22
An island of contrasts 10–11
Evidence of history 12–13
Town life and country life 14–15
Festivals and celebration 16–17
Pride in independence 18–19
A tourist take-over? 20–21
Hospitality 22

CRETE WAS 23–41
Myth and legend 24–25
Pre-Minoans and Minoans 26–27
Minoan splendour 28–29
Civilisation and catastrophe 30–31
Greeks and Romans 32
Twice Byzantine 33
Under Venetian rule 34–35
Turkish, then Greek 36–37
World War II 38–39
Life before tourism 40–41

A–Z

Irakleío 42–71
Focus On
Cretan heroes 56–57
Taking your time 64

Walks
Irakleío's highlights 52–53
Around Irakleío's Venetian city walls 65

From Irakleío to the Mesará Plain 72–107
Focus On
Olives, sheep and goats 76–77
Drink 84–85
Wildlife 96–97
Driving in Crete 102–103
Walks
Ampeloúsos to Zarós 88
Kapetanianá to Mount Kófinas 106–107
Drive
The western Asteroúsia Mountains 100–1

Ágios Nikólaos and the Díkti Mountains 108–137
Focus On
The Díkti Mountains 120–121
Icons and frescoes 129
Tradition or tourism? 135
Walks
Ágios Nikólaos 114–115
Lasíthiou Plateau 125
Drive
Coast road from Tsoútsouros to Árvi 126–127

Siteía and the East 138–163
Focus on
Islands of eastern Crete 149
Traditional music and dance 160–161
Walks
Ierápetra 145
Siteía 151
Episkopí to Thryptí and back 152
Valley of the Dead 153
Drives
Thriptís, Ornó and Siteía Mountains 156–157
Gulf of Mirampéllou 162–163

Réthymno and the Ída Mountains 164–193
Focus on
Resistance 170
Cretan caves 176–177
The Ída Mountains 192–193
Walks
Kamáres Cave 174–175
Réthymno 184–185
Drive
The old road from Réthymno to Irakleío 186–187

Chaniá 194–215
Focus on
Chaniá's museums 206–207
Walks
Around Chaniá 200–201
Chaniá breakwater by night 208

The White Mountains and the West 216–254
Focus on
Islands of western Crete 224–225
Wild flowers 227
Battle of Crete evacuations 229
The White Mountains 236–237
Monasteries 246–247
Boats and ferries 254
Walks
Ímpros Gorge 231
Rodopoú Peninsula 245
Samariá Gorge 248–249

Drives

Sfakiá to Chaniá 240–241
West coast and mountains 252–253

TRAVEL FACTS 255–272

HOTELS AND RESTAURANTS 273–283

Index 284–287

Picture credits 288

Maps and plans

Crete and three-star sights IFC
Irakleío 42–43
From Irakleío to the Mesará Plain 72–73
Agía Triáda 80
Faistós 82
Gortýs 86
Ampeloúsos to Zarós walk 88
Knosós 90–91
Kapetanianá to Mount Kófinas walk 106
Ágios Nikólaos and the Díkti Mountains 108–109
Ágios Nikólaos 112
Lasíthiou Plateau walk 125
Mália Minoan Palace 132
Siteía and the East 138–139
Ierápetra 144
Siteía 150
Episkopí to Thrypti walk 152
Valley of the Dead walk 153
Zákros Minoan Palace 158
Réthymno and the Ída Mountains 164–165
Réthymno 182
Chaniá 194–195
The White Mountains and the West 216–217

Christopher Somerville has written 15 books, mostly on walking and on travel among small, isolated communities. He also writes regularly on these and on environmental issues for the *Daily Telegraph*, *The Sunday Times* and other publications. His fascination for peoples living on islands—especially those still maintaining their traditional language, work, music, hospitality and social life in the face of modern mass tourism—has naturally drawn him to the island of Crete.

My Crete

"Chreeestopher…*kali spera*, my dear!" cries Charis Kakoulakis, shouldering through the indescribable evening crush at Irakleío Airport and enfolding me in a bearhug. Charis has not seen me for at least a month: long enough for him to have worked up a heroic thirst and a fund of gossip. We inch down the honking, dusty road into Irakleío, and find that little *ouzeri* in the shady Venetian square that only Charis knows, where over thimblefuls of *raki* and a spread of 30 tiny dishes of this and that we can plan out my next few days in Crete, the most hospitable and delectable island under the Mediterranean sun.

Twenty-four hours later I am sitting under a tamarisk tree a hundred miles from Irakleío, watching the sun dip into the Libyan Sea. A shepherd gives me a grave salute as he passes on his homeward plod with his bell-clonking flock. As the crisp smell of grilling mullet drifts from the charcoal, I let my mind slip back over the day.

Breakfast of thick yoghurt and honey, eaten at a roadside table. An early morning walk along a cobbled pathway over a mountainside fragrant with wild herbs. Among the tumbled stones of a temple built long before the birth of Christ, the discovery of a delicate shard of Minoan pottery. A plunge in a turquoise-blue sea, and a laze on empty white sands secluded between two mighty headlands. Then a picnic high on a hilltop—a bag of olives, a hunk of goat's cheese, a chunk of nutty baked bread softened with water. A dog turned up for the cheese rind, followed by his owner, a black-clad old woman gathering firewood, delighted by my few words of Greek.

In the afternoon, another discovery along a rough dirt road—faded but still beautiful Byzantine frescoes, glowing in a church half-hidden in an olive grove. A scramble into the cool depths of a cave haunted by gods. Then the hitch-hiker, a local farmer who'd invited me in…just for one glass, eh?… and the wreck of plans for the rest of the day, drowned deep in delicious, wine-embalmed slumber under a sun-warmed stone wall where cicadas were shrilling.

The taverna keeper approaches, smiling: dinner is served. Along the beach a *bouzouki* and a *lyra* play, softly. If enough people turn up, there might be a dance. It must be Crete…

Christopher Somerville

Crete Is

An island of contrasts

Crete is not a large island, only 250km (155 miles) long and just 12km (7.5 miles) across at its narrowest. But within its shores there is an astonishing variety of landscape, activities and atmospheres of old and new worlds.

Contrasts The old and the new, the sophisticated and the simple, rub shoulders in Crete. The long-established harbour towns of Irakleío, Réthymno and Chaniá have Venetian houses and waterfronts of golden stone, but there are also areas of rowdy nightclubs where modern tourism comes abruptly into focus. There are popular, crowded beaches in the north, and secluded sandy coves on the more inaccessible coasts. You can stay in a bland and expensive luxury hotel, or take your chances in a rough-and-ready village taverna. Archaeological sites range from the world-famous and much-thronged Minoan palaces of Knosós, Faistós, Mália and Zákros to unfrequented classical Greek country houses and Roman temples that are quietly crumbling away on obscure hillsides.

People Cretan people, too, exhibit a mercurial mix of temperaments—both fiery and nonchalant, eager and laissez-faire, formal and impulsive. But one thing that you can always rely upon is their unfailing courtesy and their instant, unrestrained hospitality, a hospitality that the stranger is not expected to repay, only enjoy and appreciate.

❑ Make use of the EOT (Greek Tourist Organisation) offices in Irakleío, Réthymno and Chaniá, and municipal information offices in other towns. They have information on regular and special events and celebrations. ❑

Landscape Crete's landscape is marvellously varied, with four great mountain ranges. From west to east these are: Lefká Óri or the White Mountains in the far west, Psiloreítis or the Ída range south of Réthymno, the Díkti Mountains between Irakleío and Ágios Nikólaos and the Thryptís or Siteía range out to the east. These are limestone mountains, the end of a great chain that runs down from the Balkans. The bare peaks, pale grey in summer or white with snow in winter, dominate the island. Below the peaks, the rocks are sunbaked to brown, purple and orange. Remnants of once-extensive pine and cypress forests clothe the upper ranges; below are skirts of prickly scrub,

Beneath the dramatic Díkti Mountains lies the fertile Lasíthiou Plateau, famous for its windmills, now mostly inactive

Scented, flowering herbs, including Ebenus cretica, *clothe the mountain-sides of much of the island and are particularly fine in the Cretan spring*

giving off an entrancing scent in the hot Cretan sunshine.

Lowlands Below the mountains spread the richer and more lush lowlands, strongholds of the olive grove and vineyard, cornfield and vegetable plot, orchard and nut grove. Country roads undulate from one village and small town to the next, through a green landscape that is less visited by holidaymakers but has its own easy-going, soft atmosphere. Typical of these pleasant lowlands are the lovely Amári valley, which lies south of Réthymno, the fertile length of the Mesará plain in the south of the island, and the wide country behind Chaniá and Irakleío.

Coasts The lowlands dip to flat plains along the north coast, lush and damp in the far west, sandy of beach and rocky of headland further east. Between Irakleío and Ágios Nikólaos the shoreline is largely built up, but out to the east there are many lonely stretches of rocky coastline. The south coast is far less frequented than the north, and long stretches of it—such as rugged and empty Asteroúsia and the splendidly dramatic White Mountains, which rear abruptly out of the Libyan Sea—are roadless.

❑ As little as 40 years ago it was often extremely difficult to reach the mountain villages of central Crete. Most journeys had to be made either on mule-back or on foot. The road system has greatly improved since then, but journeys on many Cretan dirt roads are still a challenge, even to experienced drivers. ❑

❑ Astivítha has pride of place among the prickly scrub plants of the Cretan mountains. It is a low, cushion-shaped bush with hexagonally arranged spikes and deep red flowers...and when you brush against a clump of it, it releases a delicious, spicy smell. ❑

Climate No matter what type of climate you prefer, Crete can provide it. Because of the barrier created by the mountain ranges in the middle of the island, there may be beautiful sunshine on the south coast while rain is sweeping the north. From January to March there is snow in the mountains and generally wild weather. April and May are warm and fresh, with flowers everywhere. June is hot, July and August hotter still, with dust and uncomfortable winds always possible. From September to October the island slowly cools down and lovely clear days bring a second flowering of the Cretan flora, before the gales and snow begin once again in November.

Evidence of history

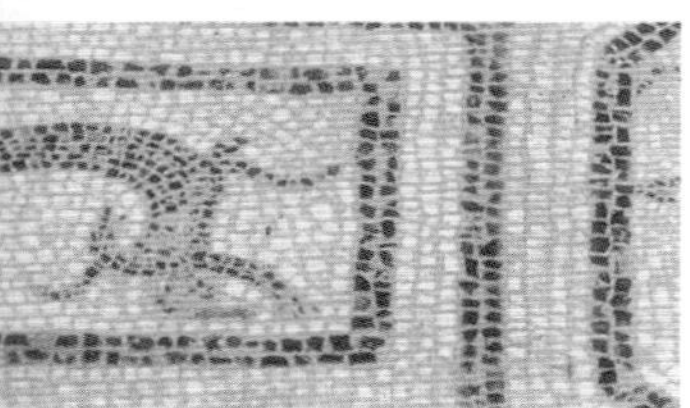

Crete's history is long, dramatic, bloody and heroic, and it has left its mark throughout the island. The world-famous sites attract the crowds, but elsewhere you may stumble across tiny painted churches, fragments of mosaics, 2,000-year-old houses, a Minoan jug handle under a stone, or a Roman column lying in a field.

Invaded island Situated as it is, at the crossroads of sea communications between Europe, North Africa and the Middle East, the island of Crete has always been a tempting plum, ripe for picking by invaders, colonisers and traders. Some have coveted the island for its natural riches of timber and fertile agricultural land; some have wanted to use it as a buffer between themselves and aggressors, others as a base for attacking enemies or as a departure-point for invasions. Crete's history is one of invasion, resistance, battle and bloodshed, interspersed with periods of calm and prosperity under a

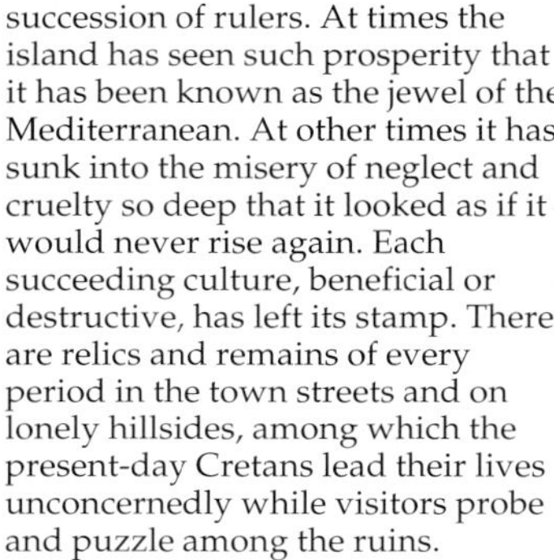

succession of rulers. At times the island has seen such prosperity that it has been known as the jewel of the Mediterranean. At other times it has sunk into the misery of neglect and cruelty so deep that it looked as if it would never rise again. Each succeeding culture, beneficial or destructive, has left its stamp. There are relics and remains of every period in the town streets and on lonely hillsides, among which the present-day Cretans lead their lives unconcernedly while visitors probe and puzzle among the ruins.

Relics of the rulers The great Minoan civilisation that rose and fell in Crete between 2600 and 1400 BC left palaces at Knosós, Faistós, Mália and Zákros, all of which are magnets for hundreds of thousands of visitors. Another is the hilltop town at Gourniá, but there are hundreds of lesser, and less crowded, sites to enjoy throughout the island. The little oval house at Khamezi, for example, is a domestic and intimate cameo set on a lonely hill. The Dorians, who ruled Crete after the Minoans, built small city-states, such

❑ Crete's steep hillsides are terraced to create level fields for cultivation. Some of the walls still in use are extremely old, dating back hundreds of years. They are patched and patched again, with stones that lie conveniently to hand, perhaps first used in Minoan times. ❑

Village life still revolves around the churches, many of which are rich with ancient decoration

One of Crete's archaeological gems, the magnificent Minoan palace of Faistós

as Polirrínia and Ítanos, in the hills and by the shore, and their house and temple ruins lie mostly unvisited. The enormous sprawling Roman city at Gortýs, where the olive groves are strewn with marble columns and fragments of pottery, also has a large basilica, built by the Byzantines, the next rulers of Crete. Byzantine artists decorated the church of Ágios Nikólaos with geometric frescos which display thousand-year-old colours that are still bright. From 1204 for 450 years the Venetians held the island and their magnificent, solid architecture is still widespread, but can best be seen in Chaniá and Réthymno. The Turks drove the Venetians out in 1669, and stayed until 1898. They built fountains and minarets, and added their own style of doors, windows and arches to the Venetian houses. War memorials, newly built mountain villages and recent rebuilding in the bigger towns are reminders of the extensive damage suffered on the island during World War II.

❑ The Church has a powerful influence on all generations of Cretans today. Young and old, even in towns, will cross themselves when they pass a church during religious festivals. The priest's teenage daughter at Méronas in the Amári Valley says, tenderly, of the 14th-century icon of the Virgin in the village church: "We look after her, because she looks after us". ❑

Cause for concern The island's best-known historic sites are suffering from the damage and erosion caused by the huge numbers of people who tramp through them. Meanwhile, the less famous sites are unprotected from the elements and have been pillaged for building stone over the years. Souvenir and treasure hunters have also been at work for countless centuries—a threat that remains today.

A bronze goddess dating from 700 BC

There are two separate and distinct atmospheres to savour on the island. There is the lively bustle of the Cretan towns, where traditional courtesies and hospitality mingle with commercial vigour and street sharpness. And there is the slower pace of the villages, where the old way of life is gradually changing.

Thriving towns At first acquaintance, the towns seem thronged and disorderly, a muddle of lorry-jammed streets and dusty shops. However, you quickly begin to identify the individual character of each place you visit. Each is distinctive, each in its own way worth lingering over if you wish to catch the full flavour of the island's thriving urban life. Some, like Ágios Nikólaos and the north coast resorts nearer to Irakleío, are essentially tourist towns, given over to servicing the visitor trade, dependent on the hotels, beaches, restaurants and night spots. Chaniá and Réthymno, which have a wealth of well-preserved Venetian architecture and a strong sense of historical and regional identity, operate a successful mixture: a thriving visitor-oriented economy and a social and cultural life that revolves round local people and affairs. In Ierápetra, the agricultural centre of the south coast, tourism and commercial activity seem to function quite separately. In Irakleío, the full-to-bursting capital of the island, business takes precedence over the desires of visitors.

These are all coastal towns that have historic commercial links to the sea and are now making the most of the seaside resort trade. Inland, in towns such as Pérama near Réthymno, or Moíres in the Mesará plain, you find a wholly rural, rough and ready, unselfconscious way of life that can be a refreshing change. It is worth stopping a day or two away from the coast to absorb an atmosphere quite unaffected by the north European visitor.

❑ In a car hire office in Odós Idomíneos, Irakleío, the man behind the desk whiles away his long afternoons by playing the dance tunes of his native village on his *bouzouki*—a lifeline in a sea of noisy streets and querulous customers. ❑

The streets of Irakleío are hectic

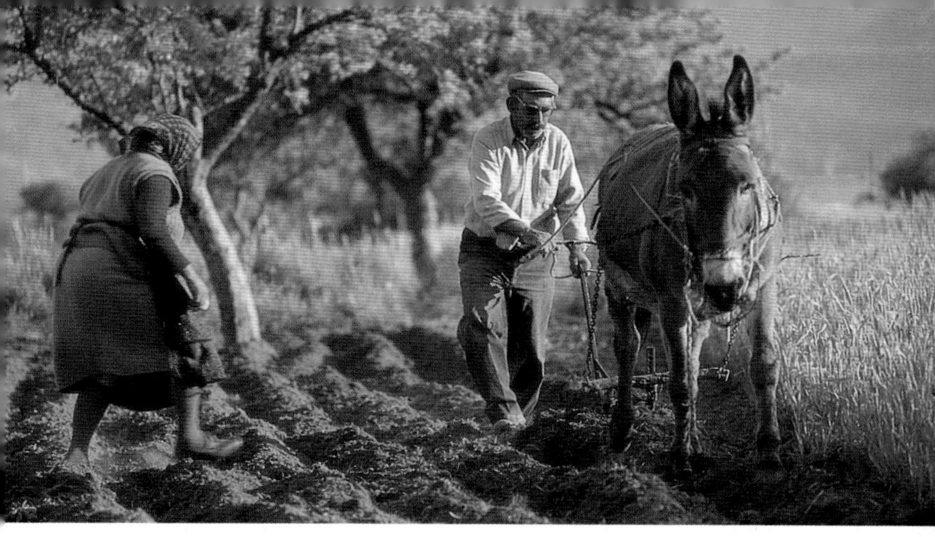

Little seems to change in the countryside

Village change and tradition Though many Cretans have left their villages in recent years to seek work and a broader outlook in the towns, the social and economic lifeblood of the island continues to pulse strongly and with heartening vigour in its hundreds of small rural villages. Each region has its own character, acknowledged almost to the point of caricature by the islanders themselves. There are the laid back qualities of the Siteía folk in the east, the commercially minded Mesarás farmers, and the proud and ferocious Sfakiots of the west. Perhaps these regional temperaments have something to do with the landscape, reflecting the gentler gradients of the east, the prosperous fertility of Mesará and the harsh bleakness of the mountainous west.

In the villages people work hard at basic agriculture with their bare hands and unsophisticated tools. Relaxation is found in a glass of *rakí*, with prolonged discussion of local affairs, and maybe a glance at the television that mutters incessantly in the corner. And it is here that you can still enjoy undiluted Cretan hospitality, see men and women going about their everyday lives in traditional dress, watch a potter creating a jar or a woman weaving a rug, in the way that such things have been done for centuries.

❑ One side effect of the flight of young people from the villages to the towns has been to deprive the old people of much of their conversational fodder...the scandalous way young folk go on. Many of the men too old to work spend a good deal of the day nodding off outside the *kafeníon*. ❑

❑ In contrast to the old men sitting outside the village *kafeníon* in magnificent idleness, the elderly women are seemingly always occupied, hobbling to and fro with buckets, toting bundles of firewood on their backs, scrubbing clothes at the water trough, peeling potatoes at their doors. ❑

Traditional dress is still a matter of pride for older men

Festivals and celebration

Something that all Cretans share is a love of celebration. Solemn religious occasions, full-blooded local festivals and village family gatherings are an excuse for singing, dancing, eating and drinking on a grand scale, all to the accompaniment of a fusillade of firecrackers.

Loud and long In his excellent book, *Crete: Its Past, Present and People,* Adam Hopkins tells the tale of a British pilot during the last days of World War II who was shocked to encounter prolonged anti-aircraft fire over Irakleío some time after the enemy had withdrawn from the town. Subsequent investigation revealed the identity of the gunners as a party of carousing wedding guests, joyfully letting off their weapons at the sky. This story sums up the Cretan attitude to celebration: make it loud and make it long. In a society where life is, on the whole, still hard and demanding, celebrations when they come are eagerly welcomed and pursued remorselessly to the end.

Lamb is frequently eaten at festivals

❑ As Easter Saturday becomes Easter Sunday at midnight, many villages celebrate with the ritual burning of the traitor Judas Iscariot. The effigy may take the form of a stuffed dummy, or appear symbolically as a floral wreath, swinging from a gallows or blazing on top of a bonfire.

After the midnight ceremonies at the church, families and friends return to their houses for a ceremonial meal. The main dish is usually lamb stewed with vegetables and herbs gathered from the mountainside. ❑

Religious festivals The Greek Orthodox faith, to which most Cretans subscribe, has a very practical attitude to worship and strong roots in everyday life and the local community. Orthodox priests are not demi-gods; they are married men who live and work with their parishioners, and play their full part in island life. In the past this has included resistance to oppressors. This special and central role of the church helps to explain why the islanders, even modern young people who may have turned their backs on church-going, flock to the many religious celebrations that take place through the year.

By far the most important of the church festivals is Easter, when Cretans will make every effort to return to their home villages from the towns and even from overseas to join in the ceremonies. On Good Friday evening the churches and streets are

The Greek tradition of decorating the church for Easter lives on in Crete, as seen here outside Chaniá

packed for the procession of the *epitáphios* or flower-decked bier. On Easter Saturday night everyone gathers at the church to pass on the candle flame that symbolises the Risen Christ. They greet each other with cries of *"Christós Anésti!"*, "Christ is Risen!", to be answered with *"Alíthos Anésti!"*, "Truly Risen!" Returning home, the master of the house will bless his threshold by making a smoky cross on the lintel with a lighted candle, after which the family celebrations can begin.

Other religious celebrations include the *paniyíria*, or saint's day, of the village church; name days when all those with the same name will gather to baptise the next generation to bear that name; and christenings at which the rôle of godparent is undertaken as a serious lifetime commitment.

Other celebrations Nowadays many towns have their own festivals. Réthymno has a Wine Festival in July, Irakleío Festival is held in high summer, Siteía holds a Sultana Festival in late August, and the Chestnut Festival at Élos occurs every year in October.

Other celebrations include Independence Day (March 25); Battle of Crete Week (May 20–27); *Óhi* or No Day (October 28), which recalls the single-word reply that the Greek leader General Metáxas gave in 1940 to Mussolini's ultimatum for a Greek alliance with Italy or invasion; and November 7–9, when fireworks at Arkádiou Monastery commemorate the devastating explosion of 1866 (see page 259).

❑ A great tradition of Easter is the battle of the red eggs. Hardboiled eggs in red-painted shells are handed round, then the contestants pair off. A player enfolds an egg in his fist and presents one end to his opponent, who brings his own egg down on it with subtle force. The egg that stays uncracked is the winner. Then the eggs are reversed, and the loser can try to gain an honourable draw. ❑

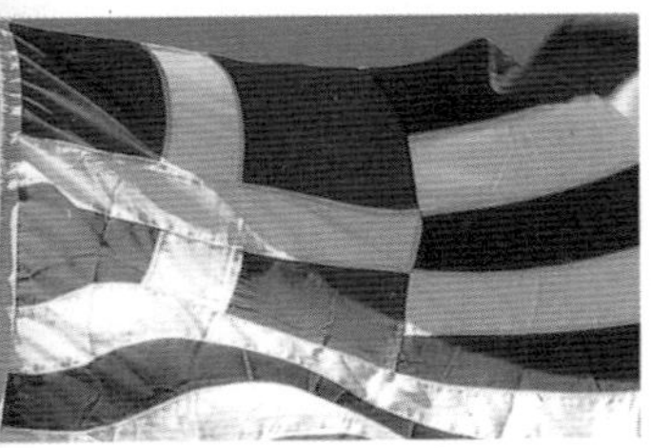

Crete's population fought, suffered and died for many years to attain political union with mainland Greece, which was finally gained only in 1913. Yet the single, most obvious, unifying characteristic of the islanders is their fierce pride in being Cretan—independent and beholden to nobody. Crete is a land apart, as every visitor quickly discovers.

Fighting and freedom "Freedom or Death!" cried the old *palikáres,* the mountain freedom fighters, as they leapt down to do battle with their Turkish rulers. "I believe in nothing. I hope for nothing. I am free", runs the inscription on the grave of Crete's great novelist, Níkos Kazantzákis. Freedom has always been the watchword of the islanders. It is something that they have both believed in and hoped for, a mighty aspiration that has brought countless imprisonments, exiles and deaths. For three thousand years they sought freedom from succeeding conquerors. After the Turks withdrew in 1898 they pressed relentlessly for the freedom to unite with Greece. They fought bitterly and with enormous courage to free themselves once more during World War II. And they united again in the late 1960s for freedom from the Greek military dictatorship.

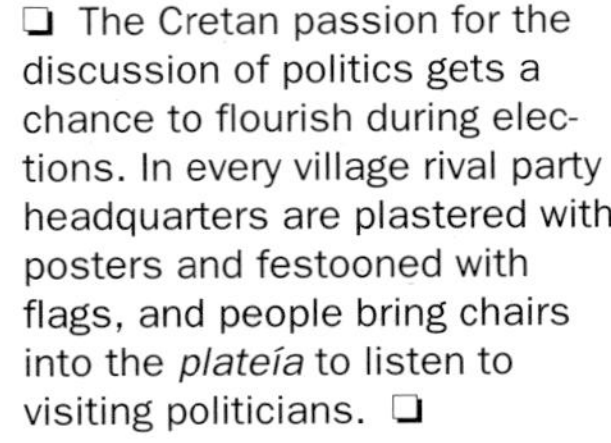

❑ The Cretan passion for the discussion of politics gets a chance to flourish during elections. In every village rival party headquarters are plastered with posters and festooned with flags, and people bring chairs into the *plateía* to listen to visiting politicians. ❑

Fighting and the search for freedom are two aspects of the character of the Cretan population which, even when constrained in calmer times, refuse to lie down. Cretans bend the knee to nobody. They may be part of a modern conservative Greece, but by instinct they are republican and liberal, not much inclined to take Athens and her regulations too seriously—still less Brussels and hers. Cretans first, and the Greeks second, is how the islanders explain themselves to outsiders.

Independence of spirit Cretan traditions of work and social life, and even the shape of the island itself, have played an important part in fostering this notable independence of spirit. Small-scale farmers and shepherds work either alone or in small groups, at a pace

Novelist Níkos Kazantzákis wrote of Crete's struggle for independence

dictated by seasons and weather rather than by a boss or commercial considerations. The villages are small, close-knit and isolated in a mountainous landscape. In the past, communications were so poor and the distances so great that natural geographical divisions created pockets of individuality, not only locally but throughout the island.

The trend of modern life may be softening these hard conditions, but the pride in independence remains. When the chips are down, as they have so often been during the island's history, Cretans display an admirable steadfastness. But there is mercury in the iron. Cretans seem more colourful and more highly flavoured than other Greeks. "All Cretans are liars", as the islanders themselves are fond of quoting; it is a crude way of saying that a Cretan can be charming and maddening, warmly concerned and shruggingly indifferent, solid as a rock and a seemingly casual breaker of appointments, all within an hour.

❑ *Kafeníon* owners fear for their television sets at election time. Tempers are quickly roused and party allegiances forcefully asserted during the party political advertisements and debates that interrupt the schedule of regular programmes. ❑

❑ One of the most powerful novels produced by Crete's best-known writer, Níkos Kazantzákis, dealt with the bloody struggle of the *palikáres* or freedom fighters against Turkish rule. As a title Kazantzákis chose the rallying cry of the Cretan patriots, "Freedom or Death!", but changed the "or" to "and" to reflect the actual theme of Cretan history, *Freedom and Death*. ❑

'Ware politics! International affairs may not appear to loom large in everyday life, but watch out for thumped tables and raised voices when politics and *rakí* mingle. You should perhaps steer clear of this territory, as outsiders do not have much of a right to a say in Cretan or Greek politics!

Politics is the meat of café talk

Any visitor to the north coast between Irakleío and Mália will be unable to ignore the changes that mass tourism has brought to Crete. But the island is trying to turn the tide, with ambitious plans for green tourism that will introduce a much-needed balance between the need for foreign currency and the ravages that low-budget tourism brings to the island's ecology and social life.

Mistakes and remedies Package tours to Crete began only in the late 1960s. Many mistakes were made in those early years. Big parcels of prime seaside land were bought up by speculators, shady hotels were run up by the score, there were non-existent or unenforced planning regulations, unsupervised jobs for the boys. Shoals of bars and discos sprang up, mostly superimposed on the northern coastline with its under-developed infrastructure.

Evidence of poor planning and building control is still to be seen today, but the authorities, under the long-range direction of Athens, have woken up to the potential disaster they have been inflicting on their lovely island. Regulations concerning the design, spacing and servicing of buildings, the layout and planning of resorts, sanitation and the hiring of seasonal staff have been tightened up. The road system has been greatly improved, especially with the construction of the modern highway between Ágios Nikólaos and Chaniá. The development of the south coast fishing villages has come under scrutiny for the first time, and there is a reluctance to grant planning permission in areas of conservation value or great natural beauty.

❑ Topless sunbathing for women has become a commonplace feature of most western European beaches, and Crete is no exception. There are many secluded spots for naturists; but visitors are well advised to behave with some sensitivity as many older Cretans do not care for the trend. As a rule, toplessness is all right on secluded tourist beaches, but should be avoided on public stretches of the town beach. ❑

In high season, every last patch of sand on Mália's beach can be taken

Green tourism Many holidaymakers these days are exploring the island, rather than simply frying on the beach. Unfortunately, at present, this often means driving in open-topped four-wheel-drive hire cars. But the advent of green tourism will perhaps see more visitors taking to the countryside on foot. The old shepherds' paths are being waymarked, better maps are in preparation, and more information is being made available. A long-distance path now runs the full length of the island, some 250km (155 miles) from end to end. Conservation of Crete's wildlife is slowly becoming recognised as a priority, and villagers are being encouraged to provide accommodation for visitors who want to stay with a family and discover more about community life.

Surviving the changes The islanders' way of life has inevitably changed in the last 25 years. With improvements to the roads, tourists have taken to the hills in hire cars, threatening the the peace and solitude of the village. Youngsters have left the remote villages for work in the city, in tourist centres or abroad. Most villagers now have electricity, running water, television, cars and aspirations. Demand for consumer goods is growing. Social divisions between the haves and the have-nots, professional and manual workers, have widened. Perceptions of wealth and glamour arrived with the tourists and with the television, changing for ever the quiet acceptance of fate. Somehow, though, the essential Cretan virtues of kindness, courtesy, hospitality and interest in the stranger, survive the onslaughts of tourists, the latest and perhaps the most invidious in a long line of foreign invaders.

❑ Nothing reflects the raw incompatibility of tourism more than the preponderance of female midriffs and uncovered male chests of the northern Europeans that jars with standard Cretan dress. Even young Cretans take care to cover delicate skin with modest fashions, and older people would never wear shorts and T-shirts. ❑

❑ Old customs, thank goodness, die hard in Crete. The authorities in Athens have recently tried to stamp out two traditions they felt reflected badly on the country as a modern nation: firstly, the enlivening of religious celebrations with a burst of firecrackers, and, secondly, the keeping open of *kafenía* and bars until the early hours. Cretans have simply turned broad backs and deaf ears to these edicts from across the sea. ❑

Crete's long monastic tradition is now under threat from dwindling numbers of novices

A characteristic that marks out Cretans, and a virtue for which they are rightly well known, is their unstinting hospitality to friend and stranger alike. This is a feature of island life that has withstood all recent changes.

Philoxénia The Greek word for this trait is *philoxénia,* love of the stranger. In Crete *philoxénia* is a social, almost a religious, obligation. The poorer the giver, the greater the pleasure in giving. There may be a return in the form of news, entertaining topics of conversation or a fresh ear to bend, but that is not the point. The impulse is a pure one.

Coffee and apples Cretan hospitality takes many forms. An Irakleío shopkeeper, resigning herself to having failed to sell you a handbag, will still offer a cup of coffee. An old woman, peeling apples on her doorstep, will hand you one as you walk by. You give a lift in your car to a homegoing boy, and his family will probably invite you in for a meal. You are benighted on the mountain, and a shepherd may offer to put you up for the night in his hut.

Water with a smile These customs have been abused by freeloaders from time to time, and in the bigger hotels and smarter restaurants *philoxénia* may by now have shrunk to a complimentary *rakí,* whose price you will find buried in your bill. But out in the country it still flourishes. Perhaps the best expression of Cretan hospitality is the simple glass of cold spring water, offered with a smile to the thirsty walker.

❑ One aspect of Cretan hospitality that visitors usually find embarrassing is the taboo on any payback gesture by the guest. You must know your host well and judge your moment before you can stand your round without causing offence. Smiles and signs of appreciation are the best way to return hospitality. Attempts at speaking just a few words of Greek will be received with pleasure: *efharistó polí* means thank you very much, *issi-yian* means good health, *polí kaló* means very good. ❑

A welcoming glass of soumadha

Crete Was

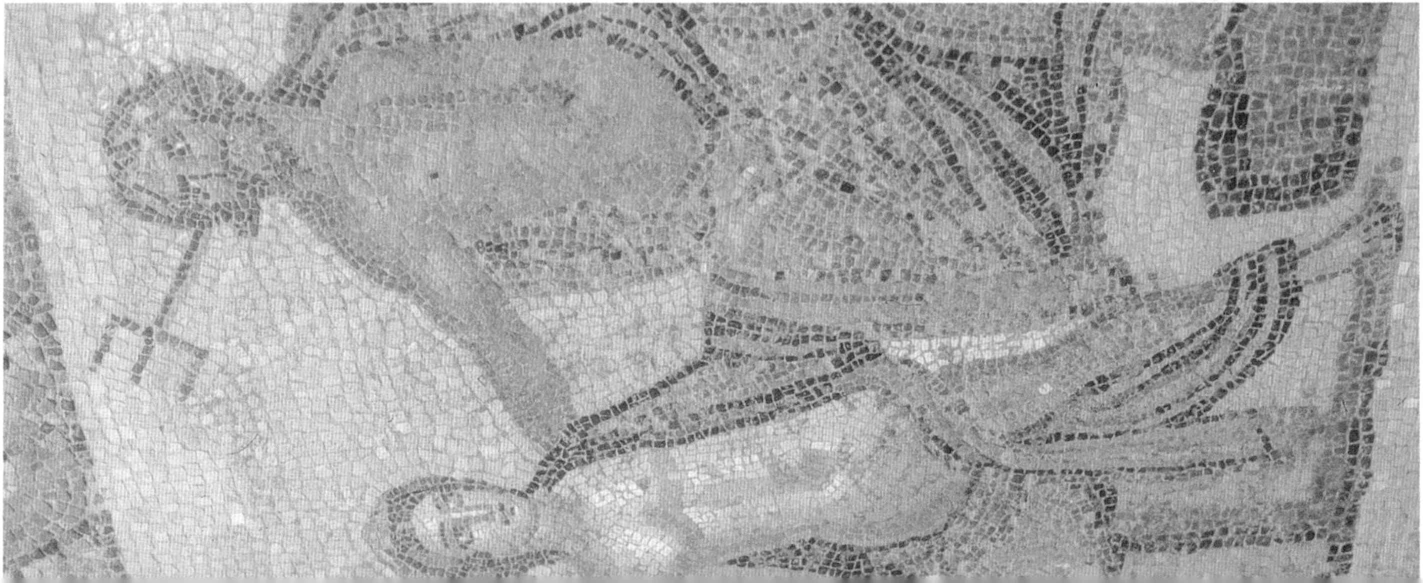

Myth and legend

Early civilisations, searching for an explanation of their origins in an unrecorded past, invested Crete with a fabulous and dramatic history. The stories make compelling entertainment; believe as much as you like.

Kronos Kronos, ruler of the gods, married his sister Rhea and begat five children whom he ate, frightened by a prophesy that he would be overthrown by his son. To protect her unborn sixth child, Rhea fled to Crete and gave birth to Zeus in the Díktaean cave above Lasíthiou. The infant was reared in the Ídaean cave on Psiloreítis. You can visit these caves and imagine for yourself how the stories came into being.

Later, Zeus, perhaps in the guise of an eagle, lay with Europa at Gortýs, and they had three sons together: Sarpedon, Rhadamanthys the law-giver, and the mighty king, Minos. When Zeus died he was buried on Mount Gioúchtas.

❑ The bull was the gathering-point for many strands of Greek mythology. The bull was the favourite animal of Poseidon the earth-shaker, it was the symbol and plaything of King Minos and the civilisation he ruled, and it was the *alter ego* of Zeus when the god of gods wished to dally with mortal maidens. It is a shame that bulls are such a rare sight in Crete these days; rams and billy-goats seem to have taken over. ❑

Minos Some have said that Minos was a just and fair king, others that he was a cruel tyrant. Certainly he was loved by his father, Zeus, who would summon him every nine years to the Díktaean cave to relearn the art of kingship. But Minos was foolish enough to try to trick Poseidon, god of the sea, who had sent him a magnificent white bull as a gift. Minos should have returned the bull as a sacrifice, but offered instead a lesser animal. In revenge, the sea god caused the king's hot-blooded wife Pasiphae to fall in love with the bull. Pasiphae enlisted the help of the master-craftsman Daedalus, who had built a wonderful, maze-like palace at Knosós for the king. Daedalus constructed a model cow, in which the libidinous queen concealed herself to be mounted by the bull. She gave birth to the Minotaur, a bull-headed monster whom King Minos consigned to the labyrinth beneath the palace. Here the beast devoured consignments of youths and maidens shipped in from Athens.

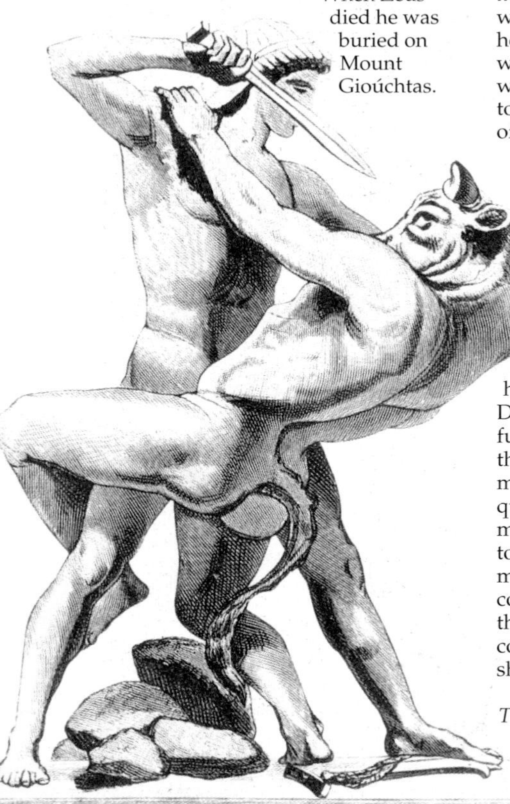

Theseus and the Minotaur

Theseus and the Minotaur Theseus, son of the king of Athens, volunteered to join a shipment of victims, enlisted the help of Ariadne, the daughter of Minos, and managed to kill the Minotaur. Theseus escaped with the princess, but apparently abandoned her after a night of passion on the island of Naxos.

Daedalus and his son Icarus fled the wrath of King Minos on home-made wings of wax and feathers. Icarus flew too near the sun, the wax of his wings melted and he fell to his death. His father went into hiding at the court of King Kokalos of Sicily. Minos followed him there to exact revenge, but was scalded to death in his bath by the daughters of the Sicilian king.

❑ Amaltheia, the resident of Mount Ída who suckled the infant Zeus and nursed him through his Cretan babyhood, is one goat at least that has made it into the annals of mythology. In some versions of the legend, Amaltheia appears as half goat and half nymph, an adoptive mother for the infant god, after his own mother Rhea had given birth to him in the secrecy of the Díktaean cave to save him from the jaws of his bloodthirsty father, Kronos. ❑

❑ A masterpeice of sheer pleasure and pace, *The King Must Die* by Mary Renault remains the best and most accessible retelling of the legend of Theseus and the Minotaur. ❑

Daedalus and Icarus

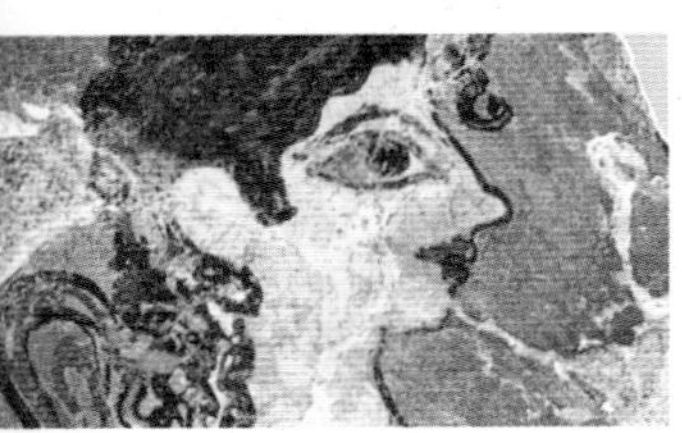

Elaborate palaces and huddled hilltop towns, priests intoning in the depths of caves, snakes wrapped round the arms of bare-breasted priestesses, golden bees hanging from a necklace, a clay jar decorated with goats and an octopus, a doe-eyed girl pouting from a wall painting, the uplifted horns of a bull—the Minoans.

Legend and fact The fame of Crete rests largely on the remains of an obscure Bronze Age civilisation unearthed at the turn of this century by a short-sighted Englishman. When Sir Arthur Evans discovered and excavated the palace at Knosós in 1900 (see pages 90–93), he brought to light one of history's most fabulous treasures, forgotten under the earth for 2,000 years and more. Evans named the palace-builders Minoans, after the mythical king of Crete (see pages 24–25), for this discovery brought together mythology and history, legend and fact. Other excavations at Faistós (pages 82–83) and Agía Triáda (pages 80–81), Mália (pages 131–133) and Gourniá (pages 122–123), were to confirm what Evans suspected—that the ancient legends of Crete were founded in reality. Folk memories existed of a sophisticated, creative, artistic and powerful society that had once flourished on the island. The excavations early this century were not the end of the story. As late as 1962 the splendid Minoan palace at Zákros (pages 158–159) was unearthed, and new discoveries are still being made in caves and on hillsides all over Crete. Libation jugs, votive figurines, statues, pots and gold ornaments are among the treasures brought to the surface in recent years. Hundreds of Minoan houses, storerooms, streets and sanctuaries lie concealed, some known to archaeologists, others unremembered and perhaps never to be rediscovered.

❑ The neolithic, pre-Minoan people (6000–3500 BC) who first settled in Crete were largely preoccupied with internal affairs. But when the island's civilisation flowered into the Minoan period or Bronze Age of Crete, the island was perfectly placed—right at the heart of the trade routes north and south, east and west, across the Mediterranean—to become an outward-going, vigorously trading and widely influential nation. ❑

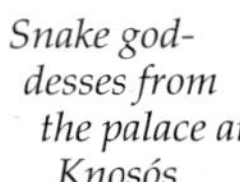

Snake goddesses from the palace at Knosós

Early days (ca6000–2000 BC) Late Stone Age people first arrived in Crete from the east around 6000 BC, and made their homes in the numerous caves of the island. As confidence grew they moved down

towards the sea, establishing a settlement where Knosós was later built and quickly developing social contacts and trade with other islands and countries across the Mediterranean. Around 3000 BC a new wave of settlers arrived from the north and east, lively-minded and energetic people who had the skills of working copper and using the

Evans's reconstruction of the queen's megaron at the palace of Knosós

potter's wheel. From 2400 BC onwards they made beautiful pottery with swirling colours and created jars carved from stone using the natural patterns of the material to harmonise with their flowing designs. These craftsmen made clay seals to mark their individuality, and built thick-walled stone houses across the island beside the land they cultivated. They brought votive offerings of clay figures and worshipped their gods in the darkness of the mountain caves.

❑ Sir Arthur Evans stamped his name on Cretan archaeological history with his discovery and reconstruction of the palace of King Minos at Knosós in 1900. But another archaeologist, the Italian Federico Halbherr, deserves to be equally well remembered. He had been in Crete for ten years when Evans arrived in search of King Minos, and had excavated a large number of sites. The discoveries at Gortýs, Faistós, the Díktaean cave at Psychró and many other places were made by Halbherr, who cut a dash in the Cretan countryside astride a galloping black horse. ❑

❑ If the appearance of a typical Minoan woman was that shown in the celebrated fresco of *La Parisienne* in the palace of Knosós—that is to say, large dark eyes, full red lips and a nose with a bump in the middle—then the old Cretan physiognomy lives on in the face of one of the guides currently showing visitors around Knosós. ❑

Minoan splendour

Around 2000 BC the Minoans began to build palaces on carefully selected sites, enormous sprawls of interconnected rooms and passages, two storeys high, cleverly lit by light wells and equipped with sanitation. The rooms clustered around great open courtyards. There were shrines, treasuries, bedrooms, dining halls, store-rooms, hallways and the throne rooms of the priest-kings who ruled the surrounding lands.

Outside the palace walls grew towns of narrow streets and tiny, box-like stone houses where the smiths and carpenters, potters and jewellers lived. Knosós was the mightiest of these settlements.

All seemed secure, but Crete was then a land of frequent earthquakes. Around 1700 BC every palace, every town and street in the island was flattened by catastrophic earth tremors. Within a hundred years, however, the palaces had been rebuilt and the towns restored, and Minoan society entered another, yet more splendid and sophisticated phase.

People of Minos From infinitely careful excavation of the Minoan palaces and towns, historians have learned a good deal about the way of life of these people. The frescoes they painted on their walls show elegant, wasp-waisted princes crowned with flowers, chains of dark-eyed dancing girls, solemn priests and cats stalking wild birds. In the most famous, from the palace at Knosós, a graceful acrobat somersaults over the back of a charging bull towards the outstretched arms of a girl. The stone vases are carved with rejoicing harvesters, boxers and wrestlers. Sea creatures swim around their elaborate jugs and long-horned wild goats are hunted across their clay coffins.

Bulls were worshipped, fêted and danced with. The bull's-horn symbol occurs again and again, as does the sacred, double-bladed *labrys* or axe. The kings, probably named Minos in succession, were gods, monarchs and politicians. Priestesses in bell-bottomed dresses had snakes as their familiars, poured libations from bull's-head vessels and may have been the power behind the throne.

Evidence shows that the Minoans ate cheese, fish, wild fruit and olives, drank goats' milk and wine,

The magnificent bull's head rhyton *from Knosós*

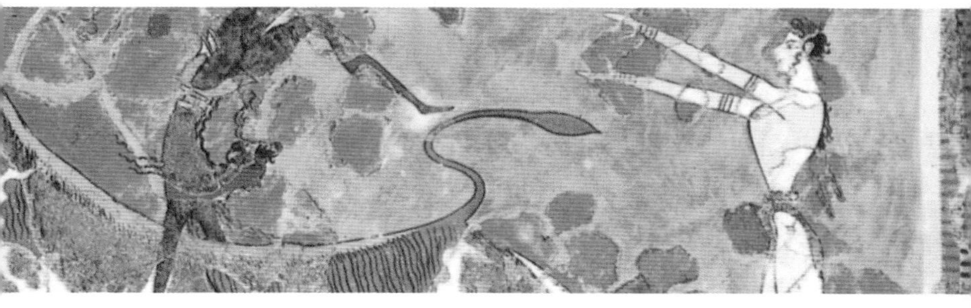

❑ Some late Minoan pottery, made after the cataclysm of 1450 BC, features a design of rearing, toppling waves. Observers also point to the sinister distortion of animal figures on seals, and to an expression of horror on the faces of clay goddesses made during this period. Fanciful nonsense? Or are these echoes of the disaster that destroyed all the palaces and towns of Crete at a single stroke? ❑

sweetened their palates with honey and sharpened them with salt and wild herbs. They kept domestic records using hieroglyphs incised into clay tablets. They took wine, corn, olive oil and timber to their trading partners and subject islands around the Mediterranean in square-sailed ships, bringing back all kinds of metal and stone for building and ornamentation.

❑ The skills of the early Minoan artist-craftsmen are seen in their symmetrical vases, carved out of solid stone in such a way that the natural patterns of the material enhanced the beauty of the product. This they achieved with tools of bronze, stone and bone and sand to rub the rough surface smooth—and endless time and patience. ❑

Part of Irakleío Museum's excellent ceramics collection

Civilisation and catastrophe

The end came around 1450 BC. Once again the palaces and towns came crashing down, felled by a disaster so sudden that the Minoans dropped whatever they were doing and ran for their lives. Was it a volcanic eruption across the sea, a tidal wave, another cataclysmic earthquake or sudden invasion? Nobody knows for certain. All the palaces burned and were abandoned, except Knosós, which lived on as a declining remnant of the golden civilisation of the Minoans.

MINOAN ERA	DEVELOPMENTS IN CRETE	DEVELOPMENTS ELSEWHERE
Pre-Palace ca2600–1900 BC	Country villas with plastered stone walls. Hieroglyphs appearing. Delicate handmade pottery, long-spouted jugs. "Vasilíki ware" pottery, mottled. Fine miniature work on seals. Gold necklaces and pins. Copper, then bronze.	ca2800 BC: **Egypt**: hieroglyphs and first stone building, the step pyramid. **Mesopotamia**: potter's wheel. ca2200 BC: **Egypt**: copper, then bronze. **Iran**: reversion to plain pottery. **Scandinavia**: primitive pottery. **Northwestern Europe**: megalithic tombs; copper produced in France.
Old Palace ca1900–1700 BC	Structured society, villas and towns. Great multi-storey palaces at Knosós, Faistós, Mália, Zákros. Frescoes, drainage, road-building, irrigation. "Kamáres ware": exquisite, painted, moulded, eggshell thin. Stone vases, metalwork, jewellery to high art. Linear A script developing. ca1700 BC: Earthquake destroys all palaces.	**Egypt**: Golden Age of Middle Kingdom. Bronze well established. **Europe**: bronze spreading, but still not reached northwest. Copper throughout. Beaker Folk taking sophistication northwest.
New Palace ca1700–1450 BC	Palaces and towns rebuilt, all services refined. Gourniá and Palaíkastro towns flourishing. Powerful god-kings, Minos dynasty. Elaboration of frescoes, jewellery, gold work, bronze and silver, stone vases. Superb "marine" decoration of pottery, but general formalisation of style. Linear A and Linear B script. Faistós Disc (only example of printing for next two millennia).	ca1670 BC: **Egypt**: invaded by Hyskos who introduced chariot. ca1650 BC: **Anatolia (Turkey)**: all-conquering Hittite Empire established. Cities walled with huge stone blocks. ca1550 BC: **Egypt** expels Hyskos, starts aggressive expansion, devises 365-day calendar; towns with houses up to five storeys high, built of mud bricks. ca1500 BC: **Britain**: Stonehenge completed.
Post-Palace ca1450–1100 BC	ca1450 BC: Fire partially destroys palaces and towns. Knosós and Gourniá reoccupied. Most other palaces and towns not rebuilt. Invading Mycenaeans take control. Native Minoan society in decline.	**Egypt**: civilisation in decline after death of Rameses III (1198–1166 BC). **Europe**: bronze throughout. **India**: Sanskrit script developing. **China**: entering Bronze Age.

What actually happened in 1450 BC? Theories abound as to exactly what it was that occurred in ca1450 BC destroying the Minoan palaces and towns on Crete.

The one link is fire, which left scorch marks at every one of the devastated palaces, villas and town streets. A tidal wave large enough to overwhelm inland as well as coastal sites would surely have extinguished fires, however widespread the inferno may have been. An earthquake would have trapped people in the ruins, but there is an almost complete absence of human remains. A combination of earth tremors, tidal wave and smothering ash would have followed a cataclysmic volcanic explosion. One such disaster occurred only 150km (93 miles) away, when the whole island of Thíra (Santorini) exploded. However, it is thought that this event took place some 50 years or so before the destruction in Crete. And in any event, there still remains the question of why Knosós escaped the demolition that all the other Minoan towns and palaces suffered?

Another explanation might be an overwhelming attack, perhaps by massed Mycenaean invaders taking advantage of their favourable position. The Mycenaeans had recently usurped the Minoan Cretans, so perhaps they turned on their former oppressors and destroyed the occupied palaces and towns. But, again, why are there no bodies to be found? And would it have been physically possible for the invaders to flatten the huge, multi-storey Minoan palaces in attacks of this sort?

Another mystery surrounds the whereabouts of migrating Cretans after the mysterious disaster. The Minoans were expert seafarers. Were they, perhaps, the Sea People who all but overthrew Egypt in 1180 BC before eventually settling in Palestine and later adopting the name Philistines? Philistine and Late Minoan pottery have strong similarities, and the Philistines always maintained that they had indeed originated in Crete. Or were the fleeing Minoans the forerunners of the Phoenicians, the Canaanite merchants who traded in exquisite coloured glass and in murex dyes manufactured from Creta shellfish? And could it have been Minoans-turned-Phoenicians who carved a double-headed axe, a sacred *labrys* of Knosós, on one of the Stonehenge pillars in far-off Britain?

A Kamarés ware krater, *used for the mixing of wine and water*

What could follow the glories of the Minoan civilisation but a steady decline? From that high peak of achievement Crete slipped slowly downwards, until it began to rise again towards the peaceful prosperity of the Romans.

Mycenaeans (ca1500–1100 BC) Around 1500–1400 BC Mycenaeans arrived in Crete from the north—a warlike people, bent on expansion. Swords and spears were buried with their dead, and helmeted warriors in chariots appear on their pottery. Did they themselves destroy the palaces of their hosts? At all events they re-inhabited the ruined Minoans towns, but the Cretan society that had been so well ordered now began to fragment.

Dorians (ca1100–67 BC) In about 1100 BC the Mycenaeans were displaced by Dorian Greeks, efficient warriors from further north, who divided Greece into 1,500 city states. Several such city states were established in Crete in the following centuries, among them Lató above Kritsá, Polirrínia in the far northwest, and Praisós in the east. Down in the south Gortýs became the most powerful settlement on the island, while the city states feuded with each other each trading on its own account across the Mediterranean.

On the Greek mainland Athens grew to eminence, while Egypt still dominated North Africa. From the one came classical influences of building and sculpture; from the other, the grim and formal Archaic style which was far removed from the Minoan lightness of touch.

❑ The decline in craftsmanship after the end of the Minoan civilisation can be seen clearly in the clumsy wheeled animal toy of the 7th century BC on display in Chaniá's Archaeological Museum. A Roman statue of Aphrodite teaching Eros to play the guitar, very warmly and expressively sculpted in the 1st century AD, shows how far, and in how different a direction, craftsmanship rose again. ❑

Roman (67 BC–ca AD 337) Then came the invading Romans, who built new temples, theatres, villas and aqueducts. Gortýs flourished, and peace came to the island. St Paul arrived briefly in AD 59, followed by St Titus, bringing Christianity and its attendant martyrdoms.

Statue of a bearded philosopher from Gortýs

One ordered empire succeeded another as Rome gave way to Byzantium. This was healthy for Crete, until the Saracens came with fire and sword. There followed more than a century of brigandage, before prosperity returned under renewed Byzantine rule.

First Byzantine occupation (ca AD 337–824) On 11 May AD 330, King Constantine declared a Byzantine empire which he promised would last a thousand years. The stronghold of the empire was Constantinople, renamed New Rome, and within seven years it had control of the Mediterranean. The Roman Empire tottered on until AD 395, when it was carved up by the triumphant Byzantines who were by this time well established in Crete. The Byzantines ran the island as a very tight ship, rigidly controlling it from Constantinople. They built round-apsed basilica churches throughout Crete, the greatest of which was Ágios Títos at Gortýs. Much of this church still stands. The island's agriculture prospered and trade increased, but trouble began to brew to the south during the 7th century as the Arabs moved steadily northwards, threatening Christian Constantinople at the heart of the Byzantine empire.

Constantine, 4th-century ruler of the Byzantine Empire

Saracens (AD 824–961) The Saracens invaded from Alexandria in AD 824, intending to use Crete as a pirate base. This they did, to great and deadly effect, attacking shipping far into the Aegean. The port below Knosós, present-day Irakleío, was known as Rabdh-el-Khandak, and was the Mediterranean's most notorious slave market. Gortýs and many of the island's basilicas were destroyed. The island lay neglected, and its Christian inhabitants were mercilessly persecuted.

❑ Crete in this era was a veritable nest of pirates and slavers, whose ships menaced the whole of the Mediterranean. Perhaps this was when Cretans acquired their reputation for being both ferocious and cunning. ❑

Second Byzantine occupation (AD 961–1204) Crete was recaptured by the Byzantines in AD 961 after a horrific siege of Rabdh-el-Khandak, during which Saracen heads were catapulted among the defenders. Byzantine landowners arrived and restored agricultural and trading prosperity; more churches were built and enhanced with frescoes.

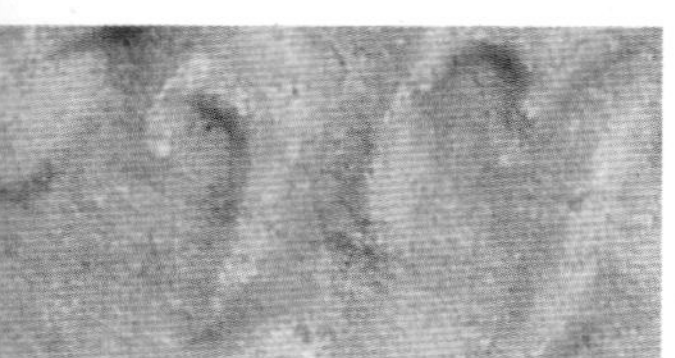

Elegant and cultured, the Venetians ruled Crete for almost 450 years, bringing unrivalled prosperity to the island. They built solidly and handsomely in golden stone, and carved their symbol, the winged lion of St Mark, on fortress walls, staring seawards towards both friend and foe.

Sold for silver By the beginning of the 13th century the Byzantine empire was in disarray, overstretched and rotting from the core. In 1204 the Fourth Crusade, composed not so much of ardent warriors of Christ as of freebooters with an eye to the main chance, took and sacked Constantinople. As the Byzantine empire had carved up the Roman empire 850 years before, so it was itself now divided up. Crete was allotted to Prince Boniface of Montferrat, leader of the Crusade, and he swiftly sold it on to Venice for 1,000 pieces of silver. Crete was to remain under Venetian rule for the next 435 years.

Prosperity and culture Venetian nobles, like the Byzantines before them, were granted estates throughout the island, and ran them feudally under the overall control of the Doge, who ruled from Candia, the name by which the capital city, and soon the whole island, came to be known. The Candy of which Shakespeare wrote was famed for its beauty and its productivity. Agriculture flourished and wine, grain, fruit and olive oil left the ports of Chaniá, Réthymno and Candia, along with timber felled across the island. The Venetians were masters of communication and trade, and Crete benefited from their commercial acumen.

Proud Venetian lions guard the fortress at Irakleío

❑ Many reminders of Venetian rule can be seen on Crete. These include the harbours at Chaniá (page 202) and Réthymno (page 184), and fortresses in Irakléio (page 59) and Réthymno (page 183). The monasteries of Hrissoskalítissas (page 228) and Arkadíou (page 171) were both built during Venetian rule. ❑

Along with increased prosperity came another flowering of Cretan culture. The Orthodox religion of the island was supplanted by Roman Catholicism, and many fine monasteries and churches, large and small, were built. Byzantine culture was still strong in Crete, and its traditions began a long fusion with emerging Renaissance expertise and a certain native Cretan energy to produce a new artistry, culminating in the superb 16th-century icon painting of Mikháil Dhamaskínos and the supreme master El Greco. Drama and poetry had a fresh impetus, too—a highlight being *Erotókritos*, an epic poem of courtly love written by Vinzétzos Kornáros towards the end of the period of Venetian rule.

Rebellions All was not sweetness and light under the Venetians, however. The feudal system imposed obligations of service, penalties and taxes, and put legal limitations on the old Byzantine families and peasants. Resentment was strong. Rebellions began not long after the new rulers came to power on the island. After an uprising in 1263 was snuffed out by reinforcements from Venice, the Lasíthiou plateau was cleared of its inhabitants as a punishment for their rôle in the revolt, and was left uncultivated for the following two centuries. Rumblings continued with a rising in about 1527, which saw the leader, a Sfakiot named Kandanóleon, executed along with his family and many supporters. The Venetians built castles on the coastal plains, while the rebels were gathering and raiding from the mountains. Periods of truce were followed by rebellions, and this uneasy state of affairs was worsened by frequent Arab pirate raids on the coastal towns. In 1538 the buccaneering Barbarossa sacked Réthymno, after which the main towns of Réthymno, Chaniá and Candia were walled and refortified.

❑ The barren nakedness of the mountains is one of Crete's most striking features. This sad stripping away of the native pine forests, exacerbated these days by the teeth of sheep and goats, was started by the Venetians who cut down enormous numbers of trees for shipbuilding and the maintenance of their great galley fleet. ❑

The Venetian walls of Réthymno

Under Turkish rule, Crete entered a period of resentful decline and neglect. Rebellions grew in number and strength, and reprisals grew in ferocity, until the Turks were forced to leave. The island then entered the last straight on the long road to freedom and enosis, *union with Greece.*

Turkish victory

The Turks attacked Crete in 1645, at a time when the Venetian empire was losing control of the Mediterranean and the vigorously expanding Ottoman empire was pushing westwards. With the first momentum of their invasion the Turks captured Chaniá, and Réthymno fell the following year. By 1647 only Candia was still in Venetian hands, along with a handful of fortified islets. As Europe stood by and wrung its hands, the Turkish noose tightened around the Cretan capital, and the epic Great Siege of Candia got under way. In 1667 they began the attack in earnest. On 5 September 1669 the defenders of Candia finally surrendered, and Venetian rule was over.

❑ Any reader of Níkos Kazantzákis's great novel set during the Turkish occupation of Crete, *Freedom and Death*, will doubtless be familiar with the *narghile* or Turkish hubble-bubble pipe. The tobacco fumes are cooled as they are drawn through water into the lungs of the smoker—or smokers, since *narghiles* can have multiple stems and be enjoyed by several friends at the same time. Every now and then, though only rarely nowadays, one is lit in a city men's club or on some devotee's balcony. ❑

Decline and neglect

Cretans see the period of Turkish rule as the nadir of their island's fortunes. Certainly great injustices and cruelties were perpetrated on the population. The Turks were not

The Turkish fleet off Candia

Mosque and fountain in Ierápetra

interested in the humdrum affairs of trade and agriculture, and never actively promoted them. They taxed the Christian islanders on the fruits of their labour and, not unnaturally, the fruit began to wither on the vine. The Christian Cretans started to convert in large numbers to Islam, for safety and to ease their burden of taxes and penalties. The new rulers preferred town to country life, but apart from converting the churches to mosques by adding minarets, erecting fountains, altering doors and windows to Islamic designs and building a few town houses, they did little to maintain the towns. Pashas or overlords ruled the three districts into which Crete was now divided, leaving law enforcement to an increasingly undisciplined and vicious soldiery. Art and literature declined, and the rich gloss of prosperity departed from the island.

❑ Protruding belts of stone run horizontally around the walls of many churches and schools built during the Turkish occupation. They were added as a reminder that Christian worship and teaching might be permitted, but only within the jurisdiction of the Ottoman rulers and the all-embracing grip of Islam. ❑

❑ Perhaps the best thing the Turks left behind was the art of the pastry cook. Try *baklavá*, a pastry triangle packed with honey and nuts, and *kataífi*, a kind of shredded wheat, also soaked with honey and filled with nuts, for a tooth-tingling, sweet and glutinous treat. ❑

From rebellion to *enosis*

Conditions like these created a hothouse for rebellion. While lowlanders lived cheek by jowl with the Turks and had to learn to get along with them, the mountain dwellers, particularly the proud Sfakiots of the west, took up arms. The heroic tales of the *palikáres* or freedom fighters were bred here. Daskaloyiánnis was flayed alive in 1770 by the Pasha at Megálo Kástro (Irakleío), and Hatzimicháli Daliánis and his followers were slaughtered at Fragkokástelo in 1828. Rebels were hanged, impaled and shot. 2,000 Cretans and Turks died in an explosion at Arkádiou Monastery in 1866. There were uprisings in 1878, 1889 and 1896. Finally, in 1898, the Great Powers of Britain, Russia, France and Italy imposed a settlement. The Turks left the island and, after further unrest and civil disobedience, the people of Crete at last achieved their dream in 1913—independence within a union with Greece.

The gunpowder room of the Arkádiou Monastery; *see pages 171–172*

History had yet another invasion in store for Crete. The German capture of the island in 1941 was followed by four years of resistance, and many horrific episodes of ambush and reprisal, a further grim chapter in Crete's bloody story.

Valuable prize Between the wars Greece was torn by struggles for power between monarchists and republicans. These quarrels were temporarily set aside in October 1940 when the Italians invaded mainland Greece, closely followed by the Germans. By spring the following year 32,000 Allied troops were in Crete, but they failed to create the impregnable fortress that Churchill had demanded. Crete was a valuable prize. The Germans wanted it as a staging post for attacks on the British Royal Navy in the Mediterranean and on Allied troops in North Africa. General Bernard Freyberg, VC, the New Zealander in command of the Cretan defences, was convinced that a German attack would come mainly from the sea. But, when it came, it was from the air.

The Battle of Crete At dawn on 20 May 1941, German paratroopers and gliders began to descend on Crete. Thousands were killed before they even reached the ground. By the end of the day the Germans had a toehold near the vital airfield at Máleme, west of Chaniá, but had mostly been contained. But due to confusion, broken communications

❑ One of the best-known figures from the World War II resistance movement still living in Crete today is George Psychoundákis. He earned international and literary fame with his 1955 account of his wartime experiences, *The Cretan Runner*, and his later translations of Homer into Cretan dialect. Psychoundákis is also remembered for the legendary stamina, toughness, humour and courage that he displayed as a young man during his epic solo journeys on foot, at the double, across scores of miles of harsh mountain, plateau and ravine, carrying messages between the scattered resistance bands. ❑

Above: war memorial in Réthymno
Left: Cretan heroes from World War II were numerous and even today are not forgotten

and a lack of reinforcements, the New Zealanders holding Máleme airfield withdrew from their positions. Soon the Germans were pouring in fresh troops and supplies. Gradually the Allies were pushed back, and the balance of the battle swung the Germans' way. British and Australian troops were hurriedly evacuated from Irakleío by the British Royal Navy. Réthymno was captured from the Australians and Greeks on 31 May. The south coast port of Hóra Sfakía saw the further shambolic evacuation of troops (see page 229). At the cost of 6,530 young lives, the Germans captured Crete.

Resistance After the Battle of Crete, many of the soldiers who had escaped to the mountains were taken off the island by submarines and small boats. Allied organisers and wireless operators were landed, to help the Cretan resistance bands that soon formed. The years of determined resistance that followed form one of the most heroic chapters in the history of Crete—pages stained with blood and tears.

Sabotage, ambushes and clandestine wireless transmissions drew down reprisals in which civilians were shot and villages were burnt. As always, the mountains became the stronghold of the resistance movement. Supplies were dropped by parachute or landed on the coast. Hunted men departed for North Africa, and replacements arrived to fill the gaps. Many Cretans went hungry and in fear, but they were nevertheless implacably opposed to the occupation.

By 1944 the Germans knew there was no future for them in Crete. In October that year they barricaded themselves in an enclave around Khaniá, and by June 1945 they had left the island.

In 1941 British soldiers work hurriedly to prepare for the air defence of Crete

❑ The Paterákis brothers from Kostoyérako, in the southwest fringes of the White Mountains, belong to one of the island's most celebrated resistance families. Mention of the Paterákis clan anywhere in the Sfakiá district will still elicit stories about the brothers: Manoli and the abduction of General Kreipe, for example, Antoni and the pothole incident, or Costis and the miraculous shot that saved a village. ❑

After the war, Crete picked itself up and set out on the road to recovery. Old ways of life resumed their measured course with traditions of work and culture that can still be encountered today by the explorer who makes a point of getting off the beaten track.

Revival In the late 1940s Crete was lucky not to be drawn into the bitter civil war that tore mainland Greece in two. There had been the potential for internecine fighting on the island between communists and non-communists, but somehow everyone held back or was prevented from initiating conflict. Gradually life returned to normal. Agriculture revived and the burned, bombed and neglected towns and villages underwent a massive and long-drawn-out scheme of reconstruction.

Village life In the early 1950s, the writer Patrick Leigh Fermor, returning to Crete to pay a call on his wartime resistance colleague and good friend George Psychoundákis, embarked on the long uphill mule-back journey to the White

❑ You do not have to venture far from the north coast beach and-hotel strip between Irakleío and Ágios Nikólaos to find many aspects of life going on much as they did before tourism invaded the island. House ovens still produce home-baked bread, home-made wine and *rakí* are on sale, cheese-makers stir cauldrons of sheep's milk in lonely huts, and black-cowled women are out on the mountainside gathering wild herbs. Such traditional activities, still the mainstay of local village life, give Crete its unique and enchanting flavour. ❑

Mountain village of Asigoniá where Psychoundákis lived. Much of rural and upland Crete was inaccessible to motor cars then, and the majority of the population was living in small, remote settlements without electricity, tap water or modern sanitation.

Donkeys are still hard at work in the country

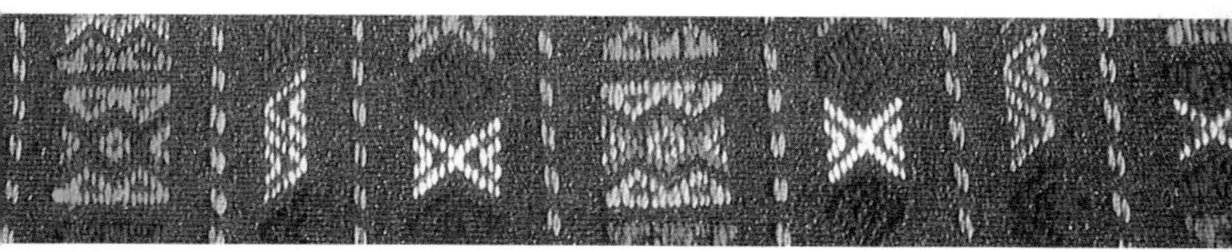

At that time, away from the towns of the north coast, people lived in a silence only occasionally interrupted by the click of a donkey's hooves, the tinkle of a spoon, or the scratch of a hoe. Village agriculture predominated, much of it subsistence gardening, but the Cretans ate simply and well on a diet of tomatoes, green stuff, potatoes, and onions grown on their own *kipos* or patch of ground. They grew their own wheat, ground their own flour, baked their own bread, pressed their own olive oil, drank home-made wine and *rakí.* Village houses had earth floors, smoke-blackened beamed ceilings under earth-on-plank roofs, an open fireplace, a storeroom with oil, wine and dried fruit in big earthenware jars unchanged in design since Minoan times. Furniture was sparse, and water came from the well or stream. Almost everyone over 30 wore traditional dress: the older women in head-to-toe black, old men in kneeboots and baggy breeches, younger men in cavalry-style jodhpurs. Most youngsters got a decent primary education in the village schools, but very few from rural backgrounds went on to secondary level. There was a basic equality of income and aspirations among the rural poor, and that meant most Cretans. Medical care was traditional and herb-based, and superstition, cruelty, generosity and realism were the mix of everyday life.

Change of character? But of course better communications, motor cars, money, television, modern facilities and the onrush of mass tourism were only just around the corner. Have they eroded the Cretan character since those days before tourists arrived on the island? Are the Cretans still volatile, warmhearted, hospitable, infuriating, easy-going, fierce, capricious, independent-minded and blackly humorous? That is something you will have to judge for yourself.

This simple open-air oven is a remnant of a vanishing way of life

❑ The backpacker, tottering through a village on his way to the mountains wearing hefty hiking boots and carrying a large rucksack, will both amuse and baffle the villagers. Cretans take to the hills burdened with nothing more than a stick and a pair of battered old shoes—and then only for purely practical reasons, such as shepherding or visiting friends in remote places, and very seldom for the perverse pleasure of taking exercise in the open air. ❑

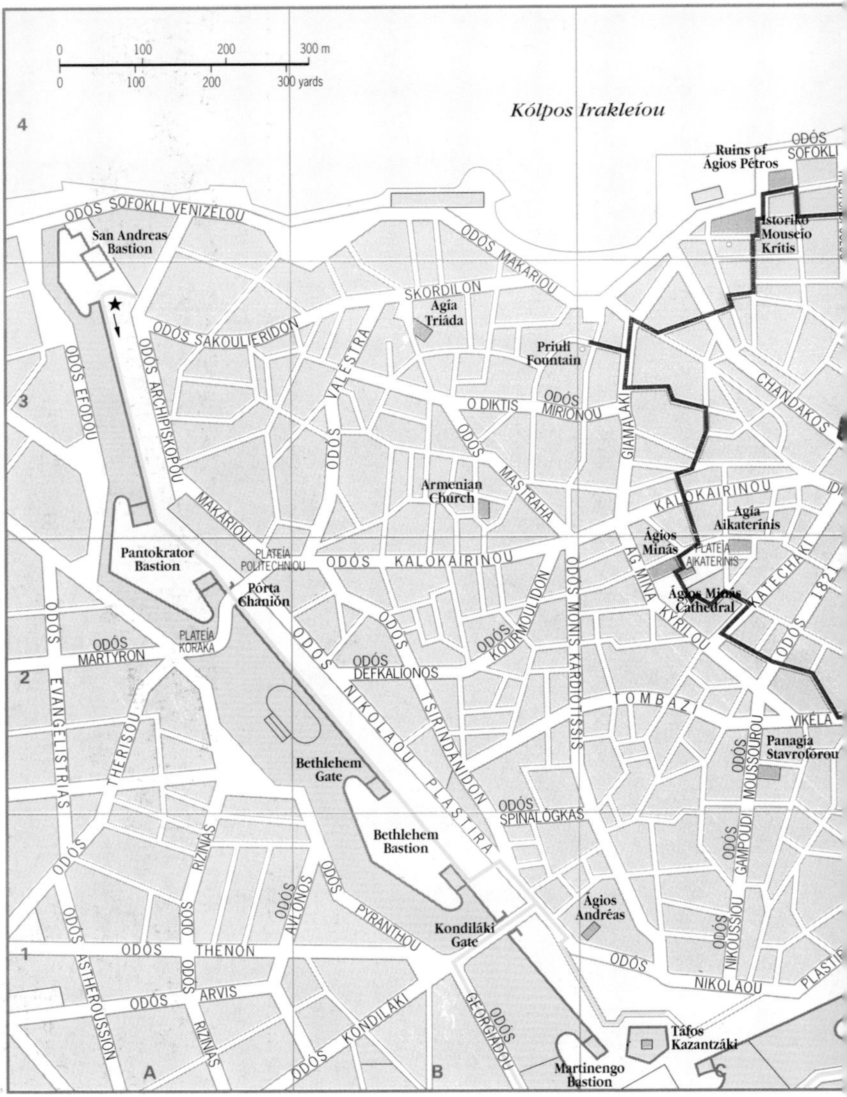

0 100 200 300 m
0 100 200 300 yards
Kólpos Irakleíou
Ruins of Ágios Pétros
Istorikó Mouseío Krítis
San Andreas Bastion
Agía Triáda
Priuli Fountain
Armenian Church
Pantokrator Bastion
Pórta Chaniõn
Plateía Politechniou
Plateía Koraka
Ágios Minás
Agía Aikaterínis
Plateía Aikaterinis
Ágios Minás Cathedral
Panagía Stavroforou
Bethlehem Gate
Bethlehem Bastion
Kondiláki Gate
Ágios Andréas
Martinengo Bastion
Táfos Kazantzáki
Odós Sofokli Venizélou
Odós Makariou
Skordilon
Odós Sakoulieridon
Odós Valestra
Odós Efodou
Odós Archipiskopou
O Diktis
Odós Mirionou
Giamalaki
Chandakos
Odós Mastraha
Makariou
Kalokairinou
Odós Kalokairinou
Odós Monis Kardiotissis
Odós Kourmoulidon
Ag. Mina
Kyrilou
Katechaki
Odós 1821
Odós Martyron
Odós Defkalionos
Odós Nikolaou Plastira
Odós Tsirindanidon
Odós Evangelistrias
Therisou
Tombazi
Vikela
Odós Moussourou
Odós Spinalogkas
Odós Gampoudi
Rizinias
Odós Avlonos
Odós Pyranthou
Odós Thenon
Odós Nikoussiou
Odós Nikolaou
Plastira
Odós Astheroussion
Odós Arvis
Odós Kondiláki
Odós Georgiadou
A
B
C
1
2
3
4

Irakleío's busy harbour (right)
Níkos Kazantzákis (far right)

A-Z Irakleío

Koúles
Palaió Limáni
VENIZÉLOU
Arsenali
Ágios Dimítrios
Katholikí Ekklisía
Arsenali
PLATEÍA KOUNTOURYOTON
EPIMENIDOU
ODÓS 25 AVGOÚSTOU
EPIMENIDOU
MALIKOUTI
Párko Gréko
Ágios Títos
AG TITOU
Sabionera Bastion
PLATEÍA ENIZÉLOU
Loggia
Kríni Morozini
Ágios Márcos
MIRAMPELOU
MIRAMPELOU
DOMINEOS
Archaiologikó Mouseío
BOFOR
PLAT. PHOKA
DAIDÁLOS
DIKAIOSINIS
Agorá
Touristikí Astynomía
PLATEÍA DAKALOGIANI
PLATEÍA ELEFTHERIAS
St George's Gate
IKAROU
ODÓS ANTHEMIOU
ODÓS ARFIMIDOUS
ODÓS 1866
EVANS
AVEROF
DIMOKRATIAS
Kríni Bembo
PLATEÍA KORNAROU
ODÓS PEDIADOS
Public Gardens
ODÓS EVANS
ODÓS PEDIAKOS
St George's Bastion
DIMOKRATIAS
ODÓS GERONIMAKI
Jesus Gate
CHARILÁOU TRIKOÚPI
PLATEÍA KÝPROU
ODÓS DRAKONTOPOULOU
Jesus Bastion
GEORGIÁDOU
ODÓS KASTRINAKI
ODÓS MISSONOS
ODÓS
D
E

▶▶▶ CITY HIGHLIGHTS

Agía Aikaterínis
page 62

Archaeological Museum
pages 48–51

Venetian fort (Koúles)
pages 59–60

IRAKLEÍO Irakleío lies midway along the northern coast, and is the centre of Crete's commercial and cultural life. A bustling modern city with 130,000 inhabitants, it immediately strikes the first-time visitor as the very antithesis of everything that Crete is famous for—peace, quiet, a relaxing atmosphere. For almost all holidaymakers, whether they come to the island by plane or by ferry, Irakleío is their first experience of Crete. Faced with the roar of traffic, the constant mess and clangour of construction works and the heat and dust of crowded pavements, most visitors want to get away from the city as soon and as quickly as possible.

WINDOWS ON HISTORY Yet even here, as in every great and historic city, there are many delights and revelations, many windows on the history and character of Crete, waiting to be discovered and enjoyed. Irakleío has an archaeological museum that many claim is the finest in Europe. It has superb Venetian squares and a massive fortress on the waterfront; it has notable churches, including Agía Aikateríni on Plateía Aikaterínis, which has an unparalleled collection of icons; it has a famous market, where you can enjoy the atmosphere of a genuine, jam-packed bazaar. All this and much more is encircled by the most outstanding medieval city walls to be seen in any Mediterranean country. There are first-class restaurants, and obscure but entirely Cretan backstreet tavernas; thumping discos and the traditional music of *lýra* and *bouzoúki*; international standard luxury hotels and inexpensive rooms to rent; sophisticated vintage

The carefully restored Venetian Loggia

CAPITAL FASHION
Irakleío's young people are intensely fashion-conscious, and the latest European clothing trends appear on the city's streets almost as soon as they do in London, Paris or Berlin. One of the many striking contrasts of Irakleío is the sight of a gleaming fashion-plate of a young man or woman inspecting a market stall shoulder to shoulder with an elderly man from a mountain village in traditional knee-boots, wide drab breeches and black shirt.

wines, tear-jerking local *rakí* and rough village wine from the barrel; bland modern shopping thoroughfares and twisting side streets where a domed Turkish doorway or a tottering Venetian town house will sharpen your focus on Cretan history.

WELCOMING GESTURES Irakleío people may shout, gesticulate, bluster and roar, for self-effacement is not the style here. Many are recent arrivals in the city themselves. Young Cretans in particular are drawn to Irakleío from their native villages in search of work, fun and a lively time. Many are on their way up in business or in the service industries that are so thick on the ground in the island capital. Some seem to have little time for the visitor in search of advice or directions. But summon up a few introductory words of Greek—*kali méra* (good morning), *kali spéra* (good afternoon), *signómi* (excuse me), *parakoló* (please), *efharistó* (thank you), *adío* (goodbye)—and you will soon break through the city sharpness to genuine politeness and a desire to help the stranger.

TAKE A WALK It would be a great shame to hurry away from Irakleío without giving this cosmopolitan and vigorous city a chance to captivate you. This process will take a bit longer, and demand a little more effort on your part, than in Réthymno or Chaniá, with their cosier and more instantly attractive atmosphere. A walk around the city will introduce you to the most important and well-known features of Irakleío, and show you many uncelebrated but intriguing nooks and corners. Here, as in all extensive and ancient cities, there is always something waiting to surprise, perhaps to shock, perhaps to delight, but always to interest you, just around the corner. Exploration of Crete begins here, in the heart of the island's least-explored and most underrated location.

Ágios Títos church

BACKSTREET CRAFTSMEN
Irakleío may seem like a big, impatient city that has thrown off its former provincialism, but first impressions can be deceptive. In tiny workshops tucked away down side streets the tradition of craftsmanship is alive and well. Opposite the church of Ágios Dimítrios between Odos Kosma Zoton and Odos Thalita, a cooper still turns out wooden barrels made by hand, exactly as his father and grandfather did.

BOOKING OFFICE
It is a good idea to take something to read with you when you visit the tourist information office opposite the Archaeological Museum. The overstretched staff, especially in the summer season, take their time to get to you. Eventually, however, your turn will come and your patience will be rewarded.

There are many good views to be had from the old walls

KIOSKS
In Iraklеío you will not take long to spot your first cigarette kiosk. An omnipresent feature of Cretan towns and villages, it is usually a little hut on the pavement, The owner skulks within its dark interior. Every wall and window is jam-packed with goods, and many have a public telephone with a meter that clicks up the charge—which you pay after your call. As well as cigarettes, the kiosk will probably sell postcards, stamps, sweets, books, magazines, newspapers, worry beads, souvenirs, lottery tickets...

SIN CITY
Iraklеío people were noted in Venetian and Turkish times for their decadence, idleness, love of luxury, fondness for drink and addiction to the pleasures of both board and bed. *Plus ça change...!*

From the Stone Age to the Saracens Neolithic people were the first to settle in the area to the east of modern Irakleío. In Minoan times there was a thriving harbour on the same site, which served the settlement at Knosós, 5km (3 miles) inland. The Roman port of Herakleium grew up on the site of the present-day harbour, trading with the southern and eastern parts of the Roman Empire. Knosós became a Roman colony during the 1st century BC. After the overthrow and partition of the Roman Empire during the 4th century AD, Herakleium continued to prosper under Byzantine rule, though Gortýs to the south had become the island's capital. In 824 the Saracens invaded and conquered Crete, destroying Gortýs and establishing their power centre at Herakleium. They fortified their new settlement with a mighty ditch, and renamed the town Rabdh-el-Khandak, the castle of the ditch. Throughout the following century the port was a base for pirate raids across the Mediterranean, but in 960 the grim Byzantine general Nikephóros Phokás landed with a polyglot army and laid siege to Rabdh-el-Khandak, underlining his determination by catapulting the heads of Saracen prisoners into the town. The siege lasted ten months, and ended with victory for the Byzantine invaders and widespread destruction of the town.

The Byzantines and Venetians After the departure of the Saracens, Rabdh-el-Khandak was renamed Khándakas, and its people reverted from piracy to relatively peaceful trading with the Byzantine empire. Stability was to last for the next 250 years. At the beginning of the 13th century, the empire of Byzantium in its turn collapsed and with the arrival of the Venetians the capital city, and subsequently the whole island, gained yet another name—Candia. From then, for 450 years, the city enjoyed a Golden Age. Fine Venetian town houses and a ducal palace were built, new churches were erected, the harbour was massively fortified, sanitation and efficient water supplies were introduced, enormous and cunningly engineered walls were built around the city, and trade with Europe, North Africa and the Middle East brought renewed prosperity.

Turkish rule All this came to an end on 5 September 1669, when the gates of the city were opened to allow the last Venetians on mainland Crete to leave the island. The city gates had been closed for 21 years during the Great Siege of Candia, while the Turks who had invaded and conquered the rest of Crete were prevented from picking this last and juiciest plum. The city started a long, dark journey of decline and tension that lasted some 250 years. Venetian churches were converted to mosques, a pasha was brought in to govern the capital and its dependent province, and the city itself received its fifth name since Roman times, Megálo Kástro, the Great Fort. Pogroms of the city's Christians, the indifference of the Turks to trade, and clandestine support within the capital for the frequent rebellions in other parts of the island all contributed to the unhappiness of Megálo Kástro. At the end of the 19th century the murder in the city of 14 British soldiers and their consul finally focused the minds of the European Powers upon Crete. The Turks were ousted, and the capital received yet another name, albeit one with echoes of the distant past—Herákleion, or Irakleío as it is known today.

BIG CASTLE
Megálo Kástro, the Big Castle, was the name by which Irakleío was known under Turkish rule. Níkos Kazantzákis retained the old name when writing of the city, both in his novels and in his long and vivid autobiographical book, *Report to Greco*.

The 19th-century Cathedral of Ágios Mínas

World War II During the Battle of Crete in May 1941 Irakleío was badly bombed as the Germans tried to dislodge the British, Greek and Australian defenders of the city. House-to-house fighting, and the bombardment of the port to harrass the evacuation of Allied troops, reduced much of the city to ruins. During the years of occupation Irakleío became a hotbed of resistance. Towards the end of 1944 the Germans withdrew from the city, and the partisans and Allied resistance workers came down from the mountains. After the war, reconstruction began to change the face and character of the old city, work that has continued to the present day. In 1971 Irakleío took over from the ancient stronghold of Chaniá as the official capital city of Crete.

BACKSTREET ARCHITECTURE
There are many modest delights of architecture to be spotted and enjoyed among Irakleío's blocks of flats and lines of modern shops. Tottering Venetian town house façades, gracefully curved Turkish window frames, ornate old doorways and curlicued iron balconies suggest that history has not departed from Irakleío, but has shifted from the main thoroughfares into the side streets and more obscure parts of town.

TOWN MOSAIC
The blueprint for much of the reconstruction of the Palace of Knosós lies in Case 25, Room II. Here you will see a set of beautiful small glazed earthenware plaques, richly decorated with colour, in the shape of Minoan house-fronts, some of them two or three storeys high. Known as the Town Mosaic, they are complete with doors and windows, and probably originally fitted together with others in one composite display.

MOTHER'S MILK
Case 55 in Room IV holds two of the small masterpieces of Minoan art: a cow giving suck to her calf, and a wild goat with great curled horns nuzzling her kids.

The Dolphin Fresco from the queen's apartment at Knosós

►►► Archaiologikó Mouseío 43E3

Plateía Elefthérias (entrance on Odós Xanthoudídou)
Open: 8–7 summer, 8–3 winter; 8.30–3 on Sunday; noon–7 Monday. Admission: expensive
This is one of the world's great archaeological collections. A renovation of the main building means that from mid 2007 only the most significant pieces will be on display in a much-reduced space. At time of print, there was no firm date for the museum to resume normal service.

Room I (ca6000 BC–ca1900 BC) These are some of the earliest artefacts discovered in Crete. There are idols, stone axe heads and bone scrapers as well as early examples of the mottled, semi-fired patterns of Vasilikí ware, notably jugs with the extended, upward pointing spouts so characteristic of early Minoan pottery and combining grace and practicality. In Case 12 is a crudely fashioned little clay bull with an acrobat curled around his left horn, and in Case 16 some exquisitely worked seal-stone carvings, including a tiny fly and dove.

Room II (ca1900 BC–ca1700 BC) Finds from Knosós include scores of votive figurines of people and animals. Case 21 contains a two-headed push-me-pull-you. There are also pottery *taxímata* (diseased arms, legs and feet) very like those stamped on silver plaques and affixed to church icons by sufferers today. Swirly decorations on great thick jars and basins in Case 27 are a complete contrast to the Kamáres pottery in Case 23, eggshell delicate and as thin as fine porcelain.

Room III (ca2000 BC–ca1700 BC) The Old Palace at Faistós contributed most of the items here, including some delicate Kamáres ware with black, red and white decorations. Pride of the room, however, is the Faistós Disc in Case 41, a flat clay disc 16cm in diameter, stamped with as yet undeciphered pictorial characters incorporating fish, shells, a ship, tools, running figures and flowers that spiral in towards the centre.

Room IV (ca1700 BC–ca1450 BC) The fine flowering of Minoan art is represented in this room, dating from the period ca1700 BC after the palaces had been rebuilt following their destruction. Nature is the main influence, with few abstract designs. Among well-known exhibits here are the two bare-breasted snake goddesses (Case 50); the finely detailed design of reeds on a jug (Case 49); the bull's-head *rhyton* or libation jug with mother-of-pearl nostrils

and rock crystal eyes (Case 51); another *rhyton* shaped like the head of a lioness; a leopard's-head axe from Mália (Case 47); an ivory acrobat caught in mid-leap (Case 56); and a very complicated and unfathomed gaming board (Case 57).

Irakleío's Archaeological Museum holds a superb collection of pottery from Knosós

Room V (ca1450 BC–ca1400 BC) Finds here are chiefly from Knosós, dating from the period immediately after the cataclysm of ca1450 BC. The decoration on pottery is beginning to turn away from naturalistic designs to something more formal and stylised. Seal stones are still beautifully carved; helpful drawings show enlarged subjects. In Case 69 are examples of Minoan scripts.

Room VI (ca1450 BC–ca1400 BC) Among the finds on display from cemeteries including Knosós, Faistós and Archánes are helmets and weapons, reflecting the advent of a more aggressive, military society. There are also some fine clay figures dancing in a circle (Case 71); elaborate jellyfish on amphorae in Case 82; and beautiful jewellery in Cases 86–8, including a ring decorated with women dancing amongst flowers, and another with figures mourning the annual death of the god of vegetation.

Room VII (ca1600 BC–ca1450 BC) Treasures include three black steatite vases from Agía Triáda palace: the Chieftain Cup (a Minoan potentate accepting animal skins); the Harvester Vase (wildly singing harvesters with flat caps bearing home sheaves of corn); and the Boxer Vase (a boxer knocked flat with his heels in the air, a wrestling match and bull-leaping). Case 101 contains the famous gold pendant from Mália depicting a pair of bees with a honeycomb.

LINEAR MYSTERY

In Room V you will find examples of the two types of hieroglyphs found at many Cretan sites. The Linear A of the Minoans is as yet undeciphered, but the Linear B, which was brought to the island by the Mycenaean Greeks shortly after the widespread destruction ca1450 BC, is reasonably well understood. How exciting it will be when someone succeeds in interpreting the secrets of Linear A, and opens a new window on the Minoan world.

ATTITUDE PROBLEM
The bronze and terracotta figures of men and women praying with one hand on the breast and the spine arched backwards probably show the actual attitude that Minoans adopted in prayer—a most uncomfortable stance. Try standing like this for two minutes!

Room VIII (ca1700 BC–ca1450 BC) This room contains finds from the great palace at Zákros, at the eastern end of the island. Tools and weapons include big saws, and there is a wonderful variety of *rhytons* or jugs. Case 111 contains a green chlorite *rhyton* burned into variegated colours and depicting a long-horned wild goat. Case 109 holds a delicate and beautiful rock crystal *rhyton* reassembled from over 300 pieces.

Room IX (ca1700 BC–ca1450 BC) Finds here are from the lesser sites in the east, and include terracotta figures in ordinary dress; tools and weapons from Gourniá (Case 127); amphorae with staring octopuses (Case 128); and marvellous seal stones with beasts, gods, thistles, goats and bull-leapers (Cases 124, 128).

Minoan pottery from the palace of Knosós

Room X (ca1350 BC–ca1100 BC) Artistic decline and a loss of vitality and originality become apparent after the destruction of the great palaces ca1450 BC. Decorations are mostly geometric and stylised, with the octopus motif being reduced to a formulaic squiggle.

Room XI (ca1100 BC–ca800 BC) There are pottery goddesses here with raised hands, stiff and crude. Case 158 has Egyptian jewellery; Case 153 shows evidence that iron was taking over from bronze. Cretan society was now changing, but old and vigorous influences were still at play. In Case 149 there are figurines of copulating couples and pregnant women, which were probably votive offerings to the goddess of childbirth.

Room XII (ca800 BC–ca650 BC) Foreign artistic influences are becoming stronger, with winged griffons and sphinx-like Egyptian figures, and eastern-looking flower motifs resembling the lotus. Case 163 has Theseus and Ariadne embracing on the neck of a vessel, a beautiful snarling lioness and a wise old horned owl.

UPLIFTED
In contrast to the backward-bending devotees, the goddesses themselves, perhaps priestesses, were represented by artists through the Minoan era standing with upraised arms, reaching skyward or maybe passing on a blessing.

Room XIII This is a collection of *larnakes* or clay sarcophagi, some with gabled tops; others may have been used as bathtubs and are complete with plug holes. Decorations include flowers, water birds, octopuses, geometric patterns, and red and black sacred axes.

Rooms XIV, XV and XVI These upstairs rooms contain restored frescoes illustrating the light, graceful and airy quality of Minoan life. Most are from the palace at Knosós and date from between 1600 and 1400 BC. They were painted directly onto wet plaster with vegetable, mineral and shellfish dyes. Men are depicted with red skin, women with white. There are bull frescoes, griffons from the palace throne room, lively dolphins from the queen's room, and the bull-leaper, somersaulting backwards over a charging bull. *La Parisienne*, a doe-eyed, carmine-lipped, carefully coiffed priestess; the saffron-gatherer; a Minoan officer and two black-skinned soldiers are all here. Others from Agía Triáda are even more vividly coloured: long-eared wild cats with bob tails watch oblivious birds feeding; a marine floor fresco shows wildly cavorting fish; a stunningly decorated sarcophagus from Agía Triáda has a bull being sacrificed while two terrified calves look on awaiting their turn.

One of several small votive offerings from Knosós

Room XVII The wide-ranging collection of the late Dr S Giamalákis includes a chubby-thighed neolithic goddess seated in the lotus position, gold jewellery, figurines with smiling faces, and a little clay shrine with two men and a dog on the roof, peering or perhaps speaking down a central shaft.

Room XVIII (ca650 BC–ca AD 400) Classical, Hellenistic, Greek and Roman cultures mingle here with wild dancers, winged figures, hunters, figures from Classical mythology, coins of bronze, silver and gold.

Room XIX (ca700 BC–ca500 BC) There are big, clumsy, solid sculptures here, in contrast with the worked bronze shields from the Ídaean Cave with projecting bosses and splendid decoration in the form of a hawk, a lion, embattled men and gods.

Room XX
Graeco–Roman sculpture lines the walls of this room, sculpture executed with a technical skill that the Minoans never approached, but they are pale and cold, devoid of the Minoan delight in the natural world. Only No 153, a rather endearing and shaggy-thighed Pan blowing his pipes, gives an echo of those warm, light-hearted people.

MODEL PALACE
For those who have visited the palace site at Knosós, and have come away unable to visualise the Minoan reality of that great jumble of stone, there is an excellent model in the Hall of the Frescos upstairs, showing the palace as King Minos must have known it.

A bronze shepherd and his rather canine sheep

Walk

Irakleío's highlights

As the capital city of the island, and the site of its main airport and ferry terminals, Irakleío may well be your first taste of Crete. Arriving tired and tense from your journey, you will almost inevitably feel a sense of let-down. It is probably best, from a scenic point of view, to arrive by ferry. Seen from the sea, the city benefits from its cradle of mountains, with the Díktaean range rising inland—snow-capped or dramatically bare, according to season. Entering Irakleío this way, you will be spared the concrete reality of the dreary suburbs with their uncompromising blocks of flats and dusty streets. Either way, it is likely that your first emotions will be confusion and a mild but definite disillusion. Irakleío is not an easy place to fall in love with. Thanks to a programme of extensive rebuilding after World War II, and to constant development during the commercial boom of recent decades, the city seems initially to have little of the historic charm that characterises Réthymno and Chaniá, its smaller and less frenetic north coast neighbours.

Bear in mind that 130,000 people live and work in Irakleío, making it a noisy, hasty and crowded place. In the high summer season you can add hundreds of thousands of tourists *en passage* to this number. Irakleío is in many ways entirely untypical of the Crete you have come to explore, but in its grimy, roaring heart the basic Cretan virtues still flourish: warmth, vibrancy, time for the stranger, an inexhaustible curiosity as to who you are and what you are up to. Many of the city's inhabitants are only first or second generation Irakleío people, and so they look to their native villages in the mountains or out along the coast for their roots and manners. Village mentality and traditions are still strong in the city. Most people in Iráklio will go out of their way to help, direct and advise you, particularly if you approach them with a few simple phrases in Greek.

In spite of comprehensive restructuring and development, Irakleío is full of

The restful courtyard of the Venetian Loggia

odd corners and reminders of its rich, violent history. A rambling walk through the old city will introduce you to the strong and idiosyncratic flavours of Irakleío past and present, which mingle to great effect inside its encircling Venetian walls. The chapter on Irakleío lists the sights of the city in the order in which you will encounter them on the walk. Allow a full day, or at least 5–6 hours. See the map on pages 42–43.

Start outside the Archaeological Museum on Odós Xanthoudídou with the tourist information office opposite you. Turn left into **Plateía Elefthérias**.

Cross Odós Xanthoudídou and keep left, then bear right around the end of the cinema block. Odós Idomíneos runs at the back of the block, parallel to Odós Xanthoudídou. Wander downhill for a detour here past dark shops in crumbling Turkish houses. The main walk follows the pedestrianised Odós Daidálos, which branches off left immediately after you round the cinema, sloping past souvenir shops, bars and restaurants down to **Plateía Venizélou**. Walk through the square and the covered passage between the restaurants, taking first right and right again to reach **El Greco Park (Párko Gréko)** and beyond, on the corner of Plateía Kallergou, the **Venetian Loggia**. Walk through here to the **City Hall** and the church of **Ágios Títos**. Cross the *plateía* and turn right down Odós 25 Avgoústou to reach the **harbour (Palaió Limáni)** and the **Venetian fort (Koúles)**. From the landward end of the breakwater cross the roundabout back to Odós 25 Avgoústou. First right (Odós Kosma Zotou) leads to a *plateía* with cafés. Turn left here to find the Church of Ágios Dimítrios, decorated with fine modern frescoes. Continue along Odós Thalita, crossing Odós Laxana. Turn right at the T-junction, left down Odós Kalokairinou, past the once ruined but now renovated Venetian Church of St Peter (Ágios Pétros) and find the **Historical Museum (Istorikó Mouseío Krítis)**.

From the museum, continue up Odós Grevenou. Take the second right, down Kalimeraki, left into Chortatsou, immediately right across Chandakos and on down Vistaki. At the end turn right, then left along Giamalaki and turn first right down Kazantzáki to the **Priuli fountain** on the left. From the fountain return up Kazantzáki. Turn right, then first left up Apokoronou, a twisting little alleyway. Keep dog-legging right and left. Odós 1770 is the next right turn; follow it round, bearing left by a tottering old building with curly iron brackets supporting its overhanging upper storey. Take the first right down Ioánnou Moirelou, cross wide Kalokairinou into Ayíon Déka, to reach **Plateía Aikaterínis**, a wide, paved square with three churches to explore.

From the steps of the Cathedral of **Ágios Minás**, bear left round the corner of the building. Turn right up Karterou, crossing Katechaki, and take first right down pedestrianised Amisou. Turn left at the bottom, cross Odós 1821 and go up Pizaniou. Bear right at the tree, and left along busy Vikéla into **Plateía Kornárou**.

Leave Plateía Kornárou and head straight up **Odós 1866**, Market Street, opposite the Turkish fountain-café. At the top of Market Street is Plateía Nikephórou Phoká. Turn right at the traffic lights along Odós Dikaiosínis Street, lined with shops ranging from tacky souvenir stalls to smart dress and jewellery emporia, and finish the walk back in Plateía Elefthérias.

Plateía Kornárou

Modern ceiling frescoes in the church of St Mary, located between Irakleío's Historical Museum and Ágios Dimítrios

►► Plateía Elefthérias 43D2

Elefthérias means freedom, and as an expression of the traditional Cretan spirit of fortitude and resistance it is the perfect name for the square where the Irakleío walk begins, Plateía Elefthérias. A mass of traffic swirls around the dusty little gardens shaded by acacias and palm trees. This used to be the city's main meeting and gossiping centre, and despite the cars and buses is still reckoned by most Irakleío people to be at the heart of their city. Cafés, hotels, cigarette kiosks and a cinema line the wide square, which at night swaps its motorised traffic, to a certain extent, for the two-legged variety.

►► Plateía Venizélou 43D3

Nearby Plateía Venizélou, better known to visitors as Lion Square, has become the hub of the tourists' Irakleío, and it is certainly a pleasant place to sit and watch the

Sadly the Morozíni Fountain rarely plays

world go by. Lion Square is traffic-free, and is peppered with cafés and restaurants as well as bakers' shops where you can buy a cheese pie or *boúgatsa,* a pastry filled with cinnamon-spiced custard, to enjoy with a cup of coffee. The focal point of the square is the celebrated **Morozíni fountain▶▶▶**, constructed in 1628 by Francesco Morozíni, the Venetian governor of Candia, as Irakleío was then known. A 16km (10 mile) long aqueduct was built to bring water from Mount Gioúchtas to the fountain, which incorporated four stone lions carved three centuries earlier. They still roar (under rather human noses) above a maritime frieze of mermaids, nymphs, tritons and winged cherubs, though the marble statue of Neptune that once surmounted them has long gone, destroyed during the Turkish occupation. Opposite the fountain stands the colonnaded porch of the **Basilica of St Mark (Ágios Márcos)▶.** Founded in 1239, twice rebuilt after earthquake damage, and later converted by the Turks into a mosque, the basilica contains a superb marble doorway decorated with clusters of grapes.

▶ El Greco Park (Párko Gréko) *43D3*

A bust of the great Cretan painter stares over tree-shaded flower beds and a children's playground with swings and slides in El Greco Park off Plateía Venizélou. Beyond the park on the corner of Plateía Kallergou stands the tall, rectangular **Venetian Loggia▶▶.** This is a reconstruction, after earthquake and war damage, of the original, which was built in 1626 by Francesco Morozíni as a pleasant gathering place for the great and good of Venetian Irakleío. The open ground floor arches are duplicated above in the window frames, and the top is balustraded and pinnacled. Inside the loggia is an open, D-shaped courtyard from which you walk through a door into the **City Hall▶** or Dimarkheíon, formerly the Venetian city's armoury, a massive construction whose far side faces the **Church of Ágios Títos▶▶▶** across a little court.

COFFEE BREAK
As midday approaches, the street waiters emerge, carrying cups of sweet Greek coffee and glasses of water from the cafés through the crowded streets to the office workers. Some carry trays balanced on one hand, others swing a pyramid-shaped tin cradle.

Irakleío possesses a number of statues and memorials to Cretan heroes. Most striking of all, in sheer size and gloominess, is the larger-than-life statue of Crete's greatest statesman, Elefthérios Venizélos. It stands at the south-eastern corner of Plateía Elefthérias.

The plaque on the grave of Níkos Kazantzákis (above)

DEMON TURKS
In icons painted during the Turkish occupation of Crete, the Roman or Barbarian soldiers shown martyring the saints are generally of unmistakably Turkish mien, with pointed hats, chin beards, pantaloons, curved sabres and slippers with upturned toes.

STREET HEROES
Cretan heroes of various wars and campaigns of resistance are frequently commemorated in street names. Among the most common are Venizélos, Daskaloyiánnis, Kandanóleon (leader of a 16th-century revolt against the Venetians), Daliánis (a mainland Greek leader who occupied Frangokástello in 1828 and was killed when the Turks retook it) and Gabriel Arkádiou, the Abbot of Arkádiou Monastery who blew up the building and everyone in it on 9 November 1866 rather than be taken by the besieging Turks.

Elefthérios Venizélos The likeness of Venizélos's statue to Lenin is often remarked on, probably more on account of the stiffness and aloofness of the pose than the individual features. Venizélos (1864–1936) is seen as the founding father of modern Greece. Cretans revere him as the local boy from Mourniés, near Chaniá, who played his part as a young man in the struggle against Turkish rule, organised the 1897 protest that led to the raising of the Greek flag, and convened the Revolutionary Assembly in 1905, which prompted the resignation of Prince George of Greece as High Commissioner of Crete. He became the Prime Minister of Greece in 1910, and three years later saw his and his island's dream of *enosis*, union with Greece, realised at last. After the Great War, Venizélos had his share of ups and downs, including long periods in opposition and the survival of an assassination attempt. The failure of his attempt to establish a New Byzantium in Turkey culminated in his resignation as Prime Minister in 1932. He was exiled when the short-lived Greek Republic collapsed, and was given a sentence of death *in absentia* when a coup failed. The newly restored King George II

Eleftheríos Venizélos brought union with Greece in 1913

pardoned him, but he never came back to Greece, dying in France in 1936. In Crete, however, the failures of his later years are disregarded. What counts is the dynamism and cool competence of the young Venizélos who brought about *enosis*.

Ioánnis Daskaloyiánnis A few hundred metres to the west stands the statue of **Ioánnis Daskaloyiánnis**, in the *plateía* of the same name. The 18th-century rebel leader was born Ioánnis Vláhos in Anópolis, on the southern coast of Sfakiot country in the southwest of the island. He embodies all the Cretan heroic attributes: he was learned (Daskaloyiánnis means John the Teacher), he was charismatic and brave, and he died a particularly nasty death. His 1770 rebellion against the Turks started brilliantly, but when support from the Russians melted away he went down to Fragkokástelo on the south coast to give himself up. The ruling pasha in Irakleío, having treated him most hospitably, took umbrage at Daskaloyiánnis's assertion that he had rebelled to set right the wrongs of all Cretans and Christians, and ordered the unfortunate hero to be flayed alive.

A well-armed Daskaloyiánnis

Nikephóros Phokás Just south of the Archaeological Museum, and outside the medieval town walls, a column beside Dimokratías Avenue commemorates a hero with an even more bloody story attached to his name. **Nikephóros Phokás** was not a Cretan but a ruthless Byzantine general who was charged with recapturing Rabdh-el-Khandak from the Saracens in AD 961. He ensured success by catapulting the heads of captured Saracens into the city, where they fell among the understandably demoralised defenders.

Heroes of arts and letters In El Greco Park, the small public gardens just off Plateía Venizélos, look for the bust of the celebrated painter who was born Doménico Theotokópoulos, probably at Fodhéle near Irakleío. Theotokópoulos (ca1541–1614) found widespread fame under the pseudonym of **El Greco**. He was an acknowledged master at marrying the spirit of the old and new, the Byzantine and Renaissance worlds.

The painter El Greco

At the southernmost tip of the medieval walls, massively simple in its setting on top of the Martinengo Bastion, is the tomb of Crete's most celebrated writer, the widely admired **Níkos Kazantzákis** (1883–1957). "I hope for nothing; I fear nothing; I am free", reads the inscription. The Irakleío-born writer became internationally famous when his novel *Zorba the Greek* was filmed. Today his other works attract equal interest. Only *Zorba* and his superb *Freedom and Death* were set in Crete, but Kazantzákis drew on his roots throughout his unorthodox, wandering life.

BIG-HEAD
The story goes that a visitor, on being shown the skull of St Titus, remarked that he had been shown the saint's skull, rather smaller than this one, the day before in a distant monastery. The custodian, not taken aback in the slightest, hastened to explain that that must have been the skull of the saint as a boy.

The Church of Ágios Títos

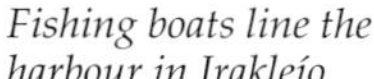

►► The Church of Ágios Títos *43D3*

The church (*Open* daily 6.30–12.30, 4.30–8) was rebuilt as a mosque after an earthquake destroyed the Byzantine original in 1856. The interior is capped by a galleried dome and has a modern iconostasis. Paintings of Cretan martyrs and scenes from the life of St Titus hang on the walls.

Titus was sent by St Paul to convert the Cretans, and he became the first bishop of the island. His body was brought to the church at Irakleío in AD 962. In 1669 the Venetians, evacuating Candia after its capture by the Turks, took the relics to Venice. They were returned to

Fishing boats line the harbour in Irakleío

The magnificent Venetian fortress still dominates the harbour

Ágios Títos in 1966. A shrine contains a gold reliquary that holds the skull of the saint; a little brown dome of bone is visible through a hole in the top of the container.

► Odós 25 Avgoústou *43D3*

Odós 25 Avgoústou is one of Irakleío's chief commercial streets, named after the day in 1898 when several Cretans were killed by Turkish soldiers just before the Great Powers enforced their withdrawal agreement on the Turks. Big, crumbling buildings at the bottom of the street, fronted in Turkish style, overlook the **harbour►►**. Irakleío's harbour has seen many centuries of fighting, destruction and bloodshed along with the steady flow of commerce that has made it the most significant place in Crete's history. One look at the enormous stone fort on the breakwater tells you the importance that the Venetians attached to securing this gateway to the island. But this harbour has been the commercial nerve-centre of Crete since it was named Herakleium by the Romans. During the Battle of Crete in 1941 the port was heavily bombed, and the British forces around Irakleío were evacuated from the mole by British Royal Navy ships at dead of night on 28–29 May. Nowadays the harbour scene is a lively one, with visitors crowding the quays and breakwater while fishermen unconcernedly continue to mend their nets and transfer their catches to the battered pick-up trucks of the fish dealers. Caïques take parties of tourists on fishing trips and out to the island of Día, whose long bulk lies offshore. The ferries from Piraeus and other islands dock at a big modern terminal to the east, so there is little to spoil the attractive old harbour.

►►► Venetian fort (Koúles) *43E4*

The Venetian fort (tel: 2810 246211. *Open* May–Sep daily 8.30–5, Oct–Apr Tue–Sat 8.30–3 *Admission: inexpensive*), a few hundred metres out along the breakwater, is an obvious magnet for visitors. Step over a metal barrier and walk into the shadow of its massive walls, and a wide view opens as far as the Psiloreítis Mountains, which are snow-capped for much of the year. The walls of the fort are many metres thick, built of enormous blocks of yellow stone eroded by centuries of wind, weather and attack. The Venetians called it Rocca al Mare, the Rock in the Sea, a name that perfectly expresses its air of grim defiance.

PRIDE OF LIONS

As a symbol of their eternal vigilance, and their pride and swiftness in retribution, the Venetians set up marble statues of the winged lion of St Mark in the walls and over the gateways of the forts they built across Crete. These Venetian lions still look seaward in poignant defiance. Many Cretan churches also bear the winged lion in tympanum carvings.

RAGING BULL
The Romans named their port of Herakleium after the Greek hero Heracles, in commemoration of the seventh labour set him by King Eurystheus of Mycenae. Heracles was sent to Crete to tame a white bull that was ravaging the island. Its owner, King Minos, had refused to sacrifice it to Poseidon as the god of the sea had demanded, and Poseidon had driven it mad in revenge. Needless to say, Heracles soon had the bull in a half-Nelson and brought it triumphantly to the astounded Eurystheus.

The Saracens built a fort on this tiny rock opposite the harbour, as did Genoese adventurers when they briefly took control of the north coast towns early in the 13th century. The Venetians, who succeeded them, constructed a stronger fortification, but this was wrecked in the earthquake of 1303, and was again rebuilt. A rocky breakwater connected it to the mainland, and another fort stood at the mouth of the harbour. After destructive raids in the 1530s by the much feared Ottoman pirate-admiral Khaireddin Barbarossa, Rocca al Mare was refortified and strengthened yet again, work that came into its own a century later during the Great Siege by the Turks. A multimillion euro renovation programme in 2006 saw underpinning of the seaward walls and bulwarks to reduced damage by the waters of the Mediterranean.

There are three imposing marble winged lions of St Mark in the north, east and south walls of the fort. The best preserved of these faces out to sea, threatening all-comers with snarling jaws and upraised wings. This sculpture, gazing out above the clicking cameras, speaks eloquently of the pride and power of medieval Venice, and of the subjugation of the island to so many succeeding conquerors. Entering the fort by the southern door, you wander through shadowy stone chambers among rusty, ancient cannon and piles of dusty cannon balls. A roughly paved stone ramp rises to the upper storey, which is laid out with a small open-air theatre and from which you can reach the crenellated ramparts. Climb up the lookout tower for a superb view over Irakleío and the mountains behind.

▶ Arsenali *43D4*

Around the east side of the harbour several tall, hollow, stone arches rise above the offices, shops and cars. These were *arsenali*, or sheds for the construction and repair of ships, which were built in the 16th century—around the same time as the re-strengthening of the fort—to service the Venetian galley fleet.

A 17th-century icon from the Historical Museum

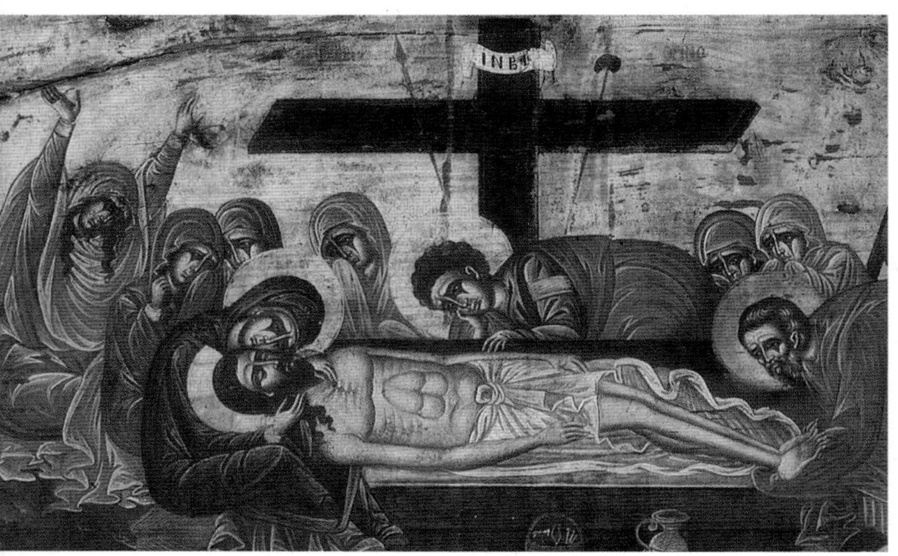

The quiet courtyard of the Historical Museum

►► Historical Museum (Istorikó Mouseío Krítis) *42C4*

The Historical Museum (Odós Lyssimachou Kalokairinou, tel: 2810 288708. *Open* Mon-Fri 9–5, Sat 9–2. *Admission: moderate*) is in a dignified Venetian town house with a Turkish fountain outside the door, opposite the Hotel Xenia. Compare the intriguing 17th-century Venetian prints of Candia in the entrance hall with the modern map before descending to the basement, where Venetian wealth and industry are illustrated in the stonemasons' craft. There are also some 18th-century Turkish mural scenes of Irakleío. On the ground floor there are icons and a beautifully restored 13th-century church fresco of a tousle-haired and heavy-eyed John the Baptist. Red-capped Sfakiot partisan chiefs line the stairs leading to the upper floor and to reconstructions of the studies of Crete's pre-eminent novelist Níkos Kazantzákis and the Crete-born wartime prime minister of Greece, Emmanuel Tsouderós. Also here are exhibitions of wartime photographs, while on the top floor you will find examples of traditional Cretan weaving and embroidery, and the re-creation of a peasant house.

► Priuli Fountain *42C2*

The nearby Priuli fountain was built in 1666 by Antonio Priuli during the Great Siege of Candia, and was embellished with Corinthian columns, a pediment, ornate side scrolls and an inscription. It stands today in the shadow of a workaday block of flats, but is still a poignant monument to the gracious living of the past.

EL GRECO

The painter El Greco was a native Cretan, born Domenico Theotokópoulos in the village of Fódhele near Irakleío in 1541. The Historical Museum contains one early painting of his, on display by itself in a room on the ground floor. This depiction of travellers on their way to the monastery of St Catherine on Mount Sinai was painted in about 1570, when El Greco had just left Crete to pursue his studies in Rome. Deep-rooted Byzantine formality and discipline show in the stiffly posed figures, but there is an altogether Renaissance depth and realism to the mountainous setting.

Ornate ceilings and candelabra in Ágios Minás cathedral

► Plateía Aikaterínis *42C2*

Plateía Aikaterínis is a wide paved square with three churches to explore: **Agía Aikaterínis;** the **Cathedral of Ágios Minás**; and the **Church of Ágios Minás**. All three are described below, but the first of these is the most notable.

►►► Agía Aikaterínis of Siniates *42C2*

Agía Aikaterínis is on your left as you enter Plateía Aikaterínis. Built in 1555, this barn-like church now houses the **Museum of Icons and Sacred Objects** (Plateía Aikaterina, tel: 2810 288825. *Open* Mon–Fri 10–1. *Admission: moderate*). Apart from the elaborately carved Venetian doorway at the west end, there is nothing particularly special about Agía Aikaterínis from the outside, but once inside you will be dazzled by the fabulous collection of Byzantine and Renaissance icons, religious texts and precious ceremonial items from churches and monasteries all over Crete.

El Greco and Mikhaíl Damaskinós A college attached to Agía Aikaterínis, an outpost of a great monastery of the same name on Mount Sinai, became Crete's most influential centre for religious and philosophical education and teaching of the arts in late Venetian times. A small painting of the mother monastery by El Greco hangs in the Historical Museum.

El Greco, born and raised in Crete, was rivalled only by his contemporary Mikhaíl Damaskinós, who studied here before going abroad to make a living and nurture his talent in Venice. Returning to Crete, Damaskinós painted a series of six superb icons in 1582–1591 for the monastery at Vrontísíou (see page 191). They were brought to Irakleío in 1800 to save them from the Turks, and now hang here in Agía Aikaterínis. They are the *Adoration of the Magi;* the *Last Supper;* the *Burning Bush,* with a sublime Virgin; *Noli Me Tangere,* with the resurrected Christ astonishing the two Marys; a semi-circle of bearded and haloed bishops at the *First Ecumenical Synod at Nicaea;* and adoring angels clustered round Christ celebrating *Holy Mass.* Brilliantly executed, wonderfully detailed and full of life and expression, these icons deserve closer study than they sometimes receive.

THE LAST SUPPER
Note the two dogs contesting ownership of a bone under the table; a little black-skinned slave bringing three bowls up from the cellar on a tray; the ornate benches which have lions' feet; and a heavy, embroidered rug which covers the table under the linen tablecloth. St John's head is on the table, cradled on his arms, a picture of dejection. Another disciple bends intently forward on one elbow, while a red-capped man leans through a curtained archway, giving a meaningful now's-the-time look to the stealthily departing Judas.

► Cathedral of Ágios Minás *42C2*

The big 19th-century Cathedral of Ágios Minás dominates Plateía Aikaterínis. Inside there is a profusion of frescoes from floor to roof, and in the centre hang fantastically elaborate chandeliers. In the shadow of the cathedral lies the little **Church of Ágios Minás►** with twin apses and bellcote. It is usually kept locked, but the custodian of the cathedral may rouse himself sufficiently to hunt out a key so that you can go in and admire the beautiful carved and painted iconostasis.

► Plateía Kornárou *43D2*

In Plateía Kornárou there is a modern sculpture of a three-headed, multi-legged horse carrying two warriors, approaching a pre-Raphaelite maiden. This is an interpretation of a stirring scene from the famous Cretan epic poem *Erotókritos* in which the eponymous peasant hero meets his nobly born lover Aretoúsa.

► Fountains *43D2*

Below and across Plateía Kornárou are two historic fountains, close together. The octagonal stone **kiosk►** was erected by the Turks to house one of the many fountains they provided around Irakleío and the other major cities of Crete, reflecting the Islamic reverence for water, so often in short supply in the religion's Middle Eastern homelands. Nowadays the graceful little building with its projecting eaves contains a very hospitable café, a welcome break on the walk. With a drink and a snack to hand, you can contrast the Turkish fountain-building style with the nearby Venetian **Bembo fountain (Kríni Bembo)**, assembled in 1588 from an odd collection of antiquities including the torso of a Roman statue from Ierápetra, various columns and carved slabs.

►► Odós 1866 *43D2*

Odós 1866, opposite the Turkish fountain-café, is one of the city's most famous, and correspondingly crowded, thoroughfares, better known as Market Street. Irakleío's present-day commercial activity is concentrated near the freight docks beyond the ferry terminal, but in Market Street, tourist-orientated though it is, you can still catch the flavour of what the bazaar must have been like in Turkish and Venetian days. Little shops line each side of the street, many of them selling souvenirs that are likely to be over-priced and of poor quality. But there are also butchers with carcasses swinging from hooks, savoury-smelling bakers, fruit shops, vendors of olives, shops crammed with leather belts and bags, and shops hung with flapping festoons of brightly coloured woven rugs and embroidered linen, some produced on village looms and needles, others definitely not. Slacken your pace or stare for more than a second, and you will invite entreaties to step inside. Haggle over the price, if you can, but don't expect to buy a genuine piece of Cretan folk art at a discount. You should find better value at the tavernas in the side lanes to the right as you walk up the street. Fotíou Theodosáki is said to have suffered a recent decline in standard and rise in prices, but it is still an atmospheric little street in which to sit at a pavement table and eat as the shopkeepers shout in Market Street a few paces away.

ADORATION
An especially tender aspect of Damaskinós's *Adoration of the Magi* is the humility with which the long-bearded, ermine-collared king bows his head to the touch of the infant Christ's chubby fingers on his bald pate.

CHEESE, PLEASE
Be sure to sample the cheeses before you buy. Stallholders will expect you to do so, and will be pleased to tell you the village where each variety was made. You will find soft *feta* cheese, waxy fat cheese and hard crumbly goat and sheep's cheeses with a mould-blue rind and a thick musky tang in the mouth.

Lively markets sell food and souvenirs

It is tempting, but a great mistake, to set yourself a punishing schedule for your holiday in Crete. There are many attractions here: the Minoan sites, the Venetian towns, the remote villages, the beaches and islands, the back-country drives and mountain hikes. But anyone who tries to hurry through timeless Crete ends up hurrying nowhere.

MAKING IT LAST
Nothing better illustrates the theory and practice of taking one's time than the Cretan ability, incredible to those from gobble-and-go cultures, to make 3cm (1.5 inches) of thick coffee and a glass of water last as long as the conversation that goes with them. Well over an hour is nothing.

The best plan is to have one or, at most, two objectives for each day, earmarking a good number of days for aimless wandering. You won't see everything this way, but what you do see, taken at leisure with no pressure of time forcing you onwards, will mean far more when you look back. It will be remarkable if a day of unplanned driving or walking does not lead you to a wealth of hospitality and conversation, to beaches and hilltops, villages and viewpoints that no guidebook could discover for you.

In the bigger towns, make for the market streets and the waterfront, and idle there, or cut up a side street into the quarters where ordinary life goes on. If a shopkeeper beckons you inside for a cup of coffee, or a glass of *rakí* is offered by someone, accept the invitation and don't hurry off. You'll learn more of Cretan life, customs and history this way than from any book or lecture. In the evening, don't eat too early; any music or dancing that takes place will probably not reach its climax until the small hours of the morning. And if you make an appointment with a Cretan, treat the agreed time as a statement of intention rather than as a fixed certainty, especially with regard to getting away again. In short, when in Crete, do what the Cretans do, and take your time. You won't regret it.

Shady café tables by the Bembo Fountain

Walk

Around Irakleío's Venetian city walls

This is a 4km (2.5 miles) stroll along the line of the old Venetian walls, with rooftop views into the old city, particularly enjoyable at sunset. Allow about two hours. See map on pages 42–43.

Almost the whole semi-circle of the medieval city walls has survived the ravages of time, war and development. Straight stretches of massively thick wall, 40m (131 feet) wide in some places, are interspersed with even thicker defensive bastions and pierced by corresponding gates. These were the strongest city walls anywhere around the Mediterranean, built from 1462 onwards on the foundations of the previous Byzantine walls, and strengthened from 1538 by the great Venetian engineer Michele Sanmichele. The walk intersperses high elevation sections along the tops of the walls with street level intervals. Staring with a 1km (0.5 mile) section.

Start at the stout, square San Andreas Bastion on the northwestern corner of the walls at the seaward end of Odós Archipiskopóu Makáriou. This is most easily reached by taking a taxi from Plateía Elefthérias. Steps lead up to the wall-top path, which runs south towards the great stone bulge of the Pantokrator Bastion. Note that the steps down to the left just before the bastion lead to a good ground-level view of the arched Pantokrator or Chaniá Gate (Pórta Chanión). Continue on the wall past the Bethlehem Bastion, looking inland to shadowy streets and across to the red dome of the cathedral. Descend to ground level by the Bethlehem Gate and continue at street level, climbing again to the top of the wall at the enormous Martinengo Bastion where you will find the simple tomb of Níkos Kazantzákis.

Return to and pass through the Bethlehem Gate and continue outside the walls for 1km (0.5 miles), noting their enormous size and strength. Beyond the busy Knosós road junction, walk through the Jesus Gate. Steps inside and to the right climb to another short wall-top section, and then descend to a road that leads to Plateía Elefthérias. A final short stretch, which as you look over the top seems sickeningly high, runs downhill from the Archaeological Museum towards the harbour.

The imposing Bethlehem Bastion

SOUR NOTES
It is a thousand pities that piped music of the blandest international kind is invading a number of Cretan hotels, including some up-market enough to know better. Why not have traditional Cretan music, if they must have music at all? Who wants to drink *rakí*, eat stuffed vine leaves or read about Crete to an irritating background of character-free, could-be-anywhere rock?

Accommodation

Visitors to Crete tend not to base themselves in Irakleío for their holiday. It is a town where an overnight stay might be forced on you at the beginning or end of a holiday by the exigencies of air or sea timetables. Since most people like to travel to and from Crete during the daytime, a demand for one-night beds has grown here, and you are more likely to find unbooked, short-stay accommodation in Irakleío than elsewhere on the island. Ask at the helpful tourist information office opposite the Archaeological Museum.

Accommodation will probably be in D and E class hotels (see page 274 for an explanation of these categories). A good number may well be too basic and uncompromisingly bare to be properly comfortable. Around the two parallel streets of Hándakos and Hortátson, which run northwest from Plateía Venizélou down towards the waterfront, there is a big selection of inexpensive rooms and pensions, along with an unofficial youth hostel at Vironos.

Reasonable, moderately priced hotels can be found to the east of Odós 25 Avgoústou, the commercial artery of Irakleío, which runs up from the harbour. There are also plenty outside the walls of the old city, a cheap taxi ride away from Plateía Elefthérias and the centre of Irakleío. Taxi drivers themselves can often recommend a hotel, and remember that you don't have to take the room if you don't like the look of it.

Generally speaking, the hotels nearer Plateía Elefthérias, the centre of Irakleío life, will be more comfortable, better appointed and more expensive. The Astoria, right on the square, is a good example of a very comfortable, expensive but central hotel. Book well in advance.

A typical budget pension in Irakleío

Food and drink

If you have just arrived in Irakleío, the chances are the city will be offering you your first taste of Cretan food and drink. If you are passing through at the end of your visit, this will be your last chance to eat and drink Cretan. So forget international cuisine and the predictable tourist restaurants around Plateía Elefthérias, and forage among the side streets for something more local in flavour.

The little restaurants in narrow Fotíou Theodosáki, between Odós 1866 and Odós Evans, are always good value, especially during the day, when the market stall-holders are eating there. Odós Daidálos, which links Plateía Elefthérias and Plateía Venizélou, is lined with unexciting restaurants, but two streets to the north, in Odós Mílatou, is the small and atmospheric *Taverna Aplo,* where the bouzoukis may be playing at 2am enjoyed by an enthusiastic and appreciative audience and where the food is fine even if the service may lack five-star polish.

Slightly more expensive restaurants can be found in Odós Kórai, parallel to Daidálos and Mílatou. *Giovanni's* and *Loukoulos* offer plenty of variety and substance.

Down by the Venetian harbour prices tend to rise, since you pay for the view. The fish restaurants are ranged here, and a stroll into the kitchen to lift lids and sniff pots is not only expected but is a wise move.

It is also worthwhile taking a taxi, or walking for about 20 minutes from Plateía Elefthérias, outside the city walls to Odós Dimokrátias, where restaurants such as *Kiriákos* specialise in Cretan food. Irakleíots eat here.

Cheaper and more basic, but extremely good value, are the *ouzéri* or small-scale tavernas. And then there are the takeaway *souvláki* or kebab stalls, and the doughnut, pastry and pie shops around Plateía Elefthérias and Plateía Venizélou, all quite safe, very nourishing and quite impossible to walk past if you are hungry.

TIRÓPITTA

Tirópitta are little round or oval pies, their flaky brown pastry cases filled with hot, soft *feta* cheese. A handful of these, eaten fresh from the counter of a *zakharoplasteío* or pastry shop, makes a sustaining and toothsome snack.

Striped fabric bags are popular souvenirs

Shopping

Irakleío offers a greater number and variety of shops than any other Cretan town. Being in the capital of the island, however, many of these sell everyday goods that are not especially appealing to visitors. There are plenty of rather expensive dress and jewellery shops in the streets that radiate from Plateía Elefthérias. Daidálos has stolen the crown of Leophóros Dikaiosíni in this regard, but fashion often changes from one year to the next.

The top end of Odós 25 Avgoústou is crammed with small souvenir shops, as is Odós Idoméneos where it joins Plateía Elefthérias behind the Astoria cinema. Pavement stalls push the same sort of things: "Minoan" chess sets, jars of perfumed creams, reproductions of classical statues and Byzantine icons. Inside the shops you will find woven and embroidered rugs, blankets, bags and tablecloths. Look for rough stitching and weaving on the reverse of the work if you want handmade goods, which will be more expensive. Pottery, modern jewellery and leatherwear, along with decorated daggers, are other favourites. For genuine antiques, try Odós Kórai, parallel with Daidálos. For knives that will actually cut, try the side streets off Odós 25 Avgoústou.

Tapes and CDs of Cretan traditional music are widely available: try the shop on the right halfway down Daidálos. Vasilis Skoulas is a master of both *lýra* and *bouzoúki*.

The most fun and colourful place for shopping is Market Street (Odós 1866), which runs north–south between Plateía Nikephórou Phoká and Plateía Kornárou. In between the food stalls there are souvenir shops, and one or two leatherware places selling at reasonable, and negotiable, prices. At the food stalls you can taste and buy fresh cheese from the mountains, delicious Cretan honey, and packets of herbs, including the famous dittany.

GLASS THAT CHEERS
If you linger more than a few minutes in a shop or at a market stall, you may well be offered a cup of coffee or a glass of something stronger. This is a pleasant gesture still occasionally met with in Irakleío, but very likely to sweeten business in the smaller towns and villages, and certainly if you intend to buy a high-value souvenir.

Pottery is often a good buy in Crete

Nightlife

Irakleío is a sophisticated modern city with a varied nightlife. There are plenty of clubs and café-bars, with several late night venues in the alleyways to the east of Plateía Venizélou and around the Archaeological Museum. The sleek modern café where you enjoy an afternoon drink may turn into a music venue at night, especially on weekends. There are far fewer of the huge non-stop music and light shows that you'll find in resorts to the east. Ittar Club on Odós Epidemidou, is the place of the moment, a nicely renovated vaulted historic building, while Flou on Plateía Daskaloyiánnis has transformed itself from disco to café-bar. Baccara on Ikarou Avenue has been a favourite for a few seasons while a relatively new arival is Desire Disco Club at Odós Arch. Makariou.

Traditional music and dancing are strong in Irakleío, owing to the large number of first-generation city dwellers who hark back to their roots. *Taverna Aplo* on Odós Mílatou often has music and singing into the early hours, and everyone joins in. There is no tabletop-dancing or plate-smashing; this is the real McCoy. Other good restaurants that put on Cretan music, singing and dancing are Embolo on Odós Máliara, Trianta-6 at 36 Handakos and Theoreion at 22 Odós Pediádos.

At present there are four enclosed cinemas. The Astoria on Plateía Elefthérias offers pretty standard Hollywood fare. There are several open-air ones near Irakleío. Those in the eastern suburbs at Néa Alikarnassós are good fun—a party atmosphere often develops among the audience.

As in all Cretan towns, the chief evening occupation is simply strolling or sitting watching the world go by. The *voltá* (evening perambulation) is still a feature of Plateía Elefthérias's shady gardens, and of the Venetian harbour. Sitting outside a café or bar, commenting on passers-by over a *rakí*, is *the* Irakleío evening pastime.

DRINKER'S DELIGHTS

"When I drink and get
drunk
I don't bother anyone.
I only celebrate my youth
And have a lot of fun."

"Would the sea were wine
And the ships were
dishes,
And the masts of the
ships
Were fried fishes!"

Cretan Mantinádes

A typical evening taverna scene, with people eating at tables set out on the street

JUNK THE JEEP
Most car-hire places have four-wheel-drive jeeps for rent. Unless you are planning some extremely bold off-road motoring, it is not worth paying extra for this kind of transport. A good hire car will cope with all but the very worst road conditions on the island. Remember that insurance may not cover the underside of the vehicle or the tyres, so check first.

Practical points

Airport The airport is 4km (2.5 miles) east of Irakleío (information tel: 2810 397800). The No. 1 bus connects the airport with the Olympic Airways office in Plateía Elefthérias (tel: 081–229191). Fixed price taxis run between airport and Plateía Elefthérias.

Banks Most banks, including the Commercial, Ionian and the National Bank of Greece, are represented on Odós 25 Avgoústou, due south of the harbour.

Bicycle hire Odós 25 Avgoústou is a good bet. Try Candia Motor at No 48 (tel: 2810 221227), and Paleologós at No. 5 (tel: 2810 346185).

Bus stations There are three bus stations operating out of the city. Station A (tel: 2810 245019) opposite the ferry terminal for buses to Ágios Nikólaos, Siteía and the east, plus Chaniá and Réthymno. Next to this is a second station (tel: 2810 220755) for city buses and Knosós services. Station B sits immediately outside the Chaniá Gate (Portá Chanion) (tel: 2810 255956) for all other services including Faistós and Mesará.

Car rental Most major car rental companies have offices at Níkos Kazantzíkis Airport including Hertz (tel: 02810 330452; www.hertz.com) and Budget (tel: 2810 344279; www.budget.com). Eurodollar also has a city centre office on Odós 25 Avgoústou (tel: 2810 243237; www.eurodollar.gr).

Car parking It is wise to park only in official parking bays between 8am and 8pm (Sundays are free). The best car park for the is on Ikaroú (the airport road).

Consulates Germany: 7 Odós Zografoú (tel: 2810 226288) UK: 16 Odós Papalexándrou (tel: 2810 224012); Netherlands: Monis Agarathou 22, Platia Agious Dimitruou (tel: 2810 343299); Norway: 15 avenue Dimokratias (tel: 2810 225991.

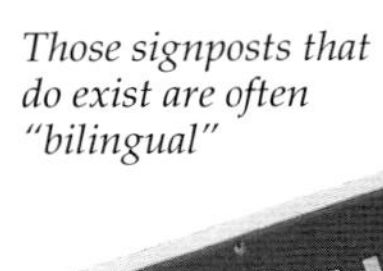

Those signposts that do exist are often "bilingual"

Ferries To Piraeus (Athens), Italian ports and Greek islands, from terminal east of Venetian harbour. Book through the shipping agencies in Odós 25 Avgoústou. Try Paleológos at No. 5 (tel: 281 0346185, www.ferries.gr).

Festival Late June to mid-September; music, plays, exhibitions, events.

Foreign newspapers Try the shops on Odós Daidálos and Plateía Venizélos.

Blue Mercedes taxis vary from ancient to modern

Gardens Plateía Elefthérias; El Greco Park; there is a long stretch of gardens in the "ditch" of the old city wall.

Hospitals Venizélos Hospital (tel: 2810 368001); University Hospital: (tel: 2810 392111).

Launderette Wash-o-Mate on Odós Mirabéllo at the first T-junction towards the harbour on Odós Xanthoudídou.

Police 10 Odós Dikeossínis (tel: 2810 283190).

Post office Plateía Daskaloyiánnis (Mon–Fri 8–8, Sat 8–2). Mobile Post Office in El Greco Park and by Bus Station A (Mon-Sat 8–8, Sun 9–6).

Roman Catholic Church On Plateía Adóniou, parallel and to the east of Odós 25 Avgoústou.

Taxis Many wait in Plateía Elefthérias.

Telephones (OTE) Area code is 2810. Main OTE office is beside El Greco Park (7.30am–11pm).

Toilets Plateía Elefthérias, opposite statue of Elefthérios Venizélos; El Greco Park.

Tourist information National Tourist Organisation of Greece (EOT) office is at 1 Odós Xanthoudídou, opposite the Archaeological Museum. It is best to visit early in the morning as queues build up. Open: Mon–Sat 8.30–3 (tel: 2810 246 299).

Tour operators Many in Odós 25 Avgoústou. Also try Christopher Travel, 59 Odós Ethn. Antistasseos (tel: 2810 221991); Cretan Holidays, 201 Odós Mafsolou (tel: 2810 331420).

Walking For all advice on walking, contact the Greek Mountaineering Club, 53 Odós Dikeosínis (tel: 2810 227609).

TAXI!
If you are caught up in a blast of Greek and it appears that a taxi service is being forced on you, or one is being arranged for you on the telephone, don't panic. It is probably only excessive use of the much-loved Greek word for OK—*endáksi*.

Akr Stavrós
Órmos Fódele
Akr Korakiás
Balí
Agía Pelagía
Akr Panagía
Achláda
Síses
Vlicháda
Moní Vosákou
Fódele
Moní Savvathianón
Kólpos
Achládes
Melidhóni
1083m
Koulоúkonas
Aloïdes
Moní Agíou Panteleímona
Rodiá
Mourtzaná
Dafnédes
Apaldianá
Theodóra
Damásta
Márathos
Ammoudára
Choumerio
Omalá
Chónos
Stróumpoulas
Kastrí
Ag Mámas
Astyráki
Kavrochóri
Kályvos
Axós
Tílisos
Gioufyrákia
Goniés
Kalésa
Anógia
Sklavokámpos
Krána
Foinikia
RÉTHYMNO
Keramoútsi
1584m
Sitáras
Korfés
Voutés
Petrokéfalo
Stavrákia
Sárchos
Giofyros
Ágios Myronas
1850m
Kouroúna
Nída
Moní Agías Eirínis
Krousónas
Psiloreítis
2456m
Idaikí Spiliá
1752m
Skínakas
Dafnés
Sivá
Profítas Ilías
Fourfourás
Vizári
Káto Asítes
Veneráto
Avgenikí
Kypárissos
1860m
Koudoúni
IRA
Kouroútes
1926m
Rouka
Ágios Ioánnis
Nithavrís
Spílaio Kamarón
Kamáres
Moni Vrontísíou
Priniás
Doúli
Ágios Thomás
Ardaktós
Vorízia
Agía Varvára
Agía Paraskeví
Vathiakó
Moní Valsamónerou
Zarós
Gérgeri
Nývritos
Megáli Vrýsi
Magarikári
Áno Moúlia
Kalochorafítis
Panagía
Mákres
Laráni
Klíma
Lagólio
Moróni
Kokkinos Pýrgos
Koutsoulídi
Ploutí
Vourvoulítis
Galiá
Roufás
Valís
Atsipádes
Tympáki
Ampeloúsos
Gortýs
Yanyáles
Vóroi
Agíoi Déka
Moíres
Stóloi
Loúres
Agía Triáda
Mitrópoli
Kapparianá
Órmos Mésaras
Faistós
Geropótamos
Mesará
Petrokéfalo
Plátanos
Péri
Vagioniá
Dionýsio
Pitsídia
Apesokári
Sívas
Pómbia
Stávies
Kommós
Lístaros
Plóra
Vasiliká Anógeia
Mátala
Vasilikí
Loúkia
Pigaidákia
Ágios Kýrillos
Moní Odigítrias
Miamoú
Moní Apezanón
Krótos
Kapetanianá
Antiskári
Koudoumás
Lassaia
Kaloí Liménes
Plateiá Peramáta
Papadogiánnis
Levín
Léndas
Akr Líthino
A
B
C
1
2
3
4
5

From Irakleío to the Mesará Plain

Día
Irakleíou
IRAKLEÍO
Néa Alikarnassós
Vathianós Kámpos
Káto Goúrnes
Goúrnes
Svoúrou Metóchi
Réma
Karteros
Elaía
Anópoli
Goúves
Chersónisos
Knosós
Knosós
Kainoúrio Chorió
Aposelemis
Kóxari
Spília
Epáno Vátheia
Kaló Chorió
Vasileíes
Galífa
Episkopí
Smári
Ágios Sýllas
Sgourokefáli
Káto Karouzaná
Kounávoi
Myrtiá
emóspila
Archánes
Moní Agkaráthou
811m
Gioúchtas
Asómatos
Sampás
Apóstoloi
Kastélli
Líthos
Pezá
Ágios Vasíleios
Ag Paraskiés
Sklaverochóri
Xidás
Vathýpetrou
Meléses
Vóni
Thrapsanó
Lilianó
Amarianó
Choudétsi
L E Í O
Alágni
Máthia
Parthéni
777m
Chouméri
Gerákí
Moní Epanosífis
Stíronas
Zinda
Arkalochóri
Nipidítos
Panórama
etaxochóri
Amourgélles
Mousoúta
Avlí
Panagía
Pártira
Áno Pouliá
Arkádes
Kasános
Charáki
Melidochóri
Pyráthi
Badiá
Ínio
Karavádos
Teféli
Vakiótes
Kastélli
Drapéti
Garípa
Parissia
Ligortýnos
Sokarás
Kalývia
Skiniás
Anapodaris
Káto Kastelliana
Demáti
Protória
Favrianá
Moní Fountádon
Mesochorió
Rotási
Chárakas
Pýrgos
979m
Asfentília
Ethiá
Achentriás
Tsoútsouros
o ú s i a
Órmos Tsoútsourou
Paránymfoi
Treís Ekklisíes
kr Martélos
0 5 10 15 km
0 5 10 miles
D
E

Looking back to Irakleío

▶▶▶ **REGION HIGHLIGHTS**

Agía Triáda Minoan Summer Palace *pages 80–81*

Faistós *pages 82–83*

Gortýs *pages 86–87*

(Palace of) Knosós *pages 90–93*

FROM IRAKLEÍO TO THE MESARÁ PLAIN There are more dramatic parts of Crete than this central section of the island. The west, for example, has the stark dignity of the White Mountains; the Réthymno area looks south to Psiloreítis and the higher peaks in Crete; Ágios Nikólaos, bustling with holiday life, backs on to the wildly beautiful Díkti Mountains with the 10,000 windmills of the Lasíthiou Plateau at their heart. The big V-shaped slice of land that lies between Irakleío and the lonely coast south of the Mesará Plain has none of these striking features. This is a relatively low-lying landscape with attractive hills, a tract of pleasant, fertile country 40km wide and about the same deep, shouldered by the great mountain ranges of Psiloreítis to the west and Díkti to the east. Only in the south does the land rise significantly. Here the long, narrow barrier of the Asteroúsia Mountains stands between the green fertility of the Mesará olive and fruit groves, and the rocky solitude of the south coast with its terrible dirt roads, isolated hamlets and stretches of rarely visited beaches and bays. There is nothing particularly awe-inspiring about any of this, but the region works a subtle magic on anyone who idles here for a few days. This spell is composed of the relatively crowd-free south coast, the smells of fruit and flowers, the unsophisticated pleasures of good local wine, easy-paced villages, vineyards and potato fields. Cretan life and landscape here is not much concerned with holidaymaking and caters mainly for local tastes and needs.

The region abounds in these unspecific delights of atmosphere and ambience. But there are particular archaeological and historical attractions to seek out. Crete's two best-known excavations of Minoan palaces are here: the seat of fabled King Minos and lair of the bull-headed Minotaur at Knosós is just south of Irakleío, and sprawling Faistós in its beautiful position above the Mesará Plain looks up the southern rise of the Psiloreítis range to the dark mouth of the Kamáres cave. A mile or so from Faistós is the excavation of the Minoan summer palace at Agía Triáda. And not far away are the extensive remains of the

Dorian city of Gortýs, where the olive groves are littered with fragments of columns and shards of pottery more than 2,000 years old. Further north is the Minoan country villa at Vathýpetrou, where the winemaking equipment survives intact, while the high and lovely peak sanctuary on the summit of Mount Gioúchtas is just outside Archánes. Near here, too, are lively and intense early 14th-century frescoes in the little church of Ágios Mikhaíl Arkhángelos, tucked away among the vineyards.

Irakleío city, of course, is the focus of the north coast of the region, along with the built-up holiday coast to the east—a seemingly unending ribbon of hotel and apartment, disco and beach bar development. But drive half an hour south and you will find yourself in the most peaceful and relaxing of landscapes, where traditional small-scale farming is carried on alongside the local industries of pottery (around Thrapsanó) and winemaking (Archánes and Dafnés).

The Mesará Plain runs parallel to the south coast, just north of the Asteroúsia Mountains, a fertile, well-watered and productive green basin, 48km (30 miles) from east to west where it reaches the Gulf of Mesará. This is Crete's best agricultural land, with unattractive plastic greenhouses and the unmemorable towns of Moíres and Tympáki. The old saying that "you can't eat scenery" applies hereabouts. Mesará farmers are well-to-do and hardworking, and their landscape reflects their priorities.

As for the Asteroúsia Mountains—in all of Crete there are no lonelier hills, no rougher roads, no wilder stretches of coastline, no mountain more satisfying to climb than Kófinas, and no monastery more welcoming in its isolation than Koudoumá.

The Mesará Plain

SIMPLE DELIGHTS

Anything elaborate or delicate that you take on a picnic is liable to be melted or mashed after it has been bumped over dirt roads or mountain tracks. It is better to take a Cretan picnic: olives, cheese, hard bread, an orange and some water. You could dine more richly, but never with more relish than on these simple ingredients in their proper outdoor setting.

UNCOMMON SEALS

Sir Arthur Evans stumbled upon the secret of Knosós in truly romantic fashion. In an antiquarian shop in Athens in 1893 he bought some seals, inscribed with hieroglyphs, which had been dug up from the still-hidden palace site in Crete. Evans had recently inspected inscribed seals discovered during the excavation of Mycenae nearly 20 years before, and immediately saw the similarities in the two sets of inscriptions. The Mycenaean seals had come from an ancient civilisation, thought to be mythical but now proved by excavation to have actually existed, so might not Crete, too, be holding similarly exciting secrets?

LIFTS

When you stop your car in a village, someone may well ask you for a lift a few miles up the road. If you agree to take them, don't be surprised if hospitality is offered at the other end.

Plastic hothouses have proliferated along Crete's south coast in recent years, forcing vegetables for the export market. Most of Crete's agriculture is, however, still village-based, and a fair proportion of it is carried out in traditional fashion: broadcasting seed by hand, horse-ploughing, irrigating with a bucket and hard labour.

Olives Of all Crete's agricultural produce the olive is clearly pre-eminent. As soon as you reach the countryside you will notice the olive groves: young trees dot the hillsides in regular rows, older groves spread their dull green cushions of foliage across valley floors and up the slopes. Olive oil and edible olives are a multi-billion-

From extra virgin to blended, olive oil comes in many forms

drachma export operation, yet still a business that relies upon thousands of experienced individual village farmers. These people know each tree, its age, its bearing capacity and its state of health. Olives have been farmed here in Crete for over three thousand years, and in some of the remoter villages there are stone presses and storage jars being used that a Mycenaean grower would have recognised.

The tree is grown from olive stones or bits of root. It may be 15 years before it produces fruit, but it may then bear fruit for many hundreds of years. A mature tree flowers in April, and the hard green olives appear in early summer. Tradition says that the oil starts to form on 20 May, the feast day of Profítas Ilías. In autumn, when the olives are black and becoming plump, large nets are laid out under the trees to catch windfalls. At Christmas the harvest begins, either with sophisticated blowing or combing machines or in the traditional way, with the whole family beating and shaking the trees.

WILD OLIVES

The original wild olive (*agría eliá*), forerunner of the present-day plump black fruit, is still to be found growing on Crete's hillsides, as it has done since before Minoan times. The wild olive's leaves are like little slips of privet, its fruit tiny and scarcely palatable. But it is a particular thrill to find it among Minoan remains, on a site where its ancestors may well have been cultivated by the Bronze Age bull-leapers.

At the oil mill, or in the family's stone press, the fruit is crushed, then pressed with hot water, which runs off as a horrible black goo to pollute nearby streams. The first pressing goes for edible and cooking oil, and the second is turned into soap or is fed to animals. What is left can be dried and burned as a pungent-smelling fuel. Excess wood from the tree itself is burned, or goes to the wood carver. Olive farming is virtually waste-free.

Sheep and goats Olive trees cannot be profitably grown on the higher slopes of the mountains. These wilder places are where the Cretan sheep and goats come into their own. They are hardy, skinny foragers, nimble climbers, voracious nibblers of anything tender and green, including the shoots of the sadly depleted native trees, which would regenerate quickly if there were no grazers on the mountains. But sheep and goats are the backbone of the Cretan upland economy. Shepherds still migrate to the high mountain pastures in early summer, living up there in *mitátos* or stone huts, in spartan and lonely conditions. In more fertile spots, such as on the Katharó plateau in the Díkti Mountains, they may be joined from time to time by their wives and children.

Lamb is the staple meat dish of Crete; goat is far less frequently on the menu. The best of the wool fetches high prices; the milk is turned into cheese, either in the stone huts by boiling in huge cauldrons and subsequent pressing in wicker baskets, or mechanically in the cheese factories of the lowlands. The crumbly white *féta* is familiar as a garnish on Greek salads. Each region has its own speciality, hard or soft, tangy or sweet.

SHEEP OR GOATS?
At first sight you may be hard put to it to distinguish between the Cretan goats and their mountain companions, the ragged-fleeced, bony sheep. Identification is easier at siesta time when the sun is high. However intermingled the two species become on the hillside, they separate into two distinct camps when the time comes to lie down and rest in the shade of the trees.

New residents take over an abandoned village

The belltower of the Church of Our Lady

CICADAS
The shrill, zithering sound of the cicada permeates all the country districts of Crete. If you can spot one of these greyish, long-bodied insects with its big wings folded like a tent across its back, notice that it doesn't, as many people believe, rub its legs together to produce that monotonous, soporific sound. In fact the noise comes from two tiny echo-chambers on the abdomen. Each contains a membrane, which the cicada vibrates with muscle spasms, thousands per minute—nature's own kazoo.

► Archánes *73D4*

Archánes, 20km (12 miles) south of Irakleío, is the most important winemaking centre in the nome (administrative region) of Irakleío. The vineyard-owners have formed themselves into the very effective Minos Co-operative, which dominates the economic life of the area. The town has reinvented itself in the last decade with a vast programme of gentrification (170 houses and of communal space) that has seen new facades on buildings, fresh cobble on roads and flowers and trees gracing the squares. The programme has won worldwide attention and has been voted second best restored village in Europe. This is a friendly place, proud of its excellent product, with most of its social life revolving around the *plateía* at the southern end of the village, where you can sample the Archánes wine by the bottle or, more cheaply, by the jugful.

The snack bar Myriophytó, on the right as you go south through the square, holds the key to the **Church of Ágios Mikhaíl Arkhángelos►►►** at Asómatos, whose beautiful 14th-century frescoes are not to be missed. Your passport will be requested as a deposit. After 1km (0.5 miles) on the Vathýpetrou road, turn left halfway along a straight stretch between vineyards. In 1.5km (1 mile) the road dips and bends left over a watercourse. The church is down to the left under two trees. A vivid Archangel Michael stands with drawn sword on the south wall; old men blow trumpets to demolish the walls of Jericho; demons ride beasts among severed limbs; an agonising Crucifixion depicts the angels covering their eyes and St John cupping his hanging head with one hand in a gesture of ineffable sorrow.

A further 3km (2 miles) along the Vathípetro road, a right turn, signposted to Gioúchtas, leads by a rough zigzag road to the 811m (266 feet) summit of **Mount Gioúchtas►►**. From here there is a wide view over the mountains of the Psiloreítis and Díkti ranges, the whole of Irakleío, a vast tract of wrinkled countryside, and a patchwork of olive groves and vineyards. A ridge connects two spurs at the summit of the mountain, and local legend suggests that Zeus may have been buried here. On the southern peak are the Church of Aféndis Christós with its four apses and numerous icons of varying solemnity, and a tall wooden cross studded with electric lights. A paved path leads to the northern summit, where a radar station stands beside the fenced and locked site of a Minoan peak sanctuary. Big squared stone blocks form the walls that support layers of terracing. There is a ceremonial space below a hollow in the rocks spanned by the massive slabs of an altar. Hundreds of items offered to the gods by Minoan pilgrims and priests, and later worshippers, have been unearthed from the space beneath the altar, including figures of humans and animals, bones from sacrifices and fragments of ceremonial vessels. A wire fence and padlocked gates prevent visitors from exploring this site.

To the northwest of Archánes, on the lower northeastern slopes of Mount Gioúchtas, lie the remains of the temple at **Anemóspila**, whose excavation brought to light remains that have raised the possibility of human sacrifice among the Minoans. An earthquake around 1700 BC entombed four bodies here: a priest and priestess, a man curled up on an altar with an inscribed bronze knife on top of his body, and another man who had been carrying a ritual vessel. Was it full of the blood of the man on the altar, shed to propitiate the earthquake spirit that buried the celebrants?

► Arkalochóri *73E3*

Southwest of Archánes, Arkalochóri is a large, busy and friendly village, the centre of a widespread country district of vineyards, olive groves and vegetable fields. An important recent discovery of Minoan origin is the Arkalochóri Axe, found in a cave nearby and now at the Irakleío Archaeology Museum.

LOCKED OUT

Many of Crete's historic sites are kept locked, even those as relatively unvisited as the peak sanctuary on Mount Gioúchtas. Finding a padlock between you and your objective is frustrating, particularly after a long, hot climb. But it is worth remembering that excavation and exploration are still taking place periodically on most sites, work which can be ruined by a carelessly placed boot or the unthinking pocketing of ancient fragments as souvenirs.

Looking back to Archánes from Mount Gioúchtas

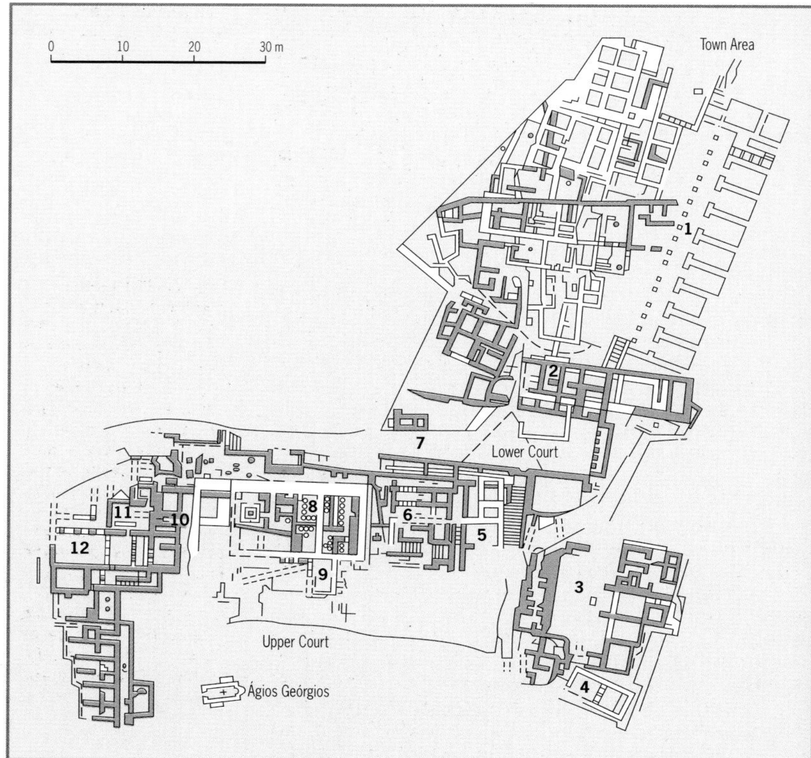

Agía Triáda Minoan Summer Palace

KEY TO THE MAP
1 shops
2 bastion/warehouse
3 Minoan house
4 shrine
5 eastern forecourt
6 reception rooms
7 *Rampa del Mare*
8 storerooms
9 loggia
10 treasury
11 archives/fresco room
12 hall

►►► Agía Triáda Minoan Summer Palace *72A2*

Agiá Triáda (Tymbaki village, tel: 28920 91360; www.culture.gr. *Open* daily 8.30–3. *Admission: moderate*) stands 3km (2 miles) west of the Minoan palace of Faistós (see pages 82–83), looking down over the Gulf of Mesará where the Geropótamos River empties into the sea between long headlands. This wonderful view may have been even better around 1570 BC when the Minoans were building here, for then the sea probably came much nearer to the rise of ground where Agiá Triáda stands. Agía Triáda was an important complex. It may well have been a summer or alternative residence for the rulers or chief priests of Faistós, and was certainly an influential centre of administration in southern Crete.

The Minoans built a road to connect Faistós with Agía Triáda. Technically this is in use as a footpath today, running around the north side of the hill between the two sites, but obscure signposting and locked gates make it a doubtful proposition.

The palace (actually something between a minor palace and an extremely grand villa) was built as a number of linked areas, connected but able to function independently. It probably stood intact for only about 120 years, before being flattened in the 1450 BC disaster—earthquake, tidal wave, insurrection, volcanic eruption or some cataclysmic combination of these—that destroyed the great palaces at Faistós, Mália and Zákros. But Agía

The Minoan Palace of Agía Triáda—still popular in summer

Triáda was reoccupied a couple of hundred years later, the town on the slopes below was rebuilt and large new buildings were put up among the ruins of the Minoan palace. In Dorian times, during the first millennium BC, there were successive shrines here. Later the Byzantine church and associated village of Agía Triáda occupied a site just to the southwest of the palace remains.

Walk down steps from the car park, through the site gate and down more steps, then bear left to the open space of the upper courtyard just below the 14th-century church of Ágios Geórgios at the top of the site. From here there is a good overview of the palace layout in front of you, with the northeast wing of the palace to your right, the west wing to the left, kitchens and storerooms further round to the west. Beyond the east wing the ruins of the town lie down the slope.

Pass the west end of the church, noting the variety of crucifix forms inscribed in its walls, and bear right through the shells of the storerooms to reach the grand apartments. In the northwestern corner of the palace, they enjoy a fine sea view and cool sea breezes. In the centre is the room where excavators disinterred the superb frescoes, including the famous one of cats hidden in bushes to stalk birds. The frescoes are now in the Irakleío Archaeological Museum. The inner angle of the palace here had two storeys and was probably used for entertaining visitors. This was where the brilliantly carved black steatite vases and libation vessels of the elated harvesters, the flattened boxer, and the haughty chieftain were found. They are now in Room VII of the Irakleío Archaeological Museum.

The paved Minoan roadway dubbed *Rampa del Mare*, the Sea Road, by the Italian excavators of Agía Triáda ran to the north of the palace wall. To the east, under the modern roof, is a group of rooms where you can sit and appreciate the coolness of the alabaster and gypsum lining slabs while considering the ingenuity of the post-catastrophe rebuilders of Agía Triáda who supplied water and took away sewage through a remarkable spillway of grooved stone between the floors of the palace.

There were no such refinements in the town, though there were basins with outlets in some of the houses that lie to the west of the pillared and porticoed market place. You can walk on the walls, above a maze of dark alleyways, speculating on the lives they must have seen.

FINE FRESCOES

The fresco painters of Agía Triáda seem to have developed the science of preserving paint to a higher level than that achieved by the painters at Knosós. The blues, yellows and reds in the *Cat and Birds* and the *Lady in the Garden* still look astonishingly rich, while the pictures themselves are just about the finest yet unearthed for detail and subtlety of execution. The remaining fragments are on view in Room XIV of the Irakleío Archaeological Museum.

The carved black soapstone Harvester Vase

The Minoan palace of Faistós

The Faistós Disc, now in Irakleío's Archaeological Museum

►►► Faistós 72A2

The Minoan palace of Faistós (*Open* daily 8.30–3. *Admission: moderate*), also spelled Phaistos or Festos, lies just south of the Irakleío–Tympáki road, 8km (5 miles) west of Moíres. It sits on a great knoll, overlooking the fertile green valley of Mesará covered with the squares and rectangles of grey stone walling. Faistós is the most dramatically sited of Crete's Minoan palaces, looking across the plain to the distant blue outlines of the Psiloreítis mountain range and the dark hole of the Kamáres cave, which can be seen clearly between two horn-like peaks.

Homer mentioned Faistós in the *Iliad* as a populous city. At the time he was writing, it had already declined since the heyday of the palace, around 1500 BC, when the city wielded power over southern Crete. The New Palace, the remains of which are largely what you see on the hilltop, was built in ca1700 BC on the foundations of an older palace three times destroyed by earthquakes and three times rebuilt. The New Palace, in its turn, was flattened ca1450 BC, in the calamity that destroyed the settlements at nearby Agía Triáda, at

Gourniá, Zákros and the other major Minoan sites on the island.

The layout of Faistós is confusing to the uninitiated and the difficulties are compounded by the absence of labelling or explanatory notices. As with all these Minoan palatial sites, the best plan is to head first for the big central court. From here you can get your bearings without too much trouble. To start your tour, however, descend the steps from the entrance gate and bear diagonally left across an uneven area, then down more steps, to turn right into the west court. Cross the court and turn to face the Psiloreítis Mountains. To your left are circular storage pits, and to your right the grand stairway, up which you walk into the *propylaeum*, a porchway and lightwell once supported on columns, the round bases of which are still there.

Go diagonally right and down some steps, then turn right into a square office room, where records would have been kept of the goods held in the long, narrow storerooms beyond. These are fitted out with hollowed-out receptacles that would have held differently shaped storage vessels. In the first chamber stands a dusty *píthos*, which looks as if it could very easily crumble into its component shards.

Now walk back through the office room into the central court, savouring the views of Psiloreítis to the north, and the far range of the Asteroúsia Mountains to the south beyond the Mesará Plain. The Kamáres cave is clearly visible on the upper flanks of Psiloreítis, and the fields of Mesará look green and well watered, contrasting with the dark spires of poplars standing alongside the white and dusty roads.

Two *píthoi* stand next to the pillars that mark the north doorway of the central court. Walk through the doorway and along a cool stone passage. Pass the colonnaded peristyle hall on your left. Descend stairs to the king's and queen's apartments on the left, sheltered by modern roofs of concrete and plastic. The hall and apartments were sited to catch the best views and the mountain breezes.

Reaching the trees at the northern edge of the site, turn right and walk along the palace walls, past a run of tiny chambers built of mud brick. In one of them, in 1903, the excavators found the Faistós Disc. A little flat circle of baked clay, only 16cm across and dating from about 1700 BC, it is stamped with a spiral pattern of symbols half pictorial and half geometric. It is obviously writing of some kind, but it has yet to be deciphered. It is now in Room III of Irakleío Archaeological Museum.

Turn right at the end across a pillared court and walk up the steps, bearing right to return to the central court.

KEY TO THE MAP ON PAGE 82

1 theatre area
2 shrine complex
3 west façade
4 ramp
5 shops
6 grand stairway
7 propylaeum
8 lightwell
9 storeroom block
10 pillared hall
11 corridor
12 lustral basin
13 pillar crypt
14 temple of Rhea
15 peristyle hall
16 lustral basin
17 king's apartments
18 queen's apartments
19 archives
20 workshops
21 furnace
22 colonnaded court
23 storage pits (cisterns)

FAISTÓS WIT

Faistós people were reputed to be the wittiest in Crete. Unfortunately none of their gems has come down to us. Perhaps, when the Faistós Disc is finally deciphered, a few rib-ticklers will be brought to light. The oldest jokes, they say, are the best ones, and these will have been maturing for 3,500 years.

WISE JUDGE

King Mínos is said to have installed his brother Rhadamanthys, revered for his wisdom and honesty, as ruler of Faistós. Rhadamanthys was also appointed arbitrator of all legal wrangles among Minos's subjects, and travelled to Knosós to exercise these judgements.

Cretans like to drink, at the right time and in the right company, though they are fairly abstemious during the day. Not every glass of colourless liquid on a kafeníon *table contains a killer dose of ferocious local spirit, as some travellers' tales would have you believe.*

RAKÍ RUB
Not only is *rakí*, sometimes called *tsikoudiá*, the drink that holds social life together in Crete, it is also recommended by the wise men and women of the mountains as a specific for chest colds, liberally applied as an external rub, and internally in the usual way.

Aqua pura In fact, the taller the glass the more likely it is to contain nothing more heady than water. Spring water from the mountains is probably the most delicious drink on the island. Places like Záros have made a good living out of bottling and selling their water, which is exported far and wide. A glass of water comes *gratis* with meals and coffee. A compliment on the local water is usually received with pleasure.

Alcohol For the harder stuff Cretans tend to stick to three tried and tested drinks: wine, beer and *rakí*. The further inland and the higher you go, the more courtesies will accompany drinking. There is likely to be a clinking of glasses together or knocking them on the table, accompanied by *iss-i-yián*, your health, or *iss-i-yámas*, health to us. Elaborate *mezédes* or appetisers may well be served too. Taking a drink with a friend or casual acquaintance is an unhurried affair, as much a matter of social ritual as of refreshment.

Wine Cretan wine has been celebrated for many centuries. Minoan, Mycenaean and Hellenic winemaking equipment has been found at several archaeological sites in the island. The press, vat and cleaning apparatus at the villa at Vathýpetrou near Archánes is particularly well preserved. When the Portuguese planted Madeira with vines in the 15th century, it was to Crete that they turned for their supplies. The Malmsey wine that was drunk across medieval Europe came from Crete.

The Greek for wine is *krasí*. There are three varieties: *mávro* (red), *áspro* (white), and *kókkino* (rosé). *Retsína*, the Greek white wine flavoured with resin that tastes to the uninitiated like a distillation of old violin bows, is not traditionally a Cretan drink, though it has been making a steady advance in recent years in response to the expectations of tourists. There are several decent bottled wines available on the island. Mínos is the most widely distributed thanks to the power of the well-organised co-operative based at Archánes that produces it.

However, the ordinary village wine is cheaper, stronger, much more characterful and complementary to the heavy, oily taste of Cretan cooking. It comes either in glass *carafes* or in metallic-pink jugs. A request for red usually produces a thick, cloudy, rose-tinted wine,

Mínos, one of the best known of Cretan wines

drawn from a plastic barrel, with a heavy, sherry-like taste. It is unsophisticated, but effective. Rosé's are found less on menus but they too have a deep rather than a pale colour and a fruity palate. White wine is a misnomer for most are a pale honey or barley coloured, always served cool from the barrel and very refreshing. Restaurant owners are proud of their local wines, which often originate in their own village. Wines from Dafnés, south of Irakleío, and from the Moulianá villages just west of Siteía, are especially well thought of.

Beer and *rakí* Beer-drinking is a recent, imported fashion. There are no specially recommended brews, but Henninger and Amstel, brewed under licence in Greece, are worth a try as a variation from the universal Heineken.

Oúzo is the traditional Greek spirit, a distillation from the mush of skin, pips and stalks left behind after wine-making, flavoured with aniseed, and drunk either neat or with water. Cretans prefer *rakí*, the same spirit without the aniseed and with more power, drunk neat from tiny glasses. In the west of Crete it is known as *tsikoudiá*. Cretans claim many beneficial properties for *rakí*, as an aphrodisiac, a soothing rub and a specific against all ills. The taste is hard to describe, but quite unmistakable. It burns all the way down, and one glass leads to another.

ROUGH WINE

Wine (*krasí*) made locally and sold from the barrel by weight, not by volume, so was traditionally ordered by the kilo and half-kilo rather than the litre and half-litre. This is changing as international standards and habits invade the island, although the word *carafe* is nearly universally understood in today's tavernas. In any case, it will probably come to the table in a battered, pink tin jug, the official wine measure of Crete.

NEAT SPIRIT

Rakí and Greek coffee compliment each other as felicitously as do brandy and French coffee, but Cretans tend to take them separately. A *rakí*, on-the-house, at the end of a restaurant meal is a very pleasant and widespread custom.

Many Cretan wine barrels are made from oak; retsína, made using pine casks, is more of a mainland tradition

FRUITFUL PLANE
One of the plane trees at Gortýs is reputed never to shed its leaves. If you visit in midwinter and find it, you will not be the first to have done so. Legend has it that under this tree, Zeus disguised as an eagle had his lordly way with Europa, a union that produced three sons: Rhadamanthys, Sarpedon and Minos.

WATERWORKS
The *praetorium* was the terminus of the great aqueduct system that brought water to Górtina all the way from the mountain springs at present-day Záros, 10km (6 miles) to the north, a notable feat of engineering.

A tangled toga or a sling?

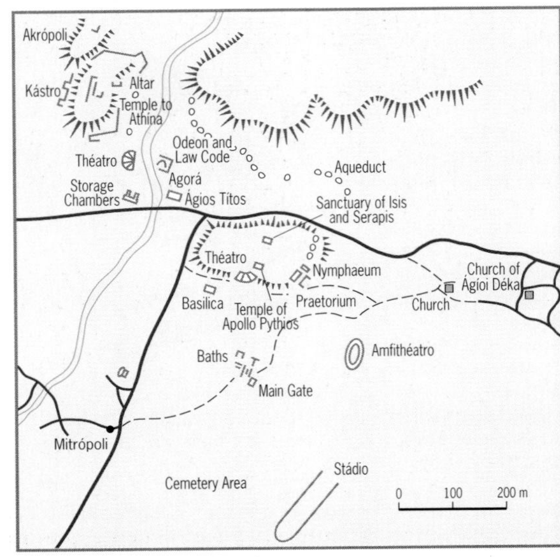

►►► Gortýs *72B2*

Your imagination will work overtime as you wander around the enormous site where the mighty city of Gortýs once stood (Agio Deká, tel: 08920 31144. *Open* daily 8.30–3. *Admission: inexpensive*). Walls, columns, pavements, baths, a theatre and even basilicas bear witness to Gortýs' influence over the best part of 2,000 years. Who knows lies under the bean fields and olive groves?

The site lies 6km (4 miles) east of Míres, about half way along the northern edge of the Mesará Plain, on the main road from Irakleío. The fertility of Mesará made it the natural location for an important city, and by the 5th century BC what had been a small Minoan settlement had expanded into a flourishing city under Dorian rule. By 200 BC Gortýs had usurped the rôle of Faistós as the most influential city in southern Crete, and after the Roman invasion of 65 BC it became the capital of the island and the centre of power for much of Egypt and North Africa. St Titus, despatched by St Paul to Crete to convert the islanders to Christianity, set up his bishopric here. During the first Byzantine occupation of the island Gortýs continued to expand and prosper right up until 824 when invading Saracens sacked the city. Partial reoccupation followed and some rebuilding, notably of the 6th-century basilica of Ágios Títos where the saint was buried, but most of the city remained a ruin.

A good way to explore the site is to start in the village of Agíoi Déka, just east of Gortýs. The church contains a magnificent old icon of the martyrdom of ten Cretan Christians in AD 250. Below it is the stone

The once-roofed theatre at Gortýs

slab on which they were executed, deeply indented with the imprints of their knees. From the west end of the church a lane leads to a low-walled footpath. Bear right to reach a red-domed chapel. Under the west end, in a gated crypt, are the tombs of the martyrs. Continue through the olive groves among fallen stone columns and outlines of walls, to pass the fenced site of the Roman governor's palace or *praetorium* with fluted, smooth or elaborately carved columns, and great walls of Roman brickwork.

Continue along the perimeter of the site, and at the first right bend keep straight on (south) through the olive groves for five minutes to find the Roman amphitheatre. Big blocks of masonry surround a hollow depression. Pottery shards lie all around: jug rims and handles, curves and discs of broken vessels. Returning, you pass the big, tiled heating chambers and stone-built rooms of the Roman baths, and the temple of Apollo Pythios with its welter of fallen columns. Make due north to reach the main road, turn left for 300m (273 yards), and pay a small fee to enter the part of the site that lies north of the road.

The big *bema* or apse of the 6th-century AD basilica of Ágios Títos stands here, beautifully preserved. From the northwest corner of the church foundations, follow the fence through the *agora* or forum, now thickly grown with olive trees, to the odeon, once a roofed theatre, with encircling square pillars of brick and a semicircle of bevelled benches. Beyond stands a modern, crescent-shaped building that protects the most important of Gortýs' many remains, a series of big stone blocks inscribed in about 500 BC with amendments to Dorian law. Written in script that runs left to right, then right to left in succeeding lines, the laws deal with rape, inheritance arrangements, divorce, allocation of property, adultery, assault and the rights of adopted children. The blocks were found by chance in 1884, when the nearby mill stream was drained.

Above and behind the odeon is the acropolis of Gortýs, with the remains of a Dorian temple to Athena, a Roman hall or *kastro*, and a mass of retaining walls.

POCKET HISTORY?

To pocket or not to pocket the shards of Cretan history? Temptation is never stronger than at Gortýs, where millions of pieces of pottery, most of it clumsy workaday stuff of no particular merit, lie tumbled across the fields and olive groves. But only experts can distinguish the extraordinary from the ordinary. The jug handle or piece of bowl rim that you take away with you might just be the fragment that, in other hands, could unlock a door to greater understanding.

Walk

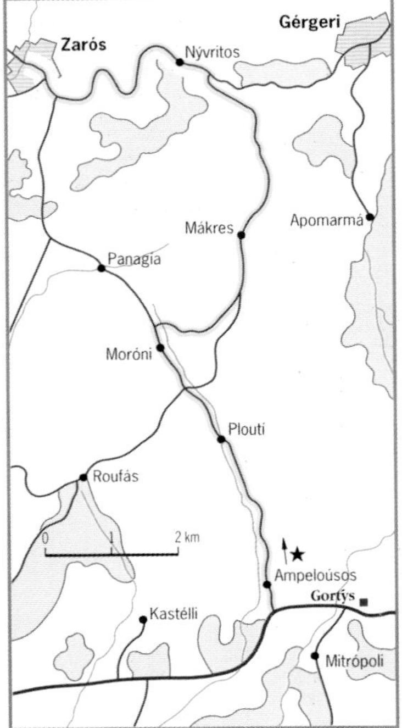

Ampeloúsos to Zarós

This is quite an easy walk from the Mesará Plain to Zarós in the foothills of Psiloreítis, following a dirt road through a slowly changing landscape (11 km/7 miles, allow 2.5–3 hours).

Many of Crete's old dirt roads, recently bypassed by new tarmac highways, have become ideal, traffic-free footpaths. This walk takes you from the Mesará Plain up through a string of seldom visited villages to Zarós, below the majestic upsweep of Psiloreítis. It follows a broad but stony old route superseded by the new road that rushes directly from Moíres to Zarós.

The walk begins in the village of Ampeloúsos, which is reached by a turning to the right off the main Moíres road 1km (0.5 miles) to the west of Gortýs. Ampeloúsos is a typical small Mesará village, where you will see farmers' motorised tricycle pick-ups parked along its streets.

Turn right half-way through the village onto the Zarós road, which quickly sheds its tarmac in favour of stones and dust. You soon leave the fruit and vegetable lushness of Mesará behind, and climb gently into a less well-regulated landscape of rock, scrub and olive groves. Flocks of grazing sheep and goats make their appearance, and you can practice your Greek greetings on the shepherds who use the road, with their crooked sticks cradled behind their necks.

The road climbs for 4km (2.5 miles) through Ploutí and Moróní, tiny villages where your arrival will provoke stares and nodded acknowledgement. At Moróni you can join the new road for a fast but busy 4km to Zarós. A better alternative is to turn right here for 4km more of rough road though Mákres to the Agía Varvára–Zarós road at Nývritos, where you turn right to reach Zarós. The big village at the foot of the mountains has plenty of tavernas. Try the local trout, and the water which has been famous since it supplied Gortýs 2,000 years ago, now bottled and exported all over Greece.

The mountain village of Kapetanianá, a little west of this walk's start point, is typical of Crete's off-the-beaten-track villages. See also opposite page and the Walk on pages 106–107

►► Kapetanianá *73C1*

Until recently, Kapetanianá, lodged high in the Asteroúsia Mountains southeast of Moíres, is certainly nobody's idea of a tourist village. However, the dirt-rough and winding road leading up to it from the Masará Plain has recently been asphalted and the village is awakening as if from a long slumber. The older villagers still rely on sheep and small vegetable plots for their living, but many of the ruined houses are now being bought by musicians and artists. The houses, most of them one-roomed, slope downhill along narrow footways to the church of Panayía. The key is kept at one of the nearby houses. The frescoes of 1401 include, on the north wall, one of Christ bending to help Adam out of the grave, and another of a calm and dignified Saviour entering Jerusalem on a donkey. On the south wall, with graffiti dating back to 1589, there is a Baptism. And from the dome of the apse the Virgin stares down gravely.

The black-garbed older women of Kapetanianá could have stepped out of one of the frescoes. Their menfolk sit in the *kafeníon* wearing head fringes. The village is the starting point for the strenuous walk to the 1,231m (4,038 foot) summit of Mount Kófinas (see pages 106–107) and 130 marked climbs can be found in the surrounding peaks.

►► Koudoumá Monastery *73C1*

Many of Crete's monasteries are on lonely parts of the coast, but Koudoumá *(Open* summer 8–7, winter 8–3) must be one of the loneliest. The Asteroúsia Mountains rear inland of Koudoumá, cutting it off from contact with the populous Mesará Plain. You can drop down to it on foot in two hours from Mount Kófinas, or drive down the tortuous basic road from Paránymfoi and Treis Ekklisiés.

At the base of the mountain there is a cluster of red-roofed buildings, a 19th-century church, the hospitable abbot (his *rakí* bites hard) and a few monks in blue working overalls. A small sandy beach, sheltered by the rocky headland of Akrotíri Martélos, lies just beyond.

PLACE NAMES

An enquiry into the meanings of place names will often throw interesting light on a locality. For example, Mount Kófinas near Kapetanianá means big basket mountain. The mountain does look like a basket upside down. And the name of the whole mountain range, Asteroúsia, reflects the clear atmosphere above these tall peaks. It means near the stars.

The lonely monastery of Koudoumá

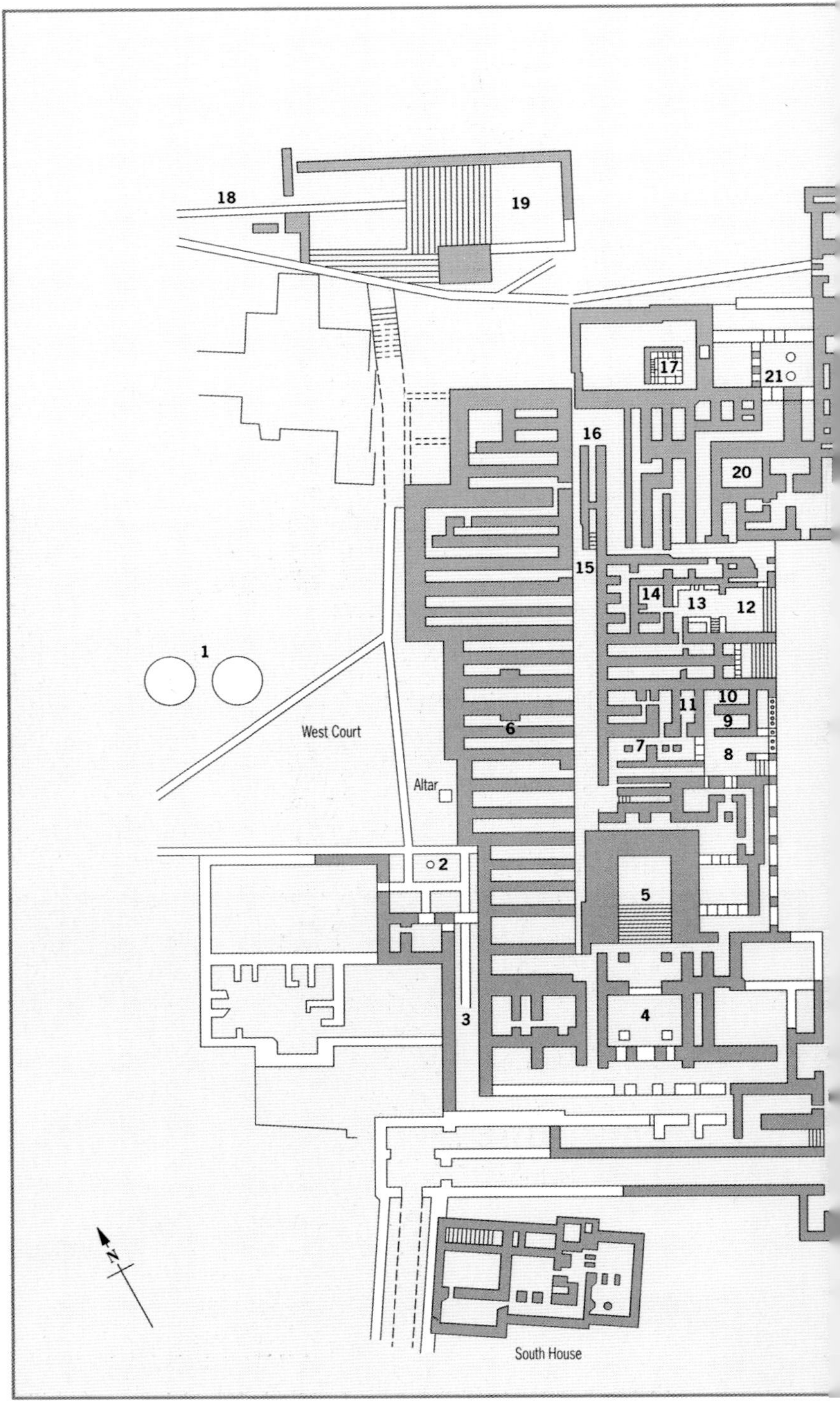

18
19
17
21
16
20
15
14
13
12
1
West Court
10
11
9
6
7
8
Altar
2
5
4
3
South House

Northeast House
23
24
25
26
27
28
29
30
31
32
33
34
35
36
37
38
39
40
41
42
43
44
45
46
entral
Court
Southeast House
0
10
20
30
40 m

KEY TO MAP ON PAGES 90–91

1 walled pits
2 west porch
3 corridor of the procession fresco
4 south propylaeum
5 staircase to *piano nobile*
6 lower storeroom block
7 pillar crypts
8 room of the column bases
9 room of tall *píthoi*
10 temple repository
11 vat room
12 antechamber
13 throne room
14 inner sanctuary
15 lower long corridor
16 deposit of tablets
17 lustral basin
18 royal road
19 theatre area
20 old keep
21 northwest portico
22 north entrance passage
23 pillar hall
24 corridor of the draughts board
25 northeast hall
26 magazines of giant *píthoi*
27 east bastion
28 court of the stork spout
29 craftsman's workshop
30 east portico
31 magazine of medallion *píthoi*
32 corridor of bays
33 east–west corridor
34 grand staircase
35 hall of colonnades
36 hall of double axes (king's megaron)
37 queen's megaron
38 bathroom
39 toilet

(continued opposite)

Tall píthoi

►►► (Palace of) Knosós *73D4*

The Minoan palace at Knosós, also spelled Knossós and 5km (3 miles) south of Irakleío, is deservedly Crete's premier tourist attraction, the one place that even a day visitor to the island should be certain not to miss. This is not to say that the site pleases everyone. It is often unpleasantly crowded with guided tours. As with all the well-known Minoan sites, an early morning visit is recommended. Controversy still rumbles on over the partial rebuilding of the palace by its original excavator, the English archaeologist Sir Arthur Evans, who used conjecture to shore up research. But a tour of Knosós (tel: 2810 231940. *Open* Apr–Oct 8–7.30, Nov–Mar 8.30–3. *Admission: expensive*) is essential for a better understanding of the other great Minoan palaces of Crete, which can seem to be a wilderness of unlabelled stone walls if you have not first had your imagination tuned in here. The best-known of Cretan myths is focused on this little knoll above the olive groves. The desperate adventure of Prince Theseus, as he fought and conquered the bull-headed Minotaur, took place in the labyrinth beneath this, the palace of cruel King Minos.

When Sir Arthur Evans unearthed the palace in 1900, what had been a fantasy was suddenly seen to be rooted in fact. A vast and intricate maze of rooms and passageways came to light. Bull's-head vases, bull's-horn roof decorations, a royal throne room, a fabulous treasure of jewellery, and brilliantly coloured and executed frescoes showed a vibrant, warm-blooded and sophisticated society in full flourish. Evans, who had long suspected that something special lay underground at Knosós, bought the site as soon as Turkish occupation of Crete ended in 1898, and struck the palace ruins in 1900.

The problem Evans had to solve was how to preserve material that was liable to fall apart after having been interred for the best part of 3,000 years. As he owned the site, and was using his own money to finance the excavations, he felt he had the right to do as he thought best. Reconstruction would at least put everything roughly where he thought it had originally stood, and would give a fair picture of how the palace had probably looked. Authenticity undoubtedly suffered from Evans's over-liberal use of concrete and perhaps over-optimistic shaping of some of the upper storeys. But better, surely, that so much should have been preserved this way than that it should have disappeared altogether.

What one sees today, fragmentary though it is with upper rooms opening onto air, flights of stairs ending nowhere, roofless halls and stark, empty chambers, is chiefly the remains of the second or new palace, constructed around 1700 BC after an earthquake had destroyed the old palace, itself built 300 years earlier. Knosós was the powerful capital of Crete in those days, the nerve centre of a Bronze Age civilisation which Evans named Minoan after its most famous king. The disastrous event of ca1450 BC—experts disagree as to whether it was another earthquake, a tidal wave or an

attack by invaders or insurrectionists—that destroyed most of the other Minoan palaces and settlements on the island seems to have affected the palace at Knosós only marginally. There was a fire and extensive damage, but the palace and its associated town continued to be used and remained a centre of influence throughout Crete for at least another 700–800 years.

A tour of the palace begins at the entrance kiosk on the well-signposted road 5km (3 miles) south of Irakleío. Here you can join one of the continuous guided tours, which is a good idea if you want to be sure not to miss anything. However, a couple of hours wandering around the site on your own will give you an excellent idea of the sheer scale and sophistication of the layout.

From the entrance gate you approach the palace across the wide west court, an open area for public markets or meetings in Minoan days. Just beyond the statue of Sir Arthur Evans, bear left to walk through the palace entrance and on into the enormous central court, some 55m by 30m (60 by 33 yards). The central court was a feature of all Minoan palaces and a focus for the entire complex. The view down the valley from here is a fine one. Far below are the remains of what may have been an arena where the Minoan bull-leaping displays took place.

At the northwestern corner of the court is the throne room, where Minos and the other priest-kings of Knosós would have performed their rituals. Just inside is a stone throne above a sunken lustral or purification basin, and in an inner chamber a copy of the wooden throne supposed to have been used by Minos himself. Stairs nearby lead to the upper storey rather speculatively reconstructed by Evans and named by him the *piano nobile*, where you will find reproductions of some of the best-known Knosós frescoes, including the celebrated bull-leaping scene now in the Irakleío Archaeological Museum.

From the east side of the central court the grand staircase leads down to the austere king's apartments, and below them the queen's apartments, where excavators found a magnificent fresco of leaping dolphins, a bath tub and a lavatory flushed by jars of water. The queen probably bathed in a glutinous mixture of ass's milk and honey. From here you can work your way north around the edge of the palace, past rows of workshops full of enormous *píthoi* or storage jars, and back along the top of the complex to tread the paved royal road that runs in a stone-sided gully past the massive walls of houses and the huge cut blocks of the palace foundations.

Ladies in Blue *fresco*

KEY CONTINUED

40 court of distaffs
41 shrine of double axes
42 corridor of sword tablets
43 house of chancel screen
44 Minoan kiln
45 house of fallen blocks
46 house of sacrificed oxen

LIGHT IN THE DARK

With its small, stone-built rooms clustered together, Knosós would have been a dark and dismal place in which to live had it not been for the ingenuity of the Minoan architects in bringing in light through the many light-wells that reflected daylight into dark corners. All the same, the palace's chief source of internal light was the naked flame of torch and lamp, with the attendant risks of disastrous fires.

PALACE THAT GREW

The labyrinthine construction of Knosós, notwithstanding the Minos legend, was the result not of planning but of centuries of gradual growth as rooms, courtyards, workshops and houses were added. Nikos Kazantzákis aptly declared that Knosós was a place where fantasy and creativity were expressed, a palace that "grew like a living organism, like a tree".

Development is creeping round the bay at Léndas

►► Léndas *72B1*

From Gortýs, on the main Moíres–Agía Déka road through the Mesará Plain, a good tarmac road brings you south towards Léndas. From Apesokári it wriggles and twists 23km (14 miles) down to a little holiday village, which appears below you as a sprinkle of white and peach-coloured buildings packed into a recess of the coastline under the eastern flank of the bulbous, craggy Cape Léndas, the Cape of the Lion. The other routes into Léndas are rough and difficult dirt tracks but now that this road has been improved the village is gradually growing into one of the better-known small resorts on the south coast of Crete. There are plenty of rooms to rent and a number of restaurants along the pebbly beach.

Léndas is a ramshackle kind of place, with nothing smart about it, and it is too remote to attract large numbers of visitors to stay, though there are plenty of day trippers in high summer. It is at its best early or late in the season. There are excellent beaches a short but bone-shaking drive to the west at and beyond Papadogiánnis, and more within walking distance along the roadless coast to the east. The slanting heights of the Asteroúsia mountains behind the resort add drama to its setting.

It must have been a long and difficult journey carrying goods inland to Gortýs from this remote bit of coast 2,000 years ago, when Léndas, then called Lebéna, was the port for the flourishing Graeco–Roman city in the Mesará. But Lebéna had been well-known for hundreds of years by then, thanks to the healing properties of its mineral springs. A Hellenistic sanctuary, with temple and baths, was built around one of the springs on the hillside just east of the harbour around the 4th century BC, and it was an important enough centre to be comprehensively restored several centuries later by craftsmen from Gortýs.

The fenced site (*Open* 15 Jun–end Oct Monday noon–3, Tue–Sun 8.30–3; Nov–14 Jun Tue–Sun 8.30–3. *Admission: free*) stands on the left of the road just before it reaches Léndas. Down the hill from the gate is a square excavation, paved with slabs, its original walls of stone blocks

PAXIMÁDHIA

In most countries, taking bread on a picnic is usually a bad move. By the time it emerges from the rucksack at lunchtime it is squashed, stale and un-appetising. Not so in Crete. Buy *paximádhia*, hunks or rings of hard-baked bread, and soften it with water to release its subtle, rather nutty flavour.

lined by the Gortýs restorers with flat, red Roman tiles. This was the Hellenistic temple to Asklepios, the god of healing. A cluster of stones at the bottom of the inner wall is all that remains of the base of a statue of the god. Two tall granite pillars rise from the temple floor, their capitals now broken off. A few metres nearer the gate the square foundations of the sanctuary treasury contain a striking Hellenistic mosaic, showing a prancing seahorse with a rippling tail. The shapes of the muscles under his white pebble skin are outlined in black, his mane and the spines along his back are picked out in red, and curling waves frame his joyfully cavorting form. The exuberance of the artist, perhaps inspired by the vivid turquoise of the sea in view from the hill, comes clearly across two and a half thousand years. Just to the east, among deep excavation trenches, stands the little brick arch that spanned the healing spring, a source until very recently resorted to by Cretans with stomach troubles.

▶ Mátala *72A1*

Mátala, on the Gulf of Mesará 15km (9 miles) southwest of Moíres, is one of those places everyone has heard of, chiefly in lurid or Utopian tales of the hippies who established themselves in the caves above the beach during the 1960s. These caves, originally Roman rock-cut burial chambers, are now empty (*Open* Apr to mid-Oct daily 8–5, mid Oct to end Mar daily 8.30–3. *Admission: inexpensive*) and the village has swapped its Shangri-la aura for modern prosperity as a full-blown resort. Mátala does have plenty of places to stay, bars, an excellent sandy beach and famously clear, fish-filled waters.

SOUVLÁKI

Beach taverna cuisine is simple, predictable and nearly always reliable. *Souvláki*, kebabs of lamb, pork or fish, grilled over charcoal and served with chips or salad, are the mainstay. Try swordfish or tuna *souvláki*. Eat them gazing out to sea and you will find that the flavour intensifies, magically.

Holiday traffic at Mátala Bay

For lovers of wildlife, Crete is a paradise. Within this comparatively small island there is an astonishing variety of habitat, from the caves, marshes and plains of the coast through scrubby hillsides and fertile lowlands to the plateaux and peaks of the high mountains. A pair of binoculars and a few good Mediterranean reference books on birds, trees, flowers and butterflies are all you need.

NAME OF THE BEAST
What should you properly call the Cretan ibex? "Wild goat" is the most commonly used term, but incorrect; *agríma*, often heard, can refer to other animals; *kri-kri* is an abominable Americanism, say the purists who prefer *égagros* (pronounced with soft, rolled g's) from the beast's Latin name *Capra aegagrus cretensis*.

POPULAR PELICANS
In spite of all the ornithological delights of Crete's wildest mountains and coasts, the island's most sought-after birds remain Níkos and Pédros, the half-tame pelicans that terrorise the waterfront at Siteía.

Between March and May Crete bursts into bloom, with carpets of wild flowers from shore to summit. Many species are indigenous to the island and, given that traditional farming practices are still so widespread, the flowers bloom extravagantly (see also page 227). A second flowering in the late autumn makes a visit in October very worthwhile. Crete is sited on the bird migration routes between Europe and Africa, and is an important landfall in spring and autumn for many species.

There are areas of coastal wetland around Tavronítis in the northwest, and at Georgióupoli, west of Réthymno that have not been drained. Others are near Fragkokástelo and around the Gulf of Mesará, west of Tympáki. These are fine sites to look for waders such as sandpipers and avocets during the migration seasons, and you will find herons, terns and marsh harriers there all year round. Feathery tamarisk trees are widespread along the coasts and beaches, and there are orchids in the sand dunes.

On higher ground For many birdwatchers, a highlight—or challenge—of a visit to Crete, is the chance to get to grips with its many species of breeding birds. April is arguably the best month, partly because those species that are migratory are likely to be newly arrived, seeking out territories and hence more visible. In addition, male songbirds are most vocal at the start of the nesting season, greatly improving the chances of finding them. Early in the season, woodchat shrikes are conspicuous, often perching on barbed wire fences from which they drop down on unspecting insect prey. By the beginning of May, the air will be filled with the calls of bee-eaters, that most colourful of Mediterranean birds. For the more advanced birdwatching enthusiast, Crete offers wonderful opportunities for observing the dozen or so species of warblers that either populate habitats ranging from open *phrygana* to woody *maquis* or pass through on migration. Often the song is all you have to go on at first, but most will

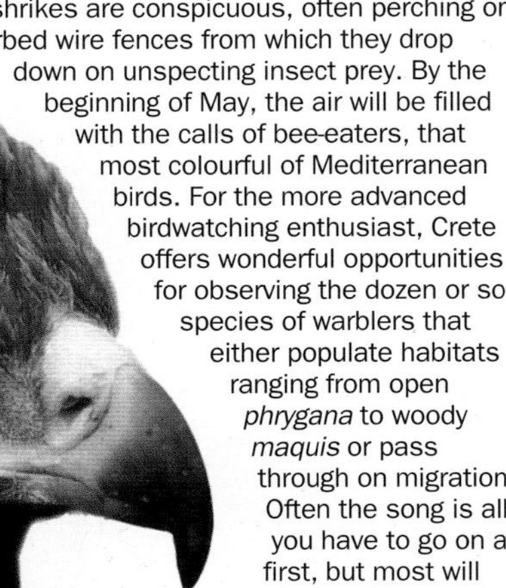

Golden eagles can be seen throughout the year—if you are lucky

The Mediterranean pine is now far less common than it once was

eventually reveal themselves to patient observers. Star of the show is the boldly marked Ruppell's warbler, a species whose entire world breeding range is restricted to the Greek islands. Griffon vultures, alpine choughs, buzzards, golden eagles and ravens haunt the peaks. In the north-east you might get a rare sighting of an Eleanora's falcon, or a big Lammergeier vulture. Even rarer is the Cretan ibex, almost entirely confined to special reserves on the offshore islands—but keep an eye open in the White Mountains, especially around the head of the Samariá Gorge.

Under threat However, all is not rosy in the Cretan wildlife garden. Pollution of watercourses by runoff from olive oil factories, use of herbicides, fouling of shores with fuel oil and rubbish, disturbance by increased numbers of visitors, are making themselves felt. The island has also suffered a 60 per cent loss of wetland habitats during the last 30 years, however' then run on with 'the most serious problem is erosion. The most serious problem is that of erosion. The visitor cannot fail to be struck by the harsh grey nakedness of the peaks and ridges. The pine and cypress forests that once covered them have been cut down over the centuries. The forests helped to create clouds and rainfall; tree roots bound the soil, which retained moisture, releasing it slowly to lower levels. Now, waterlessness has become Crete's most pressing ecological and economic concern. Herds of goats and sheep, nibbling their way unchecked across the island, allow tree seedlings no chance to grow. Recently forest fires have destroyed a significant proportion of the remaining native trees.

REPTILES
Early spring is the best time of year to see Crete's rich and diverse reptile fauna. Look for snakes and lizards, many of which will have hibernated during the winter months, warming up their bodies in the sunshine on south-facing slopes. Leave it later in the year and the reptiles avoid being active during the daylight hours for fear of overheating. Reptile enthusiasts should also keep their eyes on the skies, for short-toed eagles circling in the skies above. These impressive raptors specialise in catching snakes and can sometimes be seen flying with dead prey dangling from their bills looking for all the world like a long, leathery shoelace!

The fruits of the prickly pear are edible

The Mesará Plain is surrounded by mountains

BUSY BUGGIES
A familiar sight of the Mesará plain is the farmer's motorised buggy. Sometimes it is a three-wheeler, sometimes it has two front wheels set perilously close together. Powered by a noisy, fume-rich engine and steered with handlebars or with a tiller, the Mesará buggies take farm produce or passengers slowly along the road in their open trailers, overtaken by all other transport except the even slower but more environmentally friendly donkey.

►► Mesará *72B2*

Three mountain ranges hem in the length of the Mesará Plain: Psiloreítis to the north, the Díkti range to the east, and the lower Asteroúsia mountains to the south. Streams from the three ranges pour down to join the two great rivers of the plain, Geropótamos and Anapodáris. Mesará itself is an alluvial basin flush with rich soil thousands of years old. Well watered by streams and rivers directed into man-made irrigation channels, sheltered by the mountains and warmed by the Cretan south coast climate, the plain is the most productive agricultural area in Crete.

Older civilisations were well aware of the fertility of Mesará. The Minoans sited their palaces of Faistós and Agía Triáda on the ridge north of the plain, and the Dorian Greeks, and later the Romans, built extensively on the site of the Minoan village of Gortýs further to the east.

Descending into the Mesará Plain, you are immediately aware of its prosperity and productivity. Where Roman wheat grew, there now flourish melons, cucumbers, watermelons, tomatoes and other fruits and vegetables that thrive on plenty of sun and water. Though you might not guess it from the very ordinary-looking, rather down-at-heel buildings of the Mesará towns, the farms here are among the most prosperous in the island, trading through lively markets at Moirés and Tympáki. But a price has been paid. Wherever you look, you will see the tattered, shiny, reflective surfaces of the hothouses, and windblown shreds of plastic seem almost as ubiquitous as the Mesará wild flowers.

Mesará hothouses

► Moíres *72B2*

Moíres stands at the centre of the Mesará Plain, the chief town. As well as being the only place with a bus terminus, it has a number of eateries that serve the lorry drivers who stop here and the local farmers who flood in on donkeys, motorised tricycle trucks and in battered pick-ups to sell their produce at the rowdy street market on Saturday morning. Moirés has little of elegance or physical attraction, but as the largest Mesará town it has plenty of shops, cafés, tavernas and all the facilities needed by locals and visitors alike. There are a number of cheapish rooms to rent, too, though few visitors are attracted to the idea of staying in such a workaday place.

If this is how you feel, you will certainly avoid **Tympáki►**, 10km (6 miles) to the west and only a couple of kilometres from the shore of the Gulf of Mesará. Guide books do not have a good word to say for Tympáki. It is an unprepossessing place, for sure, and currently under threat of a proposed massive Chinese-funded commercial port. The shabby streets of run-down, post-war flats and houses each side of a long main streets is a world away from the Cretan mountain villages, but the village square just off the main drag is overarched with big, shady trees and surrounded by *kafenía* where you will almost certainly be the only foreigner. Here, as elsewhere off the Cretan tourist routes, a few words of Greek will be repayed by instant friendliness, interest and hospitality. Tympáki's Friday morning market is even louder and fiercer than that at Moíres. The frustrated lorry drivers honk more furiously at the crowds, the stallholders urge and coerce passionately over the ranks of cheap clothes and shoes and the counters packed with fresh fruit and vegetables. A night in Tympáki will not be *grande luxe* by any stretch of the imagination (the hotels are pretty basic), but a short stay here can show you a side of Crete that you will experience in very few other places—commercial, everyday, loud and unadornedly vital.

WATERING THE GROVES
Walking through the olive and orange groves of the plain, you will come across the complicated network of irrigation channels that bring water from the Geropótamos and Anapodáris rivers, helped by snaking miles of black hosepipe connected to spurting multiple valves—a reminder that even in this naturally lush and fertile region, Crete's shortage of water is only overcome by constant hard work and ingenuity.

MEANDERING IN MESARÁ
With such an abundance of dramatic mountain and coastal scenery attracting visitors to other parts of Crete, Mesará is a relatively unexplored area. Nobody will mind you walking around their fields, orchards and groves provided you bear in mind that these are their places of work. For ramblers who prefer not to encounter other ramblers, enjoyment is guaranteed.

Drive

The western Asteroúsia Mountains

This is an exciting and lonely 75km (46.5 miles) round drive in one of the least-visited corners of southern Crete, through the tumbled valleys and hills of the western Asteroúsia Mountains, and the rough but perfectly driveable coast road that skirts them between Kaloí Liménes and Léndas.

The drive explores the isolated country between the popular west-facing resort of Mátala on the Gulf of Mesará and the currently emerging one of Léndas on the south coast.

It is important to fill up with petrol and check your tyres at Moíres before setting off, since there are very few garages *en route*. The south coast road is rough and rutted, but presents no problems that the average Cretan hire car cannot tackle if driven with care. See map on pages 72–73.

Your road turns south in the centre of **Moíres** before setting off, signposted Pómbia and Mátala, towards the green and grey wall of the Asteroúsia Mountains and the big farming village of **Pómbia** cradled in the foothills. In the village fork right uphill by the church, and right again at a Kaloí Liménes sign. Soon you are above Pómbia, heading up into the hills, with enormous views opening northwards over the fruit farms of the Mesará Plain towards the massive, fissured bulk of Psiloreítis. Suddenly you crest a saddle of ground to see the Libyan Sea in front of you between the hills. At the square in **Pigaidákia**, follow the Kaloí Liménes sign to descend through the wild Asteroúsia hills, brilliant with wild flowers in springtime. A good tarmac road takes you to within a couple of kilometres of Kaloí Liménes and then the dirt starts again.

Kaloí Liménes is one of the few sheltered anchorages on Crete's south coast, guarded by three small islets offshore. This was the "fair haven" where St Paul landed in about AD 60, a captive on his way to Rome: his first contact with European soil. Paul wanted to spend the winter here, but was overruled by the centurion in charge of him, and by the ship's owner and captain. This turned out to be a fatal error of judgement, since they went on to face shipwreck in Malta. Today there are huge cylindrical oil storage tanks on one of the islets, and a clutch of hotels and tavernas on the grey sand beach, but Kaloí Liménes is still a peaceful fishing harbour with a local life of its own.

Back-track from the end of the road, and in a couple of kilometres turn right downhill past a hotel on a poor dirt road that soon improves. It clings to the puce-coloured cliffs above the half-built hotels of tiny **Plateía Perámata**. At a T-junction in

the valley beyond, turn right on to a short bad stretch and then go left, winding in and out of clefts in the skirts of the shore, covered with greenhouses and fruit and vegetable plots. There are no signposts; keep to the cliff road and ask the horticultural workers if you are in doubt.

At a T-junction above the little beach at **Papadogiánnis**, turn right to pass tavernas and drive on towards the craggy headland of **Cape Léndas**. The name means lion, and you can make out a roughly leonine shape if you try hard enough! **Léndas** (see pages 94–95), on its little bay of green sea and grey-yellow beach, is developing year by year as a resort.

The road is now tarmac again, which will come as a respite for your suspension, and climbs north into the mountains. Yellow gorse splashes the scrubby slopes, and you will likely spot eagles floating overhead. This is marvellously lonely country, where the village of **Krótos** sits in isolation. Fork right by the church beyond the village on a bad dirt road to Vasilikí. Keep straight on at the junction and on through the Mesará vineyards and olive groves to Vagioniá, Agía Déka and the road to Moíres.

The Asteroúsia Mountains are bare and lonely

Shepherds' huts dot the slopes of the Asteroúsia Mountains (left)
Even this sparse settlement (below) has its own church

Crete's road system has improved out of all recognition during the last 20 years. The new road from Irakleío west to Chaniá and east to Ágios Nikólaos has provided the north of the island with an excellent modern highway, some of it dual carriageway. Other good roads, slower but still negotiable, criss-cross the island between the larger towns, most running north–south in obedience to the lie of the land.

Shrines often denote accident blackspots

SHRINES
As soon as you embark on the Cretan roads you will notice roadside shrines erected by the families of accident victims on the fatal spot. These vary from modest tin boxes to really elaborate miniature churches. Inside are icons, flowers, lamps, candles and bottles of olive oil. At night the lighted lamps and candles in the shrines of recent victims flicker a warning as you pass.

Up in the mountains, however, and along the south coast, road conditions can still be very primitive. Tarmac can suddenly degenerate into a dirt surface, and in the more remote areas you may come across surfaces so cracked by landslips, so narrow and rocky, that you may have no alternative but to turn around and seek another route.

Maps The road maps of Crete are not much help. Freytag & Berndt's 1:150 000 Kreta map (ISBN 3707907627) is excellent for driving and touring. The Harms-ic-Verlag 1:100 000 comes in two sheets (ISBN 978-3-92468-16-0 and ISBN 978-3-927468-17-7) and is more detailed. These are not detailed enough for walking and hiking.

Vehicles Hire cars can cope with most of the dirt roads, and there are numerous rental companies all over the island. On the whole it is advisable to choose one of the reputable international firms. Four-wheel-drives are essentially for image value rather than practical necessity. Motorcycles are cheaper, mopeds and scooters cheaper still, but these can be very dangerous on the loose dirt surfaces and the lower engine capacity machines may not be able to climb the steeper hills, especially with two up. Bring your own helmet to be sure of having one.

Rules of the road In Crete you drive on the right-hand side of the road. Town drivers tend to be hasty of speed and judgement. Traffic lights flick straight from red to green, and drivers behind will beep impatiently if you do not react instantly. Motorcycles and commercial vehicles do not always respect one-way streets.

Mediterranean insouciance does not extend to the traffic police in the big towns, so it is wise to park in official parking areas.

Out in the country, white lines mark major roads. An unbroken white line in the centre of the road means no overtaking, though most local drivers ignore this. Another white line on the nearside marks a crawler lane into

Open tops give a good view—but mind the sun

which you are expected to move when being overtaken or when an overtaking vehicle is coming at you. But beware! There may be a donkey, bicycle or parked vehicle just around the corner. Pot-holes feature on all roads, and you must learn early on to watch out for them. Roadworks are frequent and rarely signposted.

Garages are usually to be found in the larger towns, but they are few and far between elsewhere, so it is a good idea fill up when you have the opportunity. Unleaded petrol and diesel are widely available. Garages rarely accept credit cards.

When they exist, traffic signs are of the standard Continental type. Some major sites, for example Foúrnou Korýfi, are poorly signposted. On main roads, signs are usually given in Greek followed by English. It is useful to know that the letters X, H, Ch and Kh are interchange-able, as in Xaniá, Haniá, Chaniá or Khaniá.

On minor roads signs may be in Greek only, and on dirt roads they are often tiny and handmade, and very hard to spot. On the south coast and up in the mountains, dirt roads are often entirely unsignposted at forks and cross-roads, so keep a wary eye on the map and be willing to backtrack and ask directions.

There are two basic rules. Firstly, for any journey on back roads, allow half as long again or even twice as long, as you normally would. And, secondly, be patient.

Mountain roads are narrow and winding

ROADWORKS

Drivers are unlikely to have advance warning of roadworks on minor and dirt roads. If you come round a corner and find the road blocked by a mound of stones or a digger, don't despair. Within a few minutes the obstruction may well be cleared. If it looks as if work is due to go on for any length of time, ask the workmen for help and someone will direct you through the obstacle course.

USES OF THE CRETAN CAR HORN 1

Greeting friends; venting rage at street blockages; summoning or repelling oncoming traffic (hard to say which, until it is too late!); calling attention to what the blarer judges to be poor driving; attracting the attention of pretty girls; announcing mounting impatience while waiting for a dilatory passenger; occupying the fingers of restless children; dispersing sheep on the road.

USES OF THE CRETAN CAR HORN 2

Never, but never, to alert other drivers to the immediate appearance of the onrushing owner around the next hairpin bend, on the wrong side of the road!

PÍTHOI

Enormous earthenware *píthoi* or storage jars, some standing up to shoulder height, are still to be seen in use in village storerooms, and as rubbish receptacles in the back streets. But the days of the *píthos* in everyday use are numbered. Modern fridges store more, keep their contents cooler and don't break when bashed into. But *píthoi* don't consume electricity, or flood the floor, or hum at night. A secondary use for *píthoi*, and one you'll see in many villages, is as chimney pots. The smaller jars are the perfect size, shape and material for the job.

Remember your hand luggage limit before you buy!

►► Thrapsanó 73E3

Thrapsanó is well signposted to the right off the Irakleío–Kastélli road. The village straggles along the side of a valley of olive groves, a rambling place of side turnings and narrow lanes. Thrapsanó has been famous for centuries for its pottery, and today the tradition is as strong as ever. There are many small workshops in and around Thrapsanó, turning out every kind of pottery from souvenirs through practical household crockery to enormous *píthoi,* waist-high earthenware storage jars whose design has scarcely changed since Minoan times. The first pottery you come to on your approach from Iráklio is that of Ioánnis Moutzákis, and this is as good a place as any to watch the skill of the potters. One turns the wheel by hand while his colleague teases and coaxes the sinuous shape of a jar or bowl out of a lump of grey clay. Fired in a kiln, the pottery flushes a rich orange colour.

► Tsoútsouros 73E1

This little coastal settlement is signposted in Káto Kastellianá, off the main Ierápetra–Áno Viánnos road. Some 11km (7 miles) of spiralling, rough road through a landscape of purple rocks and dizzying drops brings you down to Tsoútsouros.

Tsoútsouros was a lonely little place. The isolation of this part of Crete's southern coast made it ideal for the

Tsoútsouros straggles along a grey strand

daring, clandestine landings of members of the Allied resistance movement during World War II. Until recently, the village was no more than a clutch of white-painted tavernas and rooms to rent, along with a couple of small hotels, but it's sure to expand with the completion of a smooth asphalt access road from Káto Kastellianá. New property owners from around Europe have already added a slight bohemian atmosphere to the traditional Cretan feel. The grey cliffs and grey sand beach don't offer the classic holiday image, but the setting, between rocky headlands, is peaceful and lovely and the journey to get here is delightful.

► Vathýpetrou *73D3*

Following the road south out of Archánes, you reach the site of Vathýpetrou in 5km (3 miles), signposted just off the road to the right and reached by a short dirt track. Vathýpetrou (*Open* Tue–Sun 8.30–3, but may also be open at other times; ask at Café Ioúktas in Archánes. *Admission: free*) is a well-preserved example of a Minoan country villa. Everything was home-produced on the big agricultural estates, and the inhabitants of Vathýpetrou were kept busy weaving, making pottery, pressing olive oil and producing wine.

You enter the site past a shrine on your right. Continue forward to reach a low-roofed building. This may be locked, but the curator will open it for you. Inside is uniquely well-preserved winemaking equipment. You can see a big round earthenware grape press with a spout, a receptacle for the grape juice, and in the stone-flagged floor a circular basin and drainage channel for washing the feet after treading grapes.

To the right (westnorthwest) of the building is the villa's main room, with a wonderful view over a wide valley covered by a patchwork of vineyards, fields and olive groves, with snow-capped Psiloreítis beyond. To the right again stands a roofed storeroom, containing fragments of big *píthoi*. Return to the entrance by way of the villa's thick-walled living rooms.

Vathýpetrou was built on a spectacular site

Walk

Kapetanianá to Mount Kófinas

This walk is in one of the wildest parts of southern Crete, from a remote mountain village to the highest peak of the Asteroúsia Mountains, passing churches with frescoes along the way (allow about 4–5 hours). A very tough and precipitous extension (add at least 5 hours) leads down to the isolated monastery of Koudoumá on the coast and back up again!

The walk starts at the top of a rough, twisting dirt road in the high, lonely village of Kapetanianá, reached from the Moíres–Irakleío road in the Mesará Plain. Turn right in Agía Déka through Vagioniá and Loúkia, where you begin the ascent to Kapetanianá. Park beside the first buildings you come to. The church of Panagía, in the lower part of the village, has faded frescoes dating from 1401.

You could follow the dirt road directly from the car to the chapel below the peak of Mount Kófinas, but for a more interesting walk take the path that descends from the church, forking right downhill past the cemetery, for 1km (0.5 miles), to pass the church of Michális Archángelis on the right. This, too, contains faded frescoes, some dating from the 13th century and slowly being eroded by rainwater .

Two hundred metres past the church on a right-hand bend, hairpin left on a path between wire fences. Soon the lefthand fence bears off uphill to the left, but keep straight on, downhill to pass through a shepherd's gate. Scramble over the wire fence ahead and climb the hillside, crossing a dirt road. Above you there is a dry stone wall across the mouth of a cave—a shepherd's rough dwelling-place.

The domed peak of Kófinas is your aiming point as you climb to a dirt road and pass a wired sheepfold. The saddle-roofed hut inside the fence, with a white cross painted on the wall, was a church built by John the Honest, a 14th-century hermit. There are traces of fresco inside, around the base of the ruined apse.

Half a kilometre beyond, an orange scar on the hillside shows the route of a short cut. Aim directly for the saddle of ground to the left of the mountain. This will take you across the windings of the dirt road, to reach the little

The extension to the basic walk will take you to Koudoumá Monastery

chapel on the saddle. From here climb towards the biggest of the conifers above, and follow the red dots and arrows of waymarks as you scramble up among the rocks for 15 minutes to reach the chapel on the summit of Mount Kófinas (1,231m/4,038 feet). The view from here is superb, with Psiloreítis and the Díkti Mountains to the north, and the south coast a head-spinning drop below.

The return route to Kapetanianá is back the way you came. But the very strenuous extension to Koudoumá Monastery is highly recommended to strong and experienced walkers with plenty of stamina. Note, however, that it will require a further five to six hours, and involves a steep descent of 1,200m (3,936 feet), and a correspondingly steep ascent of 500m (1,640 feet). So check your watch, and your fitness, before tackling it.

Extension to Koudoumá

Return to the chapel on the saddle, bearing left downhill to the water trough. Head westnorthwest down the gully, which curves left. In ten minutes look for a stubby tree on your left, pass it and cross the scree slope on the path high on the left bank of the gully. Continue curving left under the crags of Kófinas; you will soon be heading due south with a deep gorge on your right. Descend across a stony plateau, bearing left of a wooden post on the skyline, to find red waymarks. Soon the red roofs of Koudoumá monastery will appear below. Follow the steep zigzag waymarked descent through the pines to the monastery.

From the monastery turn west, hugging the coast, for 2km (1 mile) to Agíos Ioánnis. There is a church with frescoes in the cliffs, 1km (0.5 miles) to the west. A zigzag track is clearly in view above. Follow it, or climb directly up, a very steep ascent taking a minimum of two hours, to Kapetanianá.

The wild and rocky south coast overlooks the Libyan Sea

4
Káto Goúrnes
Svoúrou Metóchi
Akr Cherónisos
Limín Chersonísou
Kólpos Malión
Goúves
Aposelemis
Chersónisos
Stalída
Mália
Mália
Sísi
Kóxari
Kaló Chorió
818m
Mochós
Seléna
Potamiés
Smári
Sfendýli
Krasí
1599m
1487m Machairá
3
Káto Karouzaná
Avdoú
Kerá
Apóstoloi
Askoí
Mésa Potamoí
Exo Potamo
Kastélli
Líthos
Sklaverochóri
Xidás
Moní Vidiánis
Tzermiádo
Pinakianó
Lilianó
Amarianó
Mésa Lasíthi
Lasíthiou
Máthia
Pláti
Psychró
Ágios Geórgios
Díktaio Andro
Avrakóntes
Kat
Geráki
Óros Díkti
Nipidítos
1414m Virgioméno
2148m
Avlí
Panagía
2
Arkádes
Kasános
2141m Afentis Christós
Katofýni
Thomadianó
Ínio
Karavádos
Vakiótes
1783m Madára
Párissia
Áno Viánnos
Skiniás
Kefalóvrysi
Káto Viánnos
Amirás
Ágios Vasíleios
Demáti
Chóndros
Favrianá
Sykológos
Keratókampos
Tértsa
Árvi
Órmos Keratokámpou
Faflágkos
Akr Sidonía
Tsoútsouros
Órmos Tsoútsourou
A
B

Anastasia and St John take a rest in Ágios Nikólaos harbour

Ágios Nikólaos and the Díkti Mountains

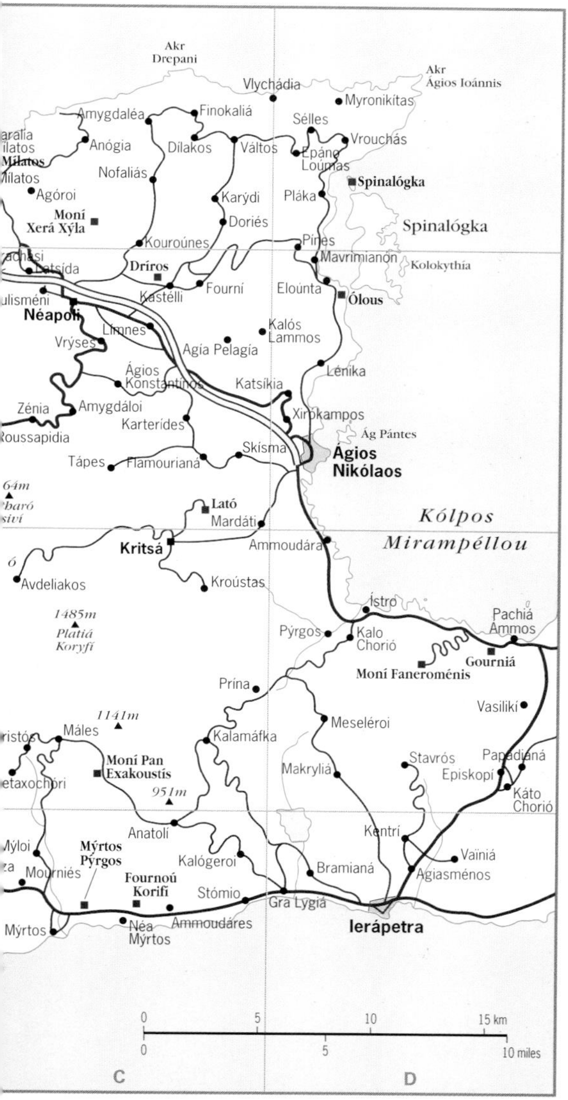

►►► REGION HIGHLIGHTS

Ágios Nikólaos *pages 112–115*

Díktaean Cave *pages 118–119*

Gourniá Minoan Town *pages 122–123*

Katharó Plateau *page 124*

Kritsá *page 128*

Lasíthiou Plateau *pages 130–131*

Mália Minoan Palace *pages 131–133*

Spinalógka Island *pages 136–137*

SHEPHERDS' GATES
The gates that shepherds install in their stock fences are flimsy grids of wire, held to the posts with a single loop. These gates are strong enough to deter sheep and goats, but will not withstand rough handling. Do remember, when you encounter one on a walk, to open it with care, and to close it securely behind you.

ÁGIOS NIKÓLAOS AND THE DÍKTI MOUNTAINS Between Irakleío and Ágios Nikólaos is a long stretch of northern coastline and a hinterland that rises to the tremendous rocky ranges of the Díkti Mountains. There is no more varied a region in Crete.

The mountains surround Lasíthiou, the best-known upland plateau in Crete—its windmills launched a thousand postcards —and Katharó, equally delightful but very little visited. The mountains themselves see only the occasional walker; solitude and face-to-face enjoyment of Cretan wildlife are guaranteed. In the flanks of the mountains quiet green valleys rise through olive groves to harsh, stony heights. Yet only a few kilometres north across the foothills is an almost continuously built-up, developed and over-exploited strip of coastline 40km (25 miles) long, where the world is at your elbow, if not occupying your sunbed.

All roads hereabouts lead to Ágios Nikólaos, the one town of any size in the region, and all excursions begin here. The town is the administrative capital of Crete's easternmost quarter, the nome of Lasíthiou. The region south and east of Iráklio is drawn towards Ágios Nikólaos for its services, commercial life and entertainment. Ágios Nikólaos became the island's premier seaside resort, perhaps because it feels free of the weight of Byzantine, Venetian and Turkish architecture that anchor Chaniá and Réthymno to the past, and it is more centrally placed than Siteía. It is not a dignified town, nor a staid one, and it is certainly not quiet. But Ágios Nikólaos is lively and has everything for the holidaymaker: buses leave for the inland towns and villages, boats depart for islands and beaches, traditional music and dancing displays break out like a rash in summer, and discos batter the night air along the restaurant-lined waterfront. Some modest and some very plush and correspondingly expensive hotels have spread along the coast to the north of the town, to cater for the hundreds of thousands of visitors who base themselves each year in Ágios Nikólaos.

The happy holiday town of Ágios Nikólaos

The Díkti backdrop

The excellent new road to Iráklio runs northwest from Ágios Nikólaos, and where it meets the coast the built-up strip begins. There are hotels, restaurants, apartment blocks, new holiday villages, gift shops, bars, discos, sports complexes and packed beaches where bodies grill flank to flank. Many Cretans will tell you of their disillusionment with this new world, which has gobbled up most of the coastline in the last 25 years with much unregulated, crass and ugly building. On the positive side, it has produced a livelihood for many local people, and it has concentrated much of Crete's more brash tourism in a clearly defined area. But welcome change is in the air. The Cretan tourist authorities, contemplating the rapacity of this brand of holiday-making, have begun to edge towards a greener and gentler view of the future of tourism in their island—refreshing thinking that is just beginning to bear fruit.

Away from the strip, there are treasures on every side for the explorer who takes a little trouble to look for them: the breathtaking frescoes at hospitable Kritsá; Spinalógka Island with its haunting history; the unfrequented shores of the northeastern peninsula and the south coast; the wriggling mountain roads up to the Lasíthiou Plateau; great caves and their legends; high and lovely Katharó; and the wild and stony beauty of the valleys and peaks of the Díkti Mountains.

WAYMARKS

Waymarking on the footpaths of Crete is an uncertain science. Splashes of red and sometimes orange on wayside rocks show the route but many have now been covered with vegetation or worn away. They have a habit of disappearing when most needed. A good point to bear in mind in the mountains is that waymarks easily visible on the way up may be tricky to spot when descending. Take a reliable bearing on a landmark you'll recognise again, if you think a waymark may be of this awkward type.

TAMARISK
The feathery tamarisk with its pale green fronds and dangling, catkin-like white or delicate pink flowers is the tree you will see most frequently in seaside towns and villages, planted to throw its whispering shade over the café terraces and nearest beach.

GREASY BUT GOOD
As a change from *souvláki* and Greek salad, invite yourself into the kitchen of your restaurant or taverna and see if they are offering *arní tis katsarólas me patátes*—lamb casserole, cooked with potatoes. With luck, or good judgement, you will be served a plateful of this greasy delight.

▶▶▶ Ágios Nikólaos *109D3*

Thanks to its vigorous tourist trade and bustling atmosphere, Ágios Nikólaos ranks as one of Crete's Big Four towns. But the town as it stands today is very much a younger sister to Irakleío, Réthymno and Chaniá, having developed its harbour and surrounding buildings only since the 19th century. You won't find in Ágios Nikólaos the glories of Venetian architecture that characterise the other three towns of the north coast. There are no strong fortifications of golden stone around the harbour, no impressive stretches of ancient city wall, and no mighty castle frowning down from a promontory. Ágios Nikólaos is a town absorbed in modern tourism, whose discos, bars and hotels have been grafted in the last 30 years onto the framework of a commercial centre that grew from almost nothing to become the capital of the Lasíthiou nome of Crete. But take the town on its own terms as a prettily sited tourist resort with all modern facilities and a lively flavour, surprisingly resilient under its enormous weight of summertime visitors, and you will find it is an excellent base for exploration of the Díkti Mountains, the coastline and the lush lowlands between Irakleío and the eastern end of the island.

Early port There was a flourishing town in Hellenistic times on the headland just south of the modern harbour, which served as the port for the Dorian city of Lató (see page 131), high in the hills 6km (3.5 miles) to the west. The

Ágios Nikólaos

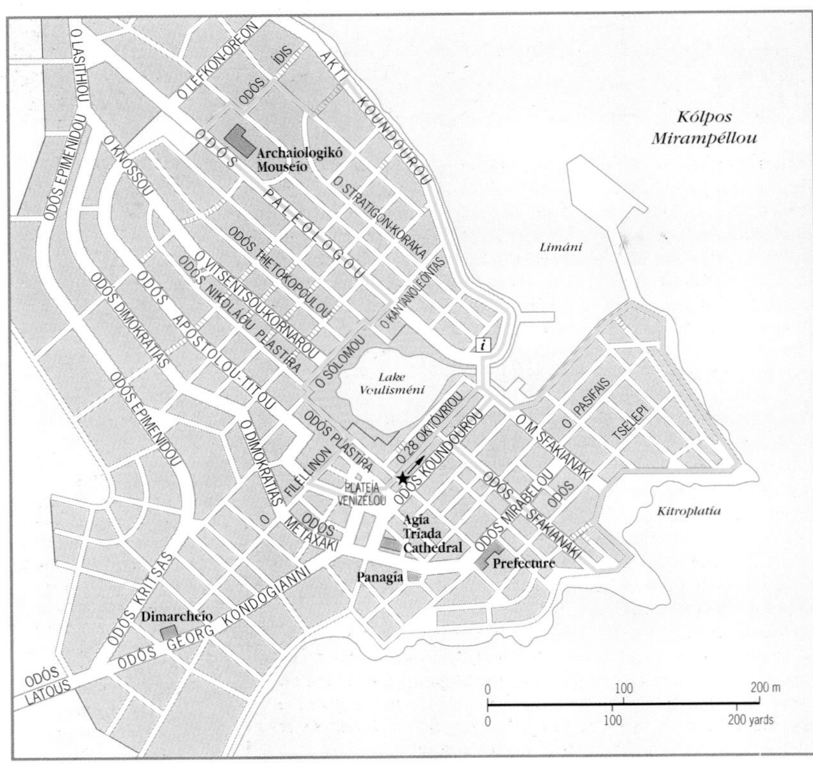

Small fishing boats supply the many restaurants

town continued to thrive during the Roman occupation, but went into a decline shortly after the Byzantine takeover of the island. The Venetians later revived it, building their fortress at Mirabéllo, inland of the old port, to guard the harbour of Porto di San Nicolo, in the shelter of the headland to the north where the Byzantine church of Ágios Nikólaos stood. Nothing remains of the fort, and there is very little to bear witness to either Venetian or Turkish rule, but by the late 19th century a new harbour nearer to the ancient port had revitalised the town.

Tourist town After the union of Crete with mainland Greece in 1913, Ágios Nikólaos became the capital of the nome of Lasíthiou, and continued its modest prosperity as a trading centre. In the early 1960s tourists began to arrive, attracted by the picturesque position of the town above the harbour and by its convenient location close to the Lasíthiou Plateau (see pages 130–131) and to nearby beaches just a short boat ride away. Since then, package holidays have filled the town with visitors, and smart hotels and apartment blocks have begun to stretch away along the coast in both directions. But, remarkably, this is not eyesore territory. Ágios Nikólaos people are relaxed and welcoming by nature, and even the most modern hotels benefit from the hilly landscape and the ever-visible sea with its backdrop of mountains.

BEACH CHARGES
Charging people for the use of a municipal beach has turned out to be a good system. Those who pay appreciate the cleanness of the sand and water, and the absence of semi-permanent colonies of campers. Those who object to paying have not far to go out of town before they find a free beach of their own.

Walk

Ágios Nikólaos

Allow about two or three hours. See the map on page 112.

The walk begins in **Plateía Venizélou▶**, the little square just inland from the harbour to which weary holiday-makers climb to relax and watch the world go by at a pavement café table. The tiny, circular central gardens with their feathery sentinel palm trees lend a green and pleasant atmosphere to the square. On the south side, at the top of Odós Elefthérias Venizélou, is the **Cathedral of Agía Triáda▶**. Its interior is entirely covered with vigorous and expressive modern frescoes, a testimony to the still flourishing tradition of Byzantine-style church painting. An old icon in faded gold and red records the adventures of St Paul.

Ágios Nikólaos caters for a large number of British visitors

From the north side of the square, walk down **Odós 28 Októvriou▶**, lined with shops selling all manner of tourist goods and souvenirs. At the bottom of the street turn right and right again up tamarisk-shaded **Odós Koundoúrou▶**, a similar, parallel street. Everyone comes to shop in these two crowded thoroughfares and, as elsewhere in Crete, you get what you pay for. Half-way up Koundoúrou, turn left up Odós Sfakianáki. Here, you are at once out of the bustle and into a quiet street between blocks of flats, each of which has a caged bird singing from the balcony. At the crest of the street a grand view opens up over the hill-encircled Gulf of Mirampéllou to the south and east of the town. A new marina and breakwater lie immediately below. At the bottom of the street turn left up steps, then descend to turn left along the long promenade that stretches right round the waterfront of Ágios Nikólaos.

The sandy beach of **Kitroplatía▶** is fringed with tamarisk trees, and the headland where the port of ancient Lató stood gives a wide view of the harbour of **Agíos Nikólaos▶▶**, scenically the chief attraction of the town. Pale, colourwashed houses lined with balconies are piled above the narrow

harbour where fishing boats and ferries lie at their moorings. Beyond stretch the swooping ridges of the hills behind the town, running down to the sea in the distance. Cafés and restaurants, gift shops and excursion boat agencies stand shoulder to shoulder around the harbour. From here you can take a boat to nearby beaches, to pirate caves and to the spectacular former leper colony of Spinalógka Island. Crowds jostle, boat touts implore, buses roar and belch fumes. Walk on northwards along the seafront promenade and after 300m (327 yards) you come to steep Odós Salamínos on your left. Climb the steps of Odós Salamínos. Turn right along Odós Stavrou, take the second left up Odós Ídis, turn right at the top and take the first left to reach Odós Paleólogou and the **Archaeological Museum▶▶** (tel: 28410 24943. *Open* Tue–Sun 8–3. *Admission: moderate*).

The Archaeological Museum is clearly laid out in chronological order through seven rooms:

Room 1 contains pre- and early Minoan finds such as stone axe heads, fish hooks, bone scrapers, some elaborate pottery from Gourniá and some clumsy pottery from Agía Fotiá. In a centrally placed case of her own in **Room 2** stands the Goddess of Mírtos, a libation vessel made between 2600 and 2150 BC in the shape of a fat-bodied woman with a long neck rising to a tiny face. Her thin arms cradle a high-spouted jug from which the libations were poured. Grid patterns in faded red, squares and triangles, decorate her body. This is a wonderfully ingenious and imaginative piece of work, testimony to the already highly developed culture of the early Minoans. Vasilikí ware and beautifully cut stone jugs are here too, and flat gold jewellery.

Room 3 contains more jewellery, some earthenware sarcophagi with marine decorations, one still housing a skeleton, and a superb green-black steatite vase in the form of a conch shell, on which two carved demons pour libations. In **Room 4** there is a funerary urn containing a child's remains. In **Room 5** the post-Minoan artefacts show a decline from Minoan skill with stiff votive figurines, some of which are in Egyptian-style headdresses.

The skull from Potamós with its wreath of golden leaves

Room 6 sees a return to the more expressive work of the Dorian period (6th to 5th centuries BC) such as tall figures with firm chins and graceful folds in their clothing, votive figures of wild boar, lions and tortoises, and some Buddha-like seated figures in various states of sexual arousal. **Room 7** contains more finds from the same period: a smiling, ample-bosomed goddess, a remarkable vase with 70 light holes, tiny decorated seal stones and, to cap the exhibition, the squashed and grinning skull of a Roman, his brows encircled with a victor's gold laurel leaves, and a silver coin to pay Charon the Ferryman beside his long teeth.

From the museum, descend Odós Paleólogou, and just before the bottom turn right along Odós Kantanoleóntas, then up steep Sólomou to walk among pines and tamarisks above **Lake Voulisméni▶▶**. This remarkable deep-water lake is reputed to be bottomless, though unromantic science has fixed its depth at 64m (210 feet). Did the goddesses Artemis and Athena bathe here? Is the lake connected by a submarine channel to the volcanic island of Santorini, causing a sulphurous steaming of its waters from time to time? Local legend says so, and you are free to believe it.

Bear left from the cliff overlooking the lake down Odós Plastíra. Halfway down turn right along Odós Filéllinon and then take third left down narrow Odós Daskaloyiánni to return to Plateía Venizélou.

The steep streets of Áno Viánnos wind up the hill

►► Áno Viánnos

108B1

The small town of Áno Viánnos lies 40km (25 miles) west of Ierápetra on the main road to the Mesará plain. This is a really delightful place. The people display an interest in and hospitality towards the stranger that are characterisitic of all Cretan hill villages. There is usually a cool breeze blowing through the streets from the mountains. Not that Áno Viánnos is truly a mountain settlement. It stands with its back to the southern foothills of the Díkti range, looking south over a beautifully green plateau. The site is superb, and the village huddles attractively at the foot of the slopes in a tight pile of white and colour-washed houses.

There is a hint of Mesará fertility in the olive groves and vineyards that spread around the village on three sides. Áno Viánnos has always been a prosperous place as the centre for the countryside east and south of Mesará. These days its influence has diminished, especially since the development of the south coast villages west of Ierápetra into a chain of ever-expanding tourist resorts. Few visitors choose to stay in Áno Viánnos, which is a pity, since this is a characterful, friendly and inquisitive village, where tiny stepped alleyways lead up the hillside into a maze of traffic-free back lanes in which conversation and glimpses into other people's lives are guaranteed.

Take any of the side lanes that rise from the main road. An easy one to identify is the one that starts opposite a

TORN TO SHREDS
Most visitors find the proliferation of plastic greenhouses along the coastal plains of Crete unsightly. This is particularly so on the south coast, whose beauty derives from the unspoiled wildness. The sea winds make merry with such easily ripped and dispersed material, and where the tatters of plastic descend after their flight, they stick on fences, on bushes and on beaches. A comprehensive clear-up would seem to be in order...

gigantic plane tree in the village centre. You will soon find yourself in labyrinthine lanes. Two churches are worth seeking out. Ask directions of anyone you meet. Ágios Giórgios has fine 14th-century frescoes, but even better is Agía Pelagía near the top of the village. The churches are usually closed so ask about the keys when you ask for directions in the village. The guardian should be close by.

The church was built around 1300, and its frescoes are wonderfully well preserved in spite of eye-gouging, face-scratching and fire damage by Turkish zealots. Some of the figures have tenderly expressive faces and graceful hands. The Passion scenes on the northwest wall are particularly moving. Other scenes are savage: harlots being embraced by snakes, and St Bartholomew, blood-red after his martyrdom by flaying, standing with his skin flung over one shoulder.

VENERABLE TREES
Many of the trees that grace the village *plateía* grow to enormous size and are several centuries old, objects of pride to the inhabitants and handy points of reference when arranging to meet someone or when giving directions. Acacia, fig and plane are the species that seem most prone to this spectacular growth.

► Árvi *108B1*

You can reach Árvi in comfort along the tarmac road that leaves the Áno Viánnos–Ierápetra road in the village of Amirás, or you can arrive in more adventurous fashion from the west by way of the rough-dirt road along the coast from Keratókambos. Árvi itself is not particularly attractive. There are rather too many abandoned vehicles about, and the landscape is festooned with strips of plastic torn that have been torn by the wind from the proliferating greenhouses. But there are plenty of tavernas and rooms to rent, a couple of hotels, some shops and a pebbly beach shaded in part by tamarisks.

Just to the east is the Árvi Gorge, 300m (984 feet) deep, a narrow, dramatic rip in the mountain wall said to have been created when the god Zeus Arvios struck the hillside. These bare grey hills attract and radiate solar heat, and Árvi is famous for its climate, which allows the local farmers to cultivate oranges, pineapples and bananas as well as the usual beans, potatoes, tomatoes and olives.

In spite of the stony nature of the beach, Árvi is an excellent spot to spend a couple of days if you are looking for sunbathing and an enjoyably lazy time. And when your energy returns you can stroll up to the monastery that clings to the mountainside near the eastern flank of the gorge (see page 127).

SASH WITH A DASH
While many items of traditional dress, such as wide-cut breeches and knee-boots, have been retained by the older men of the hill villages, the old-style cummerbund has largely disappeared. Perhaps this is because there is no call nowadays for the silver-hilted pistols and daggers that were so dashingly thrust into it by the *palikáres* of yore.

The monastery of Ágios Andónios above Árvi

The easy way to the Díktaean cave

SADDLE UP
If you decide to hire a mule for the ascent to the cave, don't be alarmed to see a hard wooden saddle across your beast's back. Padded with a blanket, it is surprisingly comfortable.

Note the traditional wooden saddle

▶▶▶ Díktaean Cave *108B2*

The Díktaean Cave (marked Díktaio Andro on some maps. Tel: 28440 31600. *Open* summer, daily 8–7; winter, daily 10.30–5. *Admission: moderate*) in Psychró village is one of Crete's most popular tourist attractions and the source of many highly coloured legends. It lies a short walk or donkey ride above the village of Psychró, on the western edge of the Lasíthiou Plateau. A turning at the west end of the village points up a side road to the car park from where you begin the climb to the cave. There is tourist clutter at its most intensive here, though the vendors are not unsmiling if you essay a few words of Greek. If you enjoy the spectacle of cursing bus drivers jammed between cars, and relish being part of a slow-moving snake of people, then visit the cave at midday in the height of the tourist season. Otherwise, go early morning and out of season, if possible.

Just above the car park you come to the departure point for donkey rides and guided tours. A guide will point out features associated with the cave legends that you may miss if you go unaccompanied. Take a sweater and wear shoes with non-slip soles, as the descent into the cave is very slippery and steep.

There is a 15-minute climb from here up a zigzag path of smooth cobbles to the kiosk where you pay your entrance fee and have another opportunity to hire a guide. Just beyond, the cave mouth opens, a big dark hole in the rock that plunges very steeply down some 65m (213 feet) to pitch-black depths. The descent is by way of a stone-cobbled path with a handrail. You will need its support, as moss, damp, and the passing of thousands of feet have polished the stones to a skidpan surface.

As visitors inch their way down, the dank

air catches at throats and brings steam from bodies sweaty from the climb to the cave. Mosses and ferns cover the walls and below in the gloom you can make out the organ-pipe shapes of stalactites hanging from the roof, and the stumpy, knobbed towers of the much larger stalagmites below them. The cave mouth diminishes to a rectangular slit of daylight, and the guides light their gas lamps as they near the floor of the cavern. Down here it is easy to understand why the Díktaean Cave, overwhelmingly dark and other-worldly, was the focus of religious worship long before Minoan times, and continued to play that rôle for thousands of years.

As you reach the bottom of the cave, a side chamber on the left,which is easy to miss, holds the chief element of the legend of the Díktaean Cave, cited as the birthplace of Zeus, god of gods. Rhea, the mother of Zeus, came here to conceal the birth of her son from her jealous husband, Kronos, who had eaten all five of his previous offspring after an oracle warned him that he would be overthrown by his son. Kronos seems not to have been overburdened with intelligence, as he readily swallowed the stone wrapped in swaddling clothes that Rhea gave him in lieu of her baby. The guides flash their torches on a stalactite with the leering face of Kronos, a stalagmite shaped like a mother and child, the ledge where Zeus was born and the nipples of rock that gave him suck.

Excavators in 1899 and 1900 discovered hundreds of pottery and bronze offerings in this little chamber. Many more were retrieved by local boys diving into the dark pool at the bottom of the cave. Local religions embraced the Zeus legend wholeheartedly, adapting it to fit with other and older gods of the cave. Somehow, echoes of these devotions still reverberate in these cold depths.

NEEDLEWORK

Among the festoons of embroidery and weaving on sale in Psychró are genuine treasures of antique needlework. Best of all are the exquisitely worked pillow and cushion covers with patterns so small they must have consumed eyesight at a terrible rate. Many were sewn together out of strips of material saved from even older covers. Look inside to admire the clever stitching that joined them, so that they appear seamless from the outside. Let price be your guide. Unless you are being duped, which is unlikely, the real thing will probably cost you four or five times as much as modern work.

Strange formations drip in the dark

Also known as the Lasíthiou Mountains, the Díkti range rises to the southeast of Irakleío and continues to the west of Ágios Nikólaos. The border that separates the administrative districts of Irakleío and Lasíthiou zigzags from across the mountains and links up the three highest peaks of the range, Lázaros (2,085m/ 6,839 feet), Aféndis Kristós (2,141m/7,022 feet) and Mount Díkti itself (2,148m/7,045 feet).

Hilltop churches are scattered through the mountains

HIPPO TEETH
Search along the silty banks of the Lasíthiou River where it winds across the Katharó plateau high in the Díkti Mountains, and you may come across the fossilised bones and teeth of hippopotamuses that roamed the plain many thousands of years ago.

SELF-FLAVOURED
The mountains are rich in wild herbs such as thyme, oregano, mint, rosemary and dittany—a pink-flowered herb that is native to Crete. Cretan sheep have the agreeable and convenient habit of flavouring their own meat as they graze.

The Díkti Mountains are impressive from wherever you see them. To the west of the main Siteía to Ierápetra road, as it cuts between the wall of Thryptí and the sloping foothills of Díkti, they loom gradually from far in the distance. To the east of the Áno Viánnos to Irakleío road they appear more abruptly. And most dramatic of all is the view to the north of the road from Ierápetra to Áno Viánnos, where weathering has cut the foothills into rounded kops, their slopes terraced both by man and by water erosion, with the bare and dry hills behind.

The central uplands of Díkti are almost entirely devoid of roads. In this barren, rocky heart of the mountains you can walk the cobbled *kalderími* and the unpaved shepherds' tracks. Or you can make the adventurous and strenuous climb to the peak of Mount Díkti, with its stupendous views. Ágios Geórgios on the southern edge of the Lasíthiou Plateau is the best place to find a guide and to stock up with water and supplies if you are going to attempt this expedition.

The Lasíthiou Plateau with its world-famous white-sailed windpumps (now mostly unfurled; see page 130) is the destination of one road that does penetrate the mountains. This wriggling route climbs southwards from the north coast just west of Mália to the pass of Selí Ambélou at 900m (2,952 feet), where it suddenly gives a full view of the plain and the high mountains beyond it to the south. The road circumnavigates the green fields and orchards of the plateau, passing Psychró and the start of the climb to the legend-haunted Díktaean Cave (see pages 118–119) before plunging off the eastern side of the plain to wind its way down to Ágios Nikólaos.

There are other, lesser-known but equally delightful upland plateaux in the Díkti range, notably Katharó high above the village of Kritsá (see page 124). There are also tiny plains south of Ágios Geórgios on the path to the summit of Mount Díkti, and northeast of Áno Viánnos towards the southwest corner of the mountains. These little plateaux, each with its solitary church and a scattering of stone huts, are the focus of summer migrations of shepherds and their flocks from the foothill villages. The heights of Díkti are inhospitable, though usually blessed with a cool breeze in summer. Snow blocks them during the winter months, there is a general lack of water and vegetation, and nowhere to stay overnight unless you happen upon a shepherd's hut. This is one of the chief strongholds of the much-sought-after herb, dittany (it was the Díkti Mountains that gave it its Latin name, *Origanum dictamnus*). This small marjoram gives a subtle flavour to stews, and an infusion makes a highly prized mountain tea. It is also said to have wonderful medicinal properties. Wounded and sick animals seek it out, as do lovesick swains for the potency it bestows.

During World War II one of Crete's most ferocious and autocratic resistance leaders, Manóli Bándouvas, had his hideout on one of the isolated upland plateaux, guarded by piratically dressed partisans. Patrick Leigh Fermor, in charge of resistance planning in eastern Crete in September 1943, smuggled the recently surrendered Italian commander General Angelo Carta across these mountains to the coast, whence the general was removed to Cairo.

KALDERÍMI

The cobbled footpaths or *kalderími* that crisscross the mountains were laboriously laid down by shepherds and packmen to guarantee passable routes through these remote uplands at all times of the year. Largely unwaymarked, unused by all but a few local shepherds, the *kalderími* still offer hundreds of miles of well-surfaced walking to anyone who takes the time to enquire and seek them out.

A stone-walled sheep corral and shepherd's hut

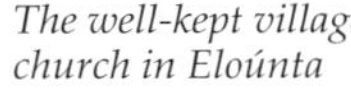

The well-kept village church in Eloúnta

► Eloúnta *109D3*

Eloúnta, also known as Eloúnda, is a pleasant little seaside resort 7km (4 miles) north of Ágios Nikólaos. Surrounded by hills, it faces a beautiful sheltered bay and is surrounded by some of the most up-market accommodation on the island. Short boat trips go to Spinalógka Island (see pages 136–137).

Towards the southern end of the village a side road leads past a lagoon with remnants of Venetian salt pans, over an isthmus and bridge to the uninhabited **Spinalógka peninsula►►**. In the water on the right of the isthmus are walls of buildings, the remains of the Graeco–Roman city state of **Ólous►**. Beyond the taverna across the causeway is a 4th-century **Byzantine mosaic►** of lively fish and geometric patterns, enclosed in the foundations of an early Christian basilica.

►►► Gourniá Minoan Town *109D2*

As with all Crete's archaeological sites, a bird's-eye view of the overall layout greatly increases understanding and enjoyment. As the road descends towards the site from Siteía, the view over the Minoan town of Gourniá will help you appreciate the help this excavation has been in shedding light on everyday Minoan life (tel: 28420 93028. *Open* Apr–Oct Tue–Sun 8.30–5.30; Nov–Mar Tue–Sun 8.30–3. *Admission: inexpensive*).

From the entrance you climb a cobbled street between box-like houses, with external walls constructed of great lumps of stone that rise to shoulder height. Inside are tiny rooms, storage chambers, outlines of doorways and passages. Many of these are the basements of long-gone houses that once stood above. Alleyways a metre or so wide wind among the houses and workshops, and if you have recently wandered around the back streets of a

CATS
Wherever fish is eaten, there are cats. They prowl in and out of the taverna terraces, watching and waiting for their chance to pounce on discarded fish heads, tails and bones. Cat-lovers, comparing the street cats of Crete with their own pampered pets at home, may be upset by the patchy fur, rickety legs and protruding ribs of the scavengers around their tables. Unfortunately, this is one of the tougher realities of everyday Crete.

Cretan mountain village your imagination will not have to work too hard to visualise the original town. Gourniá was destroyed and burned around 1450 BC in the same cataclysmic event that overwhelmed the other Minoan towns and palaces. It was excavated in 1901–1904 by a young American archaeologist, Harriet Boyd Hawes.

At the top of the long cobbled street, bear left by a tree to reach the wide, flat town court and market place, the focal point of this prosperous trading centre. Gourniá traded widely from its harbour to the north, and with Ierápetra and the other south coast settlements. The town controlled the northern end of the narrow isthmus that connects easternmost Crete with the rest of the island, and goods could be moved south by land without exposing them to the risk of the dangerous sea route round the eastern end of Crete.

From the northwestern corner of the town court, steps lead into the maze of square rooms that make up the palace of Gourniá covering the top of the hill. This was probably the seat of a local ruler who dominated the northeast of Crete. On your left are the west and south wings of the palace, with a sacrificial slab—pierced to allow the blood to drain away. There are storerooms, open halls, and a cobbled west court with a corridor running south to another room with an altar. To the north there is another court lined with square and round column bases, and beyond, on the seaward slope of the hill, there is a shrine where animal, bird, snake and human figurines were found. Descending the hill, you walk amongst more houses and workshops, including those of a carpenter and a potter.

Some of the items found at Gourniá are in the Archaeological Museum at Siteía; many more are in the Irakleío Archaeological Museum.

HIDDEN TOWN
What you see at Gourniá represents only a quarter of the town as it stood at the height of its prosperity. The land that slopes north from the hill of Gourniá towards the sea hides the remains of three times as many buildings, unlikely to be excavated now that the official site has been so clearly defined on and around the acropolis.

Part of the impressive stairway to the palace at Gourniá

DEATH WATCH
In the more traditional villages, death is accompanied by a prescribed set of rituals. A light is kept burning for 40 days and nights after the death, followed by a church memorial service every three months until the first anniversary. After that the dead person will be commemorated once a year, perhaps for many decades.

► Kalamáfka *109C2*

High on a winding mountain road between Ierápetra and the north coast road at Ístro, Kalamáfka clings between bluffs of naked rock streaked orange and black, looking south down a deep cleft over terraced lowland hills towards the Libyan Sea. This is a spectacularly sited farming and sheep-rearing village with some of the facilities you might expect of a small town and the tiny Stavros chapel sits over 200 steps above the village and offers excellent views across the rooftops. A couple of kilometres north, you reach a saddle of ground with views forward and back over both Cretan and Libyan Seas.

►►► Katharó Plateau *109C2*

The Katharó Plateau is scarcely marked on most maps, and has never had picturesque cloth-sailed windmills—which is probably the reason why this delectable saucer of green ground high at the eastern edge of the Díkti Mountains has escaped the tourist interest that centres on Lasíthiou (see pages 130–131). The plateau has no shops or other facilities, apart from a couple of tavernas that open only in summer, and is uninhabited between November and May. Yet this is one of Crete's most delightful hidden treasures, a circle of fertile land ringed by remote mountain peaks and filled with grasslands, orchards and vegetable plots, through which snakes the Lasíthiou River. A dry gully for most of the year, it rushes with water during the spring snow melt.

The road climbs west from Kritsá for 11km (7 miles) to reach the plateau. Houses which dot the slopes above the fields are occupied from 20 May each year when the vegetable and fruit growers and the wine and *rakí* makers of Kritsá settle here for the summer months.

► Keratókampos *108A1*

Isolated on the south coast between Tsoútsouros and Árvi, Keratókampos has a strip of tarmac along its single line of tavernas, rooms to rent and village houses above a narrow, sandy beach. Clear green water lies in front, and behind rears the great jagged rock tooth of Keratṓ mountain. This is a peaceful place, little affected by tourism.

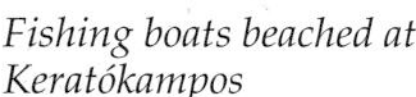

Fishing boats beached at Keratókampos

Walk

Lasíthiou Plateau

It would be a pity to visit the Lasíthiou Plateau and not venture out into the the middle of the plain among the fields and fruit orchards. Those who stick to the road that encircles the plateau see little of the traditional methods of farming that have survived here virtually unchanged by 20th-century technology. This is an easy stroll on flat roads with little possibility of getting lost, since your objective, the village of Tzermiádo, is in view all the way. This is a good way to complement your visit to the Díktaean Cave (see pages 118–119). The walk starts at Psychró, is about 6.5km (4 miles) long, and you should allow 2 hours.

Just to the right of the entrance to the cave car park is a stepped, paved path. Turn left at the road below and keep on down to the main road into Psychró by the Hotel Zeus. Cross the road and take the concrete track opposite. Soon it bears left. Turn right just beyond the bend and continue for 2km (1 mile) to the outskirts of Ágios Geórgios, walking between apple trees and corn fields. The distant mountains ring the plain and on the far side you can see Tzermiádo village under a hill crowned by a white chapel.

Turn left at a tarred road just outside Ágios Geórgios on to a wide dirt road that leads out into the middle of the plain. Here you'll see men and women breaking the ground with mattocks, ploughing with wooden horse-drawn ploughs and sowing seed from buckets—hard, primitive labour. The few remaining cloth-sailed windpumps whirl round, raising water for the irrigation channels that crisscross the plain, while the skeletons of abandoned pumps lie beside their wells.

After 2km (1 mile) turn right and immediately left at a T-junction, and follow the road round bends and over cross-roads to the road in Tzermiádo. Turn right, and bear left at the resistance memorial to reach the Taverna Kronion in the village, where you can catch the bus back to Psychró.

Hand- and machine-knitting, crocheting and weaving for sale in Tzermiádo

Drive

Coast road from Tsoútsouros to Árvi

This is a very challenging 75km (46.5 mile) drive along the south coast, in beautiful wild scenery between mountains and the sea. It features two less visited resorts and a spectacular monastery clinging to a hillside next to one of Crete's most dramatic gorges.

This is emphatically not a drive for the impatient. You should give half a day to it, and be prepared to stay in second, if not first, gear for much of the way. Sections of the road surface are very rough indeed, and there are some steep and narrow descents, which can be slippery after rain; some of these roads do not appear on several island maps (including that on pages 108–109). Your reward will be the discovery of a stretch of coastline travelled by few, with wonderful views all the way. Many sections of road have recently been widened and asphalted and this may remove some heart in the mouth moments, but shouldn't encourage you to build up speed as goats and rock falls could lie around every corner. As always, check your tyres and petrol before you set out as fuel stations are non-existent.

Driving east from Moíres on the Mesará plain, bear right beyond Ágíoi Déka through Yanyáles, Asími and Pýrgos, to leave the main road to Áno Viánnos in Káto Kastellianá, following the Tsoútsouros sign. The road spirals into the hills above some dizzying drops, between slopes of florid purple rock, with views down plunging valleys. Soon you look down on the huddle of Tsoútsouros (see pages 104–105) on a wild coast where deep water comes close inshore.

Swing left at the bottom of the descent on a rough road passing between greenhouses. Sheep graze on the flat, scrubby coastal strip, overlooked by yellow rock faces slit by narrow gorges. Keep right at a fork 3km (2 miles) beyond Tsoútsouros, and take great care on the steep descent that follows. You cross the River Anapodáris on a concrete bridge and continue through groves of olives, lemons and oranges, past lines of plastic greenhouses sheltering tomatoes and cucumbers—this is one of the sunniest spots in Crete. The

The wild coastal scenery between Tsoútsouros and Árvi

The hillside village of Áno Viánnos

pointed peak of Mount Keratő towers above a sea of sublime turquoise and the sandy beach at Keratókampos (page 124).

Keep straight ahead, twisting round difficult hairpin bends above the yellow clay cliffs. It is planned to improve this surface so there may be road works as you travel. Make time, though, to look around and appreciate the beauty of ravines, mountain slopes and purple rocks, and to notice the young shepherds on the hillsides tending their flocks with the same timeless air of monumental patience displayed by their fathers and grandfathers.

After three-quarters of an hour you descend once more to the coast and a junction with a tarmac road, signed to Amirás, which runs off to the left. Keep straight on here for 0.5km (0.25 miles) beside the bay until you come to Árvi (see page 117). Pass through the village and bear sharp right over a ford, signposted to St Antony's Monastery. After 200m (182 yards) another sign points left; park here for a walk up to the monastery.

Stroll

The rough road winds inland for 1km (0.5 miles) with superb views of the towering and exceptionally narrow gorge that widens to a Y-shape near the top, some 300m (273 yards) overhead. The buildings of Árvi Monastery cling to the face of the mountain nearby. When you reach the monastery, climb the winding steps to the church, which has frescoes and a beautiful painted iconostasis. Above the church you will find the abandoned monks' cells, which command a memorable view to the sea over a lush, tree-filled valley.

Return to the western end of Árvi and bear right on the road to Amirás. Turn left at the junction in the village to reach Áno Viánnos, piled on the southern flanks of the Díkti Mountains. You should stop here and seek out the village churches, which have rich frescoes (see pages 116–117), before continuing to Káto Kastellianá and on to Moíres.

KEY WORDS
Many churches are kept locked these days, for fear of the theft of icons and other irreplaceable treasures. Someone always has the key, but who? Most likely the village priest, perhaps a nearby householder, or a specially appointed custodian. Three useful phrases to help you in your search:
o papás (the priest);
o filakás (the custodian);
to klithí (the key).

►►► Kritsá *109C2*

Tucked into the eastern flanks of the Díkti Mountains 9km (5.5 miles) west of Ágios Nikólaos, Kritsá stands for all that is best and most typical of Cretan village life. It is a large village running uphill towards a backdrop of crags, with a wonderful eastward view downhill towards the Gulf of Mirampéllou. Many shops along the village's narrow streets sell woven and hand embroidered handicrafts. Easter here, celebrated with volleys of firecrackers, long processions and riotous parties, can be a memorable occasion. It claims to be one of the largest villages in Crete with a population of more than 2,000 people. However on 20 May each year a large proportion of the village men trek up to the lonely and beautiful Katharó Plateau (see page 124) high in the mountains west of Kritsá, and stay there for the next six months tending their vegetable and corn fields and making wine and *rakí.*

The mountainous country behind Kritsá is ideal for rough walking on *kalderími*, cobbled paths, and ancient roadways that date back to Minoan times, and for stumbling upon half-forgotten Minoan houses and Dorian settlements.

There are several notable churches in Kritsá, of which the most striking is Panagía Kerá (tel: 28410 51525. *Open* daily 8–5. *Admission: moderate*) at the bottom of the village. Here the superbly restored frescoes demonstrate the glory of Cretan Byzantine art. A 13th-century Baptism in the dome swells with sails and fish; the central nave has Salome balancing the Baptist's head on her own; in the north aisle the white-hooded souls of the dead are packed into their communal grave like bobsleigh riders; in the south aisle a marvellously sympathetic Virgin sorrows beside her inconsolable husband. These are only a few of the treasures in this unique church. Another fine church is Ágios Pnevma. The old icons in the iconostasis include some lively lions and a sinuous, upward-looking St Peter.

The ancient church of Panagía Kerá in Kritsá

Icons or religious pictures were being painted in the vivid Cretan style as far back as the 14th century. Local painters infused the formal Byzantine tradition with their own delight in earthy realities: expressions range from the sorrowful to the ecstatic, limbs are attenuated and sinuous, vigorous trees and animals are set against rocky backdrops.

A 14th-century depiction of the patriarchs in the Garden of Eden, from the church of Panagía Kerá in Kritsá (top)

Icon painting for souvenirs and for religious use

Gradually, however, the perspectives of mainland Europe's Renaissance crept in and took over. Often the icons were set in a richly carved iconostasis or wooden framework. There is a particularly superb example at Préveli Monastery. Cretans still treat their icons with reverence, kissing them on entry to the church, pushing flowers into the frames, hanging them with silver *taxímata* to solicit help and healing.

The frescoes painted on church walls and ceilings are equally lively and, because of their size and subject matter, a good deal more striking. Humour, subtlety, cruelty and tenderness fill the best of the Cretan-school frescoes from the 15th and 16th centuries. They can be found in the most unexpected places: in a crumbling cave church on the coast, in a sheepfold hut that was once a hermit's chapel, or in a rarely visited plateau church hidden in the mountains.

The Byzantine fresco arrangement seldom varies. Christ Pantokrator, Lord of All, stares down from the rounded roof of the apse, above Evangelists and Holy Fathers. Across the roof of the nave there are scenes from the life of Christ: Nativity, Baptism, Crucifixion and Resurrection. The west wall shows the Second Coming and the snake-ridden torments of the damned. Below the dado rail are military and secular saints, perhaps the founder of the church as well, while medallions on the vaulting ribs hold the heads of yet more saints.

There have been recent revivals in both icon and fresco painting, though modern treatment, rather sadly, seems to have reverted to a stiffer and more formal, and some say, less Cretan style.

MODERN ART

Do not turn up your nose at modern frescos and icons. There has been a welcome revival of the art in recent times, and the best of the modern painting is exceptionally good. Some of these new icons easily stand comparison with ancient masterpieces.

St Joachim, also from the church of Panagía Kerá in Kritsá

PUMPS PRESERVED
There are plans afoot to restore all the 10,000 wind pumps of Lasíthiou, in recognition of their enduring appeal to visitors. This is a welcome move. The hundreds of gaunt, rusting skeletons of collapsed pumps that now lie across their well-heads in the fields of Lasíthiou are a melancholy sight in this uplifting landscape. A new turbine wind farm is the 21st century version of Lasíthiou's attempt to utilise the power of the wind and the turning fins glisten in the sunlight.

Wind pump sails, made traditionally of white cloth, are becoming increasingly rare

►►► Lasíthiou Plateau *109B3*

The Lasíthiou Plateau is one of the most-visited of Crete's attractions. People make the ascent, either from Ágios Nikólaos or from the north coast road at Svoúrou Metóki, which is nearer Irakleío and gives the more dramatic initial view of the plateau, to see the windmills. It used to be a breathtaking sight in late summer, when these small wind pumps were being driven by their whirling white-cloth sails. Unfortunately, most of the wind-driven pumps now stand or lie inactive, and many of those pumps that are still working are driven by electricity.

But the plateau has more to offer than the wind pumps. This level plain of tiny green and brown fields lies between 817 and 950m (2,680 and 3,116 feet) above sea level, the only Cretan plateau at this height that is occupied all year round. The fertility of the soil, enriched by minerals leached down from the mountains and still worked largely by manual labour, is partly responsible; tourism has also brought some prosperity to the villages that lie round the perimeter road. There is the Díktaean Cave near Psychró, the legendary birthplace of Zeus (see pages 118–119); the local weaving and embroidery that flutters on clothes-lines along the road; the wild flowers that carpet the plateau every spring; and the coolness of the mountain breeze. Tzermiádo is a fair-sized village with most facilities. Ágios Geórgios is another, with an excellent folklore museum (*Open* irregular hours winter, daily 10–4 summer). It is actually a village house furnished in traditional style with loom, bread oven,

raised bed, and with a cool storeroom full of *píthoi*. There is a stable with hand ploughs, equipment for horses and a threshing board set with toothed iron blades.

Lasíthiou people have always been tough resisters. The Venetians drove them out in 1263 in response to their seditious activities, and the plain lay uncultivated for 200 years. Paduan engineers later laid out the irrigation system still worked today by the wind pumps.

The well-preserved Dorian city at Lató

►► Lató 109C3

This Dorian city site (7th–3rd century BC), 2km (1 mile) north of Kritsá, is surprisingly little visited, considering its good state of preservation (*Open* Tue–Sun 8.30–3. *Admission: free*). The city remains occupy twin hilltops, reached by way of a stepped and cobbled street that rises from the city gate, just north of the entrance to the site at the top of the road from Kritsá. Almost everything is massively built of great stone blocks: the entrance gateway itself, the guard towers on the left of the path, the deep workshops on the right with their wells, olive presses and corn-grinding querns.

At the top the street doglegs to reach the *agora* or open court on the saddle, with a rectangular shrine to Artemis and a deep cistern to the left, a little bench-lined square to the right. A wonderful view opens over a valley to Ágios Nikólaos, the ancient port of Lató. Wide steps lead up to the northern acropolis, from which you look across to the temple of Apollo on the slope of the southern hill.

►►► Mália Minoan Palace 108B4

The Minoan palace (tel: 28970 31597. *Open* Tue–Sun. *Admission: moderate*) at Mália lacks the dramatic hilly surroundings of Faistós and Agía Triáda, sited as it is on the scrubby north coast plain 37km (23 miles) to the east of Irakleío. But it has been superbly excavated by the French Archaeological School from Athens, and they are still at work here on outlying sections of the complex. The portions of the palace constructed of mud brick have been roofed over to prevent dissolution by wind and rain. There are stalls selling guide books by the entrance,

VIEW FROM THE HILL
Even if you have only minimal interest in matters archaeological, it is always worth climbing to a Cretan hilltop site for the view. Ancient settlers invariably chose their dwelling places with an eye on a good clear outlook over what was going on around them. In Crete that means, in almost every case, a superb prospect of mountain, coast and sea.

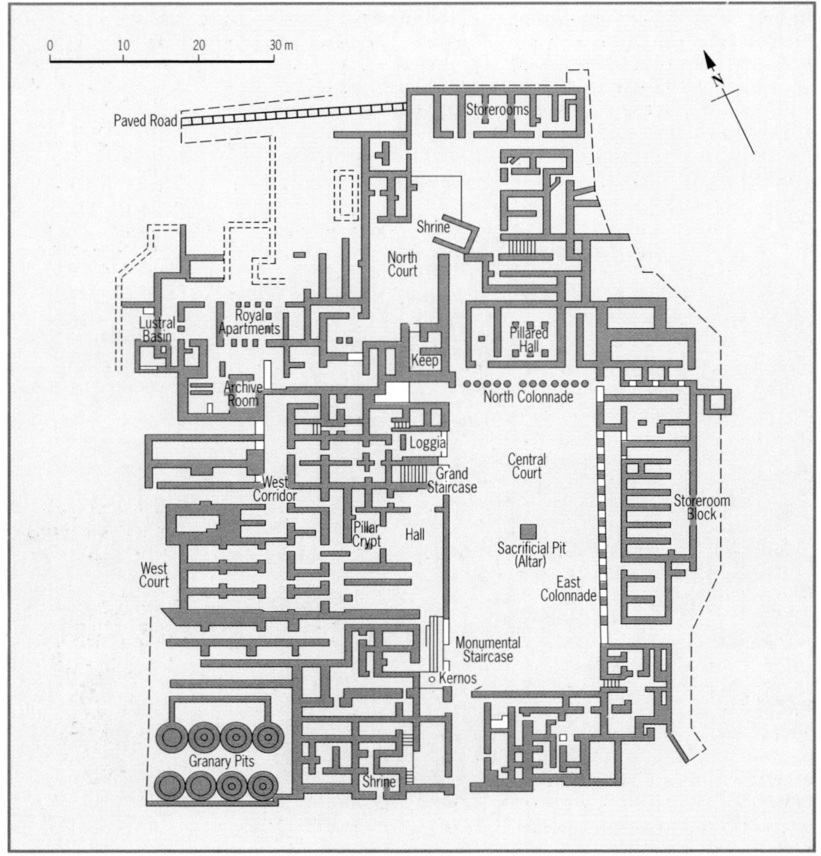

Mália Minoan Palace

GOLD PIT

If you turn left just before the palace car park and follow the road to the shore, then bear right on a footpath along the coast for a few minutes, you will come to the fenced site of Khrysólakkos, where the famous and beautiful gold bee pendant was unearthed. Locals must have known of the treasures buried here long before the archaeologists came along. Khrysólakkos means "gold pit", and the area has been so named for many years.

but refreshments are confined to a van in the car park.

The old palace of Mália was originally built some time between 2000 and 1700 BC on the site of a much earlier settlement. Around 1700 BC it was demolished by the same catastrophic event that flattened the other big Minoan palaces on Crete and, like them, it was rebuilt to enter a golden era of prosperity and influence. Then around 1450 BC came the disaster that destroyed all the palaces, except Knosós, and most of the settlements of Minoan Crete. Mália was entirely destroyed in the catastrophe, and only a few individual houses on the site were ever occupied again.

Inside the gate, turn right and right again to reach the southwest corner of the palace beside eight cylindrical stone granary pits. Follow the enormously thick walls of blue-grey stone along the south side of the palace, past a little paved shrine, to a wide entrance and a passage flagged with big slabs. It leads to the central court, the hub around which this exploration revolves.

The central court is enormous (48m by 22m/157 by 72 feet), big enough to hold thousands of people. Partially paved, it lies around a small central cavity, square-built of mud bricks, that might have supported an altar. Along the east side of the court runs a line of square pillar bases alternating with the round bases of marble columns, an arrangement echoed in many other Minoan palaces. East of here are storerooms, some uncovered and constructed of pebbles and red stone blocks, others roofed over and of crumbling yellow mud brick. The stone floors are provided with drainage canals running to sink holes, set between raised platforms that are grooved to channel away the spillage from wine and oil jars.

On the west side of the court a grand staircase rises and abruptly ends. It used to lead to the upper storey of the palace but only eleven steps remain. Just south of the staircase is the pillared hall of the west wing, and beyond it a flag-floored crypt whose square pillars are incised with the *labrys* or sacred, double-headed axe. North of the staircase, steps mount to a ceremonial platform behind which is the little room where excavators found the leopard-shaped axe and the crystal-hilted sword now in Gallery IV of the Archaeological Museum in Irakleío.

Along the north side of the central court runs a portico with ten columns, north of which is a hall with square pillars set close together. Beyond the northwest corner of the central court is the north court, with the massive wall of a *donjon* or stronghold on its south side. West of here, in a maze of rooms, were the apartments of the settlement's king and queen.

At the north edge of the palace two gigantic, finely decorated *píthoi* stand by a paved walkway. The more easterly jar is blackened by fire scorching, and dribbles of liquid carbonised in the final calamity still stain its sides. The walkway leads west to a roofed complex of sunken, thick-walled rooms, some with spillways and drain holes. The two most westerly rooms have stone benches on three sides. Palace notables may have gathered here to discuss, argue and legislate.

BODY OF EVIDENCE
A recent theory has gained a hearing, but certainly not respectability, by suggesting that the Minoan palaces were nothing of the sort, but were in fact giant necropoles or cemeteries. The almost complete absence of human remains in any of them presents something of a stumbling block to this hypothesis.

The famous gold bee pendant found at Mália

►► Mýrtos *109C1*

Said to be the southernmost village is Greece, Mýrtos sees few visitors and attracts those holiday makers wishing to get off the beaten track with a range of quiet tavernas for entertainment. The town has two ancient sites close by but both are currently closed to the public.

The first, Fournoú Korifú is an early Minoan hilltop site with a maze of tiny buildings, from which, among many pottery finds came the pot-bellied and slim-necked goddesses of Mýrtos (see page 115).

Mýrtos Pýrgos has been the subject of active archaeological research by the University of Louvain which will complete timeline work started by the British School in Athens at various times between the mid 1970s and the mid 1990s. The work is due to last until 2009. Destroyed by fire in 1450 BC Mýrtos Pýrgos still has visible paved courtyards, stone walkways, rooms are corridors.

A píthos, *also found at Mália*

Modern churches often contain modern frescoes

► Néapoli 109C3

A large, well-to-do market town 21km (13 miles) northwest of Ágios Nikólaos, just off the new road to Irakleío, Néapoli was in 1340 the birthplace of Pétros Phílargos, who was proclaimed Pope Alexander V in 1409. It later became the administrative centre of its district under the Turks, a rôle it still performs. Today it is primarily a farming town. Pick-up trucks with bales of hay jolt along the streets, and workshops repair agricultural implements. Beside the tree-shaded gardens in the main square stands a big modern church with brightly coloured frescoes of stolid and expressionless saints. In its shadow is a little old church with a vivid icon of St John the Baptist. Stroll from the top right corner of the square into the back lanes of Néapoli to find more old churches. Ágios Spirídon, Ágios Dimítrios, Agía Varvára, and Ágios Giórgios all have faded icons whose frames are stuffed with flowers and *taxímata.* Then find a café and idle over a glass of *soumádha,* a sweet and sherbet-tasting drink made locally of almonds.

► Pláka 109D4

A right turn 200m (218 yards) north of the harbour in Eloúnta (see page 122) brings you to Pláka. Nothing more than a strip of rooms to rent, village houses and tavernas, it is undeveloped and peaceful. Catch a *caïque* out to Spinalógka Island, or just sit on the shady terrace of a taverna, admiring a splendid view of the island over a plate of freshly caught fish for which the village is famed.

►►► Spinalógka Island 109D4

See pages 136–137.

►► Tértsa 108B1

Tértsa goes unmentioned in most guide books, which is scarcely surprising since this tiny line of buildings is connected to the Ierápetra–Ano Viánnos road by 11km of seemingly endless dirt track. Turn off the main road at the Sykológos sign. Where the track dips right into the village, keep left, and at a fork after 2km (1 mile) keep straight on by a concrete building, and persevere. Down on the coast at Tértsa is a tamarisk-shaded terrace overlooking a shingly beach, a few fishing boats, a taverna or two, strong homemade wine, and blissful peace—a real haven.

LOUDSPEAKERS

The advent of electricity has added a characteristic sound to the Cretan scene. The amplified human voice assails the ears of both willing and unwilling listeners: priests intone their prayers from belfries, politicians search for votes, music fans tune in to their local radio station, sellers of vegetables and fish call from their pick-up trucks. And all can be certain of a wider audience than hitherto, thanks to the power of the strategically placed loudspeaker.

The village economy is still strong in Crete, and everywhere you go you will see people working in the groves and fields, and on the mountains. But they are almost all people over 50. Increasing numbers of Cretan youngsters are leaving the villages and land. There are two main reasons for this: tourism, and the power of the modern media, in particular television.

Crete, why do you exile
Your brave young men?
Alien lands rejoice,
And you long for them.

Rise and say farewell
To your father's house;
You'll find a better one
Together with your
spouse.

Cretan Mantinádes

Left and below: sheep and shepherding still form an important part of the island's agricultural economy

These are hard times for the slow-paced, traditional villages of Crete, though you might not think so when you see their neat white outlines among freshly watered fields and olive groves. The agricultural work of the villagers has always been hard manual labour: digging irrigation channels and fetching water, transporting tools and produce by donkey, pruning, harvesting and sowing with unsophisticated implements, tending sheep through long days in the heat of summer and the cold of winter on barren hillsides.

The tourist industry of the seaside towns absorbs a large amount of seasonal labour. Less well-educated youngsters can get work as bar staff, chamber maids, hotel porters and so on. They may return to their villages during the winter, or for festivals such as Easter, but they are often discontented, bored and unwilling to help out with what they see as low-grade work. This is even more true of the better-educated young people. The world is wider for them than it was for their parents, and they aim for office jobs in local government, administration and the professions, either in Irakleío or overseas, especially in Athens.

Some young people have returned to the villages, not to pick up their parents' tools, but to use their city know-how as entrepreneurs renting out rooms, running tavernas or souvenir shops, or in small-scale manufacturing. And they are keen to entice the tourist trade to their own doorstep. Fed by television images of wealth and success, they are vulnerable to economic difficulties and to disillusionment of a kind that their village forebears, for all the narrowness of their working lives, never had to face.

Venetian defences dominate Spinalógka Island

PANTILES
One note of beauty among the harshness and desolation of Spinalógka is the old pantiled roofing of the tumbledown houses, whose red baked clay has been faded by the sun and salt wind to the most delicate shades of peach and rose pink.

QUARRIES
From the crest of the island you can see sheer-sided scars on the blunt snout of the Spinalógka peninsula. These are the remains of the quarries from which the Venetians took the stone to build their fortifications on the island.

►►► Spinalógka Island *109D4*

The history of Spinalógka Island, also spelled Spinalónga, (*Open* daily, weather permitting. *Ferry crossing: expensive*) parallels that of Crete itself: a story of stoicism, hardship, refuge, persecution, compassion and cruelty, all in a setting of harsh beauty. The position of the island, at the entrance to the long bay that leads to Eloúnta, is a glorious one, and the approach to the grim fortress walls, the terraced slopes and the symmetrical, straight-spined shape of Spinalógka is one of Crete's most memorable experiences. Soon you see that the terraces are made of ruined houses invaded by pine trees and scrub bushes, and the boatman will begin to tell of Spinalógka's more recent history, a darkness that persisted until less than 50 years ago.

Boats run to Spinalógka Island from Ágios Nikólaos, a long and fairly expensive cruise, and from Eloúnta and Pláka. You can join a guided tour. The earlier you get away the better, as crowds of visitors swarm over the island by midday, and the cruise boats pump out disco music and a tinnily amplified commentary.

On the summit of the island are the blurred ruins of an ancient stronghold. Spinalógka must always have been a prized possession, lying as it does in command of the entrance to the bay. The main fortifications that you see at the southern end as you approach, beetling stone walls, round-bellied bastions, stumpy guard towers and long runs of battlements, were built by the Venetians in 1579 when the rise of the Ottoman empire was beginning to threaten them. These fortifications were impregnable. After the Turks took Crete in 1646, a Venetian garrison remained on Spinalógka until it was ousted by treaty in 1715. Nearly three centuries later, when the Turks in their turn felt increasingly menaced by Cretan uprisings and world opinion, a town was built near the old fort as a refuge in case of trouble. After the Four Powers settlement of 1898 most Turks left Crete, but the town on Spinalógka continued to harbour a number until 1903.

Then the island entered its dark days. Leprosy was still

a virulent and dreaded disease in Crete at that time, and the position of Spinalógka made it the government's choice as a leper colony. It was near enough to shore to be supplied easily, but just far enough offshore for the contagion to be safely out of reach. The lepers were moved across to the island, housed in the old buildings of the Turkish town and then left to their life of rejection and isolation. By all accounts they were initially treated more like criminals than victims of disease. The island was run with military strictness, and its inhabitants had to do almost everything for themselves.

But things did gradually improve. More doctors were sent to join the dedicated few who, with priests and nuns, had been doing their best for the lepers. A new medical centre was built, sanitation was improved and access was made easier for the sufferers' families. In 1957 the last of the lepers was evacuated, and soon Spinalógka became the tourist attraction that it is today.

After landing on the slipway, take a left turn through a long, vaulted tunnel that leads to the ruined town. Wooden doors hang open, roofless shells of houses are filled with collapsed floor joists. Ovens, cupboards, stove pipes and partitions made of fish boxes all stand as they were left when the island was evacuated. Cypresses, pines, prickly pears, olive trees and wild roses grow among the terraced ruins on the west slope. You pass a church and the concrete doctors' hall to come to a curved Venetian redoubt at the north of the island. Just before this, a path doubles back to climb to the top of Spinalógka with bare grey rock, more crumbling fortifications, and a beautiful view of the mountains across the clear water that sealed the lepers into their island for half a century.

SISLAND REBELS

Not long after the Turks occupied Crete, a resistance movement was formed. Its members called themselves the *Khainides* and they operated from Spinalógka against the new rulers. Other branches were based on Nisos Soúda and Gramvoúsa, as all three islands were still under Venetian control at the time.

Looking towards Eloúnta from the battlements of Spinalógka Island

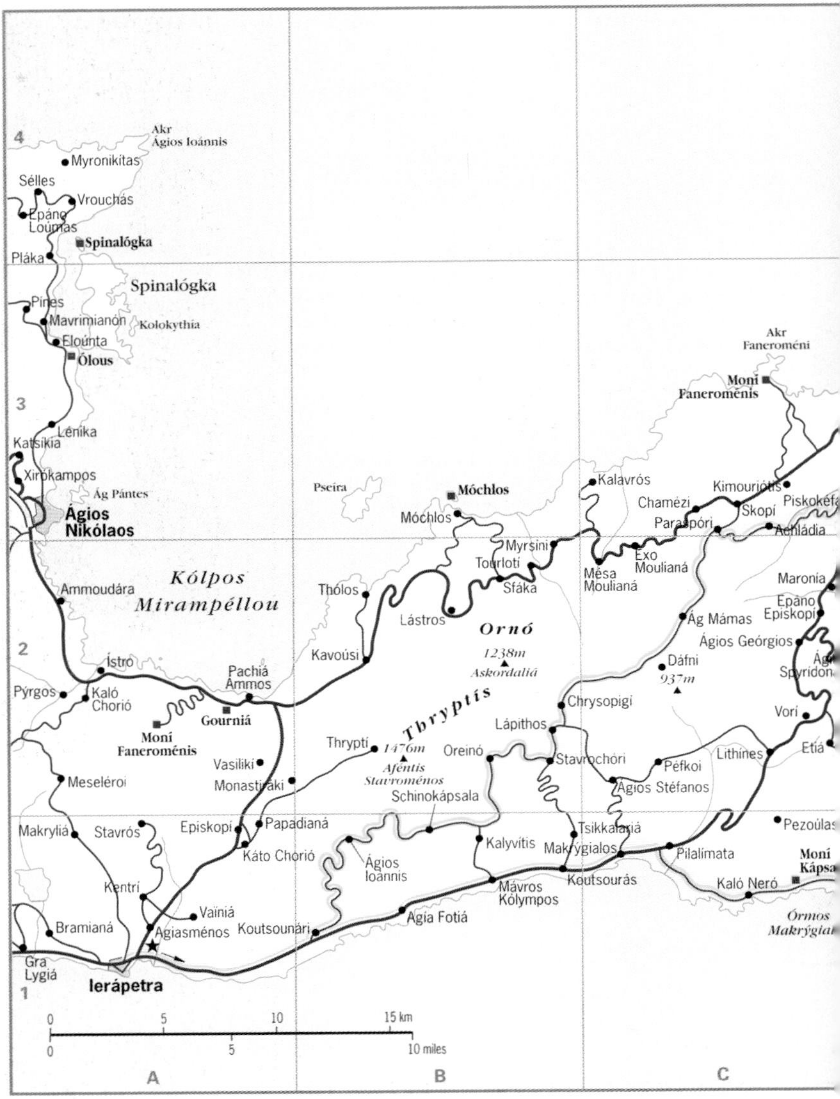

Siteía's Venetian fort was clearly built to last for centuries

Siteía and the East

Dionisádes
Dragonáda
Giannisáda
Akr Síderos
Órmos Ténda
Síderos
Elása
Akr Mavro
Ítanos
Erimoúpolis
Vái
Váï Finikodasos
Órmos Grántes
Moní Tóplou
Metoxí
Akr Vamvakia
Órmos Siteías
Grántes
Siteía
Palaíkastro
Akr Plaka
Petrás
Agía Fotiá
Roússa Ekklisía
Lagkáda
Órmos Karoúmpes
Stavroménos
Kryonéri
Chochlakiés
803m
Priniás
Kellária
Akr Avláki
Sfákia
Karýdi
Azokéramos
Adravástoi
Katsidóni
Sítanos
Áno Zákros
Zákros
Káto Zákros
Akr Zákros
Katelíónas
810m
Khandrás
Lamnóni
Zíros
Chamaítoulo
Xerókampos
Agía Triáda
Kaló Chorió
Goúdouras
Koufonísi
D
E

▶▶▶ **REGION HIGHLIGHTS**

Faneroménis Monastery *page 143*
Ierápetra *pages 144–146*
Ítanos *page 143*
Praisós *page 148*
Siteía *pages 150–151*
Tóplou Monastery *page 154*
Xerókampos *page 155*
Zákros Minoan Palace *pages 158–159*

THREE-IN-ONE
In Greek Orthodox churches the devout cross themselves with the index and middle fingertips of the right hand touching the tip of the thumb. The three-in-one signifies the Holy Trinity.

SITEÍA AND THE EAST Between Irakleío and Ágios Nikólaos the north coast of Crete suffers from an exuberantly unplanned sprawl of recent development. But once you have passed through Ágios Nikólaos everything improves: the landscape, the towns, the pace of life and the temper of the local people. Folk in the east of Crete pride themselves on their easygoing attitude to life, as much as the Sfakiots of the west congratulate themselves on their fierceness. The east has a landscape as dramatic as anywhere in Crete, and vast areas of mountain and coast with tiny, hospitable villages still very little visited by tourists. The area was little visited by tourists but several new multi-million euro developments will really put this part of Crete on the map in the next decade.

The two chief towns of the east are Siteía on the north coast and Ierápetra on the south. There are few notable Venetian buildings in either town; both went into a long decline under Turkish rule and were allowed to fall into decay. But both have quarters where you can wander among tangled old alleyways, good hotels and excellent tavernas, lively waterfronts (especially at night), and busy harbours where brightly painted fishing boats disgorge freshly caught fish that you will eat in the evening. Siteía is built on hills, giving far views over the town and harbour from the upper streets and squares. Ierápetra, by contrast, lies low on a fertile plain lined with long plastic greenhouses. These don't look pretty, but they have brought prosperity to this southeastern coast and their produce makes Ierápetra salad something to savour.

A narrow isthmus, 15km (9 miles) wide, connects the eastern end of Crete with the rest of the island. Immediately to the east rise two impressive mountain ranges: Thryptís and, meeting it at its northern end, Ornó. The formidable western face of Thryptís is cut by one of Crete's most spectacular canyons, the narrow, plunging Monastiráki Gorge. The dirt roads up into these mountains are not for the faint-hearted nor those pressed for time, but venturers into the high places will be rewarded by the sight of villages piled house on house, clinging to bluffs above enormous drops, surrounded by pine forests

In the Siteía Mountains

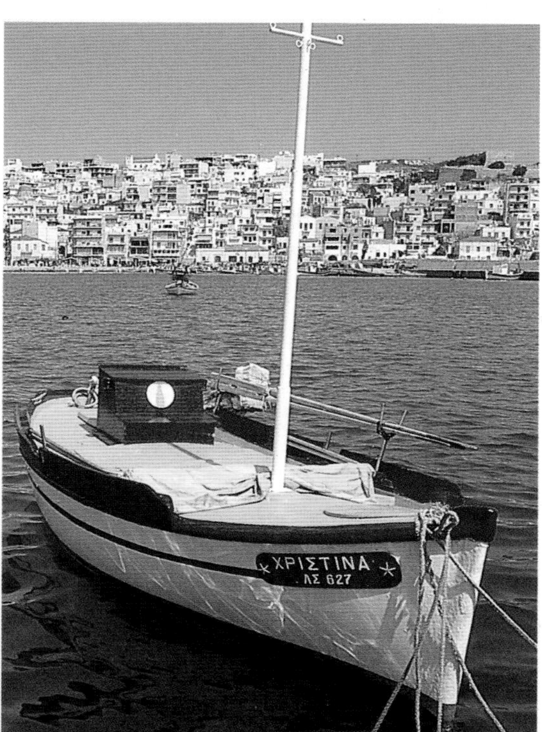

KÁTO AND _ÁNO_

When planning a day's excursion with a map, take note of *Káto* and *Áno*. *Káto* signifies the lower part of a village, *Áno* the upper part (sometimes also given as *Epáno* or simply *Ep.*). And although the village name will be shared between them, for example Káto Zákros and Áno Zákros, there is often a world of difference between the two halves, which could be several kilometres apart.

Siteía is the main port of eastern Crete

and backed by jagged ridges and peaks. Hospitality here is just as warming as the local wine.

Another valley crosses the island to the east of Thryptís carrying the main road south from Siteía to Ierápetra. Beyond this are the Siteía Mountains, which are lower than Thryptís and Ornó but still impressive, forming a great block of high country. Farming villages such as Khandrás and Zíros make the most of the fertile highlands and are very much the centre of local life. There are few concessions to tourism up here, but you'll find local people very interested in you, especially if you brave the stares and try out whatever Greek phrases you know.

The south coast is not all plastic greenhouses, although they are in evidence along much of the main road east of Ierápetra until it turns north for Siteía. As the coast turns north around the end of the island the roads become fewer. Those that do descend to the sea end in excellent beaches with a few tavernas—for example Xerókampos, Káto Zákros, where there is a superb Minoan palace, and Vái, with its famous date palm forest. The wild peninsula of Síderos pokes out from the northeastern tip of Crete; the biggest tourist complex in Greece, Cavo Sidero with six tourist villages, three hotels totalling 7,000 beds and two golf courses will break ground at its base in 2009.

There is no road along the north coast; the main highway runs inland. Little roads and tracks lead down to more isolated and delightful seaside hamlets, beaches and coves, looking out to small islands.

THRESHING FLOORS

All over the Cretan uplands you will come across circular threshing floors built among the ruins of Minoan houses, Dorian temples and Byzantine basilicas. Constructed during the last few hundred years and with a concern for matters meteorological rather than archaeological, they are sited where winds funnel and concentrate to blow away the seed husks at winnowing time.

The delightful Italianate church in Epáno Episkopí

► Agía Fotiá *139D3*

Some 6.5km (4 miles) east of Siteía on the coast road, Agía Fotiá spreads itself along the beach in a sprawl of flats and hotels—standard Cretan seaside development, which you pass by with scarcely a glance. The old village lies inland of the road, and provides a pleasant half-hour stroll through the lanes and pathways among the houses. In 1971 archaeologists unearthed the largest Minoan cemetery yet discovered, on and around a little hill overlooking the beach. The dead were buried in dug-out cavities, and in chamber tombs cut into the rock of the hill. More than 250 burials were found, together with a vast number of vases, lead amulets, a large copper knife, other weapons, fish hooks and gold sheets sealed in a lead box, evidence of the Minoans' extensive trading in a variety of metals. Some of these finds are now in Siteía's archaeological museum, others are in Irakleío.

► Epáno Episkopí 138C2

This village straddles the road south from Siteía to Ierápetra. Above the road to the right stands the graceful Italianate Church of the Panagía. The Catholic bishop of Siteía based himself here when 16th-century pirate raids made the coast a dangerous place to live. Apart from the church, the main attraction of Epáno Episkopí lies in its fine view across the terraced hills, olive groves, rocky gorges and mountains of the dramatic Pantélis Valley.

►►► Faneroménis Monastery (near Siteía) 138C3

Not to be confused with the monastery of the same name near Gourniá, this Faneroménis is reached by a winding road signed to the left off the main road about 6.5km (4 miles) before you reach Siteía from Ágios Nikólaos. Inside the tiny church (*Open* summer 8.30–5, may be closed noon–3; winter 8.30–3), a square hatchway leads to a cavern. Light a church candle and you will see a heap of skulls and bones, and icons. This was where an icon of the Virgin miraculously appeared in the 15th century and returned each time it was removed. The church frescoes were blackened in 1829 in an arson attempt by two Turks who were then stricken with fatal illnesses. Turkish bullets pierced the face of the saint who sits reading a book in one of the few fresco medallions still discernible. Around the icon nearest the cave hatch are hundreds of *taxímata* or votive plaques requesting cures for illnesses. Faneroménis offers an insight into Cretan suffering and faith, past and present, more striking than many of the island's better-preserved and more visited monasteries.

►►► Ierápetra 138A1

See pages 144–145.

►►► Ítanos 139E4

The local name for Ítanos is Erimoúpolis, the deserted city, and this is indeed a lonely place, a couple of kilometres north of Vái but far removed from its crowds and noise. Two little hills and the headland to the south across a tiny bay make up the site of the city that in post-Minoan times challenged Ierápetra (pages 144–145) and Praisós (page 148) for overall power in eastern Crete. The tablet in the wall of the church at Tóplou Monastery (pages 154–155) records the settlement of a land dispute with Ierápetra in 132 BC. Ítanos was the victor in this, but squabbles between the three had been frequent down the preceding centuries.

From the western or inland hill, with terrace walls dating from Hellenistic times well before the birth of Christ, you descend seawards into the

(continued on page 146)

MÉZEDES

By tradition, Cretans only drink alcohol if it is accompanied by *mézedes* or nibbles. In larger towns *mézedes* may be reduced to a dish of olives, but the village *kafenía* usually offer a variety, sometimes almost a meal in itself. These might include sliced artichoke with lemon, fried squid, cubes of *feta* cheese, knobs of baked bread, lupin seeds like shiny butterbeans, sweet almond bread, slices of tomato, potato or peeled apple...

SEE AND BE SEEN

Few of Crete's inland settlements lie tucked away out of sight. From earliest times it was necessary to see and be seen. That way lay safety, an insurance against surprise attack. Villages and towns stand on the edges of bluffs and outcrops, with a good view all round, situations that lend an air of the spectacular to the most humble cluster of houses.

Faneroménis Monastery

SANDY SHORE
Ierápetra's beautiful marble-paved promenade was built over a fine sandy beach. This not only did away with the beach itself, but also caused a general shallowing of the water as the tides deposited sand in a wide area just offshore. In places, locals say, you can wade out for 300m (273 yards) and still be only up to your armpits in the sea.

BEACHLESS
There is too much sand offshore, and not enough on the beaches to the west of Ierápetra. When the greenhouse building boom was at its height, and the search was on for sand to use as bedding for the greenhouse plants, these once excellent beaches became victims of countless scoop-and-grab raids, official and otherwise.

►►► Ierápetra *138A1*

Ierápetra is the largest town on the south coast of Crete, the southernmost town of Europe—and it gets more sunshine than anywhere else on the island. Superb mountain scenery forms a backdrop, and there is a long, sandy beach to the west of the town. The local people are friendly and relaxed, the local wine excellent, and there are any number of decent hotels and restaurants, and a lively night life.

Ierápetra is certainly somewhat overburdened with rather utilitarian modern architecture and it has a strongly commercial atmosphere as the centre of a large area of vegetable and fruit cultivation. But it is nevertheless a rewarding place to walk around, if you keep to the seafront and the old Turkish quarter. Its bustling and inquisitive character gives it an animated flavour unlike any other big Cretan town.

Ierápetra was the most influential town of post-Minoan Crete, trading with north Africa and the Aegean islands. The population of Ierápytna, as it was then known, had a belligerent attitude towards their neighbours, and in 155 BC the inhabitants marched north to destroy their rival, Praisós. It was the last Cretan town to surrender to the invading Romans in 67 BC. Under their rule it continued to prosper, as it did later after the Venetians had taken control. However, when the Turks captured the town in 1647, Ierápetra ran out of luck. The conquerors allowed the town to decay, and for centuries it gently declined. Now rebuilt, with rather more energy than style, and revitalised, Ierápetra enthusiastically cultivates oranges, beans, tomatoes and tourists.

Ierápetra

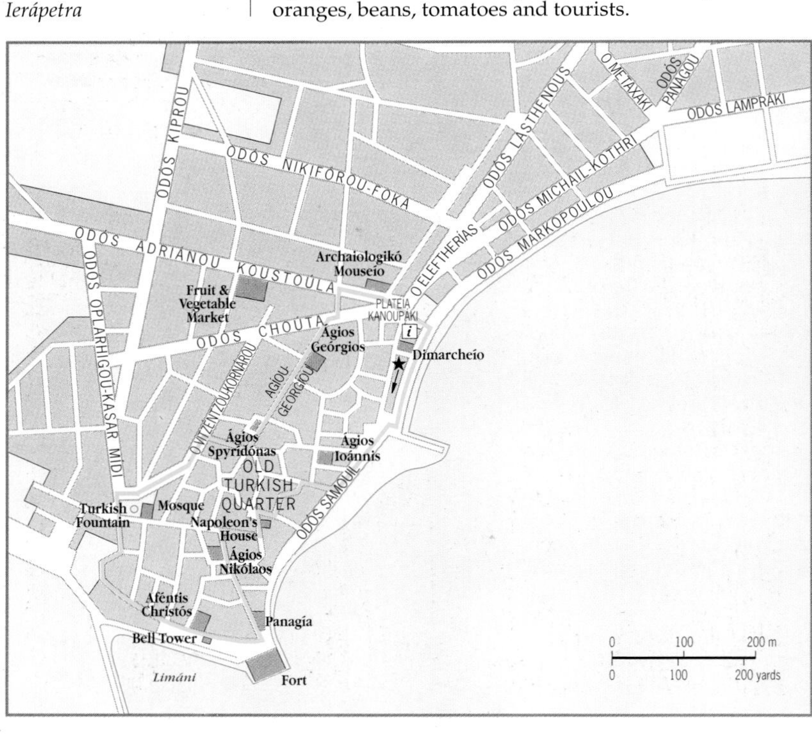

Walk

Ierápetra

Allow two hours; see map opposite.

This leisurely walk on Ierápetra's waterfront starts at the square next to the town hall. From here turn right along the seafront promenade, past the jetty from which the ferries leave, and on down Odós Samouil. Any side turning to the right will take you into the narrow paved lanes of the **old Turkish quarter▶▶**, where modern blocks of flats and tottering, balconied old houses stand quietly side by side among the potted trees and flowers. It is easy to spend half an hour roaming here, and easier still to lose all sense of direction.

Ask how to get to the fort, if you get lost, and you will come to the crenellated, slit-pierced old **castle▶** by the harbour. The Venetians rebuilt the uncompromising fortress after an earthquake in 1626, and the Turks later refortified it. Brightly painted fishing boats occupy the harbour inside a curved breakwater. A three-storey bell tower overlooks the scene, and across the road is the 14th-century church of Aféntis Christós, notable for its twin red-tiled domes.

Continue along the dusty road round a righthand bend to reach a **square▶** with a domed Turkish fountain sporting elaborate columns, dragonhead sculptures and an Arabic inscription. Beyond it stands a big Turkish mosque, with a capless minaret and inscriptions and symbols in marble.

In front of the mosque turn right along Odós Vitzéntzou-Kornárou, and second right down Odós Mamounáki into the Turkish quarter. First left brings you to a square with a blue-painted church. Take top right, Odós Ágiou Geórgiou, up to Odós Choúta. Ierápetra's **fruit and vegetable market▶** is opposite to the left and is well worth a visit in the early morning, when the artichokes, beans and aubergines are piled high. Cross Choúta and go up Odós Pagoménos, then turn right along Adriánou Koustoúla. Opposite, a few yards short of completing the walk, is the **Archaeological Museum▶**, rather dingy but home to many Minoan, Doric and Graeco–Roman bits and pieces. The pride of the collection is the Minoan *larnax* or lidded clay coffin unearthed at Episkopí. It is decorated in vigorous, primitive fashion with octopus shapes, wild goat hunts and a long-tailed horse pulling a chariot.

Turkish mosque and fountain

Relief carvings at Ítanos

FADING BLACK
Older village women dress almost invariably in black—black headscarf, black dress, black knee-socks. But it is becoming increasingly rare to see a woman under 50 dressed in this way. Uncovered hair, ordinary jumpers and even slacks are common among today's younger Cretan village women. Will the country streets and door-ways be entirely empty of those nun-like, bent old figures in 30 years time?

DRESS SENSE
The customary dress of the older men, however—tall knee-boots, drab-coloured wide breeches, black shirt, black head-fringe—is so practical, and so dashing, that its survival seems less in doubt.

(continued from page 143)
valley before climbing the eastern hill. To your right, just below the summit, lies the outline of a basilica built in the 5th or 6th century AD. A very early Christian church, it has semicircular apses in the walls of the central aisle, which is flanked by side aisles and littered with pieces of marble and stones. Looking south across the little beach with its feathery date palms, you can see other remains on the slopes of the headland.

After Ierápetra attacked and destroyed Praisós in 155 BC, Ítanos was the only other contender for control of eastern Crete. Ítanos remained influential until it, too, was destroyed, perhaps by north African or Middle Eastern pirates, well before the Venetians set foot on the island.

►► Káto Zákros *139E2*

Káto Zákros lies at the foot of the Valley of the Dead (see page 153). Surrounded by carob and olive groves, fronted by a tiny fishing harbour and a fine pebbly beach between the hard-angled jaws of the headlands, the little strip of tavernas and rooms to rent has a spectacular setting. In summer it can be uncomfortably crowded with visitors to the nearby Minoan palace of Zákros (see pages 158–159). In winter (November to February) the place is largely unoccupied. There is occasional danger from floods down the gorge after heavy rain, but the main reason for the village's desertion is simply the absence of tourists. In early spring or late autumn Káto Zákros is delightful.

►► Kavoúsi *138B2*

Kavoúsi stands above the Ágios Nikólaos–Siteía road where it turns north to skirt the flanks of the Ornós Mountains. You won't see much from the road, but for those who leave their car and walk half an hour through the tangle of lanes, up and down steps, under lemon trees and past flowers growing in wall cracks, the village provides rich rewards. There are pleasant cafés in the tree-shaded *plateía,* and three Byzantine churches. The most interesting is Apóstoli, which is decorated with faded and blackened frescoes and is reached by continuing along the narrowing lane that leads out of the square.

► Khandrás (Chandrás) *139D2*

Khandrás, on the Zíros road from Epáno Episkopí, is a working village set in well-tilled fields at the western end of the fertile Zíros Plateau. Turn left off the road just before entering Khandrás, on a dirt road signed to Stavroménos

Colourful tavernas in Káto Zákros

and Karýdi. In 1km (0.5 miles) take another dirt road to reach the poignant ruins of the village of **Voilá►►**. A brass tap still splashes water from a Turkish fountain; the remains of a Turkish tower stand on a bluff, with tesselated carvings around the doorway arch including two cypress trees—and cypresses still stand among the ruins. Above the village is the 15th-century church of Ágios Geórgios; its twin aisles contain a faded fresco of the Madonna, and an icon of St George slaying a timid dragon.

► Makrýgialos *138B1*

The sprawling resort of Makrýgialos has gobbled up the neighbouring village of Análipsi and is now a single agglomeration of hotels, shops, restaurants and car hire agents and the like. It makes a daunting introduction to the south coast when you arrive from Siteía on the Ierápetra road. There are good views west along the coast and flanking mountains, however, and the beach is sandy and long. Little bays each side of the town can be less crowded.

The lanes of Kavoúsi

WORRY BEADS

Most Cretan men have them, but few women. They can be counted one by one, flicked from hand to hand, run through the fingers, whirled round like a propeller and clicked on a table top. Older sets are made of ornately carved wood or agate, polished from long use and handed down from father to son. Worry beads. Who knows what murder and mayhem would ensue if tension and anxiety were not dissipated by these secular rosaries?

WORD PUZZLE
At Praisós archaeologists unearthed three inscriptions. They were written in Greek characters, but the language predated Greek. So far the inscriptions have not been deciphered, but there is speculation that they could be in the tongue used by the Eteocretans or true descendants of the Minoans, and might be a later version of the mysterious Linear A hieroglyphs found at several Minoan sites. If so, they may represent the best chance yet of one day receiving those unread messages from the dawn of European civilisation.

►► Móchlos *138B3*

In Sfáka village, 40km (25 miles) east of Ágios Nikólaos on the Siteía road, you turn left, signposted, to descend towards the coast, and soon see Móchlos below and to the left. The white houses of the village are sprinkled beside the sea, and Móchlos island lies just offshore.

Móchlos village is a pleasant place, not too crowded and with some friendly tavernas. You can get a boat here for the short crossing to the island, which was a peninsula before there was a rise in sea level. You can explore the excavated remains of a Minoan harbour town on the landward side, or wander off to enjoy a peaceful hour or so to yourself, looking back for a lovely view of the village of Móchlos and the mountains behind.

►►► Praisós *138C2*

Turn left in Epáno Episkopí, signposted to Zíros, some 11km (7 miles) from Siteía on the south coast road to Ierápetra, and drop into the deep Pantélis Valley. Then climb through Ágios Spyrídonas, to enter tiny Neá Praisós village with its typical kafenion—useful for a coffee on your return. The site is found a few minutes beyond the village. Follow a series of small handmade signs to find it, nestled on three small hills.

The city of Praisós occupied these hills, and it was a powerful place from Doric times (ca1000 BC), through the Hellenistic period, until 155 BC when it was destroyed by its jealous, and by now more powerful, neighbour Ierápytna, modern Ierápetra. The Eteocretans or Minoan descendants had their stronghold here on the middle hill or First Acropolis and on the further one or Second Acropolis, while the nearest hill or Third Acropolis was topped by an altar, and later perhaps a temple.

Just beyond the ruined houses there is a gate on the left. This leads to a footpath that winds clockwise to a saddle of ground between the First and the Second Acropolis. Climb the slope of the First Acropolis to your left to find the rooms and storehouses of a 3rd-century BC house, its shaped stone blocks standing out from the rough terrace walling. It faces a wonderful sea and mountain view.

Old Praisós occupied a commanding site

A scattering of small offshore islands lies around the coastline of "mainland" Crete. Some of these, such as Spinalógka, have shared in Crete's history and are a microcosm of its beauty and its turbulent past. Others are more remote and difficult to reach, but they offer a valuable retreat—for both wildlife and their few visitors—from the pressures of modern life.

The first island that most visitors see is Día, as it lies just off the harbour of Irakleío and under the main flightpath of the airport. Día was named after a nymph who was marooned on the island by Hera, the jealous sister and wife of Zeus, following a dalliance with the amorous god of gods. Diá is now one of the island sanctuaries that is home to the *égagros* or Cretan ibex, and can be visited by boat from Irakleío.

To the east is the former leper colony of Spinalógka (see pages 136–137), and behind the adjacent peninsula lie the two Kolokithía islets with humped backs and long tail-like spits. Little Pándes, off Ágios Nikólaos, is another égagros sanctuary. Pseíra, in the Gulf of Mirampéllou, has a partly excavated Minoan town and cemetery, and can be visited by boat from Ágios Nikólaos and Móchlos. Close to the coast is Móchlos island (see opposite). Off the northeastern tip of Crete rise the three Dionysádes islands of Gianisáda, Dragonáda and remote Paximádha, where the rare Eleanora's falcon breeds.

Elássa lies 5km (3 miles) off Vái beach and offers a sheltered anchorage, as it has since Dorian times. Further south at Xerókampos, there is a beautiful view out to tiny Kaválloi. Off the southernmost tip of Crete, Koufonísi lies low, deserted now, but with a long history. The island was handily placed on the sea route to North Africa and the Middle East, and the Romans established a sizeable settlement here. The Minoans had learned to crush the Murex sea snail to extract purple dye and the Romans developed the trade on Koufounísi by harvesting the extract from the living shellfish. The island can be visited by boat from Ierápetra.

Uninhabited Yaidouronísi, better known as Chrýsi or Donkey Island, is 7km (4 miles) south of Ierápetra. With its wonderful beaches, the island makes the perfect getaway destination, reached by boat from Ierápetra.

The island of Pseíra

UNTOUCHED ISLANDS
Very few of the offshore islands of Crete can be reached easily and conveniently. Apart from the regular trips to Yávdos, Día, Yaidouronísi, Spinalógka and one or two others, private and often expensive arrangements have to be made with local boat owners or fishermen. This is frustrating for lovers of small islands, but it has preserved them in their untouched state, much to the benefit of wildlife.

View from Móchlos

The fire that lightened me
Shines no more upon me.
A wind extinguished it, and
Now the darkness is on me

In the fullness of the
moon,
A tree never takes root;
Only from the tree of love
Roots and branches shoot.

Stanzas from *Erotókritos* by Vinzétzos Kornáros (1600–1677) of Siteía

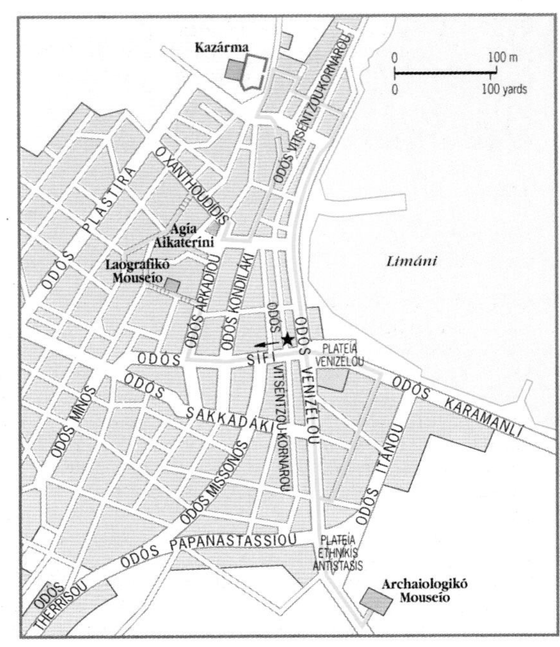

Siteía

►►► Siteía *139D3*

Siteía, with its population of about 8,000, benefits from its relative isolation from the main tourist strip of Crete's northern coast. This is a friendly, relaxed place, ideal for visitors both in and out of season. There was a Minoan settlement at Petrás, 1km (0.5 miles) east of the present town, and many excavated items from here are in Siteía's Archaeological Museum (tel: 28430 23917. *Open*: Tue–Sun 8.30–3. *Admission: inexpensive*). The Venetians walled and fortified the town and it flourished as a trading port despite its partial destruction by two earthquakes. Apart from the castle, there are few Venetian buildings to be seen. The Turks, who captured Siteía in 1651 after a three-year sea blockade, laid it waste and left it in ruins for the following two centuries. In 1879 they established an administrative centre for eastern Crete here, and laid out a new town on a grid of streets, most of which survive.

Siteía's houses look down upon its harbour

Walk

Siteía

Allow three or four hours; see map opposite.

Start at **Plateía Venizélou▶▶**, the square with formal gardens just inland of the waterfront and Siteía's focal point. Head inland up Odós Sífi past the Krystal Hotel and take the fourth turning on the right into Odós Arkadíou, where the plain older houses contrast with the Moorish arches and elaborate ironwork of the modern, the reverse of Crete's usual architectural characteristics. Turn left up the steps of Odós Perogiamáki, looking back to see harbour, bay and mountains framed by houses. At the top turn right and first right again. Descend the steps at the foot of Odós Xanthoudídis and you come to the big church of Agía Aikateríni. This is the heart of **Old Siteía▶▶▶**, a network of stepped and cobbled streets where few cars or tourists venture.

Turn down the steps of the street in front of the church and bear left along Odós Kondiláki, which narrows and rises to reach a lane below the Venetian fort. Turn right, go almost to the end, then left up the steps of Odós Nikónos to come to the **fort▶▶**. Known to Siteíans as Kazárma, the House of Arms, the hollow square fort is used in summer as an open-air theatre and enjoys a fine view over the town (a better one can be had by continuing eastwards along the path to the church and **graveyard▶▶** beyond).

A number of stepped alleyways descend from the fort to the **waterfront▶▶**, where you turn right to reach the quay. There is usually a crowd here when the boats are in. Somewhere along the shore you are bound to catch sight of the tame pelican who harasses locals and visitors alike in his quest for titbits. The beach runs east from the harbour, a long curve of sand with good bathing when the strong currents allow.

Pass Zorba's Restaurant to come to Plateía Venizélou. Turn left out of the square along shabby, bustling Odós Venizélou: a taste of workaday Siteía, lined with cafés, bakeries, ironmongers, clothes stores and music shops. At the far end cross the intersection of Plateía Ethníkis Antistásis, and in 100m (109 yards) you will reach the **Archaeological Museum▶▶** on your left (*Open* Tue–Sun 8.30–3. *Admission: inexpensive*). This is a modern building, with clearly labelled cases of finds from many Minoan and later sites in eastern Crete. Work your way clockwise round the exhibits, which include a bathtub-style coffin from Agía Fotiá, slender conical vessels from Palaikastro, long-spouted jugs and a squat bull from Móchlos. Finds from the palace at Káto Zákros (see pages 158–159) are the pride of the collection with jars, jugs, *píthoi*, cups, a wine press, and tablets inscribed with Linear A script.

Retrace your steps into Odós Venizélou. Take first right then first left down Odós 4 Septémbriou to regain the waterfront and Plateía Venizélou.

Many watersports are available

Walk

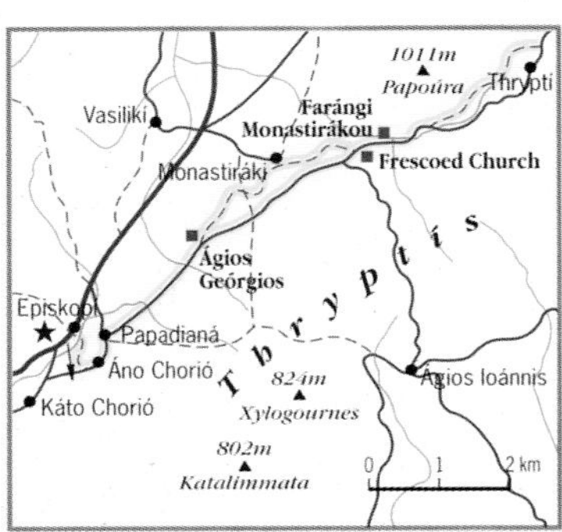

Episkopí to Thryptí and back

Allow nine hours for this demanding 20km (12 mile) walk. It leads you into the Thryptís Mountains, with dramatic views down the Monastiráki Gorge and over both Cretan and Libyan seas. Although you can get food and drink in the village of Thrypti, it's wise to carry water with you.

The sheer sides of the narrow Monastiráki Gorge

Start in Episkopí village at a little Byzantine church on the right below the Ierápetra–Ágios Nikólaos road. It has a 13th-century domed north nave and a Venetian south nave. A concrete road from the church crosses the bypass to reach a T-junction. Turn right here and after 0.5km (0.25 miles) you will come to Áno Chorió. Turn left and go up a concrete road, signposted to Thryptí, to pass a silver-domed church and climb the mountainside on a dirt road past Ágios Geórgios church. This will take about half an hour.

After 5km (3 miles) the road enters pine groves, and forks. Go left to pass a church with faded frescoes on your right. A fine view soon opens down the cleft of Monastiráki Gorge. A kilometre beyond the church, you reach a balustraded house above a left bend. After 0.5km (136 yards) there are two concrete buildings below the road on the left. In 150m (492 feet), before a right-hand bend, go left up a rough path. Keep going up and straight ahead until you reach Thryptí village, where both sustenance and a warm welcome are to be found.

Return to the church. The road bends right here. Turn right off the bend and go down on to a footpath. In 300m (273 yards) fork right at some electricity poles. After 0.5km (0.25 miles) keep right downhill to the bottom of the slope. Climb up the bank past a pine tree for 20m (22 yards). Turn right along a rising track to reach a saddle and a view over both Cretan and Libyan seas. Bear right through the pines along a stony, sunken track, descending in zigzags. In a rocky defile, hairpin right at some oleander bushes and continue downhill. You can see the track ahead by an electricity pole. In 10 minutes pass to the right of a wired enclosure and go right down a dirt road.

In another 10 minutes the road swings right at a stony outcrop. Go left along the lower of the paths, which soon forks. Go uphill, following vehicle tracks, and Ágios Geórgios church can be seen ahead and below. The track divides at the top of a valley and drops on the far side. Ten minutes later you reach Ágios Geórgios church and a dirt road down to Episkopí.

Valley of the Dead (Áno Zákros to Káto Zákros)

The Valley of the Dead lies just beyond Káto Zákros

Allow five to six hours.

This is a deep and dramatic canyon, riddled with caves where the Minoans buried their dead, through which you wind your way down 11km (7 miles) to the Minoan palace at Káto Zákros.

Leave Áno Zákros on the tarmac road towards Káto Zákros. After 2km (1 mile) the road dips into a wide valley, with a conspicuous white house on the far hillside. After a straight stretch the road bends left. Just before this, near a concrete block building on your right, turn left at a red arrow waymark along a track that curves to the right between olive trees. After about five minutes bear left onto the track that descends sharply into the Valley of the Dead. There is a steep 10-minute scramble among rocks before you reach the floor of the gorge. Ford the river and follow the trail on its left bank, waymarked with red dashes. A rough but wonderful hour's walk under the towering and twisted orange walls of the gorge, with the burial caves showing as open black mouths on both sides, brings you to a con-crete road. Red arrows point left to the palace of Zákros (see pages 158–159); Káto Zákros beach and a few tavernas are just beyond (page 146).

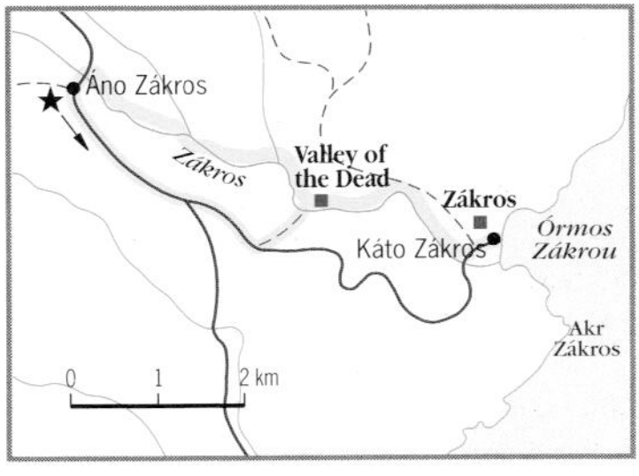

Return by the same route to the point where you scrambled down into the gorge. Continue along the right riverbank until you come to a concrete irrigation channel, which guides you up for 20 minutes to where the gorge divides and the path is blocked by a wire fence. Cross the stream and go through a shepherd's gate with a pink cloth marker. A sign points left to Zákros. After a mile you reach olive groves. Go through a second cloth-marked gate and carry on uphill between trees to cross an unmarked fence and a field. Red waymarks will take you on to Áno Zákros. Bear left at stone sheds to cross the stream, then turn right along a dirt road and you will be back in the village.

STONE MILLS
Tóplou has a well-preserved example of the thousands of stone-built windmills that served Cretans for hundreds of years until modern milling and the centralisation of bread supplies forced them into redundancy. They were sited on exposed saddles of ground, facing the prevailing wind, generally the southwest. They have the same sort of romantic appeal as the white-sailed working windpumps of Lasíthiou—or those of them that remain. There is something in their sturdy, uncomplicated lines, and the simple, graceful curve of their walls, which makes them highly attractive. And there is also a certain dignity in the usefulness that they embody. Technology has come full circle: a nearby hillside is now occupied by windmills of a new generation—a windfarm.

► Síderos Peninsula *139E4*

This entry would undoubtedly rate three stars if the peninsula was open to the public. Unfortunately for all lovers of wild and remote places, there is strictly no admission to the outermost two of the three nodes of bare, rocky land that reach out into the sea from the northeastern tip of Crete. NATO maintains a naval and military base here. After driving across the first of the three you will come to a checkpoint, where an unsmiling sentry will suggest unceremoniously that you return whence you came. This is a pity, since exploring the tracks above the cliffs, where falcons hover and only sheep and goats may venture, out to the lighthouse at the tip of the peninsula, would make one of the great wild walks of Crete.

►►► Tóplou Monastery *139D3*

Arriving at the monastery (*Open* daily 9–1, 2–6. *Admission: inexpensive*), you might well think you have come upon a Venetian fort. Tóplou has had a violent history. Founded in the 14th and 15th centuries, it was sacked by pirates in 1498 and by the Knights of St John of Malta in 1530. It was ruined by an earthquake early in the 17th century and partially destroyed by the invading Turks in 1646. Successive rebuilding has given it a square, fortress-like appearance, with high walls pierced by tiny windows surrounding the tall bell tower. Resistance has always been a characteristic of Tóplou. The name comes from the Turkish word for cannon, and during the 1821 uprising 12 monks were hanged at the monastery gate for succouring rebels. Tóplou became a meeting place for British resistance fighters and Cretan partisans during World War II, and the abbot and several of his monks were shot in reprisal.

Inside the inner gateway the central courtyard is patterned with thousands of little oval pebbles, and the monks' cells and offices rise three storeys high on all sides. Tóplou is reputed to be one of the richest monasteries in Crete, holding a vast area of land (indeed they have just leased 25ha/62 acres of this land to a development company for Crete's new super-resort Cavo Sidero), and while the ground-floor cells are bare and plain, those higher up and still

The now peaceful courtyard of Tóplou Monastery

Tóplou's icon of the Virgin

occupied are handsomely furnished. Several stone tablets are set in the walls of the 14th-century Church of Panagía Akrotirianí, the monastery's proper name. One shows a Virgin and Child. Another dates from the 2nd century BC, and records the settlement by "honest brokers", called in from Magnesia in Asia Minor in 132 BC, of a land dispute between the cities of nearby Ítanos and Ierápytna (Ierápetra) on the south coast. Inside the church a superb icon, created in 1770 by Ioánnis Kornárosm, depicts 61 miniature scenes representing the Greek Orthodox prayer *Lord, Thou Art Great*. A new museum displays a superb collection of icons and sacred objects.

EARLY AND LATE

Well-informed travellers, old Crete hands and most guidebooks will advise you to eschew Vái beach, citing it as a prime example of how tourism has spoiled a good thing. Don't be put off. Avoid the beach at peak times and, if you can, come here early on a breezy morning or on a starry evening in April or October. Lie in the shade of the whispering date palms and soak up the atmosphere of one of the island's most appealing spots.

►► Vái *139E3*

This famous beach, 6.5km (4 miles) northeast of Tóplou, is *too* famous in summer, when hordes of sun-worshippers descend in cars and coaches on the white sands that lie seaward of the feathery forest of date palms (*Phoenix theophrasti*), the largest stand on Crete of this very rare, protected palm. Legend says they grew from stones spat out by Phoenician traders—the fruit is bitter and inedible.

►►► Xerókampos *139E1*

Xerókampos has everything that Vái does not: peace, space to roam and dream, and an absence of crowds. Hidden away on the southern curve of the eastern end of the island, attainable only by a rough journey on a poor road, it offers heaven in the form of a long, unsullied beach and a couple of unhurried tavernas.

► (Áno) Zákros *139D2*

Áno Zákros is beginning to benefit from its proximity to the Minoan palace at Káto Zákros. The Hotel Zákros is plain but comfortable and friendly, and there are plenty of rooms to let in this big, unfussy village among olive groves overlooked by mountain ridges.

Looking down on the clear waters off Vái beach

Drive

Thryptís, Ornó and Siteía Mountains

This is a circular drive of about 137km (85 miles) from Ierápetra through stunning mountain scenery, winding through villages where visitors are the exception rather than the rule. Be sure to check your tyres and fill up with petrol before you set off on this all-day drive through high, unfrequented mountain country. Some of the dirt roads are very rough and there are few garages along the way.

Some of the roads in the east have been improved due to the building of a power plant on the coast in the bay of Atherinolakos, but you'll still find sections of dirt. See the map on pages 138–139.

Leave **Ierápetra** by the coast road towards Siteía, and after 8km (5 miles) turn off left through **Koutsounári**, climbing into the wild and craggy Thryptís Mountains above plunging valleys to reach **Ágios Ioánnis**, a village perched spectacularly below a crag. The road, now unsurfaced, hairpins along to **Schinokápsala**, where it forks in the village square.

Go left uphill through pine groves blackened by forest fires until you reach sleepy, whitewashed **Oreinó**, a good place to idle over coffee. The road rises beyond the village to a saddle. Immediately beyond, bear sharp right and after 0.5km (0.25 miles) turn left by an iron post to zigzag down to **Stavrochóri**, a village spread on a ledge of rock and facing down a steep valley, overlooked by the tall bell tower of its church.

Alternatively you could return from Oreinó for 2km (0.5 miles) to a major fork, and keep left back down to the left turn on the coast road at Mávros Kólympos. After 2km (1 mile) a signposted left turn at Koutsourás will bring you up to Stavrochóri.

Continue northwards to **Chrysopigí** and on through fertile upland valleys where marble outcrops shine white against the orange rocks. Beyond the side turning to **Dáfni** go left at an unsigned fork, to wind up and then zigzag down through **Paraspóri** and **Achládia**, perched, like all these villages, on bluffs, overlooking enormous views of the Ornó Mountains and the sea beyond the north coast.

At **Piskokéfalo** turn right on the Ierápetra road, and after 100m (109 yards) turn left opposite a garage. Fork right after 200m (218 yards) and continue to a T-junction. Go right here, and right again at a sign to Zoú. Keep straight ahead through **Káto Episkopí** for a diversion to the tiny, red-roofed 11th-century church of Ayíi Apóstoli. The route by way of Zoú, Sfakiá and Katsidóni is winding but well surfaced to **Sítanos**, in the heart of the Siteía Mountains. Here you bear right on a rougher road past Kateliónas to turn left on a better surface through **Khandrás** (see pages 146–147) at the edge of agricultural Zíros.

Zíros village is the centre for this hilly, largely unvisited district, and it is a place that exudes a wholly Cretan atmosphere, where the arrival of tourists is a real event. Stop and brace yourself at one of the tavernas for what follows: a very wriggling route that drops for a difficult 13km (8 miles) to the south coast at **Goúdouras**.

Leave the village and follow the road with the sea to your left around the sweeping bay until you reach **Kápsa Monastery** at the mouth of a tremendous gorge. Bear right to climb to the monastery, a beautiful, peaceful eagle's nest, high against the cliff face, looking out to sea. During the 19th century Yerondoyiánnis, an illiterate monk from Kápsa who was a champion of the local people against the Turks and a miraculous healer, built much of the monastery himself. His remains are venerated in the dark church.

Back on the road, continue through Kaló Neró to reach the highway, and turn left for Ierápetra.

Kavoúsi is dwarfed by the steep flanks of the Ornó Mountains

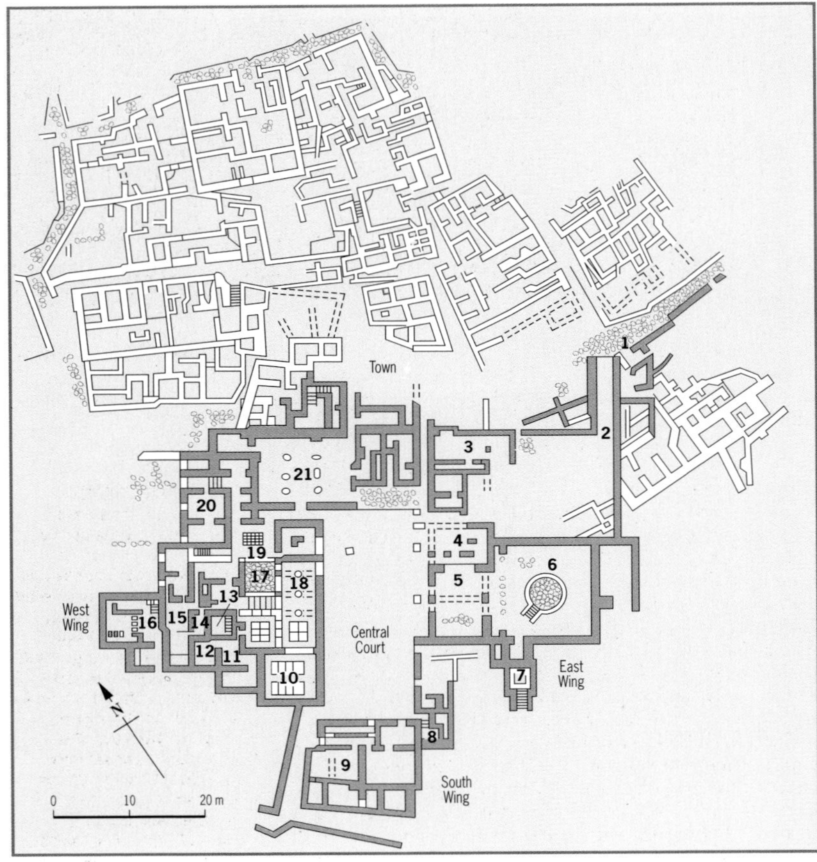

KEY TO THE MAP
1 paved road
2 main gate
3 bath
4 queen's apartment
5 king's apartment
6 cistern hall
7 spring chamber
8 well
9 workshops
10 banqueting hall
11 workshop
12 treasury
13 lustral basin
14 central shrine
15 archives
16 workshops and dye-house
17 lightwell
18 main hall
19 lobby
20 storerooms
21 kitchen

►►► Zákros Minoan Palace *139E2*

The Minoan palace at Zákros (*Open* Apr–Oct daily 8.30–5; Nov–Mar daily 8.30–3. *Admission: moderate*) is the jewel in the crown of modern Cretan archaeology. The existence of a sizeable ancient settlement at the foot of the Valley of the Dead had been suspected since the middle of the 19th century. Federico Halbherr, who excavated Gortýs, and Sir Arthur Evans, of Knosós fame, both made excavations here around the end of the 19th century. In 1901 the British archaeologist David Hogarth unearthed houses, pottery and implements from what he took to be a Minoan port. His dig came within feet of the palace itself, but the valley floor held onto its secret. In the 1930s a Cretan antiquarian, Dr Giamalákis, bought some gold items from a local farmer, who said he had found them at Káto Zákros. The doctor's collection is now in Room XVII of Irakleío Archaeological Museum, and includes a bowl and a bull's-head pendant unearthed by the farmer. Suspicion was thus rekindled that there was something down there, but it was not until 1962 that a Greek archaeologist, Nikólaos Pláton, finally located the exact site.

Zákros differs in one important respect from the other sites: after its destruction in the mysterious disaster of

The water tank at Zákros Palace

1450 BC, the existence of the palace was forgotten. Nobody came to loot Zákros. The collapsed structure lay entire under the ground, exactly as it had been at the moment its inhabitants fled and it came crashing down on their belongings, tools, pots and sacred totems. Pláton's excavation revealed by far the most complete Minoan complex yet brought to light.

Once inside the gate, climb the hill through the streets and houses of the Minoan town of Zákros, to the ruined building at the summit with walls made of double-size boulders. From here you can look down on the palace remains and compare them with the plan. When you have got your bearings (to the east lie the flat, open rectangles of the cistern hall with its circular water tank; immediately below you is the central court of the palace) return to the entrance gate and walk along the paved roadway that led from the harbour into the palace complex.

The cistern hall, part of the east wing of the palace, lies south of the first courtyard that you step down into. The cistern may have been a swimming pool or a fish tank. Today it holds murky water and is full of green plants. Bear right past the king's and queen's apartments to the big central court. In the southeast corner is a waterlogged well where the excavators discovered a jar containing 3,500-year-old olives, perfectly preserved by the water. At the northwest corner of the central court is the base of an altar. Go through the entrance to the west wing of the palace. A beautiful stone vase decorated with wild goats and scenes of a peak sanctuary was found here and is now in Room VIII of the Irakleío Archaeological Museum. A surprisingly small banqueting hall lies two rooms south of the light well, and west of that is a huddle of rooms that includes the treasury. Stone jars, clay chests and the 300 separate pieces of the famous rock crystal *rhyton* or ceremonial jug were found here. The *rhyton*, now reassembled, can be seen in Room VIII of the Irakleío Archaeological Museum. The palace archive, which consisted of wooden chests containing hundreds of clay tablets inscribed with Minoan Linear A hieroglyphs, was also found here, as was a tiny central shrine. On the western edge of the palace were a dye-house, and a latrine that emptied into a cesspit outside the walls.

Returning to the central court, walk north towards the hill to find the outlines of the kitchens and pantries which yielded animal bones, cooking pots and kitchen utensils, and a number of storerooms. Above lie the remains of the ancient town.

FINDS PRESERVED

Most of the important finds from the palace of Zákros are on display in the Irakleío Archaeological Museum. Having wandered through the actual rooms where they were found, you may decide to go back to the museum to appreciate them afresh. There is the rock crystal *rhyton* from the treasury, the ceremonial vessel from the lustral basin with its gracefully curled twin handles and brilliant natural patterning, and the conical long jar from the central court well in which olives were found preserved by the water since the destruction of the palace.

HA! GORGE

The dramatic gorge that cuts down through the hills to Káto Zákros was named the Valley of the Dead (see also the Walk on page 153) after the Minoan cave burials that were discovered there. But local people have an equally apt name for it, "Ha! Gorge". Try shouting with all your might from the bottom of the canyon and you will soon appreciate why its other name arose.

Africa, Europe and Asia all meet in the complex rhythms and haunting melodies of traditional Cretan music, which is currently enjoying a revival of popularity among the young. It is very much part of Cretan life, and can be seen and heard both in special performances devised for tourists and also as part of village life at weddings and festivals.

Dancing and music for visitors

MUSICAL MOUSTACHES
As much a part of the Cretan man's traditional dress as baggy breeches and fringed headband is the well-cultivated moustache—straggly, drooping, clipped or waxed. Some of the most luxuriant examples are seen under the noses of young musicians, the new heroes of the *lýra* and *bouzoúki*, who rightly feel themselves to be the guardians and ambassadors of Cretan tradition.

Music For an island so heavily invaded by the outside world during the last few decades, Crete enjoys a remarkably vigorous and lively tradition of music and dance. The discotheques of Irakleío, Chaniá, Réthymno and Ágios Nikólaos certainly claim plenty of custom from Cretan boys and girls in the evening, but it is both exciting and moving to walk into a bar or restaurant in the back streets of the same towns in the early hours of the morning and find the same youngsters singing their heads off, roaring out Cretan songs to the accompaniment of *bouzoúki* and guitar. There is a fierce enjoyment in such singing, an echo perhaps of the way their ancestors sang songs of defiance against the Venetians and Turks.

Singing and dancing are driven by the great triumvirate of Cretan music: the *lýra*, a three-stringed bowed fiddle that sobs and wails across the player's knee; the deep-bellied, eight-stringed *bouzoúki*; and the recorder-like flute. These days Cretans are developing a taste for their traditional tunes taken neat, without singing, but with plenty of *rakí* to fuel proceedings.

There are several parallels between the traditional cultures of Crete and rural Ireland: the hospitality, the enjoyment of the stranger, a willingness to take what the moment offers, and particularly the power of music as a social glue, an affirmation of local life and feeling. In Crete, as in the west of Ireland, musicians are well respected, and even revered. Here, too, the tradition is enjoying a revival, with plenty of excellent young musicians putting salt on the tails of their seniors. Children are encouraged to learn, and eager boys turn up, *lýra* under arm, for teaching sessions in the lobby of the Mosque of Nerantziés in Réthymno. *Lýra* and *bouzoúki* playing have traditionally been a male preserve, but increasing numbers of Cretan girls

A bouzoúki

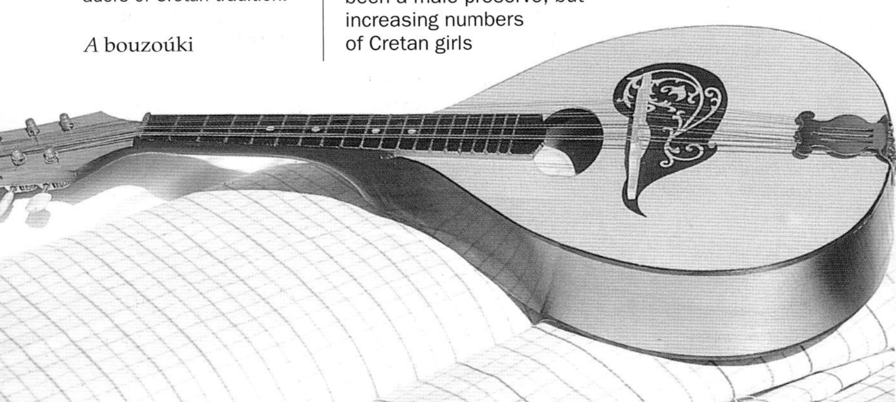

and young women are taking up the instruments these days, sharing prominence with men on the posters that announce music concerts. Many Cretan radio stations are devoted to the island's music, and Cretan television broadcasts live and recorded concerts.

This is wild music with wild rhythms, complicated and even formless to the uninitiated ear. It is music for dancing, fighting and lovemaking, a fiery meeting of North Africa, Europe and Asia. Time signatures can seem bizarre to outsiders, but once tuned in, the ears and feet suddenly find it easy to keep up. Singing can be roaring and tribal, or it can take the form of the subtle *mantináde*, a verse or series of verses in rhyming couplets, sometimes tossed to and fro between singers, often full of allusions to issues and personalities that only locals can fully appreciate. Another kind of singing is the chanted recitation of epic poems. The 17th-century *Erotókritos* of Vinzétzos Kornáros is widely known, in spite of its length, and some say that you can still hear old men recite the lament for the fallen heroes of Sfakiá, the *Song of Daskaloyiánnis*.

Dance and dress Dancing happens as and when Cretans feel moved. Nowadays, of course, it is also laid on for visitors as part of a plate-smashing, table-stomping evening out. These events will probably be your only chance to see the spectacular dances where the men spring high in the air and slap both heels against a hand. There will be stunning costumes: the women in beautifully embroidered velvet jackets looped with gold lace, white aprons, long dresses over voluminous pantaloons, and the men in baggy breeches, white boots and many metres of silver chains, which clash on superbly engraved silver daggers tucked into red sashes. Such costumes are a cockatoo display, far removed from the sombre traditional dress still worn by many village men (knee boots, tasselled black head fringe, wide khaki breeches, black shirts) and women (head-to-foot, self-effacing black for those who have suffered a bereavement).

Traditional dress may be donned for a wedding

DANCES OF DELIGHT

Cretan dances are at their most spectacular when performed by athletic young people in full traditional dress. This is most commonly seen these days at special displays put on for tourists. But there is a different, perhaps a purer, delight in witnessing, and joining in with, the dancing that goes on during festivals in village houses and courtyards. The participants may be in workaday clothes and some of them will be too old or too young or too stout to leap high. But this is where the tradition is still being passed on from one generation to the next.

HAVE A GO

Don't be shy of asking to take part in a dance you like the look of, or asking to be shown how to play a traditional instrument. If you aren't embarrassed, the performers and onlookers certainly won't be. And delighted plaudits will be yours if you can carry it off!

Drive

Gulf of Mirampéllou (Ágios Nikólaos to Siteía)

The coastline that fringes the Gulf of Mirampéllou has been nicknamed the Cretan Riviera. The road (72km/45 miles) from Ágios Nikólaos to Siteía is its corniche, twisting and turning through villages that cling to the mountainsides, above bays of wonderfully clear, shallow water.

There are several excellent vantage points from which to look back as you drive south and east from **Ágios Nikólaos** along the coast road. The town is the very picture of a Cretan resort, its houses in a graceful mound looking out on to a startlingly blue sea, which shades into green as it reaches the sandy little bays of the coastline. The road passes Ammoudára and Ístro, then after 5km (3 miles) a sign on your right to Faneroménis Monastery points up a very rough dirt road. This is a 6.5km (4 miles) diversion zigzagging up to **Faneroménis**. The monastery is built hard against a mountain cliff, facing a breathtaking view out over terraced hillsides to the Gulf of Mirampéllou. (There is a *different* Faneroménis Monastery on the coast just west of Siteía; see page 143.)

The gates to the monastery are not always open, and if not vigorous knocking and halloing will elicit an answer. A monk will guide you up the stairways of the canyon-like courtyard to the roof terrace, and unlock the door of the church built into a cave

The coast road offers spectacular views of the Gulf of Mirampéllou

above the monastery. There are some lovely old icons to see; and be sure to take a peep into the inner recess where the discovery of a mysterious icon of the Virgin led to the founding of the monastery in the 15th century.

Back on the main Siteía road, another 5km (3 miles) brings you to a side-turning to the Minoan town site of **Gourniá** (see pages 122–123). Beyond the turning the road drops to the coast at **Pachiá Ámmos**, a modest strip of shops, tavernas and hotels along a grey sand beach where a storm in 1914 exposed a Minoan cemetery, the incumbents buried in upturned *píthoi*. Now the grey, wrinkled wall of the Thryptís Mountains stands ahead, sliced by the dark crack of the Monastiráki Gorge. **Kavoúsi** village (see page 146) lies under the towering, bald peak of Mount Aféntis Stavroménos (1,476m/4,841 feet).

The road wriggles east across the foothills of Thryptís' northern neighbour, the Órno range, with memorable views over the sheer sides of Pseíra Island (see page 149) and the whole gulf. Lástros, Sfáka and Tourlotí lie like heaps of white sugar cubes on the slopes. The side road down to **Móchlos** (see page 148) branches off in Sfáka, another detour not to be missed.

Finds excavated at a Minoan cemetery in nearby Myrsini include an exquisite painted clay figurine of a priestess and a highly decorated complete three-jugged cult vessel. Both are now on display in the Archaeological Museum in Ágios Nikólaos (see page 115). The village is a tangle of old houses on tiny lanes, and the rather nondescript church encloses a far older one, of the 14th century, with some fine frescoes. If the priest is around he'll let you in.

Éxo Moulianá is one of the villages at the heart of the sultana producing region. Café owners in town may serve them as a complement to the praised local wine, which is sharp and fruity.

After a further tortuous 8km (5 miles) a sign on the right points to **Chamézi Middle Minoan House**, up a rough road for the last detour of this drive. From the main road it's a left, right, left, right then finally left at the five forks along the route to find the ruins of the house in front of you, on the crest of a hill. An oval wall encircles rooms, a tiny central court and a deep cistern. It was built around 2000 BC and is the only one discovered of this shape.

Back on the road, an uneventful 11km (7 miles) will bring you down to Siteía.

The Órno Mountains are the backdrop for this village near Móchlos

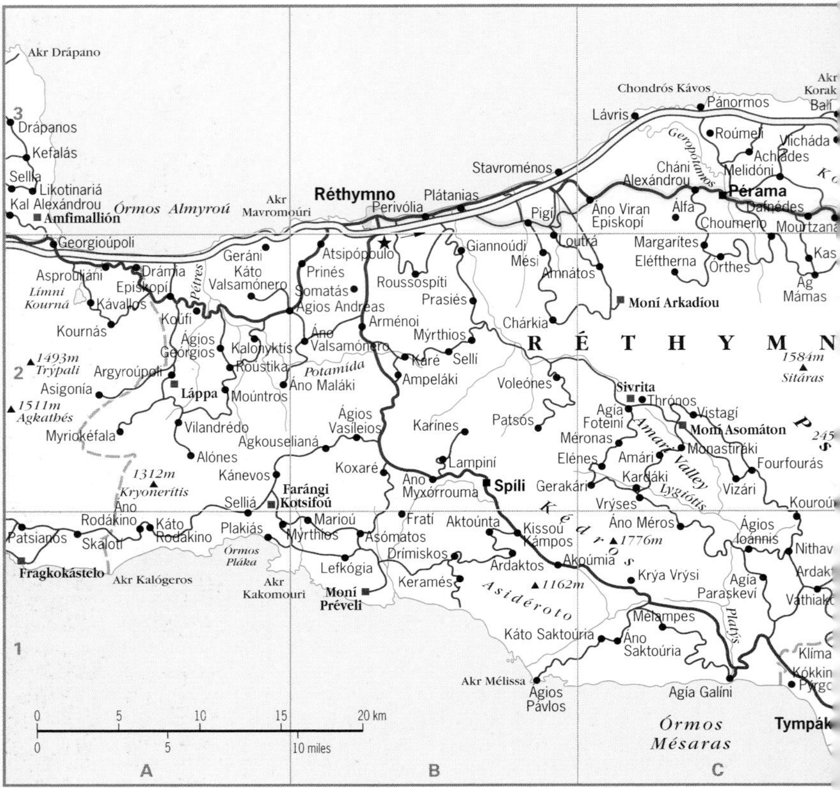

Below: Réthymno harbour   Right: Amári church

Réthymno and the Ida Mountains

Painted relief work

▶▶▶ REGION HIGHLIGHTS

Amári Valley *pages 168–169*
Anógia *pages 169 and 171*
Arkadíou Monastery *pages 171–172*
Fragkokástelo *page 173*
Nída Plateau and Ídaean Cave *pages 178–179*
Préveli Monastery *pages 180–181*
Réthymno *pages 182–185*
Valsamónerou Monastery *pages 190–191*

Old Réthymno street

RÉTHYMNO AND THE ÍDA MOUNTAINS This section of western central Crete extends along the north coast from Georgioúpoli on the Gulf of Almroú to Irakleío, and along the south coast from Fragkokástelo to Agía Galíni. The eastern part of the region is dominated by the great ragged range of the Ída Mountains, better known in Crete these days as Psiloreítis, too wild and steep to be crossed by any north–south road. In the centre lies the high and beautiful Amári Valley. To the west the land runs in broken hill ranges and valleys towards the narrowing wrist of the island and the upthrust of Levká Óri, the White Mountains of westernmost Crete.

On the northern coast, out towards the west of the region, sits Réthymno, the city towards which the entire area looks as its tourist and cultural capital. Like Crete's three other main centres, Chaniá, Irakleío and Ágios Nikólaos, Réthymno has its own particular character, a gentle and timeless one that seems to owe less to its rôle as a thriving holiday centre than to its Venetian and Turkish history, which surfaces everywhere in minarets, domes, ornate stonework, solid fortifications and sea defences. This is a town for idling away the days strolling the narrow streets and peering into shop windows, with a detail of architecture or everyday life to surprise you around every corner.

The fast coastal highway between Irakleío and Chaniá bypasses the town and takes most through-traffic straight past Réthymno. Small resorts have begun to spring up seaward of the road, but the main ribbon development is still confined to a strip east of the city. Turn inland off the new road and you find yourself immediately in quiet olive groves, fruit orchards and tumbled hills, a world away from the bustle of the coast. The old road from Réthymno to Irakleío, and the other roads further and higher inland, reveal this landscape in a leisurely way.

Above and behind these northern roads of the region towers the Psiloreítis range, nearly 32km (20 miles) from east to west. These formidable mountains rise to 2,456m (8,056 feet) at the summit of the highest peak in Crete, Mount Psiloreítis, which gives its name to the whole range. Shepherds' tracks crisscross the heights, a challenge for determined and well-prepared walkers. In the heart of these mountains lies the Nída Plateau, from which you can reach the Ídaean Cave where, legend says, Zeus, chief among Greek gods, was raised. In the southern flank of Psiloreítis is the Kamáres cave, a Minoan religious centre where delicate pottery and many other marvellous relics have been found.

Psiloreítis has been a place of refuge for resistance fighters throughout the long history of struggle against invaders in Crete. The mountain village of Anógia was razed during German reprisals in World War II, and there was more destruction along the Amári Valley, west of the mountains. This is an area of Crete much written and talked about, a truly beautiful and peaceful upland that seems green, cool and fruitful even in the heat of high summer. Olive groves, cherry orchards, woods and wild flowers abound, and there are many tiny Byzantine churches dotted around, rich in frescoes. A couple of days spent lazing along the two winding roads that flank the valley, east and west, will introduce you to a hospitable and largely unchanged way of life among the villages of Amári and the little-visited Kédros Mountains to the west.

The south coast rises dramatically from the sea. There is as yet no coastal road to connect the square Venetian coastal fort of Fragkokástelo with the lively small resort of Agía Galíni. But there are superbly sited villages to explore here—Rodákino, Ágios Pávlos, Selliá—and the historic monastery of Préveli in its peaceful cleft above the sea.

SEA HUE
An aspect of the Cretan coast commented on by all visitors from more northern climes is the superb colour of the sea, especially close inshore. There is nothing wine-dark about this southern Aegean or Cretan Sea. A combination of gently shelving sand below, strong sunlight above, and the wonderful clarity of the water gives a blue-green hue, a turquoise shimmer so vivid as to be indescribable, though many have tried.

OLD VORIZA
Driving the mountain road between Zarós and Vorízia, glance down to your left about halfway between the two villages to see Old Vorízia, a dozen roofless shells of houses, stone walls cracked and crumbling, blank windows facing down a lovely valley. These houses, now used as sheep pens, were destroyed in a wartime divebombing practice by Stukas in a reprisal gesture.

CHOOSE YOUR FISH
In the fish restaurants on Réthymno's waterfront, follow the general rule of eating out in Crete: don't order sight unseen, but walk through into the kitchen and choose something you like the look of.

WEARY LEAR
Edward Lear stayed at Réthymno in 1864, during the course of what was evidently a rather wearisome and uncomfortable visit to Crete. Sketchy representations of the town appear among the illustrations in his diary of the trip, published as *The Cretan Journal*.

The Venetian fort at Réthymno

Amári Valley memorial

CRETAN HAVERSACKS
Traditional Cretan haversacks, woven of brightly dyed wool in geometric patterns that vary from village to village, are common items on souvenir stalls. If you keep your eyes open when walking in the mountains, you may see a shepherd carrying the day's provisions in one, slung by the side or dangling from the crook of a walking stick.

Amári shepherd

►► Amári *164C2*

Amári is the capital of the beautiful high Amári Valley (see below), under the western flank of the Psiloreítis mountain range south of Réthymno. Coming south, you turn off the road to the Mesará Plain at Moní Asomáton, to reach Amári to the southwest. It is a typical mountain settlement of narrow lanes, farmyards and tiny white houses. During World War II Amári was a formidable centre of resistance to the Germans and, like its neighbouring villages, paid in blood for its stance.

Leave your car in the village square and turn right on foot up a lane that climbs to the Venetian clock tower. Spiral steps inside rise to a wonderful view from among the bells to the craggy wall of Psiloreítis. The nearby church has good modern frescoes; there are ancient ones in the Church of Agía Ánna (see opposite).

►►► Amári Valley *164C2*

Southeast of Réthymno lies the beautiful Amári Valley, filled with orange and cherry orchards, quiet villages and churches with frescoes. A selection of the valley's many treasures could begin with Thrónos at the northern end, where a well-preserved early Byzantine mosaic pavement underlies the Church of Panagía (key at the village taverna). Faces look down from faded 14th-century frescoes in the apse. The nave has 15th-century frescoes, including the body of Christ being tenderly caressed by his mother and St John. Just along the main road, the 15th-century Agía Paraskeví, isolated among cypresses in a cornfield, contains the bones of some long-forgotten saint in a glass-topped niche. Beyond here is the right turn to Amári village. In the fork stand the graceful, though crumbling Venetian buildings of Asomáton Monastery. Monastiráki on the Amári road has a beautiful small Venetian church. Amári itself has the lovely Agía Ánna, signposted to the right on entering the village. Forlorn-looking saints in the apse are dated to 1225.

Returning past Thrónos, turn left down the west side of the valley. In the three-aisled Panagía church at Méronas (key with the priest at the second large white house on the left after the church) are beautiful, faded 14th-century frescoes including Christ washing the disciples' feet and the Virgin and St John comforting each other, as well as a locally venerated 14th-century icon of a sweetly sad Virgin.

The villages down this western side were razed by the Germans and dozens of men were shot in revenge for the abduction by partisans of General Kreipe, the officer in command of Crete. Memorials in Gerakári, Kardáki, Vrýses and Áno Méros carry the names of the dead and the date of their execution, 22 August 1944. This sombre succession is relieved just to the south of Gerakári by the weather-worn but vivid late 13th-century frescoes in the ruined church of Ágios Ioánnis Theológos.

►►► Anógia *165D2*

The sloping village street is lined with the usual tavernas. You could be in and out of Anógia in a couple of minutes, but take a closer look. Almost all the buildings postdate 1944, when the village paid a heavy price for the capture and removal from Crete of the German commanding officer, General Heinrich Kreipe. As an act of retaliation, soldiers were sent to Anógia with orders to raze the town. On 15 August 1944 every house in the village was burned to the ground and every male was killed.

A museum in the lower, older part of the village shows the work of the primitive sculptor and painter Alkibíades Skoúlas also known as Grillio. His vivid painting of the sack of Anógia shows lines of villagers waiting to be shot, German mountain troops and the corpses of dead partisans. Other paintings depict the German landings at Máleme in 1941, the Turkish siege of Arkádiou Monastery in 1866, and scenes from Cretan mythology. There are also strange, monolithic, stylised carvings.

(continued on page 171)

WAR STORIES

Take time to strike up conversations with the elderly men and women of Anógia and the Amári villages. All have vivid memories of wartime. Many of the older men were partisans and can tell you astonishing tales, most undoubtedly true.

SNOW BLOCK

If you are planning to visit Anógia in the depths of winter, check on the local weather forecast first. If heavy snow is expected, be prepared to find yourself marooned in the mountains for several days or weeks as the snowfall can occasionally be deep and prolonged.

The naïve paintings and sculpture of Alkibíades Skoúlas in Anógia

If there is one word that sums up Cretan history and character, that word is resistance. And if there is one image that encapsulates the reality behind that word, it is a photograph in the wartime exhibition on the first floor of Irakleío's Historical Museum. Here a father and son stand tight-lipped against a wall, unshaven and bare-headed in the sunlight. The dark-haired young man's face is averted; his grizzled father stares straight ahead with slitted eyes, facing the gun muzzles of an execution squad that is lined up out of camera shot.

The proud face of resistance

THE CRETAN RUNNER
The Cretan Runner, by George Psychoundákis, a highly personal account of the author's experiences as a member of the resistance during World War II, is a wonderful read and a rightly acclaimed bestseller. The pages are thick with hundreds of remarkable incidents recalled by Psychoundákis, a semi-literate shepherd who became a Laureate of the Academy of Athens—a story worth telling in its own right.

This grim scene has been played out countless times down the centuries. Minoan islanders may well have been the first Cretan resisters, perhaps burning the palaces and towns taken over by the invading Mycenaeans. Ierápetrans held out against the Romans in 67 BC. Byzantines battled the incoming Saracens nearly eight centuries later. Cretans from Lasíthiou and Sfakiá harried the Venetians from their mountain strongholds. Daskaloyiánnis whipped up rebellion against the Turks in 1770. Throughout the 19th century the *palikáres* fought the Turks in one uprising after another, in 1821, 1841, 1858, 1866, 1889 and 1896. Elefthérios Venizélos held out for *enosis* in 1897 and 1905. For four years during World War II the partisans were a constant thorn in the flesh of the German forces of occupation. During the late 1960s and early 1970s, Cretans were among the Greeks who most actively opposed the military coup by the Greek colonels, refusing as far as possible to abide by martial law.

The cost of armed resistance by the militant few has been borne throughout the years by the civilian population of Crete, a cost measured in wholesale massacres, in burned villages, in women taken away to lives of prostitution, and in orphaned children. The battle-cry of the *palikáres*, "Freedom or death!", truly and succinctly tells the long tale of Cretan resistance.

A barred cell window at Arkadíou

The Venetian façade of Moni Arkadíou

(continued from page 169)

Around the square near the museum are craft workshops selling brightly coloured and patterned home-woven rugs. Up in the main street of the new village, the Old Anógian House Museum (*Open* summer Mon–Sat 8–3) displays a mass of utensils, tools, furniture and decorations typical of the traditional life that still goes on in this mountain village, which can be cut off for months from the outside world by winter snows. Little English is spoken in the village, but the hospitality is instant, and freely and proudly offered.

►►► Arkadíou Monastery *164C2*

The buildings of Moni Arkadíou (*Open* daily 8–5.30. *Admission: inexpensive*) appear as a great jumble of orange stone walls, pierced by ranks of windows and overlooked by a bell turret. In the 16th century the Venetians completely rebuilt on a much older foundation. The remaining glory of this reconstruction is the church, built in 1587 of deep yellow stone ornately carved and decorated. It stands beyond the gateway in a cool, cloistered courtyard shaded by vines. Inside the church are some striking religious paintings: a half-naked suffering Christ in Glory, a wonderful exploding Burning Bush, a pitiful Adam and Eve being expelled in misery from Eden. Around the courtyard stand the monastery buildings that have become the prime symbol of the "Freedom or Death" slogan of the Cretan resistance movement. At the time of writing, renovation work is under way.

1866 was a year of turmoil in Crete, as the islanders once more took up arms against their Turkish rulers. Arkadíou Monastery was a centre of resistance, and thousands of partisans and their families were inside the monastery in November when Turkish troops arrived to demand their surrender. Abbot Gabriel's refusal was followed by a two-day siege, culminating on 9 November in an all-out attack by the Turks. The surviving defenders gathered in

FIREWORKS
There are great celebrations at Arkadíou, and down on the coast at Réthymno, between 7 and 9 November every year, when fireworks, processions and other junketings commemorate the heroic explosion caused by Abbot Gabriel and Kostís Yiampoudákis.

KOTSIFOÚ GORGE
One of the most ruggedly beautiful yet least visited gorges in Crete lies beside the road from Réthymno to Fragkokástello. This is the Kotsifoú Gorge, just north of Selliá, an echoing, sheer-sided chasm, snaking, thrillingly narrow. You can take a rough excursion on foot from its seaward end near Plakiás.

The nightlights of the village of Agía Galíni

MAP FICTION
Road conditions in Crete have improved during the early years of the new millennium with many tracks receiving a brand new coat of asphalt, however, especially in the mountains, just because your map shows a clear route between villages doesn't mean you're going to find a pristine surface. There are still many dirt surfaces that make navigation difficult. Cretan maps may not lie, but they can be economical with the truth.

Handmade lace and embroidery for sale in Fódele

the wine storeroom where they had been keeping their gunpowder, and as the attackers broke in, Abbot Gabriel ordered Kostís Yiampoudákis to fire his pistol into the powder barrels. The store exploded, killing hundreds of Cretans and Turks.

The roofless shell of the vaulted store stands in one corner of the courtyard. Orange, grey and black wrinkles on the surface of the walls show where the heat of the explosion baked and carbonised the stonework. In the nearby refectory, where a handful of survivors hid and were quickly butchered, you can see tables scored with sword cuts and a doorway pitted with bullet holes.

► Agía Galíni *164C1*

The name means serenity, a holy calm. That might have been the case a hundred years ago when this beautiful site on the cliffs, looking out into the Gulf of Mesará, was all but uninhabited. Fifty years ago it was still a tiny fishing village, known only to a privileged band of free-wheeling foreigners. But tourism has worked on Agía Galíni since then and it's a thriving seaside holiday village, crammed with rooms to rent, car hire agents, tavernas, hotels and cafés, with a new €310 million resort with two five star hotels and a golf course being planned for the next couple of years. There are fine cliffs to east and west, clear green water beyond the little strip of a beach, and boats to other beaches, to the grottoes along the coast and to Sfakiá and Palaióchora. You take it for what it offers—sun, sand, sea and facilities.

►► Fódele *165D3*

Fódele is charmingly sited among orange groves in a valley about 19km (12 miles) northeast of Irakleío. This is a quiet place of tumbled houses, a tree-shaded square, and small bridges across a river, Fódele claims to be the birthplace of Doménico Theotokópoulos, better known as the painter El Greco (1541–1614). You can see what is claimed to be the house of his birth, a plaque to him in the village square, and copies of his paintings in the church. A strong imagination may be a better guide here than established fact, which advances equal claims for Irakleío.

►►► Fragkokástelo *164A1*

Fragkokástelo (*Open daily during daylight hours. Admission: free*) is one of Crete's most celebrated buildings: a great Venetian fortress, standing proud and foursquare on a lonely coastal site. It ought to deliver a sense of might and majesty—something more, at any rate, than the overwhelming feeling of emptiness and desolation one experiences inside its hollow, weed-grown and litter-strewn walls. The best view of the fort is from the mountain roads inland. Approached across the flat, dry coastal plain, Fragkokástelo looks unexpectedly small and two dimensional, rather like an abandoned film set.

Imagination is stirred, however, by the weather-eroded lion of St Mark that stands over the southern entrance. The Venetians built the fort in 1340, to dissuade the pirates then attacking Crete from the African coast, and as a symbol of the domination they wanted to exercise over the Sfakiot fighters in the hills behind.

Under Turkish rule the fort saw many bloody events. In 1770 the revolutionary leader Daskaloyiánnis, who had vainly trusted Russian promises to help him in his struggle, surrendered to the Turks at Fragkokástelo, and was taken to Irakleío, where he was flayed alive. In the spring of 1828, during the War of Independence between the mainland Greeks and the Turks, the Greek leader Hatzimicháli Daliánis landed in Crete and barricaded himself in Frangokástelo with 700 Cretans. They were wiped out to a man. But in Crete, history and myth are inextricably intertwined. Fragkokástelo still remembers these long-dead heroes. Every year, on a misty morning between 17 and 20 May, a ghostly procession of *drosoulítes* (dewy ones), marches a circuit of the walls. Some say they are the shades of fallen fighters, others that they are the souls of sinners not yet purged for heaven.

It is worth spending an hour walking over the plain around Fragokokástelo. The prickly bushes and scrub are home to a huge variety of wildlife including lizards, songbirds, burrowing beetles, cicadas and snails.

SCIENTIFIC FACT?
Scientists, unromantic fellows that they are, say that the *drosoulítes* are in fact mirages of people walking around on the coast of Libya, created under certain atmospheric conditions peculiar to mid-May, magnified and distorted by their journey across the sea.

The mighty Venetian fortress of Fragkokástelo

Walk

Kamáres Cave

Of all Crete's well-known Minoan sites, none is more remote and difficult to reach than the great cave of Kamáres (marked Spílaio Kamarón on the map, pages 164–165, D1). For scores of miles along the Mesará plain the mouth of the cave is visible, more than 1,000m (3,280 feet) above the plain, sited under a saddle-shaped ridge towards the heights of Psiloreítis. It looks a straightforward if steep climb, an impression also given by the short line of the path shown on maps. But the cave lies 1,525m (5,002 feet) above sea level, and to reach it involves a climb of up to four hours on a poorly-marked track that dodges about from one half-concealed paint splash to the next. The descent is even more tricky, especially in the low cloud or mist that can swirl across with little warning on even the clearest of days. The rewards of this all-day expedition, however, are great, with the echoing, atmospheric depths of

The country around Kamáres

the cave itself, the weight of history and religious ceremony attached to it, and the superb view from the heights over Mesará, spread like a promised land at the feet of the mountains.

Make this climb by yourself only if you are an experienced hill walker and you are properly equipped with weatherproof gear, hot drink, food and emergency equipment in case of difficulties. For most walkers, a better though fairly expensive alternative is to hire a guide in Kamáres village. Arrangements are informal, and the price negotiable. If you leave the village church and turn right, the *kafeníon* 200m (220 yards) along the street on the left will be able to help. Ask for Yióryio Saidákis.

Allow at least six to eight hours for the round trip.

The track starts as you enter Kamáres, a small village of tightly bunched houses 12km (7.5 miles) west of Zarós, striking uphill as a narrow lane from the right side of the road opposite the village graveyard. The bed of a stream, usually dry, takes you high up above Kamáres to some cisterns. Bear to the right, east, above the treeline and continue the steep climb to the cave.

The cave, when you reach it, is enormous. The vast entrance is 40m (144 feet) across, the roof 20m (66 feet) high, and the interior runs back some 80m (262 feet). A torch is essential if you want to investigate the furrowed recesses of the cave. The first intrepid explorer into the Kamáres cave in modern times was a local shepherd back in 1890. In 1904 Italian archaeologists came to the cave at the height of the first great era of Cretan excavations and discovered enormous numbers of pottery fragments, so exquisitely shaped and coloured that they were given their own designation, Kamáres ware. Further excavations by a British team in 1913 brought more antiquities to light, and the cave's significance as a centre of religious activity since earliest Minoan times was established.

The Kamáres cave had been a dwelling-place since neolithic times. From 1900 to 1700 BC, around the time that the Old Palaces were being built at Knosós, Faistós, Mália and Zákros, it was used for burials and religious ceremonies that included fertility rites.

The ceremonial vessels used here were made in the workshops at Faistós and Agía Triáda to the south. They were of two sorts: an early style of dark pottery decorated with red and white linear designs, and a far more delicate and elaborate type made later when the hand-turned potter's wheel had been supplanted by a faster and more sophisticated model. These designs are a superb artistic achievement, with floral motifs and mouldings, in beautiful flowing lines that complement the shapes of the vessels, using white, orange, yellow and black. Some of this later Kamáres ware is as thin as porcelain, and has been aptly christened "eggshell" pottery. Examples are displayed in Rooms II and III of the Irakleío Archaeological Museum.

Kamáres, at the start of the walk

There are an enormous number of caves in Crete. Well over 2,000 have been explored, but very many more must lie as yet unvisited. The limestone of which the island is largely composed has been eaten away by the chemical reaction of rainwater and by the flow of streams, riddling the interior structure of the mountains with subterranean passages and caverns to which a cave is only the front door.

CAVE CAUTION
Don't go in if you can't get out. Few caves on Crete have been fully explored, and most go back, and down, a lot further than they first appear to.

Cretans have lived, died, worshipped and hidden in these caves since earliest times. The caves have yielded a high proportion of Crete's archaeological finds. Legends have accrued thickly around them, many developing into Cretan mythology. Yet only the Díktaean cave above Psychró on the edge of the Lasíthiou Plateau (see pages 118–119) has become a big tourist attraction, undoubtedly because it is comparatively easy to reach. The Ídaean cave on Psiloreítis where Zeus was reared (see pages 178–179), and the caves of Artemis and of St John the Hermit, beyond Gouvernéto Monastery on the Akrotíri Peninsula (see pages 220–221), are visited by those prepared to walk some distance. The Kamáres cave above the Mesará plain (see pages 174–175), though famous for the exquisite Minoan pottery found there, is too much of a climb for all but the hardiest. The rest lie all but unvisited, guarding their secrets. A few are described here, but with a little local enquiry you can hunt down many more.

Birthplaces of the gods The cave of Profítas Ilías, the Prophet Elias, near Arkalokhóri, 32km (20 miles) south of Irakleío, makes a counterclaim with the Díktaean cave as the birthplace of Zeus. Here there must have been a cult of the *kourétes*, the shield-clashing guardians of the infant Zeus, for bronze sword blades have been excavated, along with miniature versions in gold, silver and bronze of the Minoans' sacred *labrys* or double-headed axe. Zeus, like the Cretan god of fertility, died and was reborn. On Mount Gioúchtas near Archánes, 15km (9 miles) south of Irakleío, a cave on the summit ridge is said to have been his deathbed.

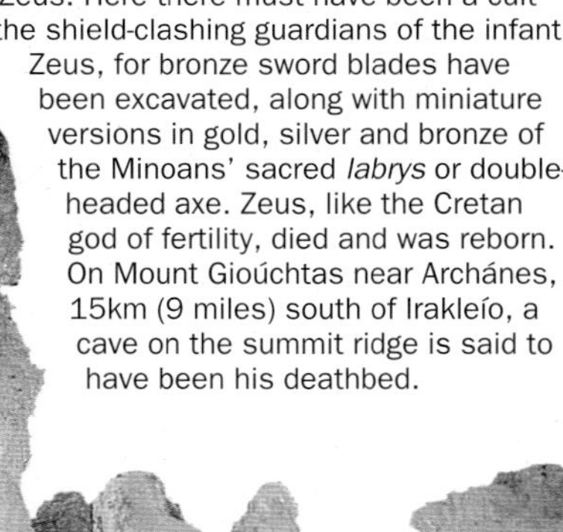

Formations that inspire legends

Caves are powerful symbols of fertility. The Ilíthia cave near Episkopí, southeast of Irakleío, has yielded several idols of pregnant women from the Stone Age. Two stalagmites have walled bases, perhaps enshrining them as phallic symbols. Ilíthia was born in the cave, daughter of Zeus's sister and wife Hera. She was also the centre of a fertility cult in a cave at Ínatos, in the beach cliff at Tsoútsouros (pages 104–105), from which came the earthenware totems of copulating couples and pregnant women now in the Irakleío Archaeological Museum.

Artemis was a fertility goddess in Graeco–Roman times, and was worshipped in the huge Skotinó cave, 5km (3 miles) southeast of Goúrnes (east of Irakleío). The cave, 160m (525 feet) deep and descending through four levels, contained three Minoan bronze statues of worshipping men, the backs of their hands pressed to their foreheads. At a later date worship was taking place in the cave of the 99 Holy Fathers at Souré, out in the wilds about 15km (9 miles) northeast of Palaióchora.

The caves were places of concealment in difficult times, but they could also be death traps. In the Melidóni cave, 4km east of Pérama, 370 Cretans were suffocated in 1824 by the smoke from brushwood fires lit at the mouth by Turkish soldiers. The previous year at the Mílatos cave, 7km (4 miles) north of Neápoli, the Turks had killed or sold into slavery 2,700 people to whom they had promised safe passage from their hiding place.

And to this day the caves attract myths, tales and legends. Did Bob Dylan once hang out with the hippie colony in the Mátala caves? If so, he has never owned up.

HONEYPOT
The unvisited, go-it-alone and do-it-yourself nature of most of Crete's caves is shown up in painful contrast by the cluster of touts, guides and donkey-drivers around the Díktaean cave's car park above Psychró. This is Crete's only popular tourist cave, a veritable honeypot that leaves all the others free.

CAVING ESSENTIALS
A torch with batteries that are not about to run out; a warm sweater; shoes with non-slip soles; a camera with flash; a ready imagination for matching fact with myth, legend and outright tall story. And always tell someone where you are going.

The cave of Agía Sofía

Cape Drapanon from Georgioúpoli

WATCHING THE POTTER
In Margarítes you are welcome to visit the potteries and watch the process. Firing time is especially enjoyable, when the little kilns puff smoke and their interiors glow white-hot.

Margarítes potter at work

▶ Georgioúpoli (Yeoryióupoli) *164A2*

Georgioúpoli—the modern spelling—sits with its back to the north coast highway, overlooking the Gulf of Almyróu. It is a relaxed resort that has grown rapidly in the last few years. There are a number of good and lively restaurants under the eucalyptus trees around the square, and hotels along the sandy beach that stretches several miles towards Réthymno. The River Almyróu empties into the sea here, and several streams flow over the sands. The village was named in honour of Prince George of Greece who had a shooting lodge here. He became High Commissioner of Crete after Turkey had been forced to grant semi-independence to the island in 1898.

▶▶ Margarítes *164C2*

Margarítes lies just north of the foothills of the Psiloreítis mountain range, and is a place where tourism has not yet seen off traditional industry. It is a pottery-making village, where you can buy anything from a tiny vase to one of the great *píthoi* or storage jars. Most of the potteries lie up the hill from the village in little stone-walled enclosures, each with a cylindrical kiln of plastered stone, crowned with a dome of firebricks. Some of the products are unashamed tourist tat, but the deep-bellied *píthoi* are direct descendants of the vessels made by the Minoans. In the village itself are colourwashed houses crowded along narrow streets, where each bend reveals a new, differently coloured perspective (sky-blue is most popular). There are handsome stone archways in the walls of the lanes, and ancient frescoes in the church of Ágios Ioánnis Prodrómos.

▶▶▶ Nída Plateau and Ídaean Cave *165D2*

The road that runs south from Anógia, climbing slowly into the foothills of the Psiloreítis mountain range, is a long and winding one. Dotted along it are the stone huts or *mitáta* of the hill shepherds. Few are now occupied, but these humble structures were home in times past to men who spent the warm months of the year up here, making yoghurt and cheese from sheep's milk. It is rugged, bare terrain. All the more surprising and welcome, therefore, when you top the final rise and look down on the Nída Plateau, a flat circle of fertile grazing land nearly 1,400m (4,592 feet) up in the heart of the mountains. Despite the modern hotel at the foot of the road to the Ídaean cave (marked Idaikí Spiliá on the map, pages 164–165), and the new ski resort not far away, this oasis in the rocky hills is still the territory of the sheep and goat herd, an elemental place covered many feet deep with snow in winter when the animals are taken down to lower and safer ground.

Beyond the hotel a rocky track, the first stage just about negotiable by car, climbs to the mouth of the Ídaean cave, a wide black slit in the side of the mountain. Archaeologists have been carrying out excavations here for many years. The cave is not open to the public, so make enquiries with the tourist office in Réthymno or Irakleío if you would like to make a visit. You will need to engage the services of a professional guide to enter the cave. The great dark chasm, 60m (197 feet) deep is filled with snow in winter, and always chilly and echoing, with stalactites dripping from the fissured roof, and mosses and ferns on the walls.

Zeus, god of gods, was raised here from babyhood, his infant yells drowned out by his guardian warriors or *kourétes* with a constant clashing of their bronze shields. It was a necessary precaution. Rhea, the mother of Zeus, had hidden her baby here to protect him from his baleful father, Kronos, who had the unsociable habit of eating his children. Cretans believed that Zeus died and was reborn each year—which is what the Minoans believed of their god of vegetation, who was also worshipped here.

The Minoans erected two enormous statues near the cave to act as landmarks for pilgrims from Faistós and Knosós. Just beside the cave mouth is an ancient stone altar, a solid slab of rock roughly shaped into a rectangle. Excavations have brought to light evidence of at least 3,000 years of worship here with finds including vases, utensils, gold jewellery, figurines and rings. Also unearthed late in the last century were a number of thick bronze ornamental shields, perhaps the core of fact around which was woven the legend of the *kourétes* and their sacred charge.

KRONOS SOAP

There is another twist to the Zeus story, making Kronos out to be a very nasty piece of work. According to this version, Kronos is the result of an incestuous union between his mother, Gaea, and her son Uranus, the ruler of the world. Kronos castrates his father/brother Uranus so that he can take over control of the world. Then he marries his own sister, Rhea, and begets five children whom he promptly eats. This is pure soap opera.

The pastures of the Nída Plateau

The atmospheric ruins of Káto Préveli

WHITE AND RED
Cretan priests and villagers take pride in keeping their churches, however remote, brilliantly whitewashed. Topped with deep scarlet domes, the little white cubes stand out sharply in the landscape, especially so when dominated by an immense backdrop of mountainside. One or two of the most-visited churches, however, look as if they have not had a lick of paint in decades. Whitewash turns grey and shabby in a very short time under the Cretan sun.

▶▶▶ Préveli Monastery *164B1*

The ruins of Káto Préveli, lower down the valley than the rest of the monastery, are closed because of the danger of falling masonry. From the roadside you can look across the decaying buildings, imagining the beauty of churches stripped almost bare during the 1821 sacking by the Turks. A tangle of ruined alleyways, flights of steps and shaded courtyards surround the abandoned church with its carved abbot's chair, stalls for 21 monks, curiously unfinished iconostasis carvings and a rather crude, half-completed icon of Christ.

Píso Préveli, by contrast, is justly famed and popular with visitors with its handsome jumble of walls, pinnacles and turrets set on a saddle of ground overlooking the sea (*Open* Jun–Oct daily 8–1 3–7; Nov-end May daily 8–3. *Admission: inexpensive*). Dating from the 16th century, the monastery was richer than Arkádiou in its heyday when, due to the unwillingness of the Cretans to allow their Turkish overlords to enjoy the fruits of their industry, the monastery benefited from gifts of olives, corn, farm produce, wine and animals. The plastered rubble walls of the monks' quarters look rather shabby, but the true glory of the monastery is the 19th-century church, which contains one of the finest examples of iconostasis in Crete. The great panel fills the end of the building, fantastically carved and filled with gilded icons. Also displayed is a golden crucifix set with diamonds, said to contain a fragment of the True Cross. Legend says that the Germans tried three times to take it to the Fatherland during the war, but the aeroplane's engines failed to start each time.

Outside the church, plaques record the gratitude of Allied soldiers from all over the world who were hidden here after the fall of Crete until they could be spirited away from nearby beaches by submarine.

In the monastery's museum there are photographs of the monks who aided resistance fighters against the Germans and the Turks. Other treasures include richly worked monastic stoles and vestments, delicate silver holy water stoups, and pilgrims' offerings of rings, necklaces and crucifixes.

PRAYER AND GUNPOWDER

In the museum at Préveli there is a black-and-white photograph, taken some time in the 19th century, of a fierce-looking brigand, swathed in belts of bullets, clutching a gun – just the sort of ruffian you wouldn't care to meet on a mountain path. A closer look reveals a crucifix around his neck. This ferocious outlaw turns out to be a 19th-century Préveli monk, Manassis Papadákis, who alternately used prayer and gunpowder as his weapons against the Turks.

Píso Préveli is a place of pilgrimage for World War II veterans

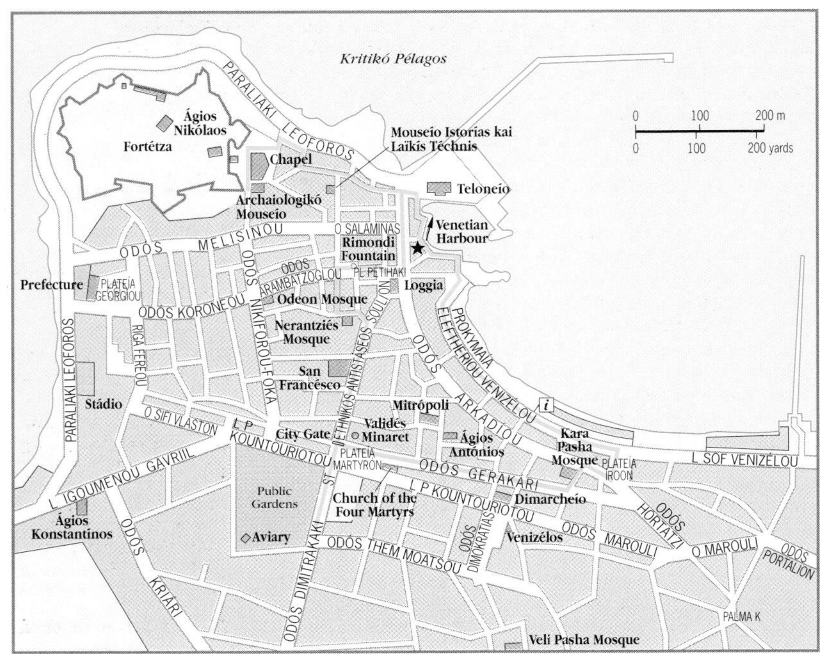

PANDELIS PREVELÁKIS
The writer Pandelís Prevelákis (1909–1986) is Crete's overlooked man of letters, perhaps because of the giant shadow cast by Níkos Kazantzákis. Prevelákis, a native of Réthymno, never achieved international status, maybe because his mixture of history, myth and fiction proved indigestible to non-Cretans. His *Tale of a Town*, written when a young man, was a big success when it was first published and is his homage to his upbringing in Réthymno. The English translation is out of print, but it is worth enquiring at secondhand bookshops.

►►► Réthymno *164B3*

Early history and the Venetians A Late Minoan settlement and the cities of both Doric Greeks and Romans underlie present-day Réthymno. Byzantium ruled the town for nearly 1,000 years. Then, early in the 13th century, four hundred years of Venetian domination began in Réthymno. These were turbulent years when pirates, most notably Khaireddin Barbarossa, the Turkish admiral and buccaneer, sacked the port, and the Venetians responded by strengthening the walls of Réthymno and building a mighty fortress. They were also civilised years of great prosperity, when the Venetians constructed breakwaters and a harbour, fine churches and houses, a splendid *loggia* where the town's aristocracy gathered, and public amenities such as fountains and gardens.

Turkish rule In 1646 Husein Pasha captured Réthymno in one swift pounce and began a 250-year period of Turkish occupation. This era of domination lasted only half as long as that of the Venetians, but was just as influential on the life of the town. The minarets and domes of Islam sprouted from the churches and public buildings of Réthymno, and the waterfront spawned a mass of cafés where the Turkish men gathered to gossip over sweet coffee and the smoke of their *narghiles.* With Muslims the dominant community, there were many cruel and bloody episodes as Christian townspeople resisted conversion to Islam. In 1821, as mainland Greeks fought their epic War of Independence against the Ottoman Empire, the Réthymno Turks reacted in fear and anger by massacring their Christian fellows.

German occupation When mainland Greek fought Turk again in 1896, the Russians took control of Réthymno as part of the agreement between the Four Great Powers. After 1913 the town, along with the rest of Crete, enjoyed a taste of independence before World War II. During May 1941 much of the Battle of Crete was fought around Réthymno. The town was one of the last to surrender, and became a centre of fierce resistance to the German occupation.

Réthymno today Réthymno is a noted seaside resort, with good bathing from the long central beach and those to either side of the town. The old town huddles below the Venetian *Fortétza,* and there are many fish restaurants and tavernas in the tall, ramshackle buildings around the curve of the Venetian harbour. Visitors, and Réthymno's smart young set, sit here to watch sun or moon glowing on the pale stone of the breakwater and the lighthouse.

Away from the waterfront you catch the living and working town of Réthymno. This is a tight maze of streets and lanes, darkly shaded between the walls of Venetian stone houses with elaborate Turkish wooden balconies. Greek Orthodox churches sport slender minarets and there are popular, crowded squares, including Plateía Pétihaki with its famous Rimondi fountain. Other streets are less frequented, such as those that run up from the harbour to the *Fortétza*, where the houses are low and cool, lacking the elegance of Venetian architecture, but exuding an individual charm. What Réthymno has to offer is a dreamy, gentle dignity that complements the warmth and spontaneity of its inhabitants.

Réthymno has always had a reputation for intellectual life, and today it boasts a Faculty of Philosophy whose students add to the lively atmosphere. In the fortnight before Lent there is a spectacular street carnival, and around Easter there is a flower festival, held in Réthymno's city park just outside the old walls. Mid-July sees the town's Wine Festival (with free sampling included in the price of a ticket), which is followed by a week of Cretan and Greek music.

LITTLE -*ÁKIS*
Much the most common ending for a Cretan surname is *-ákis*, as in Prevelákis or Kazantzákis. It is a diminutive, a fond way of saying "little"—little Prévelis, little Kázantzis—and is probably derived from the Turkish. Some Cretans say it demonstrates how fondly the Turks regarded their Cretan co-citizens; others, that the rulers used it as a way of patronising, and therefore diminishing, their subjects.

MUSIC AT THE MOSQUE
In the early evening young boys gather in the anteroom of the Mosque of Nerantziés, *lýra* and bow in hand, to be taught the first steps in playing this most Cretan of instruments.

The belltower of the castle church

Réthymno

Walk

A Venetian doorway in Réthymno

Allow about two hours. See map on page 182.

The walk starts on the waterfront, by the circular **Venetian harbour►►**, fortified between 1540 and 1570 at the same time as the city walls, after Barbarossa had sacked the town. Fix your sights on the castle, and make for it up narrow Odós Makedónias. Half-way up, turn right and then left up Odós Argyrópoulon, emerging under the walls of the **Fortétza►►►** (*Open* May–Oct, Tue–Sun 8.30–5; Nov–Apr Tue–Sun 8–7. *Admission: moderate*), a magnificent stronghold built on the promontory between 1573 and 1586. Formidable it may look, but the Turks captured it easily in 1646, and roofed in the cathedral church of Ágios Nikólaos in the centre of the fort with a dome of rough stone slabs. Various other ruinous buildings stand inside the walls. Outside the gateway a former Turkish garrison building, later a prison, houses an **Archaeological Museum►►** (Tel: 28310 54668. *Open* Tue–Sun 8.30–3. *Admission: moderate*). There is a superb view from the walls.

Return to the waterfront by way of Odós Argyrópoulon and Odós Makedónias. Sidestep from Odós Makedónias into Odós Mesolongíou. Just around the corner is the excellent **Museum of History and Folk Art►►►** (*Open* Tue–Sun 10–2. *Admission: inexpensive*). Two rooms are crammed full of traditional, everyday items from the houses of local people: clothes, tools, lyres, furniture, pottery, agricultural equipment and evocative old photographs. At the harbour the road bends sharp right. Go immediately right after the bend down Odós Arkadíou, unmarked here, to find the handsome **Loggia►►** of 1600, where Venetian nobles gathered. Tall stone columns support an old and beautiful carved timber roof. The building was derelict at the time of writing, but there are plans for renovation.

Turn right by the *loggia* into Odós K Paleológou to find the vivid and noisy **Plateía Petihaki►►** at the top. Here among the pavement tables and chatter of customers at cafés and restaurants stands the notable **Rimondi fountain►►** of 1623, with three spouting lions' heads still showing their Venetian dignity through the blurred, weather-eroded stonework. After the Turkish takeover of Réthymno in 1646 the fountain, which was named after its builder, was covered in and domed over.

The town beach in Réthymno; there are better beaches further out

Most of these additions have now fallen away.

From Plateía Petihaki continue up Odós Theod. Arambatzoglou, and turn immediately left into the narrow Odós Haril Trikoupi, with a strikingly slender and graceful minaret ahead. It was attached by the Turks to a former Venetian church, which they converted into the **Mosque of Nerantzés▶▶**, a tall, cool building, which is now a concert hall. This is one of the finest example of Ottoman architecture left on the island from the Turkish era. Turn left in front of the mosque, then right into the bustling, stimulating commerciality of **Ethníkos Antistáseos**, a street of shops that sound, smell and feel more like an open-air market. At the far end you pass through the old **city gate▶**, out of the thronged small streets of the old town onto busy Odós Gerakári.

Opposite are the **public gardens▶▶**, the setting each July for the drinking, dancing and socialising of the Réthymno Wine Festival. At other times the gardens are a haven of peace, surprisingly quiet in spite of the traffic roaring past, laid out with geometrical precision but pleasantly lush, where you can stroll under mimosa, acacia and exotic pines to the soothing sound of splashing and trickling water.

Back on Odós Gerakári, turn right towards the big modern church of the Four Martyrs, and pass the heroic **statue of Kostís Yiampoudákis▶** (see page 172), his sword half-drawn, two pistols in his belt and another in his fist—the picture of defiance. Continue along Gerakári to turn left by the old **Mosque of Kara Pasha▶** and pass through Plateiá Iróon to the seafront. Turn left here to return to the harbour.

Venetian arches hang over the streets of the old town

The old road from Réthymno to Irakleío

This leisurely 72km (45 mile) drive passes through back country, along the old high road through the hills between Réthymno and Irakleío.

If you arrive in Irakleío at the start of your holiday, you will probably be impatient to get to Réthymno or Chaniá, and will take the new road along the coast. It is a good, fast highway, but the new road does not compare with the older parallel route that runs inland and offers a slow-paced way to see the landscape and villages of the north Cretan coast with a little taste of their atmosphere. This drive, if you can plan your departure by plane or boat from Irakleío around it, makes an excellent *au revoir* to Crete, a leisurely three-hour saunter from Réthymno, or four hours from Chaniá, with plenty of time to linger over a relaxed lunch on the way.

You are sure to pass some of Crete's ubiquitous goats on this drive

See map on pages 164–165.

From **Réthymno** you drive east along the coast for 5km (3 miles) to **Plátanias** where the old road, signposted to "Mon Aradiou", turns inland from the busy new highway. Follow this and the landscape begins to rise into rolling country with olive groves. These wonderfully gnarled and stubby trees, which provide for shade sheep and goats, are often hundreds of years old. People ride along the roadside on donkeys laden with bundles of firewood, vegetables and fruit, and there are plenty of produce stalls and wayside cafés. The road winds to the east through **Loutrá** and **Áno Viran Episkopí** to come to **Pérama**, a large and thriving town that owes very little of its activity to tourism. Pérama is the commercial and social centre for this coastward country below the foothills of the Psiloreítis mountain range, which rises in great pale peaks and ridges behind the town. It is a good place to stop, stretch your legs and idle over a drink while soaking up the atmosphere of a Cretan town where life centres around local trade and conversation. It may be a bit dusty and ramshackle, but it is lively and friendly.

The road turns left to leave Pérama and enters the long east–west valley of the River Geropótamos. The lengthy range of the Kouloúkonas Mountains stands between the road and the coast. These are stark, impressive hills of pink and white rock flayed by the sun, their tops bare even of scrub. The two highest peaks of Kouloúkonas and Koutsotróulis rise to well over 900m (981 yards). The road runs through more olive groves and orchards through the outskirts of small villages where time seems to have stopped since the opening of the new road deprived them of much of the passing trade they once enjoyed.

East of **Mourtzana** you cross the river and a tributary, and come to **Apaldianá**, where the Oasis café-restaurant stands on the right of the road. This was a busy halt before the new road was built, but these days it is a genuine oasis, a refuelling and watering hole where the owner greets each customer like an old friend. This is the perfect place to spend an hour or so on the vine-shaded terrace among tubs of flowers, munching your way through well-cooked lamb cutlets, potatoes and salad, watching the bicycles, donkeys and fruit trucks trickle sleepily by between the limewashed trunks of the trees.

Beyond Apaldianá the road runs past **Doxaroú** and begins to climb over the eastward neck of the Kouloúkonas Mountains, passing through **Damásta** and curving round the base of the range to **Márathos**, whose locals claim the honey is the best in Crete. From here it passes below the 760m (2,493 foot) peak of Stróumpoulas before completing the final 5km (3 miles) into **Irakleío.**

Turkish minaret in old Réthymno

FIGHTING GRANDFATHER
In the *Report to Greco* Níkos Kazantzákis records how his grandfather went to fight the Turks in the rebellion of 1878, and was lassoed and put to death outside the monastery at Savathianá. Kazantzákis went to see the old man's skull in the monastery sanctuary "polished, anointed with sanctified oil from the watch lamp, deeply incised by sword blows".

▶ Rodákino *164A1*

Rodákino is a pleasant, quiet village on the south coast road, 27km (17 miles) east of Sfakiá. It is divided into two neighbouring but distinct settlements: Áno Rodákino perches on the mountainside, Káto Rodákino stands further down the valley. Both are backed by the steep rise of the grey mountain slope. There are little-frequented tavernas and a few rooms to rent, and there is the attraction of a rough walk down the cleft of the watercourse to the beach.

The coast here is indented with little coves and beaches with no motor access, a perfect stretch for clandestine landings. During World War II many an undercover agent came to the beach below Rodákino to be met by Cretan resistance fighters and taken away into the mountains with whatever he had brought: supplies, a wireless, gold sovereigns or simply a new set of instructions for some partisan group.

Rodákino was an important staging post for this constant, stealthy movement of men and equipment into the island, and for traffic going the other way as well. In the spring of 1944, the German commander of Crete, General Kreipe, was taken from Rodákino beach to Egypt aboard a British Royal Navy submarine, after he had been captured by partisans and force-marched across Psiloreítis. This was one of the most daring episodes of the war in Crete, and it resulted in backlash when the former commander, General Müller, returned to the island as a replacement for General Kreipe. Müller burned several villages and executed scores of Cretans in reprisal.

▶ Rodiá *165E3*

To reach the beautifully sited village of Rodiá, take the old road towards Réthymno from Irakleío and pass under the new road. After 2km (1 mile) turn right, signposted, and climb steadily for 6km (4 miles) to reach the village, tucked into the flanks of the hills 300m (984 feet) above the sea. There is a splendid view out to the east over the Gulf of Irakleío and the Cretan capital, an especially striking prospect at night, when the dark coast below twinkles with thousands of lights. The village itself is a fairly quiet place with just a couple of tavernas.

The pleasant hillside village of Rodiá

There are one or two reminders of Rodiá's more glorious past. The still impressive stonework of the façade of a big Venetian *palazzo* or country house is near the church, and outside the village, on a crag, are the ruins of a fort, the Palaiókastro, built in 1206 by the Genoese. At the time Genoa was contesting mastery of Crete with Venice, after the sack of Constantinople by the Crusaders had forced the Byzantine occupiers to leave the island. Three and a half centuries later the Palaiókastro saw the final humbling of the Venetians when they met the invading Turks here to negotiate a Venetian withdrawal from Crete. What makes Rodiá a particularly pleasant place to stop for a while is its setting in vineyards, backed by hills and far from the noise of traffic.

The carefully tended gardens of Savvathianón

►► Savvathianón Monastery *165E3*

Savvathianón Monastery is in fact a nunnery (*Open*: daily 8–1, 3–5 (later in summer). *Admission: inexpensive*), made up of a cluster of bright white buildings in a remote upland valley at the end of a rough road, signposted from Rodiá. About 20 nuns live here—a surprising number compared with the two or three inhabitants one usually finds in such isolated Cretan religious houses. The nuns pride themselves on the beauty of their gardens, the quality of their weaving and needlework, which is on sale to visitors, and the palatable flavour of their *rakí*!

The nunnery was established in Venetian times and the big Panagía church dates from 1635. A smaller and older church, Ágios Antónios, is built over the sacred grotto that inspired the founding of Savvathianón.

The imposing, four-square Savvathianón Monastery

The village of Spíli is quiet but nevertheless caters for visitors

CAR BLINDNESS
The motor car has been a great liberating agent for visitors to Crete, enabling them to go almost anywhere they want. At the same time it has drastically reduced the pleasures of discovery along the way. Driving through villages such as Spíli, one cannot possibly guess at the delights of local life and architecture that lie just off the main road. These are to be reached only on foot.

►► Spíli *164B2*

Spíli is one of those places that is very easy to miss altogether as you drive through. But this mountain village is a place where you should stop, a place which hides its character and charm around corners and up narrow alleys. Take time to wander in the maze of tangled alleyways on the hillside above the village square, where you will find donkeys tethered to fig trees, quails in cages hung on house walls, tiny courtyards shaded by orange trees, balconied houses clinging like swallows' nests to the mountainside smothered in brilliantly coloured flowers. You cannot properly appreciate Spíli until you have walked here and savoured this distinctly Cretan way of mountain living, which has remained virtually unchanged for centuries.

Down below, on the road, Spíli's village square is a delightful place with big plane trees, flowers in pots, vine leaves shifting in the breeze, and the splashing of water from a row of Venetian stone lion heads.

►►► Valsamónerou Monastery *165D1*

Only the church of Ágios Fanóurios remains of Valsamónerou Monastery, at the end of a 2km (1 mile) track from Voríza. Before you reach the monastery, ask in Voríza for the key (*to klithí*) held by the priest (*o papás*) or the custodian (*o filakás*), or you may find the gates locked when you reach the monastery entrance.

The Venetian lion's-head fountain in Spíli

The beautiful stonework round the church doorways and windows indicates that Valsamónerou was a powerful and wealthy monastery. Inside, once your eyes have adjusted to the gloom, you will see three naves, two running east–west, and a third crossing them. Here are some of the finest frescoes in Crete, glowing with startling colours, especially a vivid, ochreous yellow. These paintings date from the 14th and 15th centuries. Some say that they were worked on by El Greco and Mikhaíl

Dhamaskínos, Crete's two most celebrated painters of the late 16th century. It could just about be true, as Dhamaskínos was working at the nearby Vrontísíou Monastery in the 1580s, but there is no hard evidence. It does not matter: the paintings speak for themselves.

The faces are brown, serene and expressive, some faded, others astonishingly clear. Lines of saints stand calmly along the lower levels of the walls. Above, a 14th-century Life of the Virgin fills the ceiling. Scenes from the Life of Christ adorn the upper walls: the Three Kings follow an enormous star in a craggy landscape; St Peter walks on the water; angels hover over the stable; angels with huge wings surround a tomb; and angels with their feet drawn up support Christ on an orb of glory.

►► Vrontísíou Monastery *165D1*

Vrontísíou Monastery (*Open*: daily Apr–Oct 8–7, may be closed in the afternoon; Nov–Mar 8–3. *Admission: inexpensive*) stands in a superb location above the Zarós–Kamáres road, tucked in under steep, scrubby mountainsides alive with the sound of goat bells. Enormous plane trees shade the 15th-century Venetian fountain outside the gatehouse, where water pours from the silently howling mouths of the Four Sources of Paradise. From the monastery terrace there is a stunning view south. The church of Ágios Antónios has some finely executed 14th-century frescoes, but the chief treasures of the monastery are six icons painted in the 1580s by Mikhaíl Dhamaskínos. These were removed to the church of Agía Aikateríni in Irakleío in 1800.

The smaller and lesser-known monastery of **Ágios Nikólaos►** lies 3km (2 miles) nearer Zarós. It is a hospitable place where you may be asked to sit down and eat and drink before being shown the church with its 14th- and 15th-century frescoes.

QUITE A CLIMB
The monastery of Ágios Nikólaos has two churches, the Byzantine church that gives the monastery it's name sits just inside the walls, however, the other church, Ágios Efthimios, is a 45-minute walk into the Cretan countryside.

A guide may take you to Ágios Fanóurios at Valsamónerou Monastery

Many thousands of visitors see the Psiloreítis (Ída) mountain range from the waterfront at Irakleío, but only a few make the long and difficult trek to its highest peaks. For those with the time and stamina, the effort is repaid with a never-to-be-forgotten view over the whole of the island of Crete.

OASIS VILLAGES
The mountain villages of Crete, seen from afar amid the bright green of the fields and orchards cultivated so laboriously from the hillsides, look like wonderfully fresh, well-watered oases in a dull-coloured desert of bare rock and scrub.

For the majority of visitors to Crete, the island's four great mountain ranges are attractions admired from afar. The Thryptís Mountains towards the eastern end of the island are virtually unknown, well off the central tourist beat. Lefká Óri, the White Mountains of the west, are often braved for the Samariá Gorge, but are otherwise left untasted. The Díkti range probably sees the greatest number of visitors, thanks to the fame of the Lasíthiou Plateau and the easily accessible Díktaean cave above Psychró. The Ída Mountains, or Psiloreítis as the whole range is generally now known, see very few explorers. Yet it is the rearing peaks of Psiloreítis that one notices from the waterfront at Irakleío. It is Psiloreítis to which attaches the most celebrated incident of World War II in Crete. And it is Psiloreítis that rises to the highest peak on the island, the absolute summit of Crete.

Looking to the Ída Mountains from the Amári Valley

As a range of mountains, Psiloreítis is far less impressive than the solid block of Díkti to the east, or the extensive, craggy upthrust of Levká Óri to the west. Most of the high land of Psiloreítis, mountainous country from 1,500m (4,920 feet) to over 2,000m (6,560 feet), is confined to a lozenge-shaped area between Réthymno and Irakleío towards the centre of the island. This high land lies from northwest to southeast, and measures only about 12km (7.5 miles) by 5km (3 miles). It centres on Mount Ída, the peak also known as Psiloreítis, the highest point of Crete at 2,456m (8,056 feet).

The walk to the summit of Psiloreítis, not an especially spectacular route in itself, is nevertheless one that only a very experienced walker should undertake alone. It is usually cold at such altitudes, very often cloudy, and the excursion may involve spending a night out on the mountain. A guide on this walk is a necessity, unless you are a very well-seasoned mountain hiker. You can make arrangements in Anógia for a knowledgeable guide to accompany you from the Ídaean cave (see pages 178–179). It is a round trip of 7–8 hours to the summit. Alternatively you can ask for a guide in the village of Fourfourás in the Amári Valley on the west side of Psiloreítis (about the same time for the round trip), or in Kamáres village on the south of the range. It is a two-day round trip from the village, and about 6–8 hours' round walk from the Kamáres cave (see pages 174–175). Even better is to plan ahead and arrange a guide in advance through the Greek Mountaineering Club (EOS) office in Irakleío (tel: 2810 227609).

The reward for all this planning and physical exertion is the view from the chapel of Tímios Stavrós at the summit of Psíloreítis. There is a breathtaking panorama to all quarters of the compass and the whole island lies at your feet. Seen on a clear day at sunrise, this a prospect that will be embedded in your memory for a lifetime.

The Nída Plateau, high in the eastern flanks of Psiloreítis and reached by a long mountain road from Anógia (see pages 169–171), still sustains a summer economy of shepherding and beekeeping. A modern ski resort a short way to the west is gearing up to provide winter sports on snow-covered Psiloreítis.

As for World War II, it was across Psiloreítis that Patrick Leigh Fermor, Manólis Paterákis and other resistance members ushered the German commander of Crete, General Heinrich Kreipe, after they had captured him on 26 April 1944. For nearly two weeks the party evaded a tight German cordon around the mountains. After many close scrapes they reached the south coast at Rodákino and their rendezvous with a Royal Navy submarine.

Working the terraces on the steep slopes of the Ída Mountains

MOUNTAIN BELLS

Only one sound pervades all the Cretan mountains, the solemn, low, musical clonking of the bells strapped round the necks of goats and sheep. There is no more welcome sound to the lost walker, who can hope to find the shepherd not far away. And there is no more seductive melody to soothe one to sleep under a tree. Some shepherds claim to have their teeth set on edge if one of the bells is badly tuned. Rather a nice judgement, if it is true.

Mountain walking

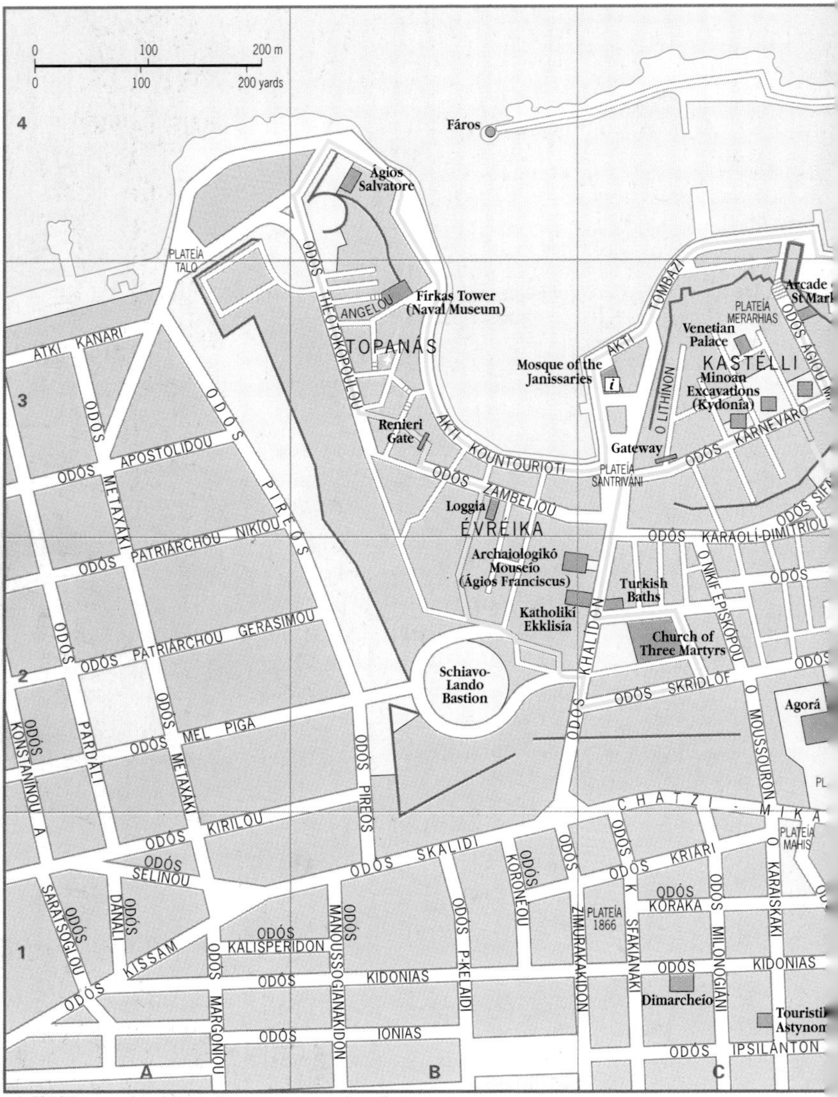

0 100 200 m
0 100 200 yards

4
3
2
1
A
B
C

Fáros
Ágios Salvatore
PLATEÍA TALO
ODÓS THEOTOKOPOULOU
ANGELOU
Fírkas Tower (Naval Museum)
TOPANÁS
AKTI KANARI
ODÓS PIREÓS
ODÓS APOSTOLIDOU
ODÓS METAXÁKI
ODÓS PATRIÁRCHOU NIKÍOU
ODÓS PATRIÁRCHOU GERASIMOU
Renieri Gate
AKTI KOUNTOURIOTI
ODÓS ZAMBELIOU
Loggia
ÉVRÉIKA
Archaiologikó Mouseío (Ágios Franciscus)
Katholikí Ekklisía
Schiavo-Lando Bastion
Mosque of the Janissaries
AKTI TOMBAZI
O LITHINON
PLATEÍA MERARHIAS
Venetian Palace
KASTÉLLI
Arcade of St Mark
ODÓS AGIOU MARKOU
Minoan Excavations (Kydonía)
ODÓS KARNEVARO
Gateway
PLATEÍA SANTRIVANI
ODÓS SIFAKA
ODÓS KARAOLÍ-DIMITRÍOU
O NIKIF EPISKÓPOU
Turkish Baths
Church of Three Martyrs
ODÓS KHALIDON
ODÓS SKRIDLÓF
O MOUSSOURON
Agorá
ODÓS KONSTANÍNOU A
ODÓS PARDALI
ODÓS MEL PIGA
ODÓS METAXÁKI
ODÓS PIREÓS
ODÓS KIRILOU
ODÓS SELINOU
ODÓS SKALIDI
CHATZI MIKALI
PLATEÍA MAHIS
O KARAISKAKI
ODÓS SARATSOGLOU
ODÓS DANALI
ODÓS KISSAM
ODÓS KALISPERIDON
ODÓS MANOUSSOGIANAKIDON
ODÓS KORONEOU
ODÓS P.KELAIDI
ZIMURAKAKIDON
PLATEÍA 1866
ODÓS K SFAKIANAKI
ODÓS KRIÁRI
ODÓS KORAKA
ODÓS MILONOGIÁNI
ODÓS KIDONIAS
Dimarcheío
Touristikí Astynomía
ODÓS MARGONÍOU
ODÓS IONIAS
ODÓS IPSILÁNTON

194

Right: Chaniá harbour
Far right: distinctive blue Chaniá ware

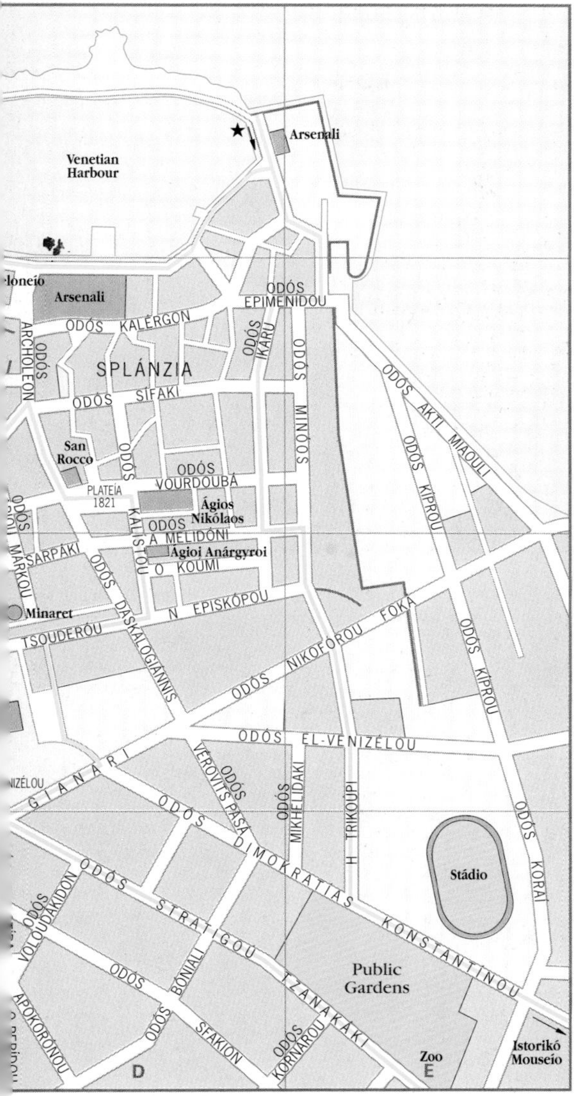

Chaniá

Venetian Harbour
Arsenali
Arsenali
ODÓS EPIMENÍDOU
ODÓS KALÉRGON
ODÓS ARCHOLEON
SPLÁNZIA
ODÓS IKÁRU
ODÓS SÍFAKI
ODÓS MINÓOS
ODÓS AKTÍ MIAOULI
ODÓS KÍPROU
San Rocco
PLATEÍA 1821
ODÓS VOURDOUBÁ
Ágios Nikólaos
ODÓS KALISTOU
ODÓS A MELIDÓNI
Ágioi Anárgyroi
O KOUMI
SARPÁKI
ODÓS DASKALOGIÁNNIS
N EPISKÓPOU
Minaret
TSOUDERÓU
ODÓS NIKOFÓROU FOKÁ
ODÓS KÍPROU
ODÓS EL-VENIZÉLOU
GIANARI
ODÓS VERÓVITS PASÁ
ODÓS MIKHELIDÁKI
H TRIKOÚPI
ODÓS DIMOKRATÍAS
Stádio
ODÓS KORAÍ
ODÓS VOLOUDAKÍDON
ODÓS STRATIGOÚ
KONSTANTÍNOU
Public Gardens
ODÓS BONIALI
TZANAKÁKI
APOKORÓNOU
ODÓS SFAKÍON
ODÓS KORNARÓU
Zoo
Istorikó Mouseío
D
E

KORALI
Snack

The view over Chaniá's rooftops to the break-water lighthouse—which seems to be shaped like a minaret

CHANIÁ Chaniá is, for most visitors, the most attractive and stimulating town in Crete. There is something special about it. Albeit somewhat crumbling and shabby in places, it has a warm, positive atmosphere allied to tremendous elegance and dignity. Chaniá owes this strong yet subtle flavour partly to its architecture: huddled streets of Byzantine, Venetian and Turkish remnants, some substantial, all of honey-coloured stone. Then there is its undisputed position as social and emotional capital of the island. Irakleío, which became the official capital in 1971, may be more prosperous, but it lacks the charm of Chaniá. And there is also its incomparable site—facing a bay and the hills of the Rodopoú peninsula, and overshadowed by the peaks of the White Mountains, which stand 2,500m (8,200 feet) above the city, snow-capped or sun-baked according to season.

PROVINCIAL CITY Chaniá wears two hats: one as a popular tourist resort, thanks to its sandy beaches and wide range of facilities, and the other dominating the life of western Crete as a self-confident city of 60,000 independent-minded inhabitants and capital of the nome of Chaniá. The town is small enough to retain an easy-going, provincial atmosphere, but is also large enough to offer something to everyone who visits. It is an ideal size to explore on foot. Across the harbour and down the maze of narrow streets and alleys are fascinating glimpses of towers, walls, minarets, domes, balconies and archways spanning at least seven or eight centuries of history. Many are in disrepair. Chaniá suffered absolute devastation at the hands of both the Turks and the Germans, and those attempting to dislodge them. The modern town built since the war has sprawled out in both directions along the coast, parts of it stark concrete, other parts eddying around splendid 19th-century houses where consuls and merchants once lived.

▶▶▶ REGION HIGHLIGHTS

Covered Market *page 205*

Evréika Quarter *page 203*

Kastélli Quarter *page 204*

Splánzia Quarter *page 204*

Topanás Quarter *page 203*

Venetian Harbour *page 202*

BEGGARS
Beggars are a feature of Cretan towns, as they are in most cities. Life can still be extremely tough for a disabled or handicapped Cretan. Hence the occasional display of infirmities and a hand outstretched for alms.

THE OLD TOWN Away from the colourful, always thronged Venetian harbour and the tight warren of streets behind it, the old town still has the little shops and workplaces of knifemakers, cobblers, leather-sellers, wood-carvers, and potters, all working and shouting among the tavernas, souvenir hawkers, restaurants and rooms to let. These thread-like alleyways and streets are always packed to the walls with strolling visitors and locals. Of Crete's four main north coast towns, Chaniá gives off the strongest savour, and the most positive and optimistic.

MINOAN TO ROMAN The city's naturally advantageous site, near the deepwater inlet of Soúda Bay, backed by fertile plains and sheltered by the White Mountains, has been occupied since neolithic times. The grandson of King Minos, the famously hospitable Kydon, founded the Minoan settlement of Kydoniá here. After earthquakes had devastated Knosós, Kydoniá became the powerbase of the Mycenaean rulers of Crete. Homer mentions the city as the place where King Menelaus lost his fleet, wrecked during its return from the siege of Troy. The Romans took Kydoniá in 67 BC, in the face of fierce resistance from the always intransigent locals. The conquerors built a theatre on the centrally placed knoll of Kastélli, and had established a flourishing city by the time Byzantine invaders ousted them in AD 352.

BYZANTINE TO VENETIAN The new rulers, using Crete as a garrison to enforce their dominance in the Aegean, fortified Kydoniá and held it for nearly 500 years. Saracens arrived from Arabia in 826, captured the city and laid it waste, completing the downfall of Kydoniá by neglect. In 961 the Byzantines returned, retook Kydoniá and occupied it until Constantinople fell to the Crusaders in 1204 and the island was sold to the Venetians. The Genoese, keen to have Crete as a cornerstone in their rivalry with Venice, took Kydoniá in 1266. But they made little headway in the rest of the island, and their capitulation in 1290 launched the city on almost 350 years of growing prosperity.

Quality gifts from the quiet back street shops?

FLOWERS FOR THE LADY?
Dark, young girls, often with a baby in the crook of one arm, prowl in and out of restaurants with buckets of tulips or roses to sell, usually targeting romantic-looking couples.

Chaniá's cathedral is set back from Khalídon

LOW LIGHTS
The medieval feel to the narrow streets of Chaniá's old quarters is due as much as anything to the lighting. Dim lamps seem to cast shadows rather than illumination.

LA CANEA Merchants, traders and other rich and confident incomers from Venice and elsewhere poured into La Canea, as the city was renamed by the Venetians. They built well and handsomely around the harbour. They walled in the knoll of Kastélli, and successfully saw off the threat from the rapacious buccaneers who cruised the Cretan coasts looking for weak points. After the determined and ruthless pirate admiral Khaireddin Barbarossa had penetrated the defences and sacked the city in the 1530s, new walls were built round the expanded town, and the harbour was fortified and provided with *arsenali,* great ship-building sheds vaulted in stone. Continued prosperity seemed assured for the wealthy trading town known as the Venice of the East. But then the wind of Islam began to blow from ancient Byzantium. The Turks, strengthening as the 17th century got under way, came storming down from the north in 1645. Yussuf Pasha and his troops made for La Canea and, after suffering many thousands of losses during a bloody siege lasting 55 days, took the city and entered on a period of dominance half as long as that of the enemy they had driven out.

TURKISH TAKEOVER Physically La Canea, or Chaniá, as it came to be known, changed little. The Turks signalled the ascendancy of Islam over Christianity by grafting domes and slender minarets onto old churches in the city and converting them to mosques. One of Chaniá's mosques still bears the name of the Janissaries, fanatically anti-Christian soldiers who had started life as Christians themselves before undergoing conversion as children. The religious and ideological balance of the city's population changed as the numbers of Muslims increased throughout the 18th century. Some were born to Turkish parents, some were willing converts, others were forcibly brought to the new allegiance.

HEADDRESS
Chaniá is the town where you will spot the greatest number of men wearing the traditional black headdress, a close-fitting woven cloth wound around the temples, with a fringe of tassels bobbing on the forehead. It gives a dashing and martial air to the wearer, almost certainly in town for the day from one of the more remote White Mountain villages, where this headgear is still standard among the older men.

The façade of the covered market—always a hive of activity inside

Gold and silver jewellery is a good buy in Chaniá

LOTTERY
On street corners, in shop doorways, around queues in public offices, on the waterfront, in cafés, along the beach—there's no part of Chaniá, or of Crete's other big towns, not penetrated by the hoarse cries of the lottery ticket sellers. A few euros in exchange for a fortune —maybe.

TURKISH TYRANTS It is tempting to cast the Turks in the rôle of bogeymen, and the Venetians as peaceful merchants. Venetians certainly perpetrated their share of atrocities against insurgent Cretans, but there is no doubt that the Turkish rulers of Chaniá outdid them. Rebellion was put down with ferocity. In 1770 the uprising under Daskaloyiánnis was crushed after the rebels reached the gates of the city, and Daskaloyiánnis was taken to Irakleío, where he was flayed alive. In the 19th century it was the same story. Chaniá was an impregnable Turkish garrison from which attacks were made on revolutionaries in the hills behind. In 1821 reports in Chaniá told of Janissaries casually shooting passersby for fun after laying bets as to whether they would drop on their faces or on their backs.

ENOSIS The mainland war of 1896 between Greece and Turkey brought new hope to the beleaguered city. In 1898 the Four Great Powers of Europe, France, Italy, Russia and Britain, took over Crete, stationing soldiers in Chaniá. The city was designated the capital of Crete, and the Turks left the island under protest. But the desire for autonomy could not be denied. Elefthérios Venizélos, the charismatic and revolutionary politician, led insurrection against the administration from his base in Chaniá, and succeeded in uniting Crete with mainland Greece in 1913.

WORLD WAR II The city saw some of the fiercest fighting of the Battle of Crete in May 1941. Allied troops, dug in around Chaniá and the Máleme airstrip to the west, shot the invaders, many of them little more than teenagers, as they parachuted in. Chaniá was bombed on 20 May, and much of the old town was burned to the ground. After the fall of Crete, resistance flourished in the city until the spring of 1945, when the Germans were driven out of Chaniá long after the rest of Crete had been recaptured.

SPOT THE LOCALS
An excellent tip, if you want to eat well-prepared Cretan food, is to assess the proportion of fair to dark heads in the restaurant. The greater the number of locals, the better and more authentic the food and wine is likely to be.

Around Chaniá

Chaniá is small enough to explore on foot, and half a day sauntering around the harbour and the old town will show you just about everything. But you are bound to be led astray, up side alleys, into shops and cafés, into conversations and offers of coffee and *rakí*. Chaniá is a convivial and friendly town, one that still has time and explanations for the inquisitive stranger. Don't expect to start in mid-morning and finish in time for lunch. It is far better to give up the whole day, lingering where the mood or conversation bids you, returning at night to the harbour to reflect on all you have seen over a meal and a few drinks.

The Venetian walls, which were built around the old town during the 16th century, now stand in only a few places, but the area covered by this walk is roughly that which they enclosed. The square of Plateía 1866 and the public gardens on Tzanakáki Street lie further south, but on a hot day you will be grateful to sit down for a few minutes under the trees in comparative peace and quiet. The sights listed on pages 202–205 are in the order in which you will encounter them on this walk.

The walk begins at the **Venetian harbour**, where all visitors to Chaniá naturally congregate. Start at the eastern or inner end of the harbour, where the breakwater joins the harbour wall. Continue around the harbour to pass on your left the **Mosque of the Janissaries**. Walk on around the curve of the waterfront to the west side of the outer harbour, to reach the **Fírkas Tower**. From the Fírkas Tower, continue round the curve of the outer harbour walkway until you come to the opening into OdósTheotokopoúlou at the top of the **Topanás quarter** of the old city.

In the old town, a fascinating maze of streets backs the harbour

Looking out to the breakwater from the Fírkas Tower

The **Renieri gate** is on your right before you reach Odós Zambelioú. Continuing down Zambelioú, you are now in the **Evréika quarter**. On your right is the **Venetian loggia**. Turn right down Odós Kondiláki to reach the **Schiavo-Lando bastion**. Turn left here to reach **Odós Khalídon**. Odós Skridlóf is directly across Khalídon.

From Skridlóf turn left down Episkopou Dorotheou, and second left to reach a little square on Khalídon with the **Church of the Trimartyre, or Three Martyrs**. Turn right down Khalídon, to reach the **Archaeological Museum**. From Plateía Santriváni, the square at the seaward end of Khalídon, turn right into Odós Karneváro and you will come to the **Kastélli quarter**. Immediately on your left, at the far end of Odós Lithínon, is the gateway to the old Venetian **archive**. The Venetian **arcade of St Mark** is on your left down Agía Márkou. Turn right up any narrow, mazy street of Kastélli to emerge on Odós Karaolí Dimitríou. Along the north side of the street stands a tall section of the Venetian city walls. Turn left and continue along Odós Sífaki, past the tourist information office, to reach Odós Daskalogiánnis.

Turn right up Daskalogiánnis and left into Plateía 1821, at the heart of the **Splánzia quarter**. From Agíoi Anárgyroi church walk south to turn right along Episkópou and on across Odós Daskalogíánnis into Tsouderoú. On your right you'll notice a slender minaret, standing in Odós Hadzimiháli Daliáni. Turn left opposite this, and walk down the east side of the **covered market**.

Turn right into Nikofórou Foká to reach the market entrance. **Plateía 1897 (**or **S Venizeloú)** is the square to the front of the main market entrance. Odós Tzanakáki runs south-east; halfway along on the left you will come to the **public gardens**. Go up Tzanakáki, over the crossroads and on into Odós Sfakianáki, and the Historical Museum is on your right.

Beyond the museum take first left, then turn left again down Odós Dimokratías past the stadium. Turn right down Trikoúpi to cross Nikofórou Foká. From here you can continue down Odós Minóos, or weave your way through Splánzia, to return to the waterfront where you started.

Landing swordfish on the quay

Mending the nets can be sociable

SOUNDS AND SMELLS
By night, music, chatter and the smell of cooking fill the streets of the old quarters. But walk into the dark, sloping residential areas, and a different Chaniá will engage your senses with a cackle of laughter or the rumble of an argument from an open window, a whiff of sewage, a waft of perfume, the crackle of a motorbike, the distant barking of a dog, and the tang of dust, sweat and sea salt.

►►► Venetian Harbour *195D4*

This protective arm of golden stone runs west, enclosing both inner and outer harbours, to end in an attractive stone lighthouse—which is an obvious target for an evening stroll. At the junction of breakwater and harbour wall stand the great stone sheds of the ***arsenali***►, built by the Venetians for the construction and maintenance of their big fleet of galleys after the sacking of the town by Barbarossa. Originally there were about 25 of these impressive buildings around the harbour, but only nine now remain. Fishing boats and yachts lie on one side of the sheltered inner harbour, and on the other is a run of restaurants and cafés, which continues unbroken all the way round the harbour. The harbour walkway is of stone, always thronged at night with visitors and Chaniá residents out on their ritual *voltá* or promenade.

►► Mosque of the Janissaries and Santriváni Square *194C3*

The Mosque of the Janissaries, domed and solid, was built in 1645 immediately after the Turks had captured Chaniá from the Venetians. Just south, at the innermost point of the harbour, is Santriváni Square, a popular meeting and eating place, named after the Turkish word for fountain, and there is a fountain, tucked away amongst the restaurants and bars. All around rise the old Venetian waterfront palaces and fine houses of the Kastélli, Evréika and Topanás quarters, many with their ground floors converted to restaurants and local craft shops.

The Mosque of the Janissaries beside the old harbour

►► Fírkas Tower 194B3

The tower's Venetian bastion houses the Maritime Museum (see pages 206–207) and hosts dancing displays. Each Sunday and on public holidays the Greek flag flies from the tower, as it did on 1 December 1913 to celebrate the union between Crete and mainland Greece.

►►► Topanás quarter 194B3

Odós Theotokopoúlou►►► is a delightful street, the backbone of Topanás, packed with old Venetian houses with wrought-iron balconies. Many have given over their ground floors to good quality craft and souvenir shops. **Odós Angelou►►** is lined with Venetian mansions. **Renieri gate►►**, at the top of Odós Zambelioú, was built in 1608 and still bears the arms of the Venetian family who paid for its construction.

DIRECT LINE
If you are self-catering in Chaniá, and have the confidence and the Greek, you can bargain directly with a fisherman for fresh fish that could have been swimming only an hour beforehand. Or try for one yourself with a line and hook off the harbour wall.

Theotokopoúlou passes through the heart of Topanás

►►► Evréika quarter 194B3

Evréika is a maze of streets with tottering, colourwashed houses, cafés and scraps of garden in sheltered courtyards. **Odós Zambelioú►►** runs between needle's-eye alleyways and flights of steps, with Venetian houses and the Venetian **Loggia►** to enjoy. The **Schiavo-Lando bastion►** is a round 16th-century tower built to defend the old city walls. **Odós Khalídon►►** is the spinal route of the Evréika quarter and the tourist heart of Chaniá, where souvenir shops stand shoulder to shoulder. **Odós Skridlóf►►►**, directly across Khalídon, is narrow and jam-packed, the traditional street of leather-sellers, where you can buy belts, bags, sandals and purses, some of which are made on the premises.

HARBOUR VIEW
One of the best of Chaniá's many breathtaking views is from the seafront promenade east of the harbour, looking west to the great Venetian wall standing massively into the sea. It is especially atmospheric at night, when the lights bring a warm, yellow-orange glow out of the stonework.

► Church of Three Martyrs (Trimartyre) *194C2*

The 19th-century Church of Trimartyre, or Three Martyrs, stands near a rather neglected, domed **Turkish bath►**. Trimartyre is the Greek Orthodox cathedral of Chaniá, an undistinguished church built by a Turk in thanksgiving for a miracle performed by the Virgin Mary that saved the life of his son. The **Archaeological Museum►►►** (see page 206) is to be found in the Venetian church of St Francis.

►►► Kastélli quarter *194C3*

The Kastélli quarter is under the knoll where the original city of Kydoniá was founded. At the entrance to Lithínon Street is the gateway to the old Venetian **archive►,** dated 1624, and a little further along the site of an ongoing excavation of Minoan **Kydoniá►**, where tombs, pavements and artefacts have been uncovered. As yet this is closed to the public. Nearby you will find the handsome Venetian **arcade of St Mark►►** and a tall section of the **Venetian city walls►►**, great pink and yellow sandstone blocks interspersed with cylindrical fragments of Greek and Roman columns.

►►► Splánzia quarter *195D3*

Plateía 1821 is the square at the centre of the Splánzia quarter, a tightly woven, characterful warren of constricted lanes and alleys full of tiny shops and half-hidden restaurants with wooden balconies and overarching upper storeys. A plaque in the middle of **Plateía 1821►►►** records the hanging of an Orthodox bishop here in that year. The plane-shaded square is surrounded by cafés where you can sit and rest, before visiting its three churches. **Ágios Nikólaos►►**, originally a monastery church, was converted into the mosque of Sultan Ibrahim under the Turks before becoming an Orthodox church in 1912—hence its twin minaret and tower. The 1630 Venetian church of **San Rocco►** stands on the north side of the square, and to the south is **Agioi Anárgyroi►►**, the Holy Poor, a 16th-century Venetian church rich in ancient icons that somehow continued to hold Orthodox services under both Venetians and Turks.

HAGGLING
The agreeable, if uncertain, Mediterranean custom of haggling over prices is not entirely dead in Chaniá's market, though more prices are fixed nowadays than hitherto. Treat this as an enjoyable game rather than with stony-faced persistence. You will probably not strike much of a bargain, but the right mixture of cheek and nonchalance will bring a smile and some extra conversation from your adversary.

CAGED BIRDS
By day, the sound of the apartment blocks is the sound of bird-song, not from wild birds, but from the sweetly singing occupants of cages hung up on the balconies.

Groceries and hardware in Splánzia

►►► The covered market *194C2*

Chaniá's covered market (Agorá. *Open* Mon, Wed, Sat 8–1, Tue, Thu, Fri 8–1, 5–8) is one of the most compelling attractions of the town. Plunge into the cool, tall, crowded and vibrant hall where all Chaniá and surrounding districts come to buy, sell and chat. The Turks had their own market, which was covered when this building was put up in 1911 closely copying the market in Marseilles—on a cruciform plan, with bays and quiet corners. The stalls, many painted with scenes of sea, land, garden and field, offer a heaped selection of just about everything that sustains everyday life: fruit, vegetables, cuts of meat, links of spicy sausages, nuts, herbs and spices, olives, myriad different cheeses and fish of every shape and size. Though you'll be invited to stop, taste and buy, there's no obligation. You can saunter around soaking up the atmosphere, then sit at a coffee stall or in one of the little restaurants tucked away at the side of the hall to enjoy the noise, smell and incessant movement. The market is one of the best free shows in Chaniá, and should not be missed. Apart from anything else, this is the best place in town to buy ingredients for your picnic.

Plateía 1897 or S Venizélou► is a wide open space roaring with traffic. Its name commemorates the year when the revolutionary committee, under the leadership of the Cretan politician and hero Elefthérios Venizélos, met on the hill of Profítas Ilías on the Akrotíri peninsula east of the city to raise the Greek flag in defiance of both Turks and the occupying Great Powers of Europe. The square is dotted with a large choice of *kafenía,* whose customers are largely locals rather than tourists, where you can sit to watch a very specifically Cretan world pass by.

►► The public gardens *195E1*

Tzanakáki Street is a modern thoroughfare lined with modern institutions. The Bank of Greece is on the corner, then Chaniá's main post office and the national telephone company headquarters, offices, clothes shops and newsagents. The street itself has none of the attractions of the old town down by the harbour, but the public gardens are a wonderfully cool, quiet and relaxed place to spend an idle hour or so, especially if you have children with you. The Turkish ruler Reouf Pasha had the gardens laid out for himself in 1870. Now there are cafés under the trees, a children's playground and a zoo with monkeys, birds and a collection of Cretan ibex. You are unlikely to see these in the wild, outside their sanctuary island of Día off Irakleío, or in the Samariá Gorge. Chaniá people come to the gardens for the folk dancing displays, evening concerts, film shows and plays put on in the open-air auditorium.

The covered market

SHADE OF ISLAM
In the public gardens you will find the elements so prized in Islamic culture and so often depicted in Islamic art: water, shade, greenery, and a harmonious and formal balance between nature and artifice.

The public gardens

Chaniá's museums put the city into context. The Archaeological Museum brings alive the ancient sites of the area; the Naval Museum illustrates the close relationship between trade and warfare; and the Historical Museum celebrates two of Chaniá's greatest heroes.

PLASTER SAINT
Mementoes of Elefthérios Venizélos are not hard to come by. Almost every souvenir shop sells plaster statuettes of the great man, myopically peering through his round-rimmed spectacles.

LABELS
In Chaniá the museums are not well labelled. Common sense, enquiry where necessary and assiduous use of guide-books will tell you most of what you want to know, but the tourist and municipal authorities are surely missing a trick, both here and in just about every other museum in Crete.

The Archaeological Museum (Khálidon 21, tel: 28210 91875. *Open* Tue–Sun 8.30–3. *Admission: moderate*). Most exhibits are from sites around Chaniá and the western end of Crete. They give a good general idea of the development of Cretan culture from the Stone Age through Minoan, Mycenaean, Greek and Roman times. Starting on the left, the first exhibits display crude pottery, both in shards and in reconstructed vessels, and tools from the late Stone Age (ca3400–2800 BC). Then come the Minoan cases, dating from ca2800 to 1200 BC. Basic zigzag and banded decoration gives way to delicate floral and swirling designs. A marine style of decoration then appears with water weeds and octopuses, before a decline from the high peak of Minoan artistry to more geometric and formal designs of giant spotted waves curled over feathery fronds and shrimp-like motifs in reds, ochres and browns.

Dorian artefacts include a toy terracotta animal on four thick wheels. Hellenic mosaic pavements feature Dionysius discovering Ariadne, and Poseidon rescuing Amymone. There is a 5th-century BC guitar-player finely drawn in red and black on a slender-necked *lekythos* or vase. Roman statuary incudes a delicately carved naked boy, and Aphrodite teaching Eros how to play the guitar.

The Maritime Museum (Akti Koundourioti, tel: 28210 91875. *Open* daily 9–4. *Admission: inexpensive*). In the Firkás Tower above the harbour, the museum houses a fascinating exhibition on the history of sea trade and naval

The Archaeological Museum is housed in a former church

warfare in and around Crete. There are ship models, photographs of 20th-century wartime episodes, including some of the World War II bombing of Allied shipping in Soúda Bay, and a collection of naval weapons ranging from early cannon to seafarers' side arms. One room has a superb collection of sea shells.

The Maritime Museum has displays on World War II

The Historical Museum, (20 Odós Sfakianáki, tel: 28210 52606. *Open* Mon–Fri 9–1. *Admission: inexpensive*). The theme here is once again "Freedom or Death", naturally epitomised by the two local heroes, Elefthérios Venizélos and Daskaloyíannis. The Venizélos room (ground floor), with its photographs of revolutionary meetings, grave portrait of the international statesman and more informal portraits of Venizélos as fiery local leader, along with his furniture and writing desk, gives a powerful impression of his importance in Crete's history, both practical and symbolic. Upstairs, Daskaloyiánnis stares nobly from his frame, the picture of defiance. Other relics of revolution include a bristling array of rebel weapons, and portraits of the leaders of some of the more famous 19th-century uprisings against the Turks.

Walk

Chaniá breakwater by night

This walk takes rather longer it than might during the daytime, owing to the roughness of the breakwater's stone surface, but it is undoubtedly one of the most rewarding that Chaniá can offer. It is best to allow nearer two hours than one, as you will certainly want to stop and admire the view from many points along the stone arm that encloses both inner and outer harbours. Watch your step—darkness adds greatly to the possibility of twisting an ankle in the dips and hollows of the great stone blocks that form the breakwater, and there are unexpected steps up and down, as well as the mooring chains and ropes of boats to step over. This is not a walk to be undertaken after one too many *rakís*!

Start from the innermost end of the inner harbour, setting your back to the Venetian *arsenali* and walking out along the narrow pathway that runs inside the length of the breakwater. It is founded on thousands of rocks tipped around the edge of the harbour in the 1530s and 1540s, when the Venetians were strengthening Chaniá in response to the violent raids of the Ottoman pirate Khaireddin Barbarossa.

Halfway along, where the breakwater thickens, stand the ruins of a fort where both Venetians and Turks would hang malefactors and rebels as a very visible example to the townspeople.

The hum of the waterfront cafés and restaurants fades to a faint murmur as you approach the slender lighthouse at the western tip of the breakwater. This was a Venetian structure rebuilt by Egyptian forces when they had stationed themselves in Chaniá between 1832 and 1840 to help their Turkish allies govern Crete after the 1821–23 uprising. From the lighthouse you can enjoy a wonderful prospect. This is not the view of the city and White Mountains that daylight shows, but the thousands of coloured lights of the waterfront reflected in the rippling water of the outer harbour. When you can tear yourself away, return along the breakwater.

The breakwater ends with an elegant lighthouse

Chaniá outskirts

The entire coastline west of Chaniá is one long sandy beach, right to the base of the Rodopoú peninsula. The first beach west of the harbour is Néa Chóra, which is sandy, with plenty of facilities, but it is often crowded and messy with litter in the high season. Kalamáki beach is a 20-minute bus ride from Chaniá, and is quieter and far less crowded, particularly if you walk on west for a few minutes. Further still you come to Agía Marína, 8km (5 miles) from Chaniá, and Platanías, 10km (6 miles) away, which has notable views to the island of Ágioi Theódoroi and the Rodopoú hills. This area has developed rapidly during the last decade with several new hotel complexes.

To the east of Chaniá there is a good beach at Kalávas on the eastern flank of the Akrotíri peninsula, and a better and more spectacular one near the big taverna at Stávros, up at the northwesternmost tip of Akrotíri.

Probably the most interesting suburb of Chaniá is out to the east, an area of elegant old villas and little, tree-shaded squares known as Khalépa also spelled Chalépa. This was where George, Prince of Greece, came to live in 1898 as High Commissioner in Crete following the departure of the Turks. The houses here, tall and solid, balconied and shuttered stand over secluded gardens, looking out over the waterfront road to the sea. It is a grand and poignant part of town.

Where Avenue Elefthérios Venizélos dips northwards to meet the sea, you pass the Hotel Doma on your right. The road forks, the airport being to the right. Turn left and you pass the walled French convent on your left, before reaching a large, immaculate house, where Prince George once lived. Opposite, on a little square, is the beautifully proportioned house where the young Venizélos lived.

GET RHYTHM
There's nothing complicated about modern disco beat, but the rhythms of the traditional music of Crete are something entirely different. Time signatures can seem impossibly complicated to the unaccustomed ear, reducing the whole tune to a formless string of notes. Watch the players' shoes as they tap out the rhythm, and follow them with your own feet or fingertips. Suddenly, and magically, it all falls into place, and order emerges out of chaos.

The modern hotels lie on the outskirts of Chaniá

REAL JAM
A welcome sight on the breakfast table at the Doma Hotel is a selection of homemade jams and marmalade. A small detail, perhaps, but one that sets up the day as no plastic square of synthetic strawberry—the norm at many establishments—can ever manage to do.

Accommodation

Chaniá has responded to its popularity with visitors by sprouting a remarkable number of rooms to rent, many of them cheap. You cannot wander in the old quarters of the town, and especially inland of the outer or western end of the harbour, without seeing literally hundreds of signs offering rooms to rent. It makes sense to book in advance during the high season, if you want something in the hotel line. Booking is also advisable between 20 and 27 May, the anniversary of the 1941 Battle of Crete.

Everyone wants a harbour view, but few want the noise that pervades the Chaniá waterfront. If you are sensitive to noise but want to rent somewhere very central, try the narrow thoroughfares of Angelou and Theotokópoulou in the Topanás quarter, and Zambelioú in Evréika, and their side lanes. You will have more peace and quiet in these old Turkish and Venetian townhouses and decent C and D (1- and 2-star) class hotels.

Further east, around the curve of the harbour, Odós Lithínon and Odós Kandanóleon in the Kastélli quarter offer more of the same; as do the tangle of streets inland of Sífaka and eastward in the line of north–south streets behind the Splánzia waterfront. The atmosphere here is shabbier but much more authentic and less touristy, with fewer restaurants and souvenir shops.

Going upmarket there is Casa Delfino, a beautifully renovated Venetian mansion with views over the town harbour. Out to the east hotels become larger, more expensive and more comfortable, particularly around the Khalépa suburb, where the Hotel Doma is the finest, though not the most expensive. This is a truly elegant building on the right of Avenue Elefthérios Venizélos, about 20 minutes' walk from the harbour. It is warm, friendly and comfortable.

The old town and harbour hotels can often be cheaper

Food and drink

It would be a pity to leave Chaniá without trying some of the local delicacies, such as roast lamb with honey glaze and the little fried cheese pies called *kalitsounia* or *tiropitákia*, filled with either sweet or salty cheese. Around Easter time these are sprinkled with mint. Sausages from the region are especially spicy. In autumn the chestnuts for which the west is famous will have ripened. Chestnut bread and cakes are very delicious. Chaniots with strong stomachs enjoy *cochlioí,* baked snails served with potatoes, helping them down with Kissámou wine.

As usual with Cretan harbour towns, Chaniá's waterfront is lined with restaurants, but these can be on the expensive side. The futher east you go, towards the inner harbour and the Kastélli and Splánzia quarters, the better the quality and the greater the number of local customers. It may be a better idea to plunge into the maze of alleyways and canyon-like streets of the old quarters behind the waterfront, and follow your nose to make your own discoveries. The *Tamám* on Zambelioú is excellent and serves Middle East-influenced food in addition to Cretan dishes. On Zambelioú, try the atmospheric Myrovolos which offers genuine Cretan and Greek dishes. Odós Kondiláki east of Zambelioú also has several good eateries. A highly recommended patisserie is *Boúgatsa* at 4 Odós Sífaki, not far from the municipal tourist office. It is named after the sweet and cheesy pastries that it sells with coffee and water from the shop next door.

There are plenty of Cretan-style fast-food stalls in Chaniá selling *souvláki* with a lick of lettuce. These are mostly around Plateía Santriváni on the harbour and at the junctions of minor with major streets near the water. Odós Daskaloyiánnis, which climbs to form the boundary between Kastélli and Splánzia, is good for cheese pie and sweet pastry shops.

For elegance and an ambience beyond the range of these, go east to Khalépa and the wide Avenue Iróon Polytechníou.

SMOKY BACON
Don't expect consideration in the matter of smoking in restaurants. Cretans smoke where and when they want to. So if you don't want the drift of tobacco smoke across your *stifádo*, choose a table outside, away from any local customers! Furthermore, smokers should note that a cigar is *to poóro*; a cigarette, confusingly, is *to tsigáro*.

Courtyard restaurants are quiet and atmospheric—and this one off Odós Zambelioú has the distinction of being in the shell of an old building

Local cheeses come in many shapes and sizes

Chaniá ware

MADE IN CRETE
In the souvenir shops you will find cheaply produced reproductions of Minoan vases, classical statues, over-excited satyrs, icons, embroidery and so on. The backstreet workshops are a better bet for a more genuine memento of Crete such as a huge-bladed knife fit for skinning a sheep (though you might have trouble with customs officers), or a pair of handmade shoes, or a hand-tooled leather purse at half the price of anything for sale in Odós Skridlóf.

Leather sandals

Shopping

In Chaniá you can buy just about everything, from *haute couture* dresses to a murderous-looking shepherd's knife. One of the city's great charms is window shopping: a dark little bootmaker's shop is next to a bridal emporium that is flanked by a trashy souvenir kiosk on one side and a blood-and-sawdust butcher on the other, while next to that is a knifemaker's and a vegetable shop that spills out onto the street.

Odós Tzanakáki, which runs southeast from the covered market, has some modern clothes shops, and everyday shops can be found in a strip just south of the west–east Skalídi–Hatzimicháli Yiannári–Nikifórou Foká road. The covered market itself is the main focus for food shopping, with a huge variety of fresh food at very reasonable prices.

Khalídon is the chief tourist trap, and the souvenirs here are no worse than anywhere else. On Odós Skridlóf, at right-angles to Khalídon, you will find leatherwork of excellent quality at reasonable prices. Leather boots are specially good value. Sfakiot shepherds buy them, and you can't get a higher recommendation than that! Handcrafted knives and tools of all kinds are well worth buying, as is the beautiful Chaniá pottery with its characteristic turquoise-blue glaze (see above), and glassware.

Local handicraft producers have banded together to form a co-operative, partly to increase their sales outlets, partly to help with quality control in a market flooded with poor products. They have an exhibition by the harbour, by the Mosque of the Janissaries, with items for sale. Better than average craft and souvenir shops are now to be found along Odós Theotokópoulou and Odós Angelou, in the Topanás quarter; on Odós Zambelioú in Evréika; and along Kaneváro in the heart of Kastélli.

Nightlife

Chaniá is a magnet for the large population of the west of Crete, as well as for thousands of tourists, and it is well provided with nightlife. There are some sophisticated cocktail and piano bars on Odós Angelou and along the waterfront going east from Plateía Santriváni: for example, the *Pallas Roof Garden*. The disco bars hereabouts are quite pricey, but they represent your best chance of catching some live dance music of the modern variety. Try *Ariádni* and the *Idaeon Andron*. The modern hotels often run their own rather stilted and soulless discos, and there are more holiday-party discos out in the beach resorts to the west.

Live traditional dance music can be found at various venues around the town and in the bigger hotels out along the beach developments to the west of town. Fly posters of traditional musicians clutching *lýra* and *bouzoúki* will appear around the streets, especially near the covered market, advertising venues. One excellent spot is the *Tzamia Krystalla* on Skalidi, with its gallery displays and live performances. One excellent spot is *Café Lyriaka* at 22 Kalergón by the waterfront, a simple little bar which really comes alive when the musicians strike up. Then the whole place and its Chaniot clientele come alive. Tables are pushed back and dancing begins, or perhaps the audience is in a mood to sit and sing along

But it is the *voltá* or traditional evening ritual of strolling and mutual sizing-up that really unites Chaniots, and the harbour is the place to be seen, either walking from the *arsenali* to the Fírkas Tower and back, or on the extremely enjoyable stroll to the lighthouse at the tip of the Venetian breakwater (see page 208). Afterwards you repair to the terraces of the restaurants along Iróon Polytechníou for a drink, well away from the hurly-burly of the harbour.

THRILLS, NOT FRILLS
Often the more elaborate the décor, the less Cretan the atmosphere. *Lyríkia* has a plain concrete floor, stark lighting and basic tables and chairs, but you don't notice these rather functional surroundings once the *lýra* and *bouzoúki* get going.

Impromptu music after dinner

COFFEE TALK
Unless you ask specifically for nescafé, the coffee you order will be the thick, fragrant brew known to the non-Greek world as Turkish coffee, but in these parts called Greek coffee, *ellenikós kafés*. It comes in a tiny cup, and the contents are usually at least one-third sludgy grounds. You'll know when you've reached them! *Métrio* is medium sweet, *glikó* is tooth-meltingly sweet, *skéto* is without sugar. A glass of water usually accompanies each cup.

NEWS FROM HOME
Visitors who crave news from home can buy foreign newspapers at many kiosks and bookshops in Chaniá. These are usually out of date by only one day, and will probably cost about three times what you would pay at home.

Practical points

Airport The airport is 13km (8 miles) east of Chaniá, on the Akrotíri peninsula. Frequent buses connect with Plateía 1866 in the centre of town, one minute's walk from the top of Khálidon. Olympic Airlines run buses to and from their office at 88 Odós Tzanakáki (tel: 28210 57701; www.olympicairlines.com). Fixed-price taxis run between the airport and Chaniá.

Banks The National Bank of Greece is on Venizélou Square (tel: 28210 28800), opposite the covered market. There are many money changers along Khálidon.

Beaches To the east: Kalávas and Stávros on Akrotíri peninsula. To the west: Kalamáki (4km/2.5 miles), Agía Marína (8km/5 miles), Platanías (10km/6 miles).

Buses Buses leave from Odós Kidoniás, at the southern end of Plateía 1866. Blue buses operate within the city; green are long-distance.

Car rental Odós Tzanakáki is the street to find the major firms. Speed Car Rentals are at 107 Khálidon (tel: 28210 45305; www.speed-rentacar.gr), and there is a selection at the airport and at the nearby resort of Agía Marína.

Car parking Basically—don't drive into the old town! There is parking around Platía 1866, and unrestricted streets south of Skalídi–Hatzimicháli Yiannári–Nikifórou Foká. The best place to park is at the western end of the harbour between Akti Kanari and the Fírkas Tower. Approach via Odós Metahaki.

Ferries To Piraeus from Soúda, 10km (6 miles) to the east. Hellenic Seaways: ticket agent is Gelasakis S.T.C., Souda Square (tel: 28210 81478; www.hellenicseaways.gr; ANEK, Platía Sophoklís Venizélos, opposite covered market (tel: 0821–27500).

Festival 20 to 27 May is Battle of Crete week. Veterans gather and the city commemorates heroism in 1941.

Foreign newspapers and books Newspapers are on sale around Chaniá at pavement kiosks and newsagents. For books try the shops in Plateía Santriváni.

Gardens There are public gardens on Odós Tzanakáki, with summer evening events and a small zoo.

Hospital General Hospital Ágios Giórgios, Mournies (tel: 28210 22000).

Layout of the city The Old City has four quarters: **Topanás**, **Evréika**, **Kastélli** and **Splánzia**. They are a mass of atmospheric, cramped and winding lanes with plenty of restaurants and cheap rooms. The main social focus of Chaniá is the Venetian harbour and breakwater—a striking semicircle of mellow Venetian architecture. Boat trips around Akrotíri peninsula into Soúda Bay; to Rodopoú peninsula and secluded beaches start from here.

Launderette Speedy Laundry on the corner of Odós Korkidi and Odós Kornonaiou (tel: 28210 88411).

Mountaineering Club (EOS) at 90 Odós Tzanakáki (tel: 28210 44647). Open 7pm–10pm.

Post office Odós Tzanakáki, opposite covered market. (tel: 28210 28444). Open Mon-Fri 7.30am–8pm, Sat 7.30am–2pm. There is also a sub-office at 10 Odós Anapauseos, open Mon-Fri 7.30am–2pm.

Police 23 Leoforos Irakleío (tel: 28210 28744).

Roman Catholic Church Plateía Mitrópolis, off Khálidon (tel: 28210 93443).

Swimming pool On the headland west of the harbour, between Fírkas Tower and Néa Chóra beach.

Taxis Mostly around Plateía 1866.

Telephones (OTE) Area code is 28210. Main OTE office is next to Post Office on Odós Tzanakáki (7am–11pm).

Tourist information National Tourist Organisation of Greece (EOT) office is at 1866 Square (tel: 28210 92943). Open 8–2. Municipal tourist office at 29 Odós Kydonias (tel: 28210 36155).

Tourist police 23 Leoforos Irakleío (tel: 28210 73333).

Tour operators Gee Dee's, 730 14 Plátanias Kydonias (tel: 28210 60411; www.Chaniá-holidays.gr); Kydonia Travel, 11–19 Odós Boniáli (tel: 28210 51660).

LOVE THE OIL
One thing you can depend on when eating out in Chaniá is the rich taste of olive oil. Anything fried or grilled, plates of chips, salads and *mezédes* will be well doused. Chaniá people like their olive oil even more than other Cretans, which is saying something. Whatever your previous attitude to this Greek water of life, you'll learn to love it, or starve!

Chaniá is small enough to allow easy orientation

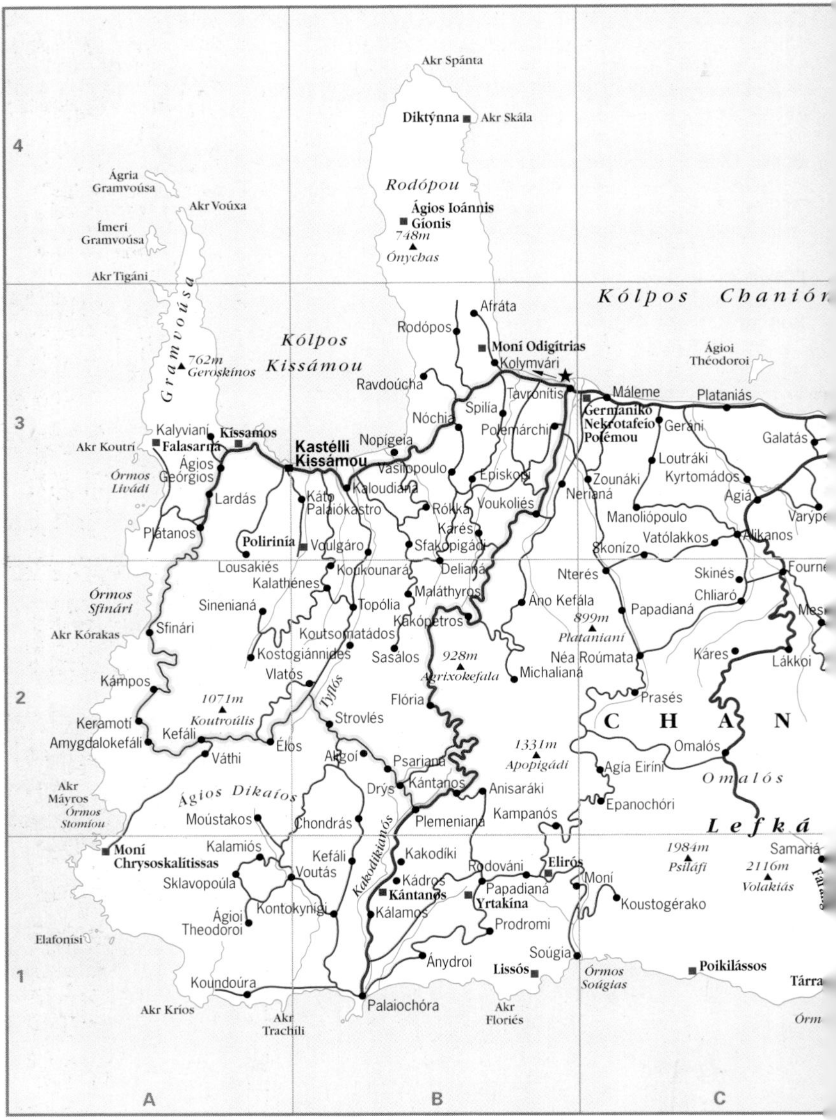

Akr Spánta
Diktýnna
Akr Skála
4
Rodópou
Ágios Ioánnis Gionis
748m
Ónychas
Ágria Gramvoúsa
Akr Voúxa
Ímeri Gramvoúsa
Akr Tigáni
Kólpos Chanión
Afráta
Rodópos
Kólpos Kissámou
Moní Odigítrias
Kolymvári
Ágioi Théodoroi
Gramvoúsa
762m
Geroskínos
Ravdoúcha
Tavronítis
Máleme
Plataniás
3
Spília
Germaniko Nekrotafeío Polémou
Nóchia
Polemárchi
Geráni
Galatás
Kalyvianí
Kíssamos
Akr Koutrí
Falasarna
Kastélli Kissámou
Nopígeia
Loutráki
Ágios Geórgios
Vasilópoulo
Zounáki
Kyrtomádos
Órmos Livádi
Episkopí
Lardás
Kaloudianá
Neriana
Agiá
Káto Palaiókastro
Rókka
Voukoliés
Manolióopoulo
Várype
Plátanos
Karés
Polirinía
Vatólakkos
Alikanos
Voulgáro
Sfakopigádi
Skonízo
Lousakiés
Koukounará
Deliana
Nterés
Skinés
Fourne
Kalathénes
Maláthyros
Órmos Sfinári
Áno Kefála
Chliaró
Sineniana
Topólia
Papadianá
Mesi
Kakópetros
899m
Sfinári
Koutsomatádos
Plataniani
Akr Kórakas
Kostogiánnides
Sasálos
928m
Néa Roúmata
Kares
Lákkoi
Agrixokefala
Michaliana
Vlatós
Kámpos
Tyflós
2
Flória
Prasés
1071m
Strovlés
Koutroúlis
C H A N
Keramotí
Kefáli
1331m
Omalós
Amygdalokefáli
Élos
Váthi
Apopigádi
Aigoí
Psariana
Agía Eiríni
Omalós
Akr Máyros
Drýs
Kántanos
Anisaráki
Órmos Stomíou
Ágios Dikaíos
Epanochóri
Moústakos
Chondrás
Plemenianá
Kampanós
Lefká
Kakodikianós
Moní Chrysoskalítissas
Kalamiós
1984m
Samariá
Kakodíki
Kefáli
Psiláfi
2116m
Rodováni
Eliros
Voutás
Moní
Sklavopoúla
Kádros
Volakiás
Kántanos
Papadiana
Koustogérako
Yrtakína
Kontokynígi
Kálamos
Ágioi Theodoroi
Prodromi
Elafonísi
Soúgia
Ánydroi
Lissós
Órmos Soúgias
Poikilássos
1
Tárra
Koundoúra
Palaiochóra
Akr Kríos
Akr Trachíli
Akr Floriés
Órm
A
B
C

Looking south over the Askífos Plateau towards the Ímpros Gorge (from the route of the drive or bus ride on pages 240–241)

The White Mountains and the West

0 5 10 15 km
0 5 10 miles

Akr Trypití
Moní Katholikó
Stavrós
Moní Agíou Ioánnou tr Gouvernétou
Akr Mavromoúri
Koumarés
Moní Agía Triáda
Órmos Kalávas
Chorafákia
Kalórrouma
Risoskloton
Kampáni
Táfos Venizélou
Profítas Ilías
Akrotíri
Pervolitsa
aniá
Korákies
Stérnes
Aróni
Polemikós Nekrotafeió Symmáchon
Soúda
Soúda
Órmos Soúdas
erivólia
Kalámi
Akr Drápano
Mourniés
Nerokoúros
Áptera
Kalýves
Pláka
Kókkino Chorió
Máláxa
Tsivarás
Drápanos
Panagía
Kontópoula
Stylos
Arménoi
Gavalochóri
Gerolákkos
Néo Chorió
Machairoi
Vámos
Kefalás
Órmos Almyroú
Kámpoi
Áyios Pándes
Káina
Likotinariá
ériso
Drakóna
Sellía
Melidóni
Kal Alexándrou
Karés
Frés
Nípos
Vrýses
Amfimallión
Georgioúpoli
Vafés
Máza
Á
Alíkampos
Asproúliani
Drámia
Límni Kourná
Kávallos
Vatoudiáris
Kournás
133m Melintaoú
2331m Griás Sorós
2218m Kástro
Kármes
1493m Trýpali
Óri
Askífou
2453m Páchnes
Ammoudároi
Pétres
Asigonía
1511m Agkathés
Myriokéfala
Ímpros
1239m
Farángi Ímprou
méli
Arádiana
Anópoli
Voúvas
Áno Rodákino
nélis
Komitádes
Foínix
Loutró
Hóra Sfákia
Patsianós
Skaloti
Fragkokástelo
Akr Moúros
Akr Kalógeros
D
E

Looking from Maláxa to the Lefká Óri

THE WHITE MOUNTAINS AND THE WEST The western end of Crete is by far the most exciting for visitors keen to get off the main tourist routes and explore. This is not to say that this region is undiscovered by tourism. Chaniá is a honeypot for visitors, and the roads of westernmost Crete are seeing a steady increase in traffic as they are being improved. But there are more hidden villages, Byzantine churches, coves, beaches, hills and valleys than in any other part of the island. And the White Mountains, the Lefká Óri, are Crete's most rugged and challenging range.

Chaniá dominates the northern part of the region; a lively, handsome old Venetian seaport which was, until quite recently, the capital of Crete and is still a place where discerning people choose to be based. Chaniá has music, dance, theatre, conversation, argument, a sense of the unpredictable, the stability of long history and the volatility of strong local temperaments. It has a confident and positive atmosphere and is a good place to wrangle with souvenir sellers by day, and sit out along the light-spangled waterfront and watch the promenaders by night.

Three peninsulas reach out towards mainland Greece from the low-lying, fertile coast. There is club-shaped Akrotíri immediately to the east of Chaniá, and the long fingers of Rodopoú and Gramvoúsa at the northwestern tip. Akrotíri offers a fine walk that connects three historic monasteries. Rodopoú and Gramvoúsa are deserted, barren places where ramblers can stretch their legs with only birds of prey, mountain flowers and sea breezes for company. From Gramvoúsa one of Crete's most spectacular roads climbs and plunges south above a coastline of little-visited bays and steep slopes, winding among villages scattered on the mountainsides, branching further south into Selínou province, the least-explored corner of Crete. There are Byzantine churches with frescoes tucked away

▶▶▶ REGION HIGHLIGHTS

Agía Triáda Monastery *page 220*

Anisaráki *page 222*

Chrysoskalítissas (Hrissoskalítissas) Monastery *page 228*

Katholikó Monastery (Akrotíri Peninsula) *page 221*

Loutró *page 235*

Omalós Plain *page 239*

Palaiochóra *pages 242–243*

Polirinía *page 244*

WEST IS BEST

The topography of Crete dictates the island's road pattern. Most roads go north to south, threading their way through the mountain ranges. All are exciting to drive, but those in the far west are by far the most spectacular, with the best coastal views and craggiest mountains—and, it might also seem to the visiting driver, the longest drops and sharpest hairpin bends.

among olive groves; capes and headlands where nobody goes; hilltop villages that give no thought to tourism; the sheltered harbours and thriving resorts of Palaiochóra and Soúgia below great mountain slopes; and the monastery of Hrissoskalítissas, where the whitewashed walls seem to grow directly out of the living rock.

Blocking the way from north to south coasts stands the truly breathtaking mountain range of Lefká Óri, the White Mountains, well named for the bare, pale limestone of which they are made. Though the summit of Mount Páchnes, the highest peak of Lefká Óri, is a couple of metres short of the top of Mount Psiloreítis, the White Mountains are more impressive than the Psiloreítis range, with a mass of close-packed, plunging valleys and slopes.

Here, as around Psiloreítis, you will hear stories of partisan refuge, revenge and struggle, not only against historic invaders, but during internecine warfare that has still not quite died out. The White Mountains are the stronghold of the famously fierce and implacable race of Cretans known as Sfakiots, people reputed to carry arms at all times and never to forget or leave unavenged an insult or injury.

A single road penetrates the heart of the White Mountains. This snaking track brings coachloads of walkers from Chaniá across the fertile plain of Omalós to the head of Crete's most famous natural feature, the 16km (10 mile) dramatic gorge of Samariá. The sheer descent into this slit in the mountains and the walk along its rocky bottom to the sea makes a trek that will rank among your most memorable, no matter where you have walked.

Southeast of the mountains crouches the Sfakiot capital of Hóra Sfákia, better known as Sfakiá, from which Allied troops were desperately evacuated after the German invasion of Crete in 1941, and from where a bus will take you on a switchback mountain road to Chaniá.

ON THE EDGE
A frequent and potentially lethal hazard of the mountain roads is the erosion of tarmac by frost, rain and weight of traffic. Chunks are bitten out of the road edge, often on the outside of a bend, directly over a drop of several hundred metres. Some, but by no means all, are outlined with a border of stones. Keep a wary eye out for these.

The Gramvoúsa Peninsula

The Venetian façade of Agía Triáda Monastery

►►► Akrotíri Peninsula *217D3*

The club-shaped peninsula of Akrotíri, some 15km (9 miles) in diameter, sticks out into the sea to the east of Chaniá, a place with a remote, island-like atmosphere.

As you enter the peninsula, signs point to the hill of Profítas Ilías, where the **tombs►►** of Elefthérios Venizélos (1864–1936, see pages 56–57) and his son Sophoklés (1896–1964) overlook a superb view of Chaniá, the sea and the White Mountains. There is no more fitting place for Venizélos, Crete's greatest revolutionary statesman, to be buried. In 1897, while Crete was under the control of the Four Great Powers (France, Italy, Russia and Britain), Venizélos convened secret meetings here that led to the raising of the Greek flag in defiance of both Turkish and European powers. The flag's standard was shot away by gunfire from the Four Powers' fleet, but the partisans continued to fly it by hand. This heroic gesture brought spontaneous applause from the naval gunners below.

The coastal village of **Stavrós►** is half an hour's drive to the north, and is not well signposted. Here you will find a perfect, circular bathing beach overshadowed by a crumpled ridge of red rock that rises abruptly from the coast, and a big taverna with a fiercely friendly owner.

From Stavrós, return to Chorafákia, bear left by the taverna and, after 5km (3 miles), turn left again to **Agía Triáda Monastery►►►** (*Open* daily 8–1, 3–7. *Admission: inexpensive*). The road sign to Agía Triáda is just *beyond* the turning, and faces the wrong way! It is not known when the monastery was founded, but some of the buildings date from the 17th century, and it presents a long Venetian façade to the road. The church across the courtyard has a wonderful iconostasis covered in faded icons and writhing with gilt foliage. A Transfiguration with the disciples being knocked head over heels is especially striking. A museum contains treasures that survived destruction by the Turks in 1821, including crucifixes, inlaid boxes, beautifully worked 17th-century silk stoles, ancient books and icons, and medals awarded to the monks for their resistance work during World War II.

CHAPEL OF THE BEAR
The little chapel at the entrance to the cave of the bear stalagmite is dedicated to Panayía Arkhoudiótissa, Our Lady of the Bear. *Arkhoúda* means bear.

ZORBA COUNTRY
If the shape of the landscape looks familiar to you when you arrive in Stavrós, it is probably a case of cinematic *déjà vu*. The rugged ridge overlooking the village was the setting for the climactic scene in the film of *Zorba the Greek*, when the pylons and cables bringing the felled trees down to the shore so dramatically collapsed—one of the classic spectacles of the cinema.

Either pick your way carefully by car, or leave it here and walk north for 5km (3 miles) up a stony road lined with beehives, among olive groves where every gnarled tree shades a goat, and up into the scrub-covered hills where **Gouvernétou Monastery►►** (*Open* daily 8–1, 3–7. *Admission: inexpensive*) stands on a saddle of ground. The Turks came here, too, in 1821, and left only a smoking ruin, burned books and icons, and a pile of murdered monks. These days Gouvernétou is a haven of peace, home to a handful of monks and an army of cats. The façade of the domed church is carved with strange, snub-nosed, howling faces. Inside is another superb iconostasis. A thick fringe of silver *taxímata* or votary plaques, stamped with the afflicted noses, eyes and limbs of the sufferers who offered them, surrounds an icon of St John.

The path to **Katholikó Monastery►►►** (a good half-hour's walk) drops from the saddle to pass a cave on the right with a chapel at the entrance and a great stalagmite in the centre. This is Artemis transformed into a bear, according to legend. Continue downhill from the cave until the path turns sharp left and you see far below you the ruined walls of Katholikó Monastery (*Open* daylight hours. *Admission: free*), astonishingly sited in a narrow ravine spanned by a bridge. This was Crete's first monastery, founded in the 11th century by the hermit St John, whose cave lies on your left as you go down. This dark, stalactite-hung hole runs 120m (131 yards) into the hillside. Pirates sacked Katholikó in the 17th century and the monks moved uphill to Gouvernétou, where their successors met their fate at the hands of the Turks.

Weathered gargoyle at Gouvernétou

Gouvernétou Monastery

WAVE DODGING
If there is a rough sea running while you wait for your boat on the waterfront at Agía Rouméli, you can while away the time watching children at their favourite game of wave-dodging. They wait until the last possible moment, then run back shrieking as the incoming wave bursts over the quay and showers them with spray.

DEADLY HOLLOW
In one of the Anisaráki olive groves stands a mighty olive tree with an enormous girth, knotted and swollen, several hundred years old and still productive, although its trunk is hollowed with age. When a file of German soldiers came through the grove in May 1941, a local man and his brother emerged from their hiding place inside the hollow tree and shot the soldiers down with their machine gun—an incident still recounted in the village.

►►► Anisaráki 216B2

The village of Anisaráki lies just off the mountain road from Kántanos to Soúgia. You might easily miss it, for Anisaráki lies sunk deep in shady olive groves, and it shows only a small portion of itself to the road. The houses are dotted around among the groves, dappled with shade as if covered with a net. The churches that are the treasure of the village are just as hard to find, standing away from the road half hidden in the olive trees. Leave your car and make your way to the village *kafeneion* to ask about access to the churches—someone will be pleased to show you around.

There are four churches in Anisaráki, each with marvellous 14th- and 15th-century Byzantine frescoes, blackened with age, in the humble shell of unremarkable stone walls. In the church of Panagía there are saints in medallion-shaped frames, a fierce red beast and a fine Archangel Michael, while outside stands a gaunt wooden gallows where an effigy of Judas is burned each Easter Saturday. In Agía Paraskeví a sorrowing Christ looks down from the roof of the apse, and there is also a wonderful Dormition of the Virgin. Christ cradles his mother's soul in the form of a baby, and a demon who has attempted to snatch the Virgin's soul holds up the severed stumps of his hands while Archangel Michael the Smiter stands by with drawn and bloody sword. More tracery and beautifully coloured figures can be found in Agía Ána. In Ágios Giórgios there is a figure of the saint riding a fine horse among other very old frescoes.

► Agía Rouméli 216C1

Agía Rouméli is spectacularly sited at the foot of the Samariá Gorge, hunched down on the shore in a cleft of the tremendous mountains that rear away skyward at its back. There are plenty of places to eat, drink and stay here, as the village is the only embarkation point to Sfakiá or Soúgia for walkers who have completed the Samariá trail. After the fall of Crete in 1941, King George of Greece was evacuated by British submarine from the beach here, after an epic journey on foot across the White

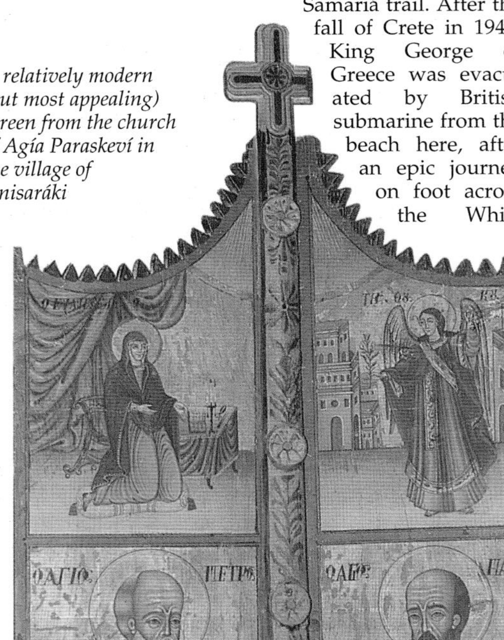

A relatively modern (but most appealing) screen from the church of Agía Paraskeví in the village of Anisaráki

Elafonísi beach, despite appearances to the contrary, can be busy in season

Mountains during which he and his party were shot at by friend and foe alike. Agía Rouméli is a stronghold of the Sfakiots, the men of these mountains who have always resisted invaders and suffered countermeasures, as witness the ruins of a Turkish fort glowering down on the village from its ridge. A mosaic pavement that probably predates Christianity surrounds the church of Panagía Rouméli, which itself stands over a temple to Apollo built when the ancient settlement of Tárra flourished here.

▶▶▶ Chrysoskalítissas Monastery *216A1*

See Hrissoskalítissas Monastery, page 228.

▶ Elafonísi *216A1*

Out of season it is well worth making the rough and dusty 6.5km (4 miles) journey south from Chrysoskalítissas Monastery to the beach and island of Elafonísi. The beach is of white sand, and you can wade out to the low-backed island just offshore to enjoy perfect peace and quiet—if you can put out of mind the events of Easter 1824, when Turkish soldiers slaughtered 850 women and children who were hiding on the island to escape being transported to the harems of Constantinople. The beach, which only a few years ago was an undiscovered paradise, is now a magnet in high season, crammed with jeeps, buses and motorbikes, while more unsightly concrete apartments and tavernas are springing up inland.

▶ Élos *216A2*

Élos lies sprawled along a series of S-bends on the mountain road to Palaiochóra, a couple of tavernas, a string of whitewashed houses smothered in flowers, all overshadowed and enclosed by olive groves and tall chestnut trees. The village is famous for its chestnut festival in October, when locals and visitors mingle to eat chestnut cake and sweets, and to dance.

SIGN OF INTENT

Bundles of metal rods poking up from flat concrete roofs are a feature of modern Cretan buldings, both finished and unfinished. They are left in place as a sign of the builder's intention to add a further storey, if and when finances allow, and to escape a government tax on finished buildings.

Several remote islands lie around the coast of western Crete with their own myths and legends. Most poignant is Gávdos, where the nymph Calypso entertained Odysseus for seven years, and died of grief when he left. Today it is still inhabited, but only just.

GRAMVOUSA REBELS
The Khainides, a resistance group dedicated to the overthrow of the Turks, used Ímeri Gramvoúsa as one of their island bases during the early years of the Turkish occupation, before the Turks themselves got hold of the fort and turned its impregnable position to their own advantage.

Paximádia and Gávdos The two islands of Paximádia lie 12km (7 miles) offshore in the Gulf of Mesará. *Paximádia* is the name for the hard-baked bread, and from the shore near Tympáki, the islands do look like two hunks of bread.

Forty kilometres (25 miles) west of the Paximádia islands, and about the same distance off the south coast, Gávdos lies isolated in the Libyan Sea. This is the southernmost landfall in Europe, a lonely chunk of rock with only the neighbouring islet of Gavdopoúla for company. A few families still cling on here, in increasing hardship despite television and radio communications. The silence, the isolation, the hard beauty of the island, the threadbare but genuine hospitality of the islanders, make a visit to Gávdos an unforgettable experience. There are a few rooms to rent, a post office and a handful of shops. A ferry plies from Palaiochóra and Soúgia all year round, and from Sfakiá from mid May to early October. Exact timings depend on the state of the weather, and the journey can take several hours. It can also be rough.

The island rises to a ridge nearly 400m (1,312 feet) high that falls to an inaccessible west coast. From the landing place a rough road leads inland to the village of Kastrí, with shops and post office, and the remains of a prison in which political dissenters were held between the world wars. Here the road splits, running north to the settlement of Ámpelos and south to Vatsianá. Beyond Vatsianá you can get down to the excellent, unfrequented beach of Tripití. Beyond Ámpelos there is another beach on the north coast, and just east of this lies sheltered Sarakíniko beach, which is about half an hour's walk from the landing place and is where most of the few visitors go. There are one or two basic tavernas.

The shallow waters of Gramvoúsa beach and peninsula

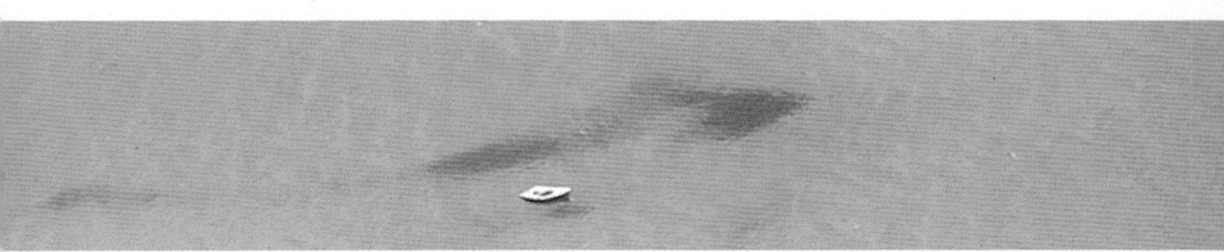

Gávdos has been inhabited since neolithic times. Odysseus is said to have stayed seven years here, under the spell of the nymph Calypso. The ship carrying St Paul was blown past the "island of Clauda" on its way to shipwreck on Malta. When the Byzantines first ruled in Crete there were 8,000 people living on Gávdos. Today there are fewer than 50. The young people have almost all gone, unwilling to face life with no mains electricity, an uncertain water supply, no job prospects, the hard labour of shepherding, and a complete absence of bright lights and fun. Mainland girls don't want to marry Gávdos boys and be obliged to live here. The crumbling, abandoned houses, the uncultivated land, the sparse supplies in the shops are all witness to a population coming to the end of its tether. Maybe modern tourism will save the day and open a new and entirely different chapter in the life of Gávdos...

Other islands Towards the top of Crete's western coast the islet of Petálidha lies off the ancient port of Falásarna. From here the Gramvoúsa peninsula points north. Off the west side of its outermost tip lie the twin islands of Ágria (wild) Gramvoúsa to the north, and closer in Iméri (tame) Gramvoúsa, with a Venetian fortress clinging dramatically to its 157m (515 foot) crest. The island saw exciting times as a Venetian stronghold against the Turks, as a Turkish stronghold against the pirates, and as a pirate stronghold against all comers. In summer tour boats leave from Kastélli Kissámou.

Off Plataniás, west of Chaniá, lies Ágioi Theódoroi, a whale turned to stone for trying to swallow Crete. You can see the cavernous mouth from the shore. It is now an *égagros* reserve. And, finally, we reach Soúda Bay in the shelter of the Akrotíri peninsula. Three nymphs lie in the narrows, having had their wings pulled off after losing a musical contest with the Muses. You may recognise them as the White Islands.

WEATHER WARNING
An essential precaution when planning a trip to Gávdos out of the summer season is to check on the local weather forecast in Palaióchora or Sfakiá, and with the boat skipper. If the weather blows up you may be marooned on the island for a day or two, so don't make hard and fast plans that depend on getting back to Crete at any particular time. By the same token, it is wise to take enough essential supplies, for example medical items, to cater for an unexpectedly prolonged stay.

Cyclists take a rest from the heat of the day to look across towards Gramvoúsa island

The dome of Gonías Monastery

►► Falasarná 216A3

A turning on the main coast road at Plátanos (see page 243) leads in 8km (5 miles) to a beautiful, curved beach of white sand, south of the headland of Cape Koutrí, where lie the remains of Falasarná (open access), once the port for the ancient Graeco–Roman city of Polirinía in the hills behind. An artificial channel runs north from where the cape curves out from the shore to reach a wide, shallow bowl in the rock, now levelled. This was Falasarná's man-made harbour, with towers and fortified walls to guard it. The city's acropolis stood on the back of the headland, with a temple to Artemis near the present day church of Ágios Géorgios. The city lay between the acropolis and the harbour, and remains include house walls, water cisterns, tombs and a mysterious, square lump of stone.

Subterranean geological upheavals stranded the old port by raising it some 6m (20 feet) above the sea. They also caused the earthquake that destroyed Falasarná.

PRIESTS AND PEOPLE
A short distance from Gonías Monastery is the Orthodox Academy of Crete, frequently visited by priests of all ages, on retreat or taking part in seminars or courses. The Cretan priest is part of his local community to a greater extent than in most European countries, which may explain why he is on the whole well regarded, and why young men are continuing to enter the priesthood here.

►► Gonías Monastery 216B3

Panagía Gonías Monastery (*Open* daily May–Oct 8–1, 3–7; Nov–Apr 8–1, 3–5), or Moní Odigítrias (Our Lady Guide), lies just north of Kolymvári village at the southeastern corner of the Rodopoú peninsula. It was founded in 1618, and the Turks battered but did not destroy it when they invaded Crete in 1645. In the 1866 rebellion Gonías Monastery had its precious library burned, but many icons and other treasures survived. The monks who show you around point out with pride the Turkish cannonballs still embedded in the walls.

The church has fine icons, and a particular treasure in the museum is a moving figure of Christ Crucified, painted by one of Crete's most celebrated 17th-century artists, Konstantínos Palaiókapas.

With more than 1,500 species of wildflowers to its name, Crete is surely one of the finest botanical destinations in the Mediterranean region. It is also one of the most dramatic. In spring visitors can discover flower-filled fields and scrub-covered hillsides set against backdrops ranging from towering mountain peaks to rugged coastal cliffs and gorges.

To make the most of Crete's wildflowers, your visit needs to coincide with the brief Mediterranean spring. Although an amazing range of flowers can be found from early February to June, April and May are the best months. By the time the tourist hordes arrive in summer, prolonged hot, dry weather has caused many species to wither and die back. For most plants, the growing season occurs during the winter months, when the weather is mild and comparatively wet.

Over the five millennia that the island has been settled, human activities such as forest clearance, fire damage and intense grazing by sheep and goats have had a marked effect upon the Cretan landscape and flora. Today, few areas could be described as entirely undisturbed and only the flora of inaccessible mountain peaks and gorges is likely to have remained unaffected.

The fact that most Cretan habitats are man-influenced in no way detracts from the stunning array of flowers found there. For botanists from northern Europe the initial shock comes when seeing farmland. In spring, even the most humble of arable fields or olive groves is certain to be a riot of colour, comprising species such as field and corn marigolds, crown daisy, pheasant's-eye and several fumitory and poppy species. Interestingly, many of these plants were once considered arable "weeds" elsewhere in Europe but now have become rare or extinct in their former range as a result modern agriculture's reliance on herbicides.

For floral diversity rather than sheer abundance the most rewarding of Crete's habitats are those where scrub predominates. Maquis—the term applied to areas dominated by tall shrubs and small trees—harbours strawberry tree, tree heather, lavenders, cistuses and spiny broom. Areas where poor soils and centuries of overgrazing have created a more open landscape of low growing and often spiny plants are termed phrygana. Here, among the sheep-pruned clumps of spiny burnet and cistuses, look for tender species such as turban buttercup, Cretan cyclamen and crown anemone. For many, Crete's crowning glory is its orchids. From late February onwards, the appearance of the appropriately named giant orchid is followed by a succession of species with intriguing names such as bug orchid, Cretan spider orchid and violet limodore. At the height of the orchid season—April and May—the keen-eyed observer should have little difficulty in finding 20 species or more, with representatives in almost all Crete's habitats.

FLORAL DIVERSITY
The key to Crete's extraordinary floral diversity lies in its complex geology. Bedrocks ranging from limestone and dolomite to sandstone and chalk encourage plants with all manner of soil-type affiliations. The island's vast altitudinal range also plays a part, and flowering plants can be found growing from sea level to the highest mountain peaks. Roughly ten percent of Crete's plants are endemic—they are found nowhere else in the world. This can be attributed in part to the island's isolation. Many are found in the mountains and include such delights as the blue-flowered *Chionodoxa cretica* and the tiny *Crocus sieberi*. However, some occur right down to sea level, arguably the best known being Cretan ebony.

Eastern yellow bee orchid

WILD GREENS
The wild greens (*horta*) found all across hillsides in Crete is part of the reason why the Cretan diet has been proved to be one of the healthiest in the world. These are packed with the vitamins, minerals and antioxidants we are all told are good for us.

►► Hóra Sfákia 217D1

The capital of the Sfakiot region of Crete lies handsomely around its harbour and is best seen from the sea at sunset when the flat-roofed white houses and hotels glow pink amid their palm trees, a scene that owes more to Africa than to Europe. These days Hóra Sfákia (sometimes spelt Chóra or Khóra Sfákion, but usually called Sfakiá) is primarily a well-provided ferry port with a good number of tavernas, hotels and rooms to rent. Boats leave from here for Agía Rouméli, Agía Galíni and the island of Gávdos. Scars of the bombing that flattened much of the town during World War II have healed, though elderly local people still recount their memories of when Sfakiá was the evacuation point for retreating Allied troops.

►►► Hrissoskalítissas Monastery 216A1

The road to Hrissoskalítissas (or Chrysoskalítissas in modern spelling. *Open* daily 8–5) has now been tarmacked and new building is beginning to appear nearby—none of it particularly easy on the eye. One hopes that none of this will threaten the peace of this unique old nunnery.

Chrysoskalítissas Monastery

Chrysoskalítissas perches high on a rocky bluff above a dusty plain on the extreme southwestern tip of the island, its blue barrel roof a landmark for many miles around. The nunnery takes its name, Golden Steps, from the 90 steps that wind up to the church and buildings on the rock. One of them is golden, but only those who have passed a sinless day can see which one. Chrysoskalítissas was founded in the 13th century, in a cave. The present-day church dates from the 19th century, and has nothing remarkable to see inside.

After visiting the monastery, take the road south through the hills to the beach at Elafonísi (see page 223) when you can enjoy a fish dinner at one of several tavernas, but beware as it gets pretty crowded with local families on summer weekends.

Father Nektários of Chrysoskalítissas

The aftermath of the successful German airborne invasion of Crete in May 1941 was a state of near-chaos among the Allied troops as the German forces advanced on their positions all along the north coast of the island.

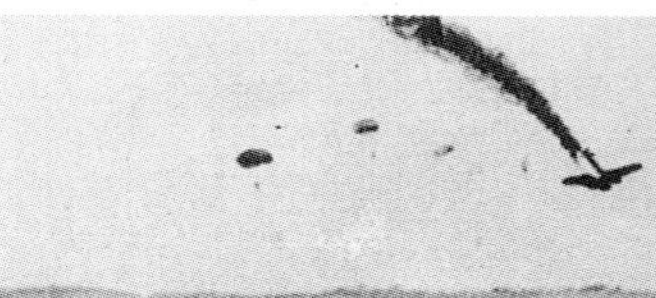

There were New Zealanders and British at Maléme and Chaniá, Australians and Greeks at Réthymno, and Australians, Greeks and British at Irakleío. Crete's road system was primitive in those days, and soon it was choked with retreating men, all moving excruciatingly slowly and under constant threat of air attack.

Réthymno held out for ten days before surrendering on 31 May, and those who could not make good their escape were captured. The British navy evacuated thousands from the end of the mole at Irakleío, taking them off by night and sustaining terrible losses during the dash for the North African coast through the dawn. But the Navy could not get into Soúda Bay to evacuate Chaniá. The troops here faced a hellish march across the White Mountains down to Sfakiá on the south coast, while brave and determined rearguard actions by separate forces of Greek and Australian soldiers held off the pursuing Germans. About 12,000 men retreated across the plain of Askífos and descended the narrow gorge of Ímvros (see page 231) in single file to reach Sfakiá.

There were appalling scenes at Sfakiá as exhausted and anxious soldiers jammed the little port. By day they had to find cover from the German bombers; for three nights running they queued to embark on Royal Navy ships, whose own crews were tired and apprehensive. Again there were heavy losses as the ships ran the gauntlet of the Libyan Sea. A fourth night of evacuation was judged to be too dangerous, and thousands of troops were left behind to be captured or to hide in the hope of escape, including all the Greeks who had fought with the Allies, and the Australians who had been holding up the pursuit.

WAUGH'S WAR
Evelyn Waugh landed at Soúda Bay in the last week of May 1941, when the Battle of Crete had already swung decisively in favour of the Germans. As brigade intelligence officer with a commando force, Waugh experienced at first hand the confusion, panic and desperation of the Allied evacuation, events he later recounted with characteristically cool insight and cynicism in *Officers and Gentlemen*, the second book in his *Sword of Honour* trilogy.

Invading paratroopers during the Battle of Crete

ÍMPROS MISTS
Fine weather cannot be guaranteed in Ímpros. Mountain and sea mists sometimes join forces to swathe the village, and at such times the *kafenía* are crowded with the elderly men who have been driven indoors from their customary roadside seats.

PRACTICAL PARTRIDGES
Town-dwellers hang caged songbirds on their balconies to exorcise the traffic noise with sweet singing. Villagers hang caged partridges outside their houses, fattening in captivity, with a rather more practical end in mind.

► Ímpros 217E1

The village stands at the top of the Ímpros Gorge (see opposite). Downgoing walkers are dropped here from buses, and those upcoming restore themselves at the end of their walk with pancakes, cheese and coffee at the big café on the main Hóra Sfakiá-to-Chaniá road.

Ímpros stands on a high plateau, surrounded by peaks of naked, dry rock. It is not a picturesque village, as many of the houses were rebuilt after the war with utility bricks, but it is an extremely characterful one, particularly if you can summon enough Greek to open a conversation with elderly Sfakiots, who have vivid memories of wartime and strong opinions on the modern world.

► Kádros 216B1

The village is reached by a left turn off the main Kántanos-to-Palaiochóra road, a couple of kilometres south of Kakodíki. At the top end of Kádros, 100m (109 yards) past a *kafeníon*, a path on the right leads to the Byzantine church of the Nativity of the Virgin, with late 14th-century frescoes still sharp in colour and detail.

►► Kakodíki 216B1

Two churches near the village are worth seeing. Enquire at any house or in the *kafeníon* for the keys. Next to the modern Agía Triáda church (up a track to the left off the Kántanos-to-Palaiochóra road) is the Byzantine church of Mikhaíl Arkhángelos (Archangel Michael). The old iconostasis is beautifully carved in wood, and the frescoes were painted early in the 14th century. Further along the track, the church of Ágios Isódoros perches on a hill from which flow springs with celebrated healing power. The frescoes are finely drawn, though some have been defaced, reportedly by the Turks. They include scenes of the torture and death of St Isódhoros, who is shown being dragged by galloping horses—although the saint seems quite serene about it all.

14th-century church near Kakodíki

Ímpros Gorge

The scrubby slopes of Ímpros Gorge

The Ímpros Gorge is not quite as spectacular as the Samariá Gorge, but it is generally uncrowded and peaceful. This is a walk you can take at your own pace.It is best if you do it early in the morning, when there are very few people about, the light is clear, and fresh smells waft from the gorge vegetation and trees. The recommended direction is uphill (inland): the slope is gradual, there is the sense of penetrating the mountains, and Ímpros village at the top has an excellent, if unprepossessing café on the main road, where you can catch a bus to Sfakiá or north across the island to Chaniá. Wear strong boots and allow at least two-and-a-half hours for the 8km (5 mile) walk.

To reach the start, leave Sfakiá on the Chaniá road, and after 3km (2 miles) turn off right through Komitádes. The Ímpros Gorge runs inland on your left, 0.5km (0.25 miles) beyond the village, from a sharp right-hand bend in the road. The boulder-strewn river bed runs between bluffs dotted with caveholes, and becomes a torrent in winter.

The rock walls soon narrow and rise, a chink in the mountainside studded with prickly bushes, figs and stunted trees among thick-leaved, water-retaining plants. The going underfoot is easy, a crunchy progress on small pebbles. Small birds call from the scrub and you might see blue rock thrushes, which breed in the gorge. You will also hear the deep musical donging of goat bells, and catch glimpses of the goats cropping grass and plants on ledges and scree slopes that look impossible to access.

The path becomes paved with rock, and the cleft narrows further, well shaded by cypresses and pines. At the narrowest point the gorge is just a sinuous slit of black-banded rock, several hundred metres high, whose walls you can span with outstretched arms: a deep, echoing chamber that is very exciting to wriggle through. Near the top the sides widen, diminish and fall away, and you walk out of the gorge into Ímpros village and the mountains.

Kántanos war memorial

KAFENÍON HEROES
The pictures that hang on the walls of the village *kafeníon* show how strongly elderly Cretans identify with the past—both national and personal. Heroes such as Venizélos and Daskaloyiánnis are flanked by fierce old *palikáres*, their sashes bristling with weapons; brides in 1920s wedding dresses; handsome young men in breeches, clutching rifles, ca1941. Compare these last with the *kafeníon* owner and his cronies—they may well be one and the same.

►► Kántanos *216B1*

Kántanos lies 20km (12 miles) north of Palaiochóra, on the main road to the northern coast and Chaniá. The village is the capital of the eparchy or province of Selínou, the most southwesterly and probably the least-visited corner of Crete. Warm winds pushing in from the sea give the province the highest rainfall in the island, and Kántanos lies in the centre of a lush and fertile area dedicated to fruit- and chestnut-growing. Olives are the keynote here. Kántanos and its many satellite villages are half hidden in the leafy, drab green groves.

The village takes its name from the ancient settlement of Kantánou, which stood just to the south and was wrecked by an earthquake. Kántanos became a well-to-do Venetian town, and later a Turkish military centre after many of the inhabitants had converted to Islam. Down the centuries, the Kántanos area has seen many ferocious battles as invaders have tried to subdue Cretan resistance. None has been as well documented, nor strikes quite such a grim note for present-day visitors, as the events of 23–25 May 1941, when Kántanos was virtually removed from the map in what Cretans speak of as one of the worst acts of reprisal of World War II.

After the capture on 20 May of the airfield at Máleme, German motor cycle troops were sent south to prevent Allied reinforcements from landing at Palaiochóra. On 23 May they were attacked in a narrow gorge to the north of Kántanos by a force of partisans, men and women from Kántanos and the surrounding villages. The Cretans managed to kill 25 soldiers in the ambush, and withdrew to their villages. Two days later, bombers arrived over Kántanos and flattened most of the village, killing many of the inhabitants. By the time German troops reached Kántanos, several days later, the partisans had retreated into the hills. The soldiers killed everyone they could find, and then reduced the village to rubble.

Almost every house in Kántanos today postdates this event. In front of the church in the centre of the village is a commemorative garden, with marble plaques recording the destruction: "Here stood Kántanos. In retaliation for the bestial murder of German parachutists and pioneers by armed men and women of the area, Kántanos was destroyed 3.6.41, razed to the ground, never to be built again." Reading this stark declaration, one wonders why the Cretans should refer to their own resistance fighters as "bestial murderers". But remember that these plaques are replicas of those erected by the Germans in the ruins of Kántanos. And the village did rise again.

► Káres *216C2*

Káres lies along the main Sfakiá-to-Chaniá road. Its main attraction lies in the view from the road above, looking down across the village's white houses and tremendous red and white church, crowned with turrets and dome, and away over the green and brown fields of the plateau beyond. All this is dominated by the pale grey heights of the White Mountains at their eastern edge.

► Kastélli Kissámou *216A3*

Kastélli Kissámou is the main centre for this remote northwestern tip of Crete. It lies along the coast road from Chaniá and commands a superb view out across the bay to the flanking peninsulas of Rodopoú and Gramvoúsa. Kastélli Kissámou served the inland Doric settlement of Polirinía (see page 244) as a port, and the Venetians fortified it as a prosperous harbour. But little remains of these former glories. It is a working town nowadays, concentrating on its local businesses and market. Its few streets are busy and not much concerned with tourism, though there are a number of hotels and rooms to rent, along with a sprinkling of tavernas around the little fishing harbour. This is a good place to base yourself for a couple of days if you are sated with the tourist clamour of the coastal strip and would like to taste an unaffected, bustling Cretan town.

KAFENÍON COWARDS

Many visitors are reluctant to enter the *kafeníon*, especially the outwardly drab and nondescript version most often found in the villages. Reasons for this hesitancy vary: people may be unsure of their welcome as outsiders, handicapped by their lack of Greek, or simply unnerved by the stern stares of the customers. Be bold: a cheerful *khérete!* (hello!) will put everyone at ease. And if you want to talk, someone will probably have enough English (or German, French or even Italian in the east) to start up a conversation.

The main square of Kastélli Kissámou

Flowers adorn Kefáli's balconies

► Kefáli *216A2*

Kefáli commands one of the best views on the straggling road that skirts the western coast of Crete. The village perches 5km (3 miles) inland in the neck of a tree-lined valley that plunges away to a distant sea 430m (1,410 feet) below. It is a rough, stony road in and out of the village, but worth pursuing as the church at Kefáli contains some of the best Byzantine frescoes in the area. Park your car near the *kafeníon* on the right as you come from the north, and follow a narrow path beside the *kafeníon* to drop through back alleys past tiny farmyards full of turkeys and

Early frescoes (and more modern votive offerings) at Kefáli

cockerels. The path winds around, but eventually brings you out in front of the little church of Metamórphosis tou Sotírou, Transfiguration of the Saviour. In the dark interior, haloes and eyes stand out startlingly from the faded figures in the early 14th-century frescoes, painted at a time when the resurgence of Byzantine culture under Crete's Venetian rulers was at its height. Visitors have scratched their graffiti dates in the walls; some date back 400 years.

►► Khóra Sfákion *217D1*

See Hóra Sfákia, page 228.

►►► Khrisoskalítissas Monastery *216A1*

See Hrissoskalítissas Monastery, page 228.

► Lákkoi *216C2*

The village is spectacularly sited high in the mountains, where the road from Chaniá begins to zigzag and climb in earnest up the northwestern face of the White Mountains towards the Omalós Plateau and the top of the Samariá Gorge. Lákkoi is famous for honey and for clear, aromatic mountain air. In winter it can be cut off for weeks by snow, but in summer a cool breeze blows over the red-roofed village. The road snakes tightly among the tavernas, but the best view is over to the left as you climb from Chaniá, a really breathtaking prospect of the red-and-white village church with its dome and minaret perched on the back of a knife-edge ridge, above dizzying drops to the valley below.

Ten kilometres (6 miles) towards Omalós there is a roadside plaque commemorating the death on 28 February 1944 of Sergeant Dudley Perkins, known to Cretan resistance fighters as Captain Vasilí, a formidable New Zealander who commanded a band of partisans in Sélinos province, in the southwestern corner of the island. Vasilí was said to have killed more than a hundred Germans. The ambush that killed him here robbed the partisans of a genuine hero, honoured as few others by the coveted title of Captain.

►►► Loutró *217D1*

A very rough path connects Loutró with Sfakiá and the outside world but it is by boat that most people come. The charming coastal village retains the character of a place very much closed in upon itself, clinging to the theatre of rock at its back. There are tavernas and rooms to rent on the harbour that is Loutró's shopfront, looking to the ferries from Sfakiá to the east and Agía Rouméli to the west for its continued existence as a quiet holiday town under the slopes of the mountains. Viewing Loutró from the sea, you appreciate its past importance as a safe natural harbour, the only one on the entire southern coastline of Crete.

The ancient port of Foinix lay just beyond the western headland of the bay of Loutró. The Alexandrine ship carrying the captive St Paul to Rome could not enter this "haven of Crete", and was driven on to shipwreck on Malta. Some Roman, early Byzantine and Venetian ruins stand on the headland, as does the church of Sotíros Khristós, Christ the Saviour, which contains 14th and 15th-century frescoes.

Foinix was the port for **Anópoli►**, once a powerful Roman town, which sits high in the mountains above Loutró. There is a statue here to a famous son of Anópoli, the Cretan resistance hero Daskaloyiánnis (see page 57).

NICKNAMES

For reasons of security, and because foreign names sat awkwardly on Cretan tongues, Allied resistance workers in Crete were given nicknames. Sergeant Dudley Perkins was Vasilí and other well-known foreign agents were Yánni (Jack Smith-Hughes), Aléko (Xan Fielding), Aléxis (Sandy Rendel), Manóli (Geoffrey Barkham), O Tom (Tom Dunbabin), and Micháli (Patrick Leigh Fermor, later to become a celebrated and brilliant writer). Their exploits, along with those of the Cretan resistance fighters, have been detailed by George Psychoundákis in his notable book *The Cretan Runner.*

ILL WIND

"And because the haven [*Kaloí Liménes*] was not commodious to winter in, the more part advised to depart thence also, if by any means they might attain to Phenice, and there to winter; which is an haven of Crete, and lieth towards the south west and north west.
And when the south wind blew softly, supposing that they had obtained their purpose, loosing thence, they sailed close by Crete.
But not long after there arose against it a tempestuous wind, called Euroclydon.
And when the ship was caught, and could not bear up into the wind, we let her drive."

(Acts of the Apostles, XXVII, 12–15)

The White Mountains (or Levká Óri) are aptly named. The bare limestone heights stand out in pale magnificence against the blue Cretan sky in summer, truly white with snow in winter. The impression is always of bareness and whiteness, a pure and hard landscape, stunningly wild and beautiful from the sea or from the rooftops of Chaniá.

SFAKIOTS ACCORDING TO SITEIA
Natives of Siteía at the other end of the island, styled as soft, easy-living and easy-going easterners, regard the Sfakiots with a mixture of admiration, fear and incomprehension. A Siteía man, explaining the characteristics of Sfakiots, employs three gestures: a ferocious scowl, a clenched fist and a rotary movement of the index finger of his free hand against the side of his head.

Looking into the Samariá Gorge from Omalós

This is the wildest country in Crete, the harshest and most primitive, where traditional ways of life and thinking cling on tenaciously in the face of tourism and the modern world. In spite of the fame of these mountains, they see far fewer visitors than the Psiloreítis and Díkti ranges further east. This is partly due to the distance from Irakleío, partly to poor road access, partly to the lack of holiday towns around the extremely beautiful but forbiddingly steep coastline. Sfakiá is not much more than a small ferry port, and only Soúgia at the end of long and winding roads offers anything in the way of modern holidaymaking facilities.

The southern coastline of the White Mountains is the most isolated and dramatic in Crete. Between Soúgia and Sfakiá it soars from lonely beaches and craggy headlands up to the heights of the mountains, smooth slopes that tower magnificently above the Libyan Sea. This is 25km (15.5 miles) of roadless, virtually unvisited coastal splendour. Wandering by foot along the White Mountain coast, you can follow dirt roads and tracks inland to remote villages. For example, in Ágios Ioánnis above the harbour village of Loútro, or Prodrómi northeast of Palaiochóra, you will be welcomed as a rare visitor. There are historic sites where no crowds gather such as the Hellenistic city-state of Lisós west of Soúgia (see page 251) and that of Arádiana beyond Anópolis. There is Poikilássos, 6km (4 miles) east of Soúgia and really accessible only by boat, and the ancient port of Foinix west of Loutró, which the ship carrying St Paul could not enter during the voyage that saw the saint wrecked on Malta (see page 235).

The central massif of the White Mountains is the most extensive spread of high ground in Crete, a great barrier of mountains rising to the peak of the range, Mount Páchnes. At 2,453m (8,046 feet), Páchnes is just three metres lower than Psiloreítis, but even more difficult to reach. You can climb north from the tourist pavilion at the head of the Samariá Gorge for about an hour and a half to reach the climbers' hut of the Greek Mountaineering Club (EOS, tel: 2810 227609), and continue from there on up to the central peaks. A guide is essential. Great gorges cut down to the coast through these mountains. There is celebrated Samariá, of course (see page 248–249), Ímpros (see page 231) and others. There are flat, fertile plateaux, too, such as Omalós (see page 239) and Askífos on the Chaniá-to-Sfakiá road.

The entire area is best known for its status as the homeland of the Sfakiots, proud and warlike people who have feuded, raided and resisted down the centuries. Daskaloyíannis, ill-fated leader of their 1770 revolt against the Turks (see page 57), stands as their symbol. But there is a dark, doomed side to their ferocity and independence of spirit. Feuding depopulated many Sfakiot villages during the 18th and 19th centuries, and their resistance during World War II exacted a fearful price in reprisals. Old men in the White Mountains still dress in full Sfakiot fig, though these days without a pistol in their belts (not a visible one, at any rate). This anecdote is telling: the Sfakiots went to God to complain that they had nothing but rocks to live on, only to be reminded that the rest of Crete was cultivating its softer lands just for them.

SHEPHERDS' STICKS
Shepherds' sticks are not used solely as crooks. Bags can be hung from them for ease of carrying, and edible plants can be dug up with their points. They can clean boots, thrash dogs, point out paths to strangers, support ruminative chins, poke fires, and kill scorpions. The best are made of iron-hard *prinos* wood. Many have sinuous or spiral shafts. When not in use, they are usually carried horizontally across the shoulders. A good stick, the shepherds say, is the best friend you can take to the mountains.

The road from Káres to Sfakiá winds over the plateau towards the Ímpros Gorge

FACE OF A FIGHTER
In George Psychoundákis's book *The Cretan Runner* there is a photograph of Manólis Paterákis in his sheepfold near Kostoyérako, taken after the war. Paterákis wears a wartime battledress blouse. From under his beret an eagle's nose arches between deep-set eyes. The cheeks are hollowed and lean. The mouth, though smiling in the picture, can easily be imagined setting into a thin line of determination. It is a formidable face.

► Maláxa *217D3*

Maláxa sits about 8km (5 miles) southeast of Chaniá on the old mountain road that snakes inland to Néo Chorió and Vrýses. There are excellent views of the north coast from the town and an atmosphere of genuine Cretan life. Cavers and hikers find the village a useful base for exploring the local caves of Achlodolakki and Grai because it has a range of tavernas serving excellent local food.

► Máleme *216C3*

Máleme lies 16km (10 miles) west of Chaniá, along the coast road. Ribbon development has rather spoiled this low-lying coastline, though the road is fringed with thickets of a giant reed (*Arundo donax*) and orange groves that hide some of the recent building. To the right of the road on the western edge of Máleme lies the airfield, now operated by the Greek Air Force, that became the hinge on which turned the fortunes of the Battle of Crete in 1941. When German paratroopers began landing on 20 May, a force of New Zealanders under Lieutenant-Colonel Andrew was in possession of Hill 107, overlooking Máleme airfield, an essential target for capture by the invaders. A lack of information led to the New Zealanders pulling back from the hill, which the Germans then occupied the following day. Now their airborne troops could land, though under fire and sustaining casualties. Within

The German War Cemetery at Máleme

three days, German fighter planes were operating from Máleme, reinforcements were arriving, and the long Allied retreat to Sfakiá was under way.

Inland of the coast road is the immaculately tended **German War Cemetery►►** where nearly 4,500 young men lie, most of them killed as they parachuted in. An irony of fate saw two of the resistance's toughest fighters, George Psychoundákis and Manólis Paterákis, eventually appointed to take care of these graves. The setting could not be more poignant as the site overlooks the waters over which the young parachutists were carried before their fatal final jump. Casualties were heavier than expected, so much so that the Germans never used large-scale parachute drops again during World War II.

Hikers in the narrowest part of the Samaria Gorge

►► Moní Odigítrias *216B3*

See Gonías Monastery, page 226.

►►► Omalós Plain *216C2*

Coming south from Chaniá to reach the head of the Samariá Gorge, the road passes across the dead flat Omalós Plain, 1100m (3,608 feet) above sea level, a roughly triangular, fertile saucer of ground set among mountains that climb to 1830m (6,002 feet) and more. In spring the area is blanketed with acres of wild flowers, including many species of anemones, plus butterflies and insects. The pollen imparts a wonderful flavour to the local honey. Villagers stay up here each summer, tending herds of goats and sheep (which have startling red fleeces coloured by the earth) and cultivating patches of corn, potatoes, vegetables and tomatoes. In winter the plain is deep in snow, and in spring the meltwater sluices down off the hills, bringing with it the minerals that make the Omalós soil so fertile, flooding the plain until it drains down a huge plug-hole of a cavern.

In spite of the rash of ugly and out-of-place hotels and tavernas that have recently appeared along the road, Omalós has a remote feel to it. The plain, at the meeting point of many tracks across the White Mountains, was always a centre of insurgence against the island's foreign rulers. The little church to the left of the road was built by Khátzi Mihális Yiánnaris, a celebrated 19th-century leader of resistance against the Turks, in gratitude for his deliverance from a Chaniá prison. His simple house stands nearby, not far from his grave.

CRETAN SAUSAGES
Cretan sausages or *loukánika* are generally delicious. You can have them *kapnistá* (smoked), *vrastá* (boiled) or *tiganitá* (fried). The spicy, heavy taste and slightly greasy texture are always good, and can be a gourmet's delight if you strike lucky.

PLAIN COLD
Omalós can be genuinely cold, particularly at night and towards winter. Frosts and snow are commonplace here. Bring warm clothing with you if you intend to explore the plateau between September and May.

Grazing the Omalós Plain

Drive or bus ride

Sfakiá to Chaniá

After the thrills of the walk down the Samariá Gorge and the sea journey from Agía Rouméli to Sfakiá, the prospect of returning by road to Chaniá may seem rather tame. But the mountain road from Sfakiá to Chaniá is no mundane route. This is one of the most exciting drives in Crete, and as you may well be in a coach you will also be able to take full advantage of the views—if you can stay awake for the 70km (43 miles)...

The Sfakiá to Chaniá road is a wriggling succession of climbs, falls and hairpin bends, with superb views of the White Mountains and their high plateaux. The route is well engineered and maintained all the way, but will provide nervous drivers with some hair-raising moments. Not for nothing are the bends of the road liberally studded with the tin shrines that mark the sites of fatal accidents. Samariá Gorge walkers are spared the responsibilities of driving as they enjoy the dramatic scenery from the bus that plies regularly between Sfakiá and Chaniá—definitely the best way to travel this road.

Three kilometres east of **Sfakiá** the upward twists begin as the road doubles back and forth, climbing beside the open lips of the **Ímpros Gorge** (see page 231) on your right. Turn and look out of the back window of the bus for a wonderful view over the Libyan Sea to the distant island of Gávdos 37km (23 miles) offshore. The road climbs through thick stands of pine trees to reach **Ímpros** village (see page 230), a straggle of houses and tavernas surrounded by hills, a place famous for the resistance of its inhabitants to the many invaders of Crete down the centuries.

Now the driver's work begins in earnest as he hauls the bus round one sharp bend after another. As oncoming cars appear with Cretan suddenness and *insouciance* in the middle of the road, he swings over to place the bus wheels with cool precision right on the margin of tarmac and empty space, with tremendous drops below.

As the only good route providing north–south communication in this part of the island, the Sfakiá-to-Chaniá road has played a full part in Cretan history. Older people in the villages along the road well remember the interminable lines of exhausted Allied soldiers limping down to Sfakiá during the Battle of Crete, some of them lucky enough to be taken off by the ships of the Royal Navy, others destined to be left to face capture or months in hiding among the mountains or in the monasteries.

Roadside shrines may mark the sites of past accidents—so speed past them at your peril

At the highest point of the route, 760m (2,493 feet) above sea level, the villages of **Petrés**, **Ammoudári** and **Káres** (see page 233) lie along the road, above the little square fields of the Askífos Plateau, over which the grey heads of the mountains rise on all sides. The tightly packed houses are sheltered by fig and walnut trees. The bus squeezes round the hairpin bends between the buildings, the conductor standing amidships to talk the driver through the obstacle course. Free and frequent use of the blaring bus horn clears the road, eventually. Cretan bus drivers eschew reverse gear, with even greater tenacity than their car-driving cousins.

The road begins to fall from the summit, passing the Karés ravine where Turkish troops twice came to bloody grief at the hands of Sfakiot

Bees forage amongst the scented herbs on the hillsides

fighters: firstly, in 1821 during Crete's armed rising in sympathy with the mainland Greeks' War of Independence; and, secondly, in 1866 as an act of retribution against the Turkish soldiers who had captured Arkádiou Monastery and sparked the famous and terrible gunpowder explosion that claimed around 2,000 lives.

The bus makes its way down to flatter country, to reach the plane trees, waterfalls and slow-paced streets of **Vrýses**, a pleasantly shady village famous for yoghurt and honey. Soon the excitement of the mountains is behind you as the bus driver swings west on to the coast road and puts his foot down for Chaniá.

FRESH ORANGE
The orange juice served for breakfast by many Cretan hotels and cafés is a noxious sweet liquid tasting more of chemicals and saccharine than of fruit. If you want the real thing, freshly squeezed, ask for *portokáli limós*, and you could back up your request with a mime if the waiter looks baffled.

►►► Palaiochóra *216B1*

Winding down out of the mountains on the main road from Chaniá, you approach Palaiochóra (also Paleochóra), the Bride of the Libyan Sea, down a long avenue of eucalyptus trees, a rather splendid introduction to what is one of the most welcoming and enjoyable small resorts on Crete's south coast. Palaiochóra sits on the neck of a small peninsula that juts out a few miles east of the most southwesterly point in Crete, and if you come during the day there is still the feeling of having arrived in a bit of a backwater. The magnificent mountains behind, and the headlands east and west that hem in the town, contribute to this cosy, enclosed atmosphere.

At night along Venizélos Street, the main street of Palaiochóra, things come alive. Venizélos and the other small streets that run down to the sea are crammed with tavernas, bars and discos, nothing horribly loud or down-market, but with a real sense of fun and colour that is impossible to resist. Dionysos Restaurant on Venizélos Street offers a good choice of menu. Go into the kitchen and pick what looks good. Pork *stifádo* with a creamed aubergine salad is a speciality, but there are many other dishes. If you are sitting outside a restaurant, make sure you check which establishment actually owns the table. In Palaiochóra, as in many Cretan tourist resorts, the tables are jammed so close together along the pavements that only different patterns of tablecloth tell you which table belongs to which restaurant.

Caravella restaurant in Palaiochóra

The rooftops of Palaiochóra

There are plenty of hotels in Palaiochóra and also inexpensive rooms to rent. Breakfast at one of the cafés along the east beach is a memorable experience if you are there in time to see the sun rise over the mountains and bay. This beach is pebbly, and not as popular or crowded as the wide beach of clean sand to the west of the promontory, crowning which is a square of golden stone walls, all that remains of Palaiochóra's Venetian fort. The fort was built in 1282 after a serious uprising in western Crete. Rebels captured it briefly 50 years later, and the admiral-corsair Khaireddin Barbarossa destroyed it in 1579, before the Turks finally took it after a siege in 1653. Nowadays there is nothing to see at the fort by way of architectural or historic interest, but the view over roofs, domes, peach- and cream-coloured walls and flowery courtyards to the mountains and sea is reason enough to climb up here. Inland from the fort is a maze of tiny streets bright with flowers and shaded with eucalyptus and tamarisk. Seaward of the fort on the very tip of the southern promontory is a sparkling new marina which attracts sailors from around the Greek islands.

Palaiochóra's waterfront is the departure point for boats for Soúgia, Agía Rouméli and Sfakiá, as well as to Elafonísi beach round to the northwest. A quay on the east side is where the little fishing boats, pointed fore and aft, land their catch.

PARTY LINE
The noisiest public telephone in Crete might well be the one in the middle of Venizélos Street, especially at night when Palaiochóra's unofficial street party takes place.

► Plátanos *216A3*

Plátanos is 11km (7 miles) west of Kastélli-Kissámou on the coast road, and is a good place to stop and refresh yourself before the long and spectacular climb across the mountainous coastline of western Crete. The Milos taverna by the watermill is well known for its good food and peaceful atmosphere. It is worth taking the side road to wind past the village houses where old men and women sit out under the trees, enjoying a wonderful view over the roofs of Plátanos towards the roll and rise of the back of the Rodopoú Peninsula. In the village church there are faded frescoes and some icons.

SHOWER SHOCKS
The fittings of Cretan hotel showers may come as a shock to the unforewarned. There are rarely curtains; the user is trusted to direct the water in the general area of the tiles. A plastic stool is often provided so that you can make your ablutions while seated, a notion that makes up in pleasurable decadence what it lacks in practicality. Soap and towels are the responsibility of the guest in smaller establishments, so look before you lather!

The remains of Polirinía

GET A HAT
The sunhat is not only a practical necessity when walking in the Cretan countryside. It is also a powerful aid to social intercourse for gentlemen explorers. Raising the hat while intoning greetings always brings a smile from older people, not of hilarity, as might be the case elsewhere, but of genuine pleasure at the courtesy.

▶▶▶ Polirinía *216A3*

Polirinía (open access) lies back in the hills 7km (4 miles) south of the coastal town of Kastélli Kissámou, which served as its port in Doric and Roman times over 2,000 years ago. A signposted road turns off left from the eastern end of Kastélli Kissámou's bypass to reach the village of Áno Palaiókastro. You have to leave your car here if you want to walk up through the paved streets of the village to the top of the rise. A track on the left brings you up to the Church of the 99 Martyrs, built largely of slabs retrieved from the ruins of the former settlement and fortifications, some with their inscriptions still legible. The church's foundations are four times as old as the building itself. These great cut stone blocks originally supported a Hellenistic temple built around 400 BC.

The city was founded around the 6th century BC on this naturally fortified site, guarded by steep slopes falling to sheer rock walls and deep gullies. In Hellenistic times Polirinía was fortified with massive walls strengthened by curved bastions. After the Roman invasion of 67 BC the city entered a new phase of prosperity, was refortified and given a water supply by way of Hadrian's Aqueduct. The rock-cut channels can still be seen, along with cisterns, walls, houses cut into the rock one above another, and tombs hewn into the hillsides and rock faces.

After the Roman occupation the city entered a period of decline, and may have been sacked when the Saracens invaded Crete in AD 824. But after the Byzantine reconquest in AD 961 Polirinía was revived, and when the Venetians took control of the island in 1204 they refortified parts of the site, notably the acropolis. A path, waymarked in red, leads from the church to the ruins of walls and towers on the peak, and a really spectacular prospect of both north and south coasts.

Walk

Rodopoú Peninsula

This is a long, tough and lonely walk in the mountainous interior of the uninhabited Rodopoú Peninsula, with an isolated church as the focal point. The twin peninsulas of Rodopoú and Gramvoúsa frame the Gulf of Kissámou at the northwest corner of Crete. There is very little shade on this challenging circular walk on Rodopoú, so it is vital to take a sunhat, sun cream and plenty of water. Wear strong boots, too, as the track is very rough. Allow a minimum of six hours for this strenuous 19km (12 miles) walk.

Rodopoú is a quiet, end-of-the-road village where you will get both stares and greetings. Park by the church and walk north, climbing all the time on a stony road that gets steadily rougher, twisting through a baked, dusty landscape of grey rock, stubby prickly plants and dry gullies, everything absolutely quiet and lonely. The ridges and small peaks of Rodopoú rise all around, with birds of prey floating above. Nobody lives out here. You have the long peninsula entirely to yourself.

After 6.5km (4 miles) the road forks by an old cistern, where a faded sign in Greek points left to Ágios Ioánnis. You can see the way from here. The track changes colour from grey to red, and passes through a narrow gap between blasted-out bluffs in the hillside, to emerge with a breathtaking view over the rocky, crumpled western face of Rodopoú.

Far below, tiny against the immense backdrop of coast and sea, lies the little red-roofed church of Ayíos Ioánnis Yíonis, set among trees in a walled plot. Tens of thousands of people come here each 28 and 29 August, to witness the christening of boy babies with the name of the church's patron saint.

Make your zigzagging way down to the church, and then continue on a rough and steep footpath. Fork left after 4km (2.5 miles) to return over the neck of the peninsula to the village of Rodopoú and what will be a very welcome cold drink.

Rodopoú village

The independent explorer, studying the map, will soon pick out the monasteries of the island. Where the roads shrink away to dirt tracks, descend to a lonely coast or come to a full stop among the mountains, there you are likely to see the prefix Moní next to a church symbol and almost certainly a good distance from the nearest settlement.

MONASTERY RULES
Monasteries vary in the behaviour they request from visitors. There is often a ban on shorts, and photography may be prohibited inside the church. Many of the monasteries close for a few hours in the middle of the day, and visitors are asked not to pry into the living quarters of the monks or nuns.

FORTHRIGHT ABBOT
Abbots may be religious leaders but in Crete they have also been a powerful political force, especially during times of strife from invasion by the Turks to invasion by the Germans during WWII. Many stood strong and refused to acquiesce, and this strong leadership continues in monasteries in the present day.

Monastic life is not easy

A life of prayer and contemplation demands isolatation and Crete is not short of this. Once the island supported over 1,000 monasteries. Most were very small and fewer than 50 survived the first years of Turkish rule. Today only 40 monasteries of the Greek Orthodox faith are active, some enjoying prosperity, some in decline.

The monastic tradition in Crete is a long one. Well over 1,000 years ago hermits were established in caves and remote corners of the island. There was an upsurge in the prosperity of the monasteries in Venetian times, with many Roman Catholic settlers converting to the Orthodox faith and building splendid churches and monastic quarters. A good number of these still stand. Arkádhiou, in the hills southeast of Réthymno, is probably the best known, thanks to the bloody drama of its history (see page 171). Others include the famous resistance centre of Préveli on the south coast (see page 180–181), Agía Triáda on the Akrotíri peninsula (see page 220), Tóplou in the northeast (see pages 154–155) and Vrontísíou on the southern flanks of Psiloreítis (see page 191).

These monasteries can face the future with a degree of confidence. Fewer young Cretan men and women are opting for a monastic way of life, as is the case all over the Christian world, but establishments such as Préveli and Agía Triáda, with a steady stream of coach-borne visitors and museums filled with superb treasures of art and craft, have more than a toehold on financial security. The Abbot of Toploú is reputed to be one of the richest men in Crete, if holdings of land can be taken to represent actual wealth. The leasing of a vast tract of monastery land for the building of Cavo Sidero resort has ensured financial security for the community into the next century.

However, monastic life is seldom easy. It is at the more obscure and less frequently visited monasteries, tucked away on the coast or in the hills, that the inmates have a struggle to keep going. Such monks and nuns work hard. They can be seen in their working habits, sleeves rolled up, digging and cleaning or dressed in finely embroidered robes making their religious observances. Looking at the sparse furnishings and the simple meals of monasteries like Faneroménis near Gourniá (see page 162), Árvi on the coast south of Áno Viánnos (see page 127) or Kápsa to the east of Ierápetra (see page 156), one sees evidence of a spartan lifestyle, lived in the hard light of reality. This is very much in accordance with Greek Orthodoxy, particularly the Cretan variety, demonstrating close practical links between the religious and the secular.

When it has come to fighting and resistance, the monasteries of Crete have never kept themselves above the strife. Arkádiou and Préveli were both eager to conceal and help evacuate Allied soldiers after the Battle of Crete. Abbot Silignákis of Toploú was shot, along with a dozen of his monks, after the discovery of a radio transmitter in the monastery. Agía Triáda was destroyed by the Turks in 1821, and Gonías Monastery on the Rodopoú peninsula (see page 226) proudly shows off the Turkish cannon balls embedded in its walls.

Vidhianís on the Lasíthiou Plateau, ancient Katholikó on Akrotíri (see page 221) and Káto Préveli stand empty. But remote Koudoumá on the south coast (see page 89) and Chrysoskalítissas (Hrissoskalítissas) in the west (see page 228), still dispense warm hospitality, and would never dream of turning away a benighted stranger.

SHAKEN, NOT STIRRED
Cretan monks, living as they do in some of the remotest parts of the island, face a long drive over rough roads whenever they venture abroad from their monasteries. Poverty and bad road conditions usually conspire to make early wrecks of the monastery's transport. It is not rare to see a couple of monks bouncing around in the cab of an old pick-up truck more dilapidated than any local farmer would tolerate.

Women, too, choose a contemplative life

Walk

Samariá Gorge

This is the classic adventure walk of Crete, and one that hundreds of thousands of visitors take every year. It is a 16km (10 mile) linear hike in scenery unequalled anywhere else in Crete for sheer drama, and is a walk you will remember as long as you live. Five or six hours should see you through the Samariá Gorge in comfort, and leave time to dawdle along the way—as you will certainly want to do. There are no particular difficulties, provided you wear strong boots and take the staple water, sunhat and suncream, but a few points must be borne in mind. There are no escape routes from the gorge. Once you have begun, you have either to see it through or return, painfully, to the

Starting the descent into the gorge

start. From Agía Rouméli at the foot of the gorge there are no roads out, so you must decide either to stay the night there, or to reach the village in time to catch the boat to Sfakiá or Sóugia, from where buses take you back to Chaniá. These run until quite late in the evening during the summer (Jul–Sep), but less often in spring and autumn. Always check times before you set out. Plan your timetable carefully. Chaniá to Samariá Gorge to Agía Rouméli and back to Chaniá (see pages 240–241) makes a very long day. And note that the gorge at midday in the summer is one long procession of tourists and school parties. The gorge is usually open from 6am to sunset, and the earlier you set off the better (*Entrance to National Park: expensive*). From November to April there is no access, as the river at the bottom becomes a dangerous torrent.

Start at the tourist pavilion at the head of the gorge. The initial descent is as breathtaking as you could wish, zigzagging 600m (1,968 feet) down a precipitous pathway known as the *xilóskala* or wooden stairway, which is what it was before the crowds began to come. The huge scree and rock faces of 2,080m (6,822 feet) Mount Gíiyilos stare down through gaps in the pines and cypresses, which scent the sharp mountain air with a delicious sappy smell. At the bottom is a picnic area where you will find the river, a trickle through dry boulders in summer but a rush of wild water after the snows have melted. A tiny plain stone church, Ágios Nikólaos, stands beside the river, which you cross and recross under eucalyptus and chestnut trees. Stupendous grey corries curve away to the east as you approach the abandoned village of Samariá. Its few houses were evacuated in 1962. It was always a resistance centre. The Turks never managed to take it, and it proved to be a nest of vipers for the Germans during World War II. There are fountains here and picnic tables under the trees. Across the gorge is the little white church of Óssia María, built in 1379, after which both village and gorge were named.

Now comes the drama. The gorge deepens and steepens into sheer rock walls, the sides falling together until you can almost feel them snap shut. Thick bands of white quartzite and black rock writhe along the cliffs, and the sky narrows to a chink overhead. At last the path, twisting over the pebbles, threads its way through the *sideróportes*, or iron doors, walls of rock less than 3m (10 feet) apart that tower well over 300m (984 feet) into the sky. Everyone spreads their arms as they go through here, but the opening is just too wide to span.

By comparison, the final few rocky kilometres are unimpressive. They bring you out at the lower entrance gate, where freshly squeezed, ice-cold orange juice is for sale. This nectar will nerve you for the final 2km (1 mile) down to Agía Rouméli and your boat.

The stream is this tame only in the summer months

ROUGH LANDING
A group of Allied resistance members who arrived by night on the beach near Soúgia on 27 November 1942 had a landing to remember. They had to swim to shore through storm waves from their wrecked boat, and most of their supplies were lost *en route*. They spent a miserable cold and wet night on the beach. At dawn they found themselves under the guns of the Paterákis clan from nearby Kostoyérako, who had almost shot them by mistake during the night. The Greek submarine that had brought the new arrivals had omitted to tell anyone that they were coming.

► Sfakiá 217D1

See Hóra Sfákía, page 228.

► Sklavopoúla 216A1

Sklavopoúla stands 640m (2,099 feet) above sea level, 16km (10 miles) back in the hills north of Palaiochóra, an all-but-unvisited village at the breezy summit of a very rough road. Slav mercenaries were granted land here by a 10th-century Byzantine emperor, and gave their name to the village. There are wonderful views over miles of plunging hill country where roads lie like coils of string. Sklavopoúla is utterly quiet and peaceful, its houses dotted around three churches: Ágios Geórgios, Sotíros Khristós or Christ the Saviour, and the Panagía, Virgin Mary, contain Byzantine frescoes. Panagía's are particularly fine. Ask about keys at the *kafeníon* in the square.

To reach Sklavopoúla, turn off the road from Palaiochóra in the sleepy, tree-lined village of **Voutás►**, beside the first *kafeníon* on the left. About 2km (1 mile) up the Sklavopoúla road from the village, you pass a side track on the right into **Kalamiós►**. It is worth turning aside for half an hour to enjoy this traditional and secluded hamlet of whitewashed houses scattered among olive trees with bulbous trunks and shading leaves. The women still fetch the water from a stone trough. A path leads up to a tiny Byzantine church whose dark interior is lined with faded frescoes.

►► Soúda Bay 217D3

Soúda Bay is Crete's best natural harbour, a deepwater inlet 15km (9 miles) by 3km (2 miles) separating the southern shore of the Akrotíri Peninsula from the north coast east of Chaniá. The view of water, ships and the Akrotíri hills from the coast road is beautiful, but the bay saw some of the bloodiest episodes of the Battle of Crete in May 1941. West of the port of Soúda lies the spectacularly sited and very moving Allied War Cemetery, with 1,497 graves of those who died defending Crete, some as young as 16.

Looking down on the Akrotíri Peninsula and Soúda Bay, still used by visiting naval vessels

Peaceful Soúgia Bay

► Soúgia *216B1*

Soúgia is hidden away on the south coast, 70km (43 miles) southwest of Chaniá at the end of a very long and winding road that skirts the westernmost flanks of the White Mountains. This little fishing port used to be one of the best-kept secret delights of Crete, visited only by those in the know, seekers after the simple pleasures of taverna, beach, coast and mountain walks, and a sight of one of the least-known Byzantine mosaics in the island. Nowadays, however, thanks to development of the settlement and an improved road, Soúgia has taken on the characteristics of a popular, if not yet too overcrowded, small resort. It is still an excellent bolthole for a couple of quiet days, and as a base for expeditions on foot.

The village lies beside the mouth of the Soúganos River, fronted by a great double sweep of pebbly and partially sandy beach fringed with feathery tamarisk trees and backed by the rise of the mountains. Some 2,000 years ago Soúgia served as the port for the Graeco–Roman city of Elirós, 5km (3 miles) back in the hills to the north. A few shaped stones and slabs remain of the Roman port just to the east of the river mouth. The Byzantine mosaic, incorporating peacocks and deer, has been removed to Chaniá Archaeological Museum from its position under the fairly modern church just west of the village. The mosaic was discovered and the church built on the advice of a Soúgia man, who saw it all in a dream while sleeping on the site.

A short way to the west of Soúgia are the remains of the ancient city of **Lissós►►**. Foundations of a theatre, some tombs with barrel-vaulted roofs, a temple to Asklepios, the god of healing, and a fountain from which issued a curative spring can be reached by a short boat trip or by a walk of about one and a half hours (start in Soúgia by crossing the gorge, then follow the waymarked track).

HARD NUT

The Venetian fort on the little island of Nísos Soúda at the mouth of Soúda Bay proved as hard a nut for the Turks to crack as did the other island fortresses around the shores of Crete. A garrison was still holding out here almost 50 years after Francesco Morini had surrendered Candia (Irakleío) to the Turks. The new rulers of Crete did not finally get their hands on this tiny symbol of Christian intransigence until 1715.

Drive

West coast and mountains

This sometimes hair-raising, always thrilling, full-day circuit is one of the most spectacular and least-travelled routes that Crete has to offer. It is a 320km (184 mile) circular drive from Tavronítis; add 40km (25 miles) each way between Tavronítis and Chaniá.

The coastal road going west from **Chaniá** is pleasant enough as it runs straight and flat behind the shore to Tavronítis and on inland to regain the coast at **Kastélli Kissámou**. It is not until you reach **Plátanos**, 11km (7 miles) to the west, and see the mountains of westernmost Crete rise in front of you, apparently barring the way, that you begin to appreciate how the road from here on south might justify its fame as one of the prime scenic routes of Crete. Yet this is, as yet, a little-driven road. Its remoteness from the centres of tourism, and the enticing fact that it doesn't really go anywhere, both have something to do with its lack of traffic, as does the haphazard way its surfaces switch from tarmac to rough stone and back again. Going south the drops are mostly on the driver's side of the road, and the tarmac often does literally drop into space. As the few cars you meet will probably be well over in the middle of the road, and on a blind corner, great care and a moderate speed are essential. Cretan hire cars are fairly robust, and with careful driving there should be few problems. Do note the number of tin shrines beside the road, commemorating accident victims. Petrol stations are also few and far between, and even the most modern tyres can suffer punctures from sharp stones.

From Plátanos the road climbs to slumbrous **Sfinári**, perched among the hills above a pebbly beach, where there are a couple of hopeful signs advertising rooms to rent. The road winds upwards on rock ledges, across the foothills of the mountains between groves of olive trees and oleanders, past hillsides covered with vegetation either thick-leaved or covered with prickles—typical of dry country, although this part of Crete is in fact one of the wettest. Villages such as **Kámpos**, **Keramotí** and **Kefáli** (see page 234–235) are small and mostly poor with goats, chestnut trees and

You will pass tiny mountain villages, such as Keramotí…

olives on the outskirts, one store and a *kafeníon* in the narrow street of red-roofed, white-washed stone houses under the trees, men riding donkeys, and women tilling vegetable patches. The newer houses are along the road, and the older dwellings are tucked away down side tracks, in among the olives, all dwarfed by the huge slopes of the mountains, looking down to an undeveloped, unspoiled, secluded coastline a couple of kilometres below. Stop in these villages, try a couple of words of Greek, and you will be met with warm hospitality.

There is a good stretch of tarmac through **Élos**, and after 5km (3 miles) you turn off right across the River Tíflos to pass through **Strovlés**. Two kilometres further, and you take the roughest of dirt roads to the left to **Algoi** and **Drýs**, and on through shady chestnut groves in steep, hidden valleys, zigzagging and switchbacking along the hillsides, at last descending to turn left on the Palaiochóra-to-Chaniá road at Plemenianá.

From here it is a 40km (25 mile) drive north to the coast road at Tavronítis, but take your time. There are two neighbouring villages high in the mountains at **Floriá** to explore. Apáno Flório and Káto Flório both have Byzantine churches with frescoes. The road surface is better as you wind on down, sometimes with a distant sea view in front of you, to **Voukoliés**. The Saturday morning market is a long-established tradition, but by the time you reach Voukoliés the traders will probably have packed up. If not it's the perfect opportunity to stock up for an afternoon picnic.

The last few kilometres pass orange groves and roadside melon stalls, before you reach Tavronítis.

...which can be reached only on foot

For thousands of years the islanders of Crete have recognised the many advantages of travelling by sea. Small coasters continue to provide an essential link between those communities, especially on the island's isolated south coast, which can only be reached by boat. Those visitors who are prepared to negotiate can often arrange to tag along with the crew.

PAY YOUR WAY
If you miss your connection, it may be possible to negotiate a ride with a local fisherman. What you pay depends on whim. Sometimes a couple of drinks or even a present of cigarettes, for example, may be enough. At other times you may be charged well over the odds. If this happens, bear in mind that you are probably the only lucrative catch he will make all week.

Sun decks give unobstructed views of the coast

Sea travel is an everyday fact of life for Crete. Only a few years ago the majority of visitors arrived by ferry from Piraeus. The south coast of the island between Palaiochóra and the Gulf of Mesará, with almost no west–east road communications, still relies on the ferries. The harbours and coastal villages have not entirely given up fishing in favour of tourism. Indeed the two are complementary on an island surrounded by excellent fishing waters. And yachting, dinghy sailing and windsurfing are all on the increase in and around harbours such as Irakleío, Réthymno, Chaniá, Ágios Nikólaos, Siteiá and Palaiochóra.

The big ferries, to the mainland of Greece and those on the Palaiochóra–Soúgia–Agía Rouméli–Sfakiá–Agía Galíni run, operate to reasonably reliable timetables. If you are lucky at the end of your walk through the Samariá Gorge, you may sail from Agía Rouméli with the splendidly theatrical skipper who has the habit, when upset, of dashing his cap in fury on the deck. Where the ferries cannot get passengers ashore, even with their modern let-down ramps, the *caïques* will sail. These boats vary in size and carry both passengers and supplies. Some have facilities, some are purpose-built, others are converted from fishing boats or double between the two roles. The *caïques* have a more cavalier attitude to the clock. Prices on the whole are fixed by general agreement among the boat owners, and local competition keeps them reasonably low.

Where neither ferries nor *caïques* go, you can usually arrange to be dropped by a small private vessel or fishing boat. Try asking around on the waterfront. Take time to appreciate the beautiful lines of the traditionally built boats, brightly painted in primary colours, with pointed sterns and curved wooden tillers. This design has been essentially unchanged for thousands of years, in spite of the electronic fish-finding gear that some now carry.

Travel Facts

Arriving

By air

Scheduled flights originating outside Greece may involve a change in Athens. Charter companies fly direct from other European countries. Flight time from Athens to Crete is a little under one hour. Olympic Airlines (www.olympicairlines.com), the Greek national airline, operates from Athens. Olympic offer special economy rates to students and others. Aegean Airlines (www.aegeanair.com) also flies throughout Greece and the islands and Sky Express (www.skyexpress.gr) based at Irakleío connects various southern Greek Islands. In winter schedules are reduced. For flights in from June to September, book early.

The neat building belies the chaos within Irakleío Airport

Crete has three passenger airports: Irakleío, Chaniá and Siteía. Irakleío handles 90 per cent or more of the holiday flights. The airport has an information desk (tel: 2810 397800), the major car hire firms, and good bus and taxi connections with the capital. Crete's western airport at Chaniá handles fewer passengers, and has recently been upgraded with improved facilities. Siteía is the smallest of the three. In Feb 2007 the Greek government announced plans for a new larger airport to be built close to Irakleío. This will be the main air portal for the island.

The best way to travel round the Aegean

For travellers from outside North America, Olympic Airways offers flights to Athens from New York, Toronto and Montreal. Delta Airlines (www.delta.com) flies to Athens from New York, Cincinnati, Atlanta, LA and Salt Lake City.

By sea
The two main shipping lines are Minoan (tel: 2810 399800 www.minoan.gr) and ANEK (tel: 2810 222481 www.anek.gr). Most ferries depart from Piraeus, the port of Athens, sailing to either Irakleío or Chaniá. ANEK also run a service to Réthymno. Sailings usually leave Piraeus in the early evening, arriving 10 or 12 hours later. Some sailings leave Piraeus early in the morning for an early evening arrival in Crete. As with air travel, it is Irakleío that sees most of the holiday traffic. Sailing into Chaniá early in the morning as the sun lights the snowy peaks of the White Mountains is a treat.

There are also sailings to Irakleío from the port of Yíthio on the south coast of the Peloponnese peninsula southwest of Athens.

By car
You can drive to Piraeus and bring your car across to Crete on the ferry. The cross-Europe drive will take several days. If you bring your own car, you will need an EU or international driving licence, your car registration documents and a nationality sticker. EU residents do not need Green Card insurance, but it is essential to have full, comprehensive insurance before driving on Crete.

By train and coach
Taking the train to Piraeus or another port of embarkation, or to Athens airport, is a fairly relaxed way to travel. Package tour coach operators have beaten well-worn paths to the same destinations, but the long drive, as in a car, can be tiring.

Customs regulations
Citizens from outside the EU may bring the following items duty free:
200 cigarettes, or 50 cigars or 250g of tobacco;
1 litre of spirits or 2 litres of wine;
50g of perfume.
There are severe penalties for exporting antiquities from Greece without an export certificate. Your own customs regulations may prevent you from importing products made from animal skin or bone so check before buying.

Passports and visas
EU visitors need an identity card. UK and all other citizens need a valid passport. No visa is needed for a stay of up to three months by visitors from EU countries, Canada, New Zealand or Australia. Extended stays can be authorised by contacting the "Aliens Police" or local police station. Visitors whose passports contain a stamp from the Turkish part of Cyprus may be refused admission.

Travel insurance
Travel insurance is vital for belongings, changes to itineraries, health problems and emergencies. EU citizens are entitled to medical treatment provided by the Greek state. To get this you must be have a European Health Insurance Card (EHIC). In the UK this can be obtained online on www.ehic.org.uk or tel: 0845 605 0707. Travel insurance is still advised.

Visit early to avoid the tour buses

The higher you go, the later spring starts

Essential facts

When to go

April and May are definitely the best months to be in Crete. It is springtime, the flowers are at their most spectacular, the crowds have not yet begun to arrive, and the islanders are slowly expanding from their winter insularity. The absolute zenith is probably the Greek Orthodox Easter celebrations and the weeks that follow. June is a good time too, but it is getting hotter. The "autumn spring" in September–October is also lovely, with fewer visitors, but some hotels and restaurants are closing down for the winter by then. Winter is a wonderful time for fluent Greek speakers who like a *triste solitude* and don't mind basic amenities. And there are always fine, clear days. The heat, dust, noise, crowds and general impatience of late July and August should be avoided, unless you have to dovetail plans with school holidays.

Climate

From January to mid-March there will be snow on the mountains, gales and rain, with some beautiful clear days. The average temperature is 12–13°C (54–55°F). The Cretan spring comes between mid-March and May, warm with coastal breezes and flowers everywhere. The temperature rises from 13–14°C (57–59°F) in mid-March to 20–21°C (68–70°F) in May. By June it is getting hotter (23–25°C/73–77°F) with still, dry days, but snow can still cover the high peaks. July to September is the Cretan summer, with a peak of heat in August (26–27°C/79–81°F, sometimes hotter). The rocks and sand are baking hot, and the powerful *meltémi* wind from the northwest raises sand on north coast beaches and dust on the roads. The island is very arid at this time, and crowded. The south coast is probably the best place to be. The temperatures begin to drop to around 24°C (75°F) by the end of September. From October to mid-November there is often a second flowering. The island is tired and relaxed now and is looking brown and dry, with temperatures dropping to around 15°C (59°F). Mid-November to December sees the onset of gales and rain with snow later in the mountains. There will be a few wonderful fresh days, especially on the south coast, and the temperature falls to between 13 and 14°C (55 and 57°F).

National holidays

31 December and 1 January, New Year's Day. Cakes with lucky coins, midnight shooing of devils out of houses.
6 January, Epiphany. Youths dive for crosses blessed and thrown in sea. Fonts and springs are blessed, and demons exorcised.
25 March, Greek Independence Day. Town parades.
Carnivals take place during the two weeks before Lent in Irakleío and Réthymno.
On Clean Monday (the last Monday before Lent), meat is foresworn and houses are cleaned.
Holy Week sees fasting.
Easter is between one and four weeks later than western Easter, and sees memorable, emotional celebrations (see pages 16–17).
Ascension Day. Parades with dancing and fireworks.
1 May, Labour Day. Spring celebrations with picnics and flower gathering to make wreaths for house doors.
20–27 May. Battle of Crete commemorations at Máleme and Chaniá.
26–27 May. Anniversary of 1821 War of Independence at Sfakiá.
24 June. Feast of St John the Baptist.

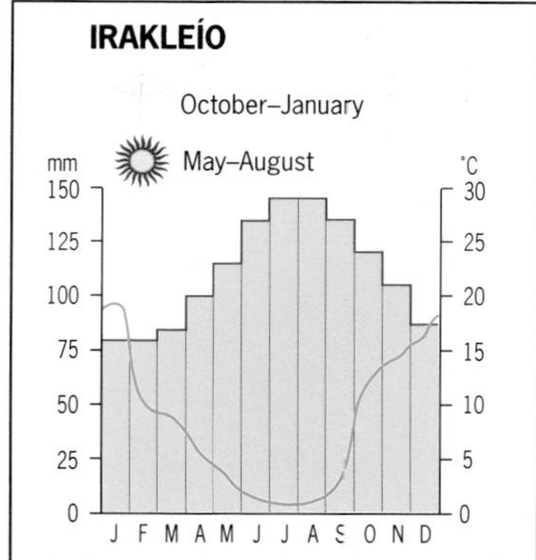

Midsummer celebrations with fireworks. 1 May wreaths thrown onto bonfires, which some Cretans leap.
July–September. Cultural Summer in Chaniá with concerts and arts exhibitions.
30–31 July. Wine Festival in Voúves
July–August. Irakleío Festival with many cultural events.
Mid-August. Siteía Sultana Festival.
15 August. Assumption of the Virgin Mary with services, music and dancing at churches, monasteries and villages.
20 August. Honey Festival in Afrata
29 August. Commemoration of the beheading of St John the Baptist. Christenings and gatherings of those named Ioánnis at churches dedicated to the saint.
Late October. Élos Chestnut Festival.
28 October. Óhi Day. Celebrating Greek pride in their "No" to Mussolini in 1940.
7–9 November. Commemoration of the 1866 Arkádiou Monastery explosion. Fireworks and celebrations at Arkádiou and Réthymno.
25–26 December. Christmas is a low-key affair, and demons abound.

Time differences
Greece is 2 hours ahead of Greenwich Mean Time (GMT). Greek summer time (GMT + 3 hours) starts on the last Sunday in March, winter time the last Sunday in September.

Money matters
Crete uses the euro (€) which is Greece's official currency. Banknotes come in denominations of 5, 10, 20, 50, 100 , 200 and 500 euros, and coins in denominations of 1, 2, 5, 10, 20, 50 cents and 1 and 2 euros.

Banks
Banks are usually open Monday to Thursday 8–2, Friday 8–1.30. In big tourist resorts some may be open later, and on Saturdays. Most Greek and some foreign banks have branches on the island. It is advisable to change money and travellers' cheques at a bank or post office, as commission is usually lower and rates better than in hotels, *bureaux de change* or travel agents. The EOT (Greek Tourist Organisation) offices will also change money. Take your passport as identification. Euros can also be obtained from cashpoint machines outside certain banks in the larger towns.

Credit cards
Access, Visa and American Express are usually recognised in the larger souvenir outlets, car hire agencies and up-market restaurants at the coastal resorts, but you may find that there may be an extra charge for using cards. In small villages and remote areas you will need to use cash. This is particularly important if you are driving as fuel stations away from the north coast very rarely accept credit cards of any kind. Small hotels and most tavernas will also only accept cash.

Many bank staff speak English

Getting around

Car rental

Most visitors to Crete rent transport when they arrive on the island. This obviates the need for a tedious drive across thousands of miles of mainland Europe, and is quick and easy to arrange. Car rental on Crete is not especially cheap, but savings can be made if hire is part of a package or fly-drive deal.

The major car rental firms are represented in the four big towns of Irakleío, Chaniá, Réthymno and Ágios Nikólaos, as well as in other large towns. The better hotels will fix you up with a rental car on request. In Irakleío most major car rental companies maintain offices at Níkos Kazantzákis Airport including (tel: 02810 330452; www.hertz.com) and Budget (tel: 281 0344279; www.budget.com), however Eurodollar also has a city centre office on Odós 25 Avgoústou (tel: 281 0243237; www.eurodollar.gr). Caravel car rental is an independent company that is well represented across Crete. They will deliver and pick up cars to your hotel, at any airport or port. Their main office at at Odós 25th Avgoústou in Irakleío (tel: 2810 245345/cross island number is tel: 6937 200391; www.caravel.gr).

You will be asked to show your driving licence, which must be a full licence held for at least a year. The lower age limit for hiring a car is 21, but some firms may require you to be 23. Hire prices are comparable to most other European countries. Out of season, bargain for reductions.

Four-wheel drives are fun, but mark the occupants as tourists...

Local companies compete with the big internationals

Do satisfy yourself that the deal you strike includes full, comprehensive insurance. Cretan roads are always liable to spring nasty surprises, and it is far better to pay more and drive with peace of mind.

By the same token, check tyres for wear, windscreen washer bottles for water, battery and oil levels, and ask what that flashing red light on the dashboard means *before* you drive away. If you hire from a major company, these checks should have been carried out already. Four-wheel-drive vehicles, although they cut a rugged dash, are not really necessary. Provided you hire a car with an engine over 1100cc, there are few dirt roads you cannot negotiate with care.

Petrol and diesel cost roughly the same as on mainland Europe, but trying to find petrol in remote districts of the island, which means anywhere away from the north coast holiday strip and the bigger towns, is a needle-in-a-haystack business. The golden rule is always to fill up when you have the opportunity, and not to set off with a nagging doubt about the car. Check it, or get it checked, first. Away from towns and the coast, garages can close at round 7pm, and sometimes earlier on Saturdays. On Sundays only the bigger garages in the main towns are open.

Driving tips
These are mostly covered on pages 102–103, Focus on Driving in Crete. The absolute basics that you need to remember are: some roads are unmade-up, narrow, steep and winding; allow plenty of time; be patient; be prepared to turn back. And note that placenames in this guide, on your map and on road signs may be spelt in several different ways.

Breakdown
ELPA is the Greek motorists' aid organisation. Several other motoring organisations, for example, the AA in the United Kingdom, is affiliated to ELPA. If you are a member of this organisation, you will benefit from ELPA'S free breakdown service (tel: 104 00). If you are not a member of an affiliated organisation, dial 154 for assistance. Also call the car hire firm. Do remember to make a note of their number before you drive away from their premises!

Bus and coach travel
Bus travel on Crete is probably the best-value, euro-per-kilometre, way of getting around the island. The buses, run under the loose organisation of the KTEL group (www.bus-service-crete-ktel.com), are inexpensive and reliable, though journeys can be hair-raising on the more frisky sections of road,

particularly in the mountains. The service along the new road between the four main towns of Chaniá, Réthymno, Irakleío and Ágios Nikólaos is fast and frequent. From these big towns, local services run to the smaller country towns and to most villages. Local tickets are bought on the bus. Long distance tickets are sold in an office at the bus station, usually marked *Praktoreíon.* On Sundays the service is reduced, and in winter the timetable changes. Local tourist information offices have details and timetables.

There are several bus stations in Irakleío. Station A (tel: 2810 245019), at the ferry port operates services to the east. Station B (tel: 2810 255956), just outside the Chaniá Gate, serves the south and west. A final station (tel: 2810 220755) controls city buses and Knosós services. Chaniá bus station is at Odós Kidonías, just south of Plateía 1866; for information tel 2821 093306/093052. Réthymno bus station is at 44 Odós Moátsu, on the corner with Odós Dhimokratías; for information call 2831 022212/022785. Ágios Nikólaos bus station is on the shore at the bottom of Odós Sofoklís Venizélos; call 2841 022234 for information.

Fires are a real problem in the dry season

There are numerous coach tours to destinations all over the island, often with a cultural event thrown in: dancing, music, plate-smashing, waiter-smooching, and so on. These can be good fun if you're with the right people and in the mood. Some Irakleío operators are: Adamis (tel: 2810 222303); Cretan Holidays (tel: 2810 331420; www.cretan-holidays.gr); Sbokos Tours (tel: 2810 229712; www.sbokos.com); Zeus (tel: 2810 398655; www.zeus.gr).

Flights

Domestic flights leave from Chaniá (tel: 28210 83800), Irakleío (tel: 2810 397800) and Siteía (tel: 28430 24424) airports. Destinations include Rhodes and other islands in the Dodecanese and Cyclades groups to the north of Crete.

Motorcycle and bicycle hire

To hire a motorcycle you must be at least 19 years old, and for anything over 50cc you will need a full driving licence. The same lower age limit applies to scooters and mopeds. Though these are cheaper by far, they won't be able to tackle the many steep ascents on dirt roads that you will meet if you want to explore the Cretan hills. But for tootling around the resorts, they're fine. Crash helmets may or may not come with the bike—most likely not. You should bring your own, or insist on the hire place producing one. It is not worth taking any risks on the poorer roads and it is also illegal not to wear one. If a helmet is not forthcoming, move along to the next hire place. There are plenty to choose from!

Bicycle hire is increasing in popularity and mountain bikes are ideal for the difficult roads and hilly landscape. There is no charge for bringing your own bicycle to the island. Alianthos in Irakleío (tel: 28320 32033; www.aliathos-group.com), Greenways in Réthymno (tel: 28310 72440; www.greenways.gr), Moto Express in Khersonísos (tel: 28970 248760; www.motoexpress.gr).

As ever, youth hostels are a cheap option

Sea travel

There is a lively trade in passengers and goods from most ports and harbours in Crete, both formally and informally. The island's main shipping companies are Minoan (78 Odós 25 Avgoústou, Irakleío, tel: 2810 229602; www.minoan.gr) and ANEK (33 Odós 25 Avgoústou, tel: 2810 222481; www.anek.gr).

Irakleío has services to Piraeus (Athens), Kós, Kálimnos, Íos, Náxos, Rhodes and other Aegean islands; also Ancona and other Italian ports. Contact the shipping lines direct; many have offices in Odós 25 Avgoústou above the Venetian harbour. Shipping agents, for example, Paleológos Shipping Agency, 5 Odós 25 Avgoústou, tel: tel: 2810 346185; www.ferries.gr. Réthymno also has sailings to Piraeus. Contact Odeon Travel at 25 Odós Peleologou (tel: 28310 57610).

Ágios Nikólaos has ferries to Piraeus, the Dodecanese and the Cyclades. Try Byron Travel at 4 Odós Akti Koundourou (tel: 28410 28480).

Chaniá has a service to Piraeus from the port of Soúda, 10km to the east with buses every 15 minutes. Contact Hellenic Seaways (tel: 28210 81478; www.hellenicseaways.gr).

Irakleío and Siteía have sailings to Piraeus, Rhodes, Pátmos, Kos and Kálymnos. Try Dikta Travel at Odós Koranroy (tel: 28430 25080).

Kastélli Kissámou is the departure point for the Peloponnese ports of Gytheion, Kalámata and the island of Kíthira.

There is also a good, regular south coast service between Palaiochóra, Soúgia, Agía Rouméli, Sfakiá and Agía Galíni. Details can be obtained from local tourist offices.

Student and youth reductions

There are no official International Youth Hostelling Federation affiliated establishments on Crete, however there are some family run hostels and a whole range of inexpensive rooms for rent around the island. A student card will get you reductions on Olympic Airways flights into Greece, entrance fees to museums and archaeological sites, and on some tours. Check with tourist information offices.

Taxis

Taxis are widely available, and can get you to many of the parts the buses cannot reach. Town taxis operate fixed-price journeys within the towns. In other cases, agree both the price and destination before you get in. Fares are normally shown on boards at airports, and some town centres. You may be able to use a taxi to connect two ends of a walk, or to fill in a gap in the bus timetable.

The ubiquitous newsagent-cum-sweet seller; this one is in Irakleío

Communications

Media

Newspapers Most major foreign newspapers and some magazines are available in the big seaside towns; buy them (a day or two old) at street kiosks, big hotels, newsagents and bookstalls or the airport. The mark-up can be three or four times the cover price, and is stamped on the front page.

Television Some concerts of traditional Cretan music are broadcast, along with a great many hoary American films, subtitled or dubbed to interesting effect. Do yourself a favour and choose a *kafeníon* without a television if you want to enjoy the atmosphere and chat. Some four- and five-star hotels offer Sky News, BBC News 24 or CNN.

Radio Cretan and Greek music pours out of the radio; just twiddle the dial. Some local stations carry tourist information in English in the season. With perseverance you will pick up the BBC World Service, the Voice of America and also US Forces radio.

Post offices

Post offices are open 7.30–2.30 weekdays, in Irakleío and Chaniá 7.30am–7.30pm. Other big towns may stay open later, and at weekends. The main post offices are: Plateía Daskaloyiánni, Irakleío; Odós Tzanakáki, just

Don't rely upon postboxes being emptied every day

up from the covered market in Chaniá; Odós Moátsou in Réthymno; Odós 28 Oktovrioú in Ágios Nikólaos; Plateía Kothrí in Ierápetra; Odós Therissoú in Siteía.

Post offices (*takhydromeíon*) sell stamps (*grammatósima*), as do pavement kiosks and shops. Post offices will also change money and cheques. Parcels can be collected only from a parcels office, and should be sent from a main post office. Air mail letters take from three to seven days to reach European destinations, seven to ten days to the US, and 10–14 days to Australia and New Zealand. Postcards should be written as soon as you arrive if you want them to beat you home! *Poste restante* at main post offices will hold letters for up to a month. Take your passport when you collect, to identify yourself. Post boxes are yellow.

Telephones

The Cretan telephone system works well, and is modern and efficient. Phones in hotel lobbies may seem to be free, but check your bill on leaving! Most better-class hotels have telephones in the bedrooms, on which you can make local and international calls, at a price.

The big cities are well provided with telephone booths, and almost every town and substantial village has one. These operate by telephone cards bought from OTE offices and most street kiosks (*peripteros*). They can be used for both local and international calls. Metered phones are also available at the kiosks. Some cafés display a sign: *tiléfono me metrití*. You make your call (to anywhere in the world), and the owner reads the cost from the meter.

You can also phone from Greek Telephone Organisation (OTE) offices. Main offices are in El Greco Park, Irakleío (3-5 Odós Tzanakaki'); Odós Tzanakáki next to main post office, Chaniá (10 Odós Sfakianak); Sfakianáki, Ágios Nikólaos (22 Odós C. Sifi, Siteía); Odós Kondiláki, Siteía; and Odós Koráka, Ierápetra.

Area Codes:

Irakleío 2810
Chaniá 28210
Réthymno 28310
Ágios Nikólaos 28940
Siteía 28430
Ierápetra 28420

Internet cafés

Internet cafés are common in all the main towns and tourist resorts. Some hotels have Internet access in the rooms or in a dedicated point within the complex.

Essential phrases

Yásoo	Hello
Kalí méra	Good morning
Kalí spéra	Good evening
Kalí níkhta	Good night
Adío	Good-bye
Né	Yes
Óhi	No
Parakaló	Please
Efharistó	Thank you
Póso káni?	How much?
Poú eené…?	Where is…?
Parakaló, o drómos ya…?	Please can you tell me the way to…?
Meh léne…	My name is…
Katalavéno	I don't understand
Iss-iyían!	Cheers!
Parakaló, mípos miláte…	Do you speak…
Anglikí/Yermoniká	English/German/
Galiká/Olanthiká	French/Dutch
Ispaniká	Spanish?
Voíthia!	Help!

Keeping abreast of the news

Always take plenty of water with you

Emergencies

Crime

Crete is a conservative, tight-knit society with strong moral standards, and there is very little crime on the island. Any perpetrator is much more likely to be a fellow-tourist than a Cretan. Almost all crime is restricted to petty pilfering from tents, hotel rooms and unlocked cars, so the usual precautions with regard to locking doors, and keeping tempting valuables out of sight, should ensure you a trouble-free stay. Lost property is almost certain to be where you left it, or being looked after by someone nearby. This especially applies to children. If you are really worried, contact the Tourist Police.

If you lose your passport, driver's licence or other important documents, tell the police as soon as possible, and also your consulate. If you will be making an insurance claim for stolen or lost property, be sure to ask for and keep a copy of any police report.

Be aware that drug dealers, even of small amounts, could face life imprisonment. The younger the person supplied with drugs, the stiffer the penalty for the supplier. People found in possession of small amounts for personal use can be jailed for a year. This applies to soft as well as hard drugs.

Sexual harassment is generally restricted to enthusiastic observation, but if you are really pestered, say "*Parátame!*" ("Go away!") .

Nude bathing, while technically punishable by a fine or even a short jail sentence, is not hotly pursued. There are many nudist beaches on Crete's coasts, usually remote from tourist centres. But you will certainly offend many Cretans if you appear before them only in Mother Nature's garb on a public beach.

Police

The regular police wear green uniforms, and deal, usually politely, with normal police business. The tourist police wear grey uniforms, which display national flags indicating the languages the wearer speaks. Their job is to advise visitors.

Consulates

Germany, 7 Odós Zografoú, Irakleío. tel: 2810 226288; 64 Odós Daskaloyiánni, Chaniá, tel: 28210 688876. **Great Britain**, 16 Odós Papalexándrou, Irakleío, tel: 2810 224012. **Netherlands**, Monis Agarathou 22, Platia Agious Dimitruou, Irakleío, tel: 281 343299. **Norway**, 15 avenue Dimokratias, Irakleío, tel: 281 0225991.

Emergency telephone numbers

General emergency 100 or 112
First aid/ambulance 166
Tourist Police 171
Breakdown 154 (104 00 if affiliated to ELPA)

Accidents and trouble

Keep as calm as possible; stay at the scene; don't make a statement unless you are sure that it is to a fluent speaker of your native tongue; telephone the tourist police or the regular police, depending on the circumstances. Be prepared to be detained for up to 24 hours, and be sure to contact your consulate.

Health

The only vital precautions to take are against sunburn, which can strike even on windy, cloudy days. Bring a sun hat, sun cream, dark glasses and after-sun lotion. Drink plenty of liquid at all times, particularly during a walk.

Crete has one variety of poisonous snake, one kind of poisonous spider and a population of scorpions. All three shun the limelight, and you are most unlikely to see any of them. Dogs bark a lot but rarely bite, and rabies has not been recorded. A stick deals with dogs; insect repellent deals with mosquitoes.

All tap and spring water is drinkable. Check that your tetanus, polio and typhoid immunity is up to date, but vaccinations are not absolutely necessary.

Doctors and pharmacies

All big towns have English-speaking doctors. Pharmacies (*farmakí*) display a red, blue or green cross and have staff skilled in diagnosis and remedy. A 24-hour rota operates, details of which will be found on the pharmacy door.

Hospitals

There are hospitals at Irakleío, Chaniá, Réthymno, Ágios Nikólaos, Siteía and Ierápetra.

There is very basic free care for EU nationals (with an EHIC, see page 257), but it is safer to have comprehensive health insurance which includes a flight home.

Don't forget to wear sufficient skin protection to cope with the strength of the Mediterranean sun

Other information

Accommodation

For camping, youth hostelling and self-catering holidays between June and September, prior booking is essential. Out of season you may well strike an excellent bargain on the spot.

Camping

The main camp sites are at Gouves near Irakleío, Ierápetra, Mália, Khersónisos, Mátala, Agía Galíni and Palaiochóra. Others are scattered around the coast. For full details contact Panhellenic Camping Association (tel: 210 3621560; www.panhellenic-camping-union.gr). Facilities are generally unadorned, but sites are clean and all basic requirements are present. There is usually a shop or taverna.

Camping on unofficial sites is technically forbidden and recently there have been attempts to tighten up this regulation, owing to the selfishness of a few campers who have fouled beaches and left litter behind. However, as with most aspects of life on Crete, what the official eye does not see the official heart does not grieve over. There are many wonderful beaches, headlands and flowery plateaux in Crete, far from prying eyes. The essentials are to ask permission at the nearest taverna, as they may well let you camp on their land if you eat your meals with them; and to clear up scrupulously.

Youth hostels

Youth hostelling is a good way to stay in Crete on the cheap. There are hostels in Irakleío at 5 Vironos between the bus station and Odós 25 Avgoústou, tel: 2810 286281; at 33 Odós Drakoniánou, Chaniá, tel: 28210 53565; at 45 Odós Tompazi, Réthymno, tel: 28310 22848; at Malia, tel: 2810 285075; on the western edge of the village of Plakias, tel: 28320 32118 ; www.yhplakias.com; and at 4 Odós Therísou, Siteía, tel: 0843-22693. For information contact the Greek Youth Hostel Association, 75 Damareos Street, Athens, Greece (tel: 00 30 210 7519530).

Self-catering

There has recently been a great upsurge in provision for self-catering holidays. Villas and apartments can be found in all the main visitor centres, and in many other towns and villages. Local tourist information offices will have details. The travel pages of most major European newspapers carry advertisements for the large number of companies offering self-catering accommodation in Crete as well as private ads. GNTO offices in European cities can also help with suggestions and addresses.

Visitors with disabilities

Cretans are interested in other people and ready to help when needed, but the island is very short on provision

Camping on Elafonísi beach

CONVERSION CHARTS

FROM	TO	MULTIPLY BY
Inches	Centimetres	2.54
Centimetres	Inches	0.3937
Feet	Metres	0.3048
Metres	Feet	3.2810
Yards	Metres	0.9144
Metres	Yards	1.0940
Miles	Kilometres	1.6090
Kilometres	Miles	0.6214
Acres	Hectares	0.4047
Hectares	Acres	2.4710
Gallons	Litres	4.5460
Litres	Gallons	0.2200
Ounces	Grams	28.35
Grams	Ounces	0.0353
Pounds	Grams	453.6
Grams	Pounds	0.0022
Pounds	Kilograms	0.4536
Kilograms	Pounds	2.205
Tons	Tonnes	1.0160
Tonnes	Tons	0.9842

MEN'S SUITS

UK	36	38	40	42	44	46	48
Rest of Europe	46	48	50	52	54	56	58
US	36	38	40	42	44	46	48

DRESS SIZES

UK	8	10	12	14	16	18
France	36	38	40	42	44	46
Italy	38	40	42	44	46	48
Rest of Europe	34	36	38	40	42	44
US	6	8	10	12	14	16

MEN'S SHIRTS

UK	14	14.5	15	15.5	16	16.5	17
Rest of Europe	36	37	38	39/40	41	42	43
US	14	14.5	15	15.5	16	16.5	17

MEN'S SHOES

UK	7	7.5	8.5	9.5	10.5	11
Rest of Europe	41	42	43	44	45	46
US	8	8.5	9.5	10.5	11.5	12

WOMEN'S SHOES

UK	4.5	5	5.5	6	6.5	7
Rest of Europe	38	38	39	39	40	41
US	6	6.5	7	7.5	8	8.5

for disabled people, islanders and visitors alike. You will find offices on upper floors, steps and staircases, hard-to-use lavatories and so on. Out and about in town, the pavements are often cracked, or non-existent, or blocked by parked vehicles, and cobblestones are a constant hazard. Zebra crossings are ignored by drivers. In the countryside roads are often steep and rough; paths are always lumpy with stones.

New buildings such as museums and hotels must meet European standards and will be accessible. The key to a successful trip is planning, and it is especially important on an island where not much information is available, even to native people with disabilities. Contact your own home country organisation. They will have information on holidays catering specifically for people with disabilities, and, if you prefer to explore independently, they may be able to put you in touch with someone who has firsthand experience of Crete and its challenges.

Among your other preparations, you will need to take all medicines and the equipment you require, a wheelchair servicing kit, and a thick skin—the more rural your wandering, the more penetrating the stares and murmurings. This is not rudeness, merely curiosity.

In the UK, Holiday Care Services (tel: 0845 124 9971; www.holiday-care.org.uk) offers information for travellers with mobility problems. In the US contact Society for Accessible Travel & Hospitality (SATH; tel: 212 447 7284; www.sath.org).

Electricity

Electricity on Crete is at 220 volts A.C. Two-pin plugs are used, so bring an adaptor for three-pin appliances.

Etiquette and local customs

Greetings in Greek are always received with pleasure, and mark you out as someone who has taken some trouble. In Crete, courtesy breeds courtesy. A handshake on meeting and saying goodbye is good form, but be careful never to wave your palm at a Cretan, as this can be taken as an insult.

Speak when entering a *kafeníon* or passing a seated person. It is good manners for the person on the move to start the exchange. *"Kalí méra"*, "good day", will do very well.

You will not be permitted to pay back hospitality by buying your round. All that is required from you is a smile and some praise of Crete and your entertainment, in sign language if necessary. To be offered hospitality with a family is an honour. Taking them a present is acceptable if you are going to have a meal. If the woman of the house seems to be doing all the work and feeding everyone but herself, she is! Accept the custom, and eat what you are offered, individually or from a common dish.

Always ask permission before photographing people. Resentment can be caused by insensitive and patronising photographers.

Tipping is acceptable. Give a euro or two to a taxi driver, 10 to 15 per cent at a restaurant, and what you judge for a hotel chambermaid.

Everyone displays curiosity, so answer back and be nosy yourself!

Opening times

EOT tourist offices are open Monday to Friday, 8am–2pm, 5pm–8pm; Saturday and Sunday, 8–2; high season 8am–10pm.

Post offices open Monday to Friday, 8am–2pm, most places; 8am–7pm, main towns and resorts. Mobile post offices in large resorts may be open later.

Banks open Monday to Thursday, 8am–2pm, Fri 8am–1.30pm. In high season one bank also opens 5pm–7pm, and on Saturdays, for changing money in Irakleío, Chaniá, Réthymno and Ágios Nikólaos.

OTE telephone offices mostly open 7.30am–10pm.

Shop hours vary widely according to place, season and inclination of the owner. Officially they are open Monday, Wednesday and Saturday, 8am–2.30pm, and Tuesday, Thursday and Friday 8am–2pm, 5.30am–8pm. In high season, many resort shops are open all week to very late hours.

Pavement kiosks are also often open from dawn to midnight.

Restaurants are open from 1pm to 3pm and from 8pm to the early hours and tavernas in resorts right throughout the day.

Kafenía are open from when you arrive to when you depart.

Photography: Digital peripherals (cards and batteries).

Some Internet cafés have equipment to enable you to post images on the web or send them by e-mail. Film is becoming hard to get and will be expensive. Always check the sell by date of any film you find.

You can hire video equipment in the bigger of the north coast resorts, but at a hefty price.

Photography is not permitted in churches, nor in the vicinity of the naval base at Soúda, nor around the Síderos Peninsula in the northeast, site of another base. Large notices remind you of this.

Most museums permit photography but charge a fee, which doubles or trebles if you use a tripod. Some exhibits may be off-limits to photographers, but these will be clearly labelled. Archaeological sites may or may not charge you for taking photographs.

Places of worship

Almost all places of worship on Crete are Greek Orthodox. Anyone is welcome to attend a service, but be aware that in rural districts women with flimsy clothing, shorts or short skirts will undoubtedly offend local worshippers. If you have not attended a Greek Orthodox ceremony before, you are in for a treat, especially during the spectacular, often chaotic, celebrations around Easter time (see pages 16–17).

There are Roman Catholic masses on Saturday and Sunday, in the cathedrals at Irakleío, Chaniá, Réthymno and Ágios Nikólaos. No Nonconformist or Jewish services of worship are held.

Toilets *(toualéta)*

Public lavatories are usually sited in or near town parks or *plateía*. These can be dark and smelly, of the big-drop variety, or, more rarely, a pleasant and reasonably modern surprise. Bring your own lavatory paper. *Kafenía*, restaurants, tavernas, and bus stations usually have facilities. The hotels almost invariably have a better standard, and all the better class hotels have en-suite facilities. A golden rule is to use the hotel lavatories before setting out for the day.

Crete's ageing plumbing system cannot cope with the demands made on it, especially in the high season. Conquer instinct and put lavatory paper, once you have used it, in the bin provided. Do not flush it down the lavatory pan unless you are of the Noah persuasion.

Women travellers and people travelling alone

Crete is, on the whole, an easy place for women to travel around alone. Provided that you do not behave in a manner that invites attention, you will be treated with respect. You are more likely to meet with curiosity and concern. It is not usual for Cretan women to be unattached, either to their family or husband, so questions will be asked about why you are not married or where your children are. It is also unlikely that you will be allowed to eat alone in a local restaurant—you will be invited to join the family eating at the next table, and the questions will start all over again...

Topless sunbathing is widespread, but if you are alone it will probably be seen as an indication that you are somehow available and will, unfortunately, attract the beach wolves or *kamaki* (harpooners) as they are known here. It is best not to strip off unless you are happy with the company. Similarly, wearing very short shorts, or going sleeveless into churches, can cause tutting, particularly from the local women. Priests too will be dismissive; the men just stare. The advice, therefore, is to be aware of the cultural differences, and to respect Cretan values.

Colourful tie-dye and batik wraps

Tourist Offices

The National Tourist Organisation of Greece (GNTO, known locally as EOT—"*áy-ot*"; www.gnto.gr) has several offices in Crete. All are helpful, if overworked in high season. They arrange guides, tours and accommodation, provide information, brochures, maps and timetables, give details of festivals, celebrations and events. Make the EOT office your first port of call in a new town. There are municipal offices, too.

GNTO (EOT) offices in Crete:
At the **airports.**
Irakleío 1 Xanthoudídou Street, Platea Elefthérias (opposite the Archaeological Museum), tel: 2810 246106.
Chaniá 40 Kriári Street (Pantheon Building), tel: 28210 92943.
Réthymno Avenue Elefthérios Venizélos, tel: 28310 29148.
Ágios Nikólaos 20 Aktí I Koundoúrou, tel: 28410 22357.
Siteía Plateía Iróon Polytéchnichou, tel: 28430 24955.
Ierápetra (in high season) beside Hotel Ítanos on Plateía Venizélos, and sometimes at Plateía Kanoupáki, on the waterfront, tel: 28420 28721.

GNTO offices overseas:
London 4 Conduit Street, W1S 2DJ, tel: 0207 4959300.
New York Olympic Tower, 645 Fifth Avenue, Suite 903, New York, NY 10022, tel: 212 4215777.
Also in Amsterdam, Athens, Australia, Canada, Copenhagen, Germany, Madrid, Paris, Rome, Sweden.

Lending a helping hand

Hotels and Restaurants

HOTELS

The classification of hotels is undergoing profound change. The government is moving from the official Greek system to the more internationally understood star rating for hotel services and quality. The old system classified hotels from E (the lowest rating) through D, C, B and A, with an L rating for luxury properties. The B and C ratings roughly translate to a 3 star rating under the old system. At present you may find hotels rated under either system.

The highest class hotels will be expensive but not excessively so by European standards. Those built in the 1970s and 80s have little character and are often block-booked by tour operators, but several boutique hotels have emerged to offer fantastic facilities and a little more character. Previous booking is essential between July and September.

Many small less luxurious hotels are family run concerns, clean and friendly with en-suite accommodation and often with a restaurant attached. The lowest class of room may have few facilities but will always be clean and during the summer season and at major festivals may be the only accommodation that remains unbooked. Prices for all but luxury accommodation is fixed by the government.

Most hotels will ask for your passport to complete forms for the government.

Private rooms are classified from A to C. A class may often be a distinct cut above a moderate C class hotel, though only half the price. Private rooms are in private houses, all checked by the Tourist Organisation for cleanliness and comfort if they carry a classificaion. You may have to pay for a hot shower.

There are thousands of villas and furnished apartments in Crete that are not under the aegis of the Tourist Organisation. Travel agents will book you into these, but many also advertise on the Internet.

If you arrive without accommodation, general rules are always to inspect before you accept; ask to see another type or price of room if you do not like what you are offered; book several months ahead for July and August; out of season, bargain for reductions

In the countryside, if you are stuck without accommodation, ask at the nearest taverna or *kafeníon*; a little persistence will almost invariably procure you some sort of shelter for the night.

Since standards can vary within Greek Tourist Organisation categories, and these categories are revised year to year, a rough price guide is used below:
€ under €75; €€ between €75-€150
€€€ more than €150

IRAKLEÍO

The code for Irakleío is 2810

Capsis Astoria (€€€)
5 Plateía Elefthérias
tel: 0343080; www.capsishotel.gr
City centre location belies the quiet comfort of this well-appointed and long-established hotel. Service is friendly and very helpful, the hotel was renovated in 2001, and the social heart of Irakleío is right on the doorstep.

Galaxy Hotel (€€)
17 Leofóros Dimokratias
tel: 238812
www.galaxy-hotel.com
Modern hotel of several storeys with a clean, sleek design in the public areas though the rooms aren't quite as slick, though still comfortable. A good range of services and what's claimed to be the largest pool in the city.

GDM Megaron (€€€)
9 D Beaufort
tel: 2810 305300
www.gdmmegaron.gr
This splendid 1930s building overlooking the waterfront was converted into a luxury hotel in 2003. It's a magnificent amalgamation of historic yet right up to date. There's a health club, a cute roof pool and a hip restaurant.

Lato (€€€)
15 Odós Epimenidou tel: 228103; www.lato.gr
Award winning boutique hotel with sleek modern décor smart design and internet access as standard. There's a superb roof garden with cocktail bar, a gym, steam room and Jacuzzi. Well situated near to but far enough away from the bus station, and a short walk to the centre and the Archaeological Museum. If you get the right room there are stunning views down on to the Venetian harbour.

Marin Dream Hotel (€€)
12 Odós Doukas Mpofor tel: 2810 300019
www.marinhotel.gr
Renovated in 2005 with a sharper style and up-to-the-minute internet connections, this is another trendy setting option for the capital. The communal areas have sumptuous sofas and there's a great café/bar. The rooms are small but it's all nicely finished.

Youth Hostels (€)
5 Odós Víronos, just north of El Greco Park (family-run) tel: 286281
24 Odós Chándakos tel: 280858
Both are clean and pleasant, and just a few minutes from the centre.

IRAKLEÍO REGION

Agia Pelayia

Happy Cretan Hotel (€–€€)
71500 Irakleío tel: 2810 811289
www.happycretan.com
Well appointed character apartments and studios with Cretan charm but modern conveniences including Internet access, electronic key and air conditioning. There are sea views from most of the terraces or balconies. Amenities include a Jacuzzi, spa, pool and fitness centre on site along with a restaurant.

Ano Archanes

Villa Archánes (€€–€€€)
70100 Archánes tel: 2810 3907780
www.maris.gr
Beautifully renovated villa in this mountain village

makes an ideal base for walking and hiking with six apartments (small kitchenette) and a taverna serving local dishes with fresh seasonal ingredients. There's a small pool on site.

Kerasia

Villa Kerasia (€€)
Tel: 28250 32690 (low rate call from UK is 0871 871 2891); www.CreteTravel.com
An exceptional small (eight rooms) stone country mansion hotel about 20 minutes south of Irakleío in the country. Décor is modernist and very comfortable and there is a pool, restaurant and bar on site. This is a fantastic option for those seeking an intimate atmosphere and a good option for the price.

Limin Khersonísos

Creta Blue Suites (€€€)
Odós Ipsilantou, Koutouloufari
tel: 28970 29157; www.cretablue.com
Set in the hills above the north coast, the Creta Blue is a family owned boutique suites-only hotel with 28 units set like a small, whitewashed, mountain village overlooking the infinity pool. Rooms are simple but luxurious with design elements taken from traditional Aegean architecture.
Silva Maris (€€€)
70014 Irakleío tel: 28970 22850
www.maris.gr
A modern but very tastefully designed hotel, simply furnished and built in "Cretan Village" style, at the eastern end of the town adjoining the beach. A small-scale development with two-storey buildings, low stone walls and small "piazzas" in subdued Mediterranean colours. An excellent base to combine sunbathing, nightlife, archaeology and exploration of the mountain backdrop.

Mália

Hotel Mália Studios & Apartments (€)
70007 Irakleío tel: 281 0213378
www.maliastudioshotel.com
Mália is a coastal resort known for its 24-hour summer fun. It's raucous and young, so you have been warned. This small hotel offers good value accommodation close to all the action. You'll need to pay extra for air-conditioning.

Mátala

Hotel Zafiria (€)
70200 Irakleío tel: 28920 45366
www.zafiria-matala.com
The largest hotel in the centre of this small resort, the Zafira makes a good base for both the beach and evening activities. There are good basic Greek style rooms with balcony or terrace.

Piskopiano

Amazones Village Suites (€€)
Odós Lykou, 70014 Irakleío
tel: 2897 030190
www.amazoneshotelsgreece.com
This small typically styled hotel features rooms, studios and suites with kitchens and living rooms set around a central pool area. Good level of facilities. There's a restaurant on site but the units are well equipped for self-catering.

Zarós

Eleonas (€€)
70002 Zarós tel: 28940 31238
www.eleonas.gr
Ten sympathetically styled individual "chalets" set a village style in 10ha (25 acres) close to Zarós. The units each have an open fire, terrace, CD player and satellite TV and there's a taverna on site with Internet access. A very peaceful retreat with touches of luxury.
Idi (€€)
70002 Irakleío tel: 28940 31302
www.idi-hotel.com
Stunning views of Psiloreítis from this comfortable modern hotel set among trees above Zàros village. Swimming pool, own taverna above a millstream, Cretan music and dancing evenings, hardworking and obliging owners. A good base for excursions.

ÁGIOS NIKÓLAOS

The code for Ágios Nikólaos is 28410

Apollon (€€)
9 R Kapetanaki tel: 23023
Follow Odós Filéllinon southwest from Lake Voulisméni. Not cheap, but its position in a quiet square just ten minutes from the waterfront, is a recommendation if you do not want noise at night.
Minos Beach Art Hotel (€€–€€€)
Akti Ilia Sotirhon, approximately 3km (2 miles) north of Ágios Nikólaos tel: 22345
www.slh.com
A beautiful position on a private beach owned by the hotel. This is probably the place to spend an unruffled few days if money is not an issue, since the Minos Beach is just about as luxurious and exclusive as a Cretan hotel can get.
Mirabéllo Village (€€€)
approximately 4km (2.5 miles) north of Ágios Nikólaos tel: 28400; www.iberostar.com
Another extremely luxurious and well-appointed hotel, spread over a cove and headland. Every kind of facility from a nightclub to sailboarding, outdoor and indoor pools with supervised games for children. Expensive, but not monstrously so considering the range of enticements on offer.
Pension Perla (€)
4 Odós Salamínos tel: 23379
Pleasantly situated on the seafront promenade a little north of the harbour. One of the quieter pensions, clean and efficiently-managed.
St Nicolas Bay Hotel (€€€)
Thessi Nissi, 72100 Ágios Nikólaos
tel: 25041; www.stnicolasbay.gr
One of the island's mature luxury resorts, the St Nicolas Bay is still an exceptional hotel. The styling is typically Aegean with beautifully accessorised rooms, suites and villas. There's a state of the art Elemis spa and many bungalows have pools.

ÁGIOS NIKÓLAOS REGION

Ammoudara

Lato Hotel (€)
72100 Ágios Nikólaos tel: 2841 024581
www.lato-hotel.com.gr
Small family run hotel with 37 well kept air-conditioned rooms, pool, restaurant and bar.

Eloúnta

Blue Palace (€€€)
72053 Eloúnta tel: 2841 065500
www.bluepalace.gr
Listed in Tatler's Top 101 Hotels of the World in 2006, the Blue Palace certainly offers exceptional accommodation, facilities and service including an internationally recognised spa and five restaurants, but this is certainly reflected in the room rates.

Eloúnda Beach (€€€)
tel: 2841 063000; www.eloundabeach.gr
One of Crete's most luxurious hotels. Accommodation either in hotel building or in bungalows on the private beach. A good place to splash out for an extravagant few nights, with every service and facility you would expect at top prices.

Néapoli

Néapolis (€)
1 Odós Evangelistrias tel: 28410 033966
This inexpensive clean and friendly hotel is a useful stand by in this busy part of Crete if you are touring and accommodation is elusive or very expensive in the coastal resorts. There's genuine Cretan life on the doorstep in the town.

Sissi

Castello Village (€€)
72400 Lasíthiou tel: 2841 071367
www.castellohotels.com
Pretty multi-coloured and multi-level apart-hotel that's designed to mimic a mountain settlement. The units are well finished and equipped with kitchenettes, though there are also several restaurants on site. The hotel sits 350m (318 yards) from the sea but has several cosy swimming pools.

Xerokambos

Hotel Mikro Village (€–€€)
72100 Lasíthiou tel: 2841 028500
www.mikrovillage.com
This small hotel has simple but spacious rooms with kitchenettes and balconies set around a verdant garden. The pool is a good size and there's a gym and sauna.

SITEÍA

The code for Siteía is 28430

Arkhontikon (€)
16 Odós Kondiláki tel: 28177
Near the Metiháki steps leading down to the waterfront, this hotel is at the end of a shady back street artery. Clean and quiet, it is well- located for the nightlife, bars and restaurants on the front.

Itanos (€)
4 Karamanli tel: 22900
Large family owned hotel on the waterfront overlooking the bay in the centre of the town. The décor is a little utilitarian, however offers good value for money.

Krystal (€–€€)
17 Odós Kapetan Sífi tel: 22284
www.ekaterinidis-hotels.com
Halfway up the hill that leads to the upper town, the Krystal is quiet, friendly, if rather old-fashioned and family run.

Hotel Denis (€–€€)
60 Plateía Elefthérios Venizélos tel: 28356
North of the *plateía* andbehind the most popular restaurants and bars. This well-kept place is in the midst of an evening atmosphere which is either lively or rowdy, according to your point of view.

Youth Hostel (€)
4 Odós Therísou tel: 22693
A little way out of town along the Irakleío road. Friendly and lively; compares well with Crete's other youth hostels.

SITEÍA REGION

Agia Fotia

Eden Rock Hotel (€€)
72300 Lasíthiou tel: 2842 061370
www.edenrock.gr
Neat and tidy family run hotel with a pretty pool and gardens leading down to a public beach. The owners have a full programme of activities, Cretan dishes at the restaurant and home produced raki at the bar. Prices are for half board.

Ierápetra

El Greco (€€)
42 Odós M Kothri, on the promenade
tel: 28420 28471
Highly recommended seafront hotel, family owned and run. Exceptionally helpful and friendly staff, pleasant décor, comfortable. Own restaurant on the promenade.

Koutsounári

7km (4 miles) east of Ierápetra

Club Creta Suites (€€)
72200 Lasíthiou tel 2842 061915
www.cretasuites.com
Designed like a traditional Cretan mountain village, all bare stone and traditional fabrics, these suites offer a cosy place to stay. There is an excellent restaurant on site serving Cretan dishes but no pool. There is a four night minimum stay.

Koutsounari Traditional Cottages (€€)
tel: 28420 61815; www.traditionalcottages.gr
These beautiful reconstructions of traditional Cretan homes have bed slabs, furnishings, beams and gardens. Selt-cater, or use Koutsounari's own taverna. Minimum stay one week.

Kató Chório

Istron Bay (€€€)
Ístro tel: 28410 61303; www.istronbay.gr
Large, expensive and luxurious. Everything you could want from a modern top hotel: superb position on cliff over sandy bay that is nominally for the use of residents only; nightclubs; shops;children's and adults' swimming pools; watersports; tennis; bars; discos; Cretan evenings.

Móchlos

Sofía *(€)*
72057 Lasíthiou tel: 28430 28177
Unfussy hotel in a quiet position down on the Bay of Mirampéllou, with a good view out to Móchlos Island from the seafront rooms. A pleasant base for exploring this craggy coast between Pachiá Ámmos and Siteía.

Nakou

Nakou Village (€€–€€€)
72200 Lasíthiou tel: 2842 061815
www.traditionalcottages.gr
Twenty one exquisite studios and apartments taking the best elements of Greek design combined with modern accessories. There's a lovely pool and a restaurant on site. Minimum stay one week.

Palaíkastro

Hotel Hellas (€)
75100 Lasíthiou tel: 28430 61240
A first-rate pension in this large, rather back-of-beyond village at the eastern tip of Crete. Clean, welcoming and comfortable.
Marina Village (€)
75100 Lasíthiou near Angathiá on road to sea tel: 28430 61284
This simple family run hotel a couple of kilometres east of Paliakastro was renovated in 2005. The two-storey box styling offers single, double and family rooms. There's a tennis court and a pool.

Zákros

Pension Poseidon (€)
72300 Lasíthiou Káto Zákros tel: 28430 93385
Plain, inexpensive rooms overlooking the beach of this beautifully sited and unfrequented single-strip hamlet below the Minoan palace.
Hotel Zákros (€€)
72300 Lasíthiou Áno Zákros tel: 2843 0933799
On the main *plateía* on the way to Zákros Minoan palace. Bed and breakfast only, but good tavernas nearby. Very plain from outside, but friendly and quite comfortable.

RÉTHYMNO

The code for Réthymno is 28310

Adele Mare (€€€)
Adelianos Kambos Platanes tel: 71803
This is a good, expensive international beach hotel about 4km (2.5 miles) east of Réthymno, with its own sandy beach, apartment houses set in landscaped grounds and a big hotel building fronting the swimming pool.
Fortezza (€€)
16 Odós Melissinou tel: 55551
www.fortezza.gr
Close to Réthymno's impressive Venetian Fortress—indeed, just below the walls. Convenient for the city but away from the crowds, and no need to go to the beach as the hotel boasts both courtyard and swimming pool.
Ideon Hotel (€€)
10 N. Plastira Square tel: 28667
www.hotelideon.gr
A pleasant, modern hotel overlooking the waterfront in the old town. All rooms have a balcony. Swimming pool, lounge and restaurant.
Mythos Suites Hotel (€€–€€€)
12 Plateía Karaoli tel: 2831 053917
www.mythos-crete.gr
This beautifully restored mansion in Karaoli Square in the heart of the old town has elegant suites and studios with comfortable traditional furnishings with internet access and kitchenette. A great place to spend a few days at the heart of the resort action but the hotel doesn't have a pool or restaurant on site.
Porto Réthymno Hotel (€€€)
52 Leofóros S Venizélou tel: 2831 050432
www.sterlinghotels.com
Stylish modern high-rise hotel on the water's edge, 700m from the centre of town. Facilities include outdoor and indoor pools, fitness room, gym, sauna, dive centre and a range of watersports.
Youth Hostel (€)
41 Odós Tombázi tel: 22848
In a street running south from the old city gate. A big, well-run and welcoming hostel, with all the basic facilities. One of Crete's best.

RÉTHYMNO REGION

Agia Galini

Sky Beach Hotel €)
Troullimos Mihalis, 74056 Réthymno
Tel: 28320 91415; www.skybeach.gr
A small property whose suites and apartments tumble down the hillside offering each room a view of the bay. There are steps down to the beach, which may not suite the young or inform. Furnishing is simple.

Ágios Pávlos

Ágios Pávlos (€)
Tel: 2832 071104
www.agiospavlos.gr
One of those Cretan secrets, trembling on the brink of development. For the moment, the hotel and apartments look out on a practically perfect, pristine bay. Simple, clean and very Cretan hospitality.

Balí

Balí Beach Hotel & Village (€€€)
tel: 0834–94210; www.balibeach.gr
The part-pebble, part-sand beach is overlooked by this comfortable, modern hotel: All facilities; private stretch of beach. Prices compare favourably with other upmarket hotels.

Missiria

Creta Palace (€€€)
74100, Réthymno tel: 28310 55181
www.grecotel.gr
Beautifully designed large luxury hotel with elegant yet up to the minute Cretan style and luxurious fittings. Standard rooms are refined, but there are also private bungalows and villas for families or couples wanting more privacy. The word "palace" in the title tells the story.

Pánormos

Creta Marine (€€€)
74100 Réthymno tel: 28340 51290
www.aegeanstar.com
Set on a seaside cliff around three bays, the Creta Marine is styled like a Cretan village though its one and two storey buildings are set around an enormous pool. The differing styles of the units shows a fine attention to detail and there's a full programme of sports and activities.

Pánormo Beach (€€)
tel: 28340 51321
The hotel is on a sheltered and sandy cove tucked below the new road. Easy-paced and comfortable, with a good view over the village and bay. Especially enjoyable early or late season.
Villa Kynthia (€€€)
tel: 28340 51102
A beautifully restored 19th-century mansion offering individually styled rooms and private courtyard with small swimming pool. Located equidistant between Réthymno and Irakleío. Perfect for a relaxed touring holiday.

Plakiás

Lamon (€€)
74060 Réthymno tel: 28320 31425
www.lamon-hotel.gr
Set across the road from the beach at this fast-growing south coast resort west of Agía Galíni. Quieter location than the waterfront, though not as picturesque. A very clean, pleasant, moderately priced hotel.
Plakiás Bay (€)
74060 Réthymno tel: 28320 31951
www.plakiasbay.com
A small family run hotel, very friendly and with good home cooking. Set at the far end of the village on a headland overlooking both towering mountains inland and a beautiful bay. A ten-minute stroll along the beach into the centre of Plakiás for a taverna meal, and a slightly longer, romantic walk back in the moonlight. Heaven.

Scaleta

Creta Royal (€€€)
74100 Réthymno tel: 28310 71812
www.aegeanstar.com
Set on 700m of long sandy beach, the Creta Royal is a luxury hotel with 100 rooms set overlooking the pool and ocean. There's a good range of activities including sports and an entertainment programme, so it's a good option for families who want a touch more class. Prices are for half board.

Spíli

Green (€)
74053 Réthymno tel: 0832–22225
www.greenhotel.gr
Both hotel and village are a delight. An excellent base for exploring the mountains and coasts of the Kédros range. Extremely well-run and friendly bed and breakfast place; clean and comfortable, and furnished with eccentric reading matter.

CHANIÁ

The code for Chaniá is 28210

Casa Delfino (€€€)
9 Odós Theofanus Tel: 87400
www.casadelfino.com
This delightful 17th century harbour-side mansion has been tastefully renovated and now offers 21 luxury suites set around an elegant courtyard. The owner has used the finest materials to create modern yet comfortable interiors, and the delights of Chaniá old town old just beyond the gates.

Doma (€€)
124 Elefthérios Venizélos tel: 51772
www.hotel-doma.gr
This handsome old building on the edge of the elegant Khalépa quarter has housed the British consulates and embassies. Everything at the Doma is unfussily spot-on.
Nostos Hotel (€€)
42-46 Zamelio
tel: 94743; www.nostos-hotel.com
This small hotel in the Evréika quarter is set in one of the major pedestrian alleys only a couple of minutes from the harbour. Rooms are basic but clean, with air conditioning. Some have balconies.
Porto Veneziano (€€)
Aktíi Enoseos Palaio Limani tel: 27100
www.bestwestern.com
An excellent position right next to the Venetian *arsenali* at the eastern end of the inner harbour, with views from the balconied rooms, over fishing boats to the lights of the waterfront.

CHANIÁ REGION

Akrotiri Peninsula

Perle Resort Hotel and Health Spa Marine (€€€)
Stavros Akrotiriou, 73100
tel: 2821 039400; www.perle-spa.com
Luxurious hotel completed in 2002 with thalassotherapy and wellness programmes and fitness centres. Rooms have a classical elegance whilst spa takes design elements from the Near East.

Kalýes

Kalyves Beach (€€)
Apokoronou tel: 28250 31285
www.kalyvesbeach.com
Set right on the sandy beach near the centre of this bustling, large coastal village. It also sits alongside a fast-flowing river which, unusually for Crete, flows all year round. Picturesque setting, next to a trout-filled stream with resident local ducks—a change from barking dogs. Serves one of the best frappés the island has to offer.

Kolymbari

Grand Bay Beach Resort (€€€)
73006 Chaniá tel: 2824 083380
www.grandbay.gr
This elegant modern low-rise resort hotel has around 130 rooms of various sizes set overlooking the beach. There's a large pool and fitness centre restaurant and snack bar.

Loutró

Porto Loutró (€–€€)
tel: 28250 91433; www.hotelportoloutro.com
Wonderful central position in the curve of houses, and as clean and fresh as you could wish, though by no means *grande luxe*.

Máleme

Neos Omalos (€€)
tel: 28210 67269; www.neos-omalos.gr
An excellent base for exploring the White Mountains or the Omalos Plateau at your leisure. Spring is a beautiful time of year to pay this area a visit, with its wild flowers, blue skies and snow-

covered mountains. However, the nights (and even the days) can be cool at this time of year, therefore a warm hotel, with central heating, is an essential. A very good range of fresh Cretan food in the taverna and a large log fire to warm your toes if the *raki* hasn't done so already.

Palaiochóra

Hotel Lissos (€)
12 El Venizelou 73001 Pelekanos
tel: 28320 41122; www.lissos-hotel.gr
A better-class pension completely renovated in 2005. On the main street, which means it can be lively at night.

Platanias

Porto Platanias Beach Resort (€€€)
73014 Chaniá tel: 2821 038800
www.portoplatanias.gr
Set in the lea of rolling hills this large resort has a good sandy stretch. Accommodation ranges from doubles to maisonettes and suites suitable for families. Good range of facilities for all ages.

Pergamos

Pergamos Village (€)
Rapaniana Kolimbariou tel: 28240 22944
www.pergamos-hotel.gr
Simple whitewashed two storey complex with a good sized pool, the Pergamos Village is inexpensive Greek accommodation at it's best.

Sfakiá

Vritomartis (€€€)
at Komitádes, 3km (2 miles) east of Sfakiá
tel: 28250 91112
Efficient, plush hotel, much frequented by German visitors. Serve-yourself meals, chalet accommodation, own section of beach, swimming pool, acres of cool marble, pleasant staff.

Xenia (€)
On the west side of the harbour in Sfakiá
tel: 28250 91202
A smallish hotel, one of the string of Xenia hotels established by the government. The usual good standard of cleanliness and comfort, and a handy position a little away from the waterfront with a good view up the town and over the harbour.

Soúgia

Pikilassos (€–€€) *tel: 28230 51242*
A comfortable and welcoming hotel, set back a little from the front in a quieter position. A pleasant atmosphere and its own good taverna. Worth paying a little extra for.

Vlatos

Milia (€–€€)
Milia, Vlatos, 73012 Chaniá
tel: 2821 046774 ; www.milia.gr
This traditional mountain settlement surrounded by hills has been transformed into a small eco-resort. Rooms are simple and the electricity supply irregular, but this is a place to totally unwind and forget about the 21st century. The hotel sits on a working farm and the produce is used in the excellent restaurant on site. The whole concept is to go back to the way life used to be lived on Crete, and guests can join in with activities on the farm.

RESTAURANTS

Mass tourism has increased the number of places to eat out in Crete. It has also separated tourist restaurants from places where the locals go. Tourist restaurants offer roughly the same range of prices and dishes across the island. Local restaurants may be a little cheaper, pay less attention to décor, but offer a more characterful approach to cooking.

All the Big Four towns—Irakleío, Chaniá, Réthymno and Ágios Nikólaos—have expensive restaurants offering international cuisine that are often attached to hotels. These can be excellent, or pretentious. Tourist restaurants often have coloured photographs of the dishes on offer displayed outside, and multilingual menus. You cannot really go wrong in these places, but after a while the unadventurous approach can pall. The local restaurants will be found up side streets, away from popular areas such as the harbour. Ask the hotel receptionist or owner where they would choose if they were going out to eat good Cretan food. Or assess the Cretan:tourist ratio of customers. These restaurants, like tavernas, will always be only too happy to show you the dish of the day in the kitchen.

The good, plain tavernas are often a better bet than any of the foregoing if you are after a characterful, inexpensive meal of local cooking, cheerfully served with strong local wine from the barrel. There is at least one in all but the tiniest villages and they are always family-run. A *psarótaverna* specialises in fish dishes. Fish is often surprisingly expensive for an island so dependent on the sea for a living. An *ouzéri* is a small version of a taverna, often offering an astonishingly varied *mezédes* or hors d'oeuvres in lieu of a formal meal. And the *souvláki* stall, selling takeaway kebabs of meat or fish, is always a good cheap way to fill up the empty corners. Fast food restaurant chains selling burgers, fried chicken and pizzas can nowadays be found in all the main towns.

IRAKLEÍO

Erganos (€€)
5 Odós Georgiadi tel: 285629
Erganos is leading the way as a new generation of traditional Cretan taverna, you'll find locals enjoying the food here and there's sometimes live music. A good place to try local dishes.

Erotokritos (€€)
109 Odós A Papandreou tel: 252426
Another new taverna that reassures lovers of Greek food that traditions aren't being lost. The food is tasty without being presumptuous and the house wine delicious.

Giovanni's (€€)
12 Odós Kórai tel: 346338
Justly popular, which also accounts for slow service. Nice dark panelled interior, or eat outdoors on Odós Kórai's paved roadway. Imaginative cooking with touches of sophistication. Try their mouth-tingling *stifádo*. Talkative owner with excellent English.

Goody's (€)
Michelidaki 6 tel: 341091
Greek fast-food that locals will eat.

Kiriákos (€€€)
45 Odós Dimokratías, just outside city walls to the southeast tel: 224649
Knowledgeable Irákliots come here to appreciate well-cooked *stifádo*, stuffed vine leaves, and cabbage in egg and lemon sauce, along with a characterful house red wine.

Klimátaria (€€)
Plateía Viglas tel: 346483
This is one of a number of restaurants along this pedestrian lane which connects Plateía Elefthérias and Plateía Venizélou. The Klimatária is, however, the one most frequented by Cretans along this very touristy road.

Loúkoulos (€€€)
Odós Kórai tel: 224435
Very popular with a younger and better-heeled clientèle. Adventurous Italian cooking with a touch of Cretan character. Considered to be a smart place to see and be seen eating.

Odós Aigaiou (€€€)
Corner of Odós Aigaiou & Odós Spinaki tel: 241410
Renowned fish restaurant with views out across the harbour, this is one of the most expensive traditional eateries in the capital but has a loyal clientele for its attention to detail.

Ouzéri (€)
On south side of Plateía Daskaloyiánnis tel: 226286
Shaded tables on the pavement. Simple menu, but enormously varied *orektiká* (hors-d'oeuvres), which are the best bet and make a complete meal in themselves. Good village wine, too.

Pagopoieion (€€–€€€)
Plateía Ágios Titus tel: 346028
One of the fashionable places to sit and have a coffee and meze snacks (or a full meal), the eatery is housed in an old ice factory. Food is Greek and Italian and there's a good selection of wines.

Psária (€€)
At bottom of Odós 25 Avgoústou
Popular with locals and tourists alike for its fish specialities, but the real attraction is the wonderful view over the *voltá* strollers to the Venetian fort, and the fishing boats in the harbour.

IRAKLEÍO REGION

Archánes

Myriophytó (€)
on the plateía *at the southern end of the village Tel: 2810 751441*
Friendly owners serve unexceptional but well-cooked food on a pleasant, leafy terrace overlooking the square. In Archanes, drink the dark red local wine by the carafe. Key to superbly frescoed church of Mikhaíl Arkhángelos kept here.

Ano Khersonísos

Konaki tou Mougavia (€€)
One of many restuarants in the pretty main square of the village, where they host regular Greek evenings. Typical taverna food and wine, and only a short ride from Khersonísos resort.

Ta Petrino (€€)
Odós ta Petrina tel: 28970 21976
The epitome of an excellent Greek family owned tavern, the grilled meats are delicious, served with meltingly tender potatoes roasted in olive oil plus a range of mezede dishes. Many ingredients are home produced, as is the after dinner raki.

Koutouloufari

Fabrica (€€)
Centre of the village tel: 28970 23981
A lovely tradition stone house that's been transformed into a 21st century *kafeneion*. The restaurant serves crepes and coffee during the day on the shady terrace but turns into a candlelit restaurant at night where crepes are supplemented by meats from the grill or curry.

Rodia or Rogdia

Ouzerie Kegos (€)
Top of the village tel: 2810 841393
A new ouzerie in the old tradition, Kegos serves lovely fresh mezedes and excellent ouzo and you can also drink in the views from the terrace. A nice place for a relaxing hour or two in the afternoon.

Tsoutsouros

Petra & Fos (€–€€)
72200 Lasíthiou tel: 28910 92345
A great place top drop in for lunch while you're touring, the sandwiches are fresh and there are sizzling stone baked pizzas, plus the usual Greek choices. In the evening the restaurant continues the pizza theme but also serves grilled meats.

ÁGIOS NIKÓLAOS

Itanos (€€)
1 Odós Kyprou, just southeast of Plateía Venizélou tel: 28410 25340
Off the tourist waterfront, and excellent value if you want a real Cretan atmosphere, pleasant sevice and good, plain food. Popular with locals.

La Strada (€€)
5 Odós Plastira tel: 025841
Delicious Italian cuisine with over 30 different types of pizzas plus excellent antipasto and delicious desserts, this makes a reliable change from Greek taverna food.

Migomis (€€€)
20 Odós Plastira tel 28410 24353
High above Lake Voulisméni and overlooking the town, this elegant restaurant has a terrace and interior dining room. The menu is Italian, and of excellent quality. It's a perfect place for a romantic meal and there's live piano music in summer.

Ormos (€€€)
Ormos, 72100 Ágios Nikólaos tel: 28410 24094
Classy and expensive restaurant attached to Hotel Ormos. Highly praised cuisine with Greek food only one of the options.

Pelagos (€€)
Corner of Odós Koraki and Katehaki tel: 025737
Located in a neo-classical house and patio garden a little way back from the seafront. Seasonal menu specialises in fish dishes.

Synantisi (€€)
69 Odós Ath Sereti on the right off the Eloúnta road tel: 2294 022647
Good food and village wine, friendly waiters and expansive cook. Surprisingly quiet position. A popular local taverna beyond the normal visitor circuit.

ÁGIOS NIKÓLAOS REGION

Elounta

Kalidon (€€)
72053 Eloúnta tel: 2841 041451
Perhaps Crete's only floating restaurant the Kalidon sits on pontoons in the bay at Eloúnta. The menu offers standard seafood and Greek staples. There's a land-based dining room for those who suffer from sea-sickness!

The Old Mill (€€)
Hotel Elounda Mare tel: 2841 041102 www.eloundamare.gr
This high-class restaurant is recognised as one of the best in Greece with high standards of cuisine and service and a menu that pushed the boundary of modern fusion food. The décor is a superb rendition of an atmospheric olive mill.

Vritomartes (€€)
Schisma, Eloúnta tel: 28410 41325
Set on an artificial island at the heart of Eloúnta, the Vritomartes specialises in fish and prices that aren't as fancy as some other places in town. The owner has his own boat and his morning catch then goes on sale in the restaurant.

Tzermiádo

Kronio (€€)
Near where you wait for the bus that circumnavigates the Lasíthiou Plateau tel: 2844 022375
This is a friendly place with a young owner who has built the reputation of his restaurant in the last few years. It's considered the best on the plateau. Excellent Cretan cuisine without a fancy price tag.

SITEÍA

Kalí Kardiá (€€)
On Odós Emmanuel Foundalidóu. the next street up from and parallel with Odós Vinzétzos Kornárou
Locally caught fresh fish is a big speciality here, preceded by huge and varied hors d'oeuvres and lubricated with excellent local wine.

Mixos (€€)
105 Odós Vinzetzos Kornarou tel: 2843 026515
One of Siteía's gems, frequented by local people, either eating the good Cretan-style food or idling over the village red wine that seems darker, stronger and more irresistible here. A real find, and good value.

Neromílos (€€€)
A couple of kilometres east of the town tel: 2843 025576
Very highly recommended as much for its stunning view, looking out over the Bay of Siteía to the Dragonáda Islands, as for its local and adventurous food flavoured with spices and garlic. This one is certainly not for the shallow-pocketed.

Zorba's (€€)
Plateía Kosma Zotou tel: 2843 022689
If you are going to eat "tourist" while watching the world strut by, then Zorba's is probably the place to do it. Acceptable Greek food served by dashing waiters. Not particularly good value for money, perhaps, but the lively hub of Siteía's holiday nightlife. Good for lunch too.

SITEÍA REGION

Chiona (near Itanos)

Kakavia (€€)
Tel: 2843 061227
One of a selection of restaurants in this tiny resort but Kakavia concentrates on Cretan cuisine and fresh seafood, rather than international dishes—the name means 'fish soup' in Greek. Definitely worth spending some time in the kitchen choosing what you want to eat.

Ierápetra

Kastro Ouzeri (€)
78 Odós Stratigou Samouil tel: 2842 028218
Enjoy a few glasses of raki and some Cretan nibbles as you watch the world go by here.

Napoleon the Great (€€)
20 Odós Samoúliou tel: 2824 022410
An excellent, local restaurant, friendly and informal, whose plain décor belies the delicious food served here. Try their fish soup—fish and soup come separately—and ask for local wine.

Taverna Konaki (€€)
32 Odós Sratigou Samouil tel: 2842 024422
Traditional family-owned taverna by the beach. There's a good choice of well-cooked local dishes.

Kato Zákros

Taverna Akrogiali (€€)
Tel: 2843 026893
This shady restaurant skirts the water's edge and serves a pleasing variety of dishes plus freshly caught seafood. Another place to where you may want to linger for the whole afternoon.

Khandrás

Kafeníon (€)
On the right of the plateía *as you go south through the village*
Well worth a stop. Excellent *mezédes* with very inexpensive drinks. Locals play cards, chat and snooze in the dark interior of this archetypal Cretan village café.

Palaíkastro

Elena's (€€)
Plateía Palaiokastrou tel: 2843 061304
This is a very pleasant place for lunch if you have most of the afternoon to idle over your lamb cutlets, salad and wine. Definitely long on flavour and ambience, but short on speed and formality.

Mythos (€–€€)
Tel: 2843 061243
Tasty local cuisine with a good range of mezede titbits washed down with local wine. There are tables on the roadside terrace or in the stone clad interior that looks a little like the markings on a giraffe—don't let that put you off eating here.

Xerókampos

Kastri (€–€€)
One street back from the seafront
Tel: 28430 26715
Grilled meats and fish in the family run restaurant just off the waterfront, this is a very traditional style taverna worth seeking out.

Liviko View (€)
Tel: 2843 027000
Good and substantial cooking at reasonable prices. The owner uses olive oil, fruit and vegetables from the family farm. This is good substantial cooking at reasonable prices and there's a nice terrace for alfresco dining.

RÉTHYMNO

Plateía Petiháki

This is the square round the Rimondi Fountain, the less expensive and more spicy of Réthymno's two dining centres. There is always bustle, shouting and laughter around here. The restaurants and cafés here are always busy, most of them much of a muchness.

Avli (€€€)
Odós Xanthoudidou 22 (at Odós Radamanthys)
A Venetian house with large, verdant courtyard is the setting for probably the best restaurant in town. Cretan and Mediterranean cuisine, with seasonal specialities.

Cavo d'Oro (€€€)
42 Odós Nearchou tel: 2831 024446
www.cavodoro-rethymno.com
It's true that you pay a little extra to eat in the harbour in Réthymno but Cavo d'Oro is a reliable choice. Seafood is a speciality but the menu is extensive. Take a table at the water's edge.

Samaria (€–€€)
Odós E Venizélou tel: 2831 024681
Much frequented by locals the Samaria offers reliable inexpensive grills, salads and wine from the barrel. Vegetables come from the owner's garden and there's a choice of seafood. The sheltered courtyard is a wonderful place for a leisurely lunch.

Thalassographia (€€€)
33 Odós Kefalogiannidon
Tel: 2831 052569
Thalassographia has a large open terrace with views over the sea and towards the old fortezza. Greek and European cuisine.

Veneto (€€€)
4 Odós Epimenidou tel: 2831 056634
This lovely vaulted dining room and courtyard of this 15th century mansion makes an atmospheric place to eat and the Cretan dishes are delicious. There's a wine list of over 150 choices.

RÉTHYMNO REGION

Agia Galini

Taverna Kosmas (€–€€)
74056 Chaniá (in the centre of the village)
Tel: 2832 091222
Three generations of the Linoxilakis family have been in the hospitality business in Agia Galini. Since 1996 Kosmas and his German born wife Ines have been in charge. This is a good honest eatery in the Greek tradition.

Armeni

O Alekos (€–€€)
74100 Réthymno tel: 2831 041185
An unpretentious family kafeneion that serves a limited daily menu, which you know will be ultra-fresh and tasty, accompanied by wine by the barrel. There is a totally non-touristy atmosphere but an authentic Cretan experience.

Georgióupoli

Arkádi (€€)
70007 Georgióupoli tel: 2825 061166
A very good spot to enjoy an evening meal looking across to the lights of Georgióupoli sparkling along their waterfront.

Goumes (5mins from Réthymno)

Maistros (€€–€€€)
Odós Akrotirou tel: 28310 25492
This bar/restaurant has passable Greek and Continental food, plus fresh seafood, but is really mentioned because of the fantastic sunset views it offers from the tables in the gardens. It's only a short distance from Réthymno and could be the end point for a very nice walk from the town.

Missiria

Taverna tou Zissi (€–€€)
63 Odós Mahis Kritis tel: 2831 028814
Popular local taverna specialising in spit roast lamb and chicken served meltingly tender. There's a whole range of excellent local dishes, however, including rabbit stew and juicy veal in tomato sauce with wine from the barrel. There's a large courtyard or spacious dining room.

CHANIÁ

Antigoni (€€)
Akti Enosseos corner Dukalianos
tel: 28210 45236
This longstanding favourite has recently received a new lick of paint, but the owners haven't changed the successful menu and still concentrate on the freshest seafood plus local dishes. Follow the locals here—they know what they're doing.

Apostolis (€€€)
6 & 10 Odós Akti Enosseos (on the old port)
Tel: 2821 043470
Renowned in Greek circles of cuisine, Apostolos Apostolakis keeps a very traditional kitchen and menu, with delectable slow cooked stews plus the ubiquitous seafood. The views of the old port are almost as good as the food.

Dino's (€€€)
2 Akti Enoseos Tel: 2821 041865
An excellent place for well-cooked and imaginative fish dishes, as long as your pockets are reasonably well lined. In a prime position on the inner harbour, near the Venetian *arsenali*, away from the noisiest part.

Karnagio (€€)
8 Plateía Katehâki tel: 2821 053366
A long-established old favourite in the very heart of the Kastélli quarter. Set in a quiet location a little way back from where the inner and outer harbours join. Very good food, a warm atmosphere and excellent wine served by the jug.

Konaki (€€)
40 Odós Kondilaki tel: 2821 097130
This family owned restaurant has been in operation for over 20 years and is set in a pretty Chaniá mansion with a cosy terrace. There's an extensive menu of Cretan, Greek and European dishes.
Myrovolos (€€€)
19 Odós Zambeliou
Tel: 2821 091960
Set in a traditional Venetian building in the old town the menu includes delicious stuffed vine leaves, grilled meats and, to finish the meal, creamy local yoghurt topped with honey.
Nykterida (€€€)
at Korákies, just on the neck of the Akrotíri peninsula, a short taxi ride from Chaniá
Tel: 2821 064215
A good restaurant recommended by locals in the know, serving well prepared Cretan food as well as a more pan-Mediterranean menu. Varied selection of sophisticated and village wines. Garden with wonderful views across Soúda Bay. Sometimes has traditional music and is used by tour companies for Cretan evenings.
Tamam (€€)
49 Odós Zambelíou tel: 2821 096080
This is another justly popular place and a former Turkish bath. Tall, plain interior with tables on two levels, or alternatively cramped outside on the pavement of a narrow street. Really well-cooked local food is on offer. Try their sausages, lamb stew and local wine. Street cats may wander in and out. A relaxed restaurant where your meal can be spun out for hours.

All along Odós Sífaka there are several good **pavement cafés** (€) selling cheese and sweet pies along with the usual Greek coffee and glass of water. These all face the ruins of the ancient city walls, in one of Chaniá's quieter streets.

CHANIÁ REGION

Galatas
Taverna Elia (€–€€)
Close to the town stadium
Tel: 28210 31720
Family owned typical taverna serving excellent grilled meats, fresh fish and mezedes. Try the grilled feta or the zingy tzatziki (garlic dip) with a crispy fresh salad. Owner Elefteria also serves the horta (wild greens) that doctors have said is so good for us.

Grameno Beach
Grameno (€–€€)
In the centre of the settlement
Tel: 2823 041505
A nice shady pergola with lots of greenery is the dining area for this family owned restaurant. Ingredients for many dishes are produced on the family farm including olive oil and vegetables. The meat is sourced from local producers. Traditional cuisine.

Kalives
Kritiko (€€€)
Tel: 2825 031096
Situated on the seafront just beyond the main square of the village. Housed in a refurbished stone building with patio and veranda, Kritiko offers more upmarket surroundings than the usual taverna. Seafood and traditional local dishes predominate. Live piano music in season.

Kalyviáni
Kafeníon (€)
Just above the church. This is an absolutely archetypal *kafeníon* with old men playing cards outside, very cheap drinks and nothing at all to do but sit back and stare at the shimmering rocks of the Gramvoúsa Peninsula.

Loutró
Blue House (€€)
Enthusiastically recommended for its well-cooked fare and pleasant service. A favourite for its good view over the peerless harbour.

Maleme
Persama Taverna (€€)
73014 Maleme tel: 2821 062145
It's hard to see the entrance of this taverna, just a couple of hundred metres from the beach, for the verdant flowers and trees, and the shade is provided by a canopy of vines. The menu is classic Cretan with local ingredients.

Palaiochora
Cosmos Taverna (€€€)
On the ridge at Platanías, 73014 Platanías
Tel: 2821 068558
A delightful restaurant with a terrace with panoramic sea views, the Cosmos is a level above the family taverna with elegant décor and table settings plus a fusion menu with attractive food presentation.
Galaxy (€€)
Tel: 2823 041059
www.chaniagalaxy.com
Galaxy has been open since 1980 and concentrates on fresh seafood but also has traditional dishes and pizzas. Set on the town beach it's a pleasant place for a lazy lunch or dinner.

Platanías
Milos Taverna (€€)
14km (8.5 miles) west of Chaniá
tel: 2825 091433
This has been popular for many years. Excellent food in a garden with ducks and peacocks and an old water mill.

Vlatos
Milia
73102 Vlatos tel: 2821 046774
A trend-setting ecological restaurant, part of the Milia eco-friendly village, Milia serves excellent Cretan cuisine taken either from the hotel farm or from local sources. The menu changes from day to day but there's always a supply of delicious fresh bread to accompany the food.

Vrýses
Many little **cafés** on the main street sell the famous local honey and yoghurt—mouthfuls of heaven.

A

accommodation
  camping 268
  hotels 243, 274–8
  self-catering 268
  youth hostels 263, 268
Aféndis Christós 79
Agía Aikaterínis 62
Agía Ána 222
Agía Ánna 169
Agía Déka 86
Agía Fotiá 142
Agía Galíni 172
  accommodation 277
  eating out 282
Agía Marína 209
Agía Paraskeví (Amári Valley) 168
Agía Paraskeví (Anisaráki) 222
Agía Pelagía (Áno Viánnos) 117
Agía Pelagía (near Irakleío) 274
Agía Rouméli 222–3, 248, 254, 283
Agía Triáda (Ágios Nikólaos) 114
Agía Triáda (Minoan palace) 80–1
Agía Triáda (Kakodíki) 230
Agía Triáda Monastery 220, 246
Agía Varvára 134
Agíi Anargyri 204
Agíi Apóstoli 156
Agíoi Theódhoroi 225
Ágios Antónios (Savvathanon Monastery) 189
Ágios Antónios (Vrondísion Monastery) 191
Ágios Demétrios (Iráklio) 53
Ágios Demétrios (Néapoli) 134
Ágios Fanóurios 190
Ágios Giórgios (Anisaráki) 222
Ágios Giórgios (Néapoli) 134
Ágios Ioánnis (Asteroúsia Mountains) 107
Ágios Ioánnis Prodrómos 178
Ágios Ioánnis Theológos 169
Ágios Ioánnis (Thryptí Mountains) 156
Ágios Ioánnis (White Mountains) 237
Ágios Ioánnis Yíonis 245
Ágios Mikhaíl Arkhángelos 78
Ágios Minás (Iráklio: cathedral) 62
Ágios Minás (Irakleío: church) 62
Ágios Nikólaos 14, 110, 112–15, 162
  accommodation 275
  Archaeological Museum 115
  Agía Triáda 114
  eating out 280
  harbour 114–15
  history 112–13
  Kitroplatía 114
  Lake Voulisméni 115
  Odós 28 Októbriou 114
  Odós Koundoúrou 114
  Plateía Venizélou 114
  walk 114–15
Ágios Nikólaos (Chaniá) 204
Ágios Nikólaos Monastery 191
Ágios Pávlos 167
Ágios Pnevma 128
Ágios Spirídon 134
Ágios Títos (Górtina) 87
Ágios Títos (Iráklio) 55, 58–9
Ágios Geórgios 125, 130–1
Ágios Giórgios (Áno Viánnos) 117
Ágios Giórgios (Sklavopoúla) 250
Ágios Giórgios (Voilá) 147
Agría Gramvoúsa 225
agriculture
  olives 76–7
  sheep and goats 77
  terraced hillsides 12
  threshing floors 140
airports and air services 256, 262
Akhládia 156
Akrotíri Martélos 89
Akrotíri peninsula 218, 220–1
Aligí 253
Allied War Cemetery 250
Amári 168, 169
Amári Valley 11, 166, 168–9
Ámpelos 224
Ampeloúsos 88
Amirás 127
Ammoudára 162
  accommodation 275
Ammoudári 241
Anemóspila 79
Anisaráki 222
Áno Méros 169
Áno Rodákino 188
Áno Viánnos 116–17, 127
Áno Viran Episkopí 186
Áno Zákros 153, 155
  eating out 282
Anópoli 235
Anógia 167, 169, 171
  accommodation 277
  eating out 282
  Old Anógian House Museum 171
Apáno Flório 253
Apladianá 187
  eating out 282
Apóstoli 146
aqueduct system 86
Arádiana 237
Archaeological Museum (Ágios Nikólaos) 115
Archaeological Museum (Ierápetra) 145
Archaeological Museum (Irakleío) 48–51
Archaeological Museum (Chaniá) 204, 206
Archaeological Museum (Réthymno) 184
Archaeological Museum (Siteía) 151
Arkádiou Monastery 171–2, 246
Arkádiou, Gabriel 56, 171, 172
Arkalochóri 79
Archánes 78
  accommodation 274
  eating out 280
Árvi 117
  accommodation 275
Árví Gorge 117
Árví Monastery 127, 246
Askífos 237
Asomáton Monastery 169
Asómatos 78
Asteroúsia Mountains 74, 75, 89, 100–1

B

Balí 277
Bándouvas, Manóli 121
banks 259, 270
Barkham, Geoffrey 235
Basilica of St Mark 55
Battle of Crete Week 17
beaches 113
beggars 196
bicycle hire 262
boats and ferries 254, 256–7, 263
bus and coach travel 261–2
bus ride: Sfakiá to Chaniá 240–1

caged songbirds 204, 230
caïques 254
camping 268
Cape Koutrí 226
Cape Léndas 101
car hire 70, 102, 260–1
Carta, General Angelo 121
caves 176–7
  Artemis, cave of 176
  Díktaean cave 118–19, 176
  Ídaean cave 167, 179
  Ilíthia cave 177
  Ínatos 177
  Kamáres cave 167, 174–5, 176
  Melidóni cave 177
  Mílatos cave 177
  Mount Gioúchtas 176
  Profítas Ilías 176
  St John the Hermit, cave of 176
  Skotinó cave 177
  Souré 177
Chandrás *see* Khandrás
Chaniá 14, 195–215, 218
  accommodation 210, 277–8
  Agíi Anargyri 204
  Ágios Nikólaos 204
  airport 214
  Angelou Street 203
  arcade of St Mark 204
  Archaeological Museum 204, 206
  arsenali 202
  banks 214
  beaches 214
  breakwater 208
  buses 214
  car hire 214
  car parking 214
  Church of Three Martyrs (Trimartyre) 204
  city layout 214
  covered market 205
  eating out 211, 215, 283
  Evréika quarter 203
  ferries 214
  festival 214
  Fírkas Tower 203
  foreign newspapers and books 214
  Historical Museum 207
  history 197–9
  hospital 214
  Kastélli quarter 204
  Khalídon 203
  Kydoniá 204
  launderette 215
  lighthouse 208
  Maritime Museum 206–7
  Mosque of the Janissaries 202
  nightlife 213
  Odós Skridlóf 203
  outskirts 209
  Plateía 1821 204
  Plateía 1897 205
  police 215
  post offices 215
  practical points 214–15
  public gardens 205, 214
  Renieri gate 203
  Roman Catholic church 215
  San Rocco 204
  Santriváni Square 202
  Schiavo-Lando Bastion 203
  shopping 212
  Splántzia quarter 204
  swimming pool 215
  taxis 215
  telephones 215
  Theotokopoúlou Street 203
  Topanás quarter 203
  tour operators 215
  tourist information 215
  Turkish bath 204
  Venetian archive 204
  Venetian city walls 204
  Venetian harbour 202, 203
  Venetian loggia 203
  walks 200–1, 208
  Zambelioú Street 203
Chrysoskalítissas *see* Hrissoskalítissas 228
Church of 99 Martyrs 244
Church of Trimartyre 204
churches: keyholders 128
climate and seasons 11, 258
coastline 11
consulates 266
conversion charts 269
crafts
  frescoes and icons 129
  haversacks 168
  needlework 119
  potteries 104, 178
credit cards 259
Cretan Runner, The 170, 228, 235
crime 266
currency 259
customs regulations 257

Dáfni 156
Daliánis, Hatzomocháli 56, 173
Damaskinós, Mikhaíl 62, 63, 190–1
Damásta 187
dance, traditional 161
Daskaloyiánnis, Ioánnis 57, 173

Díktaean cave 118–19, 176
Díkti Mountains 10, 110, 120–1
Diá 149
disabilities, visitors with 269
Donkey Island 149
Doxaroú 187
Dragonáda 149
dress, traditional 41, 110, 146, 161, 198
Drís 253
drives
  coast road (Tsoútsouros to Arví) 126–7
  Gulf of Mirampéllou (Ágios Nikólaos to Siteía) 162–3
  Réthymno to Irakleío 186–7
  Sfakiá to Chaniá 240–1
  Thryptís, Ornó and Siteía Mountains 156
  west coast and mountains 252–3
  western Asteroúsia Mountains 100–1
driving in Crete
  accidents 266
  breakdowns 261
  car hire 70, 102, 260–1
  car horn, use of 103
  documents 257
  maps 102
  petrol and diesel 261
  road signs 103
  rules of the road 102–3
  tips 102–3, 219, 252, 261
Dunbabin, Tom 235

E

Easter 16–17
El Greco 57, 61, 62, 172, 190–1
Elafonísi 223
Elássa 149
electricity 269
Elirós 251
Élos 17, 223
Eloúnta 122
  accommodation 275
emergencies 266–7
emergency telephone numbers 266
entry regulations 257
EOT (Greek Tourist Organisation) offices 10, 272
Epáno Episkopí 143
Episkopí 152
Erimoúpolis (Itanos) 143, 146
erosion 97
Erotókritos (epic poem) 34, 62, 161
etiquette and local customs 269–70
Evans, Sir Arthur 26, 27, 75, 92, 158
Éxo Moulianá 163

F

Faistós 82–3
Faistós Disc 83
Falásarna 226
Faneroménis Monastery 143, 162–3, 246
ferry services 254, 256–7, 263
festivals and celebrations
  Easter 16, 17
  national festivals 17, 258–9
  religious festivals 16–17
  town festivals 17
Fielding, Xan 235
Finikiá 235
fireworks 171
flora and fauna
  astivítha 11
  birdlife 96–97
  cats 122
  cicadas 74
  date palm 155
  dittany 96–7, 121
  Eleanora's falcon 149
  ibex 96, 97
  pelican 96
  tamarisk 112
  trees 117
  wild flowers 96, 227
  wild herbs 120, 121
Floriá 253
Fódele 172
Foinix 237
food and drink
  beer 85
  bread 94
  cheeses 63
  coffee 214
  Cretan sausages 239
  drinking water 267
  fruit juice 242
  lamb casserole 112
  mézedes (nibbles) 143
  olives 76–7
  oúzo 85
  picnics 75, 94
  rakí 84, 85
  restaurants 211, 278–83
  souvláki 95
  sweet pastries 37
  tirópitta (savoury pastries) 67
  water 84
  wine 84–5
footpaths 21, 111, 121
Fourfourás 193
Fournoú Korifí 133
Fragkokástelo 173
frescoes 129

G

Gavdopoúla 224
Gávdos 224–5
  Ámpelos 224
  Kastrí 224
  Sarakíniko 224
  Tripití 224
  Vatsianá 224
George, Prince of Greece 178, 209
Georgióupoli 178
  accommodation 277
  eating out 282–3
Gerakári 169
German War Cemetery 239
Giamalákis, Dr 158
Gianisáda 149
Gonías Monastery 226, 247
Gortýs 13, 86–7
Goúdouras 156
Gourniá 122–3
Gouvernétou Monastery 221
Gramvoúsa 218
Gramvoúsa Peninsula 218, 227
Greek Mountaineering Club 71
green tourism 21
Gulf of Almiróu 178
Gulf of Kissámou 227
Gulf of Mirampéllou 162–3

H

haggling 204
Hal Gorge *see* Valley of the Dead
Halbherr, Federico 27, 158
Hawes, Harriet Boyd 123
health advice
  drinking water 267
  insect pests 267
  medical treatment 267
  pharmacies 267
  sunburn 267
  vaccinations 267
historic sites 12–13, 79, 131
Historical Museum (Irakleío) 61
Historical Museum (Chaniá) 207
history of Crete 24–41
  armed resistance 170
  Byzantine occupation 13, 33–4
  catastrophe (1450 BC) and decline 31
  Greeks and Romans 32
  Mycenaeans and Dorians 12–13, 32
  myth and legend 24–5
  pre-Minoans and Minoans 26–31
  Saracen invasion 33
  Turkish rule 13, 36–7
  union with Greece 37
  Venetian rule 34–5
  World War II and after 38–41, 229
Hogarth, David 158
Hopkins, Adam 16
Hóra (Chóra) Sfakía 228, 229
hospitality 22
hospitals 267
Hrissoskalítissas Monastery 228

I

icons 129
Ída Mountains 10, 166–7, 192–3
Ídaean cave 167, 179
Ierápetra 140, 144–5
  accommodation 276
  Archaeological Museum 145
  castle 145
  eating out 281
  market 145
  Turkish quarter 145
  walk 145
Ilíthia cave 177
Iméri Gramvoúsa 224, 225
Ímpros 230, 240
Ímpros Gorge 231, 240
Ínatos 177
Independence Day 17
Irakleío 42–71
  accommodation 66, 274
  airport 70
  Archaeological Museum 48–51
  Arsenali 60
  Agía Aikaterínis of Siniates 62
  Ágios Demétrios 53
  Ágios Minás62
  Ágios Minás (church) 62
  Ágios Títos 55, 58–9
  banks 70
  Basilica of St Mark 55
  Bembo fountain 63
  bicycle hire 70
  bus stations 70, 262
  car hire 70
  car parking 70
  City Hall 55
  consulates 70
  eating out 67, 279–80
  El Greco Park 55
  ferries 70
  festival 70
  foreign newspapers 70
  Fotíou Theodosáki 63
  fountains 61, 63
  gardens 70–1
  harbour 59
  Historical Museum 61
  history 46–7
  hospitals 71
  launderette 71
  Lion Square 54–5
  Market Street 63, 68
  Morosini fountain 55
  Museum of Icons and Sacred Objects 62
  nightlife 69
  Odós 1866 63, 68
  Odós 25 Avgoústou 59
  Plateía Aikaterínis 62
  Plateía Elefthérias 54
  Plateía Kornárou 62
  Plateía Venizélou 54–5
  police 71
  post offices 71
  practical points 70–1
  Priuli fountain 61
  Roman Catholic church 71
  shopping 68
  statues and memorials 56–7
  taxis 71
  telephones 71
  toilets 71
  tour operators 71
  tourist information 45, 71
  Venetain loggia 55
  Venetian city walls 65
  Venetian fort 59–60
  walks 52–3, 65
irrigation channels 99
islands *see* offshore islands
Ístro 162
Ítanos 143, 146

K

Kádros 230
kafeníon 233
Kakodíki 230
Kalamáki 209
Kalamávka 124
Kalamiós 250
Katáthas 209

kalderími (footpaths) 121
Kalivianí 227, 283
Kaloí Liménes 100, 280
Kalýves 278
Kamáres 175, 193
Kamáres cave 167, 174–5, 176
Kámbos 252–3
Kandanóleon 56
Kándanos 232–3
Kapetanianá 89, 106
  eating out 280
Kápsa Monastery 156
Kardáki 169
Karé ravine 241
Káres 233, 241
Kastélli Kissámou 233
  accommodation 278
  eating out 283
Kastrí 224
Katánou 232
Katharó Plateau 110, 121, 124
Katholikó Monastery 221, 247
Káto Episkopí 156
Káto Flório 253
Kató Chório 276
Káto Préveli 180, 247
Káto Rodákino 188
Káto Zákros 141, 146, 153
  eating out 282
Kaválloi 149
Kavoúsi 146, 163
Kazantzákis, Níkos 18, 19, 47, 57, 93, 188
Kédros Mountains 167
Kefáli 234–5, 252–3
Keramotí 252–3
Keratókampos 124
  accommodation 275
  eating out 280
Khainides (resistance movement) 137, 224
Khalépa 209
Khamézi Middle Minoan House 12, 163
Khandras 141, 146–7
  eating out 281
Khóra Sfakíon *see* Sfakiá
Khrisí 149
Khrisoniyí 156
Khrisoskalítissas *see* Hrissoskalítissas
Khrysólakkos 132
Kitroplatía 114
Knosós 26, 90–3
Kolimbári 278
Kolokithía islets 149
Kotsifoú Gorge 166
Koudoumá Monastery 89, 107, 247
Koufounísi 149
Kouloúkonas Mountains 187
Koutsounári 156
  accommodation 276
Kreipe, General Heinrich 169, 188, 193
Kritsá 128
  accommodation 275–6
  Ágios Pnevma 128
  eating out 280–1
  Pangyía Kerá 128
Krótos 101
Kydoniá 204

L

Lake Voulisméni 115
Lákkoi 235
landscape 10–11
language
  Cretan surnames 183
  essential words and phrases 265
  Káto/Áno (lower/upper) 141
  Linear A and Linear B scripts 49, 148
Lasíthiou plateau 110, 125, 130–1
Lasíthiou River 120, 124
Lástros 163
Lató 131
Lear, Edward 167
Leigh Fermor, Patrick 40, 121, 193, 235
Léndas 94–5, 101
leper colony 136–7
Lefká Óri 10, 219, 236–7
Limín Khersonísos 274–5, 280
Límnes 281
Lisós 237, 251
long-distance path 21
lottery 196
Loúkia 106
Loutrá 186
Loutró 235
  accommodation 278
  eating out 283
lowlands 11

M

Makrígialós 147
Maláxa 238
  eating out 283
Máleme 238–9
  accommodation 278
Málía 131–3
  accommodation 276
maps 102
  see also Contents
Márathos 187
Margarítes 178
Maritime Museum 206–7
Martzaná 187
Mátala 95
  accommodation 275
media 264
medical treatment 267
Melidóni cave 177
Méronas 169
Mesará plain 75, 98, 99
Metamórphosis tou Sotírou 235
Mikhaíl Arkhángelos 230
Mikhális Arkhángelis 106
Mílatos cave 177
Mirsíni 163
Mírthios 282
Mírtos 133
Mírtos Pyryos 133
Moíres 14, 99
  accommodation 275
Móchlos 148
  accommodation 276
monasteries 246–7
  Agía Triáda 220, 246
  Ágios Nikólaos 191
  Arkádi 171–2, 246
  Árvi 127, 246
  Asomáton 169
  Faneroménis 143, 162–3, 246
  Gonías 226, 247
  Gouvernétou 221
  Hrissoskalítissas 228, 247
  Kápsa 156, 246–7
  Katholikó 221, 247
  Káto Préveli 180, 247
  Koudoumá 89, 107, 247
  Préveli 180–1, 246
  Savvathanon 189
  Toploú 143, 154–5, 246
  Varsamónero 190–1
  Vidianís 247
  Vrontísiou 191, 246
Monastiráki 169
Monastiráki Gorge 140–1, 152
money
  banks 259, 270
  credit cards 259
  currency 259
Moróní 88
Mosque of the Janissaries 202
Mosque of Kara Pasha 185
Mosque of Nerantziés 185
motorcycle hire 102, 262
Mount Aféndis Stavroménos 163
Mount Díkti 120
Mount Gíyilos 249
Mount Keratό 126–7
Mount Kófinas 89, 106, 107
Mount Páchnes 219, 237
Mount Psiloreítis 167
Mount Gioúchtas 79, 176
mountain ranges 10–11
  Asteróusia Mountains 74, 75, 89, 100–1
  Díkti Mountains 10, 110, 120–1
  Ída Mountains (Psiloreítis) 10, 166–7, 192–3
  Kédros Mountains 167
  Kouloúkonas Mountains 187
  Levka Óri (White Mountains) 10, 219, 236–7
  Ornó Mountains 156
  Siteía Mountains 10, 141, 156
  Thryptís Mountains 10, 140–1, 152, 156
Moutzákis, Ioánnis 104
Müller, General 188
Museum of History and Folk Art 184
music, traditional 160–1, 209
myth and legend 24–5
  Amaltheia 25
  Daedalus and Icarus 24, 25
  Heracles 60
  Kronos 24, 119, 179
  Minos 24–5, 25
  Theseus and the Minotaur 24–5
  Zeus 24, 25, 86, 119, 176, 179

N

narghiles (hubblebubble pipes) 36
national holidays 258–9
Nativity of the Virgin, Church of 230
NATO naval and military base 154
Néa Chóra 209
Néapoli 134
  accommodation 276
needlework 119
Néos Mírtos 133
newspapers 264
Nída Plateau 167, 178–9, 193
Nísos Soúda 251
nude bathing 266

offshore islands
  Agioi Theódoroi 225
  Agría Gramvoúsa 225
  Dragonáda 149
  Diá 149
  Elássa 149
  Gavdopoúla 224
  Gávdos 224–5
  Gianisádha 149
  Iméri Gramvoúsa 224, 225
  Kaválloi 149
  Kolokithía islets 149
  Koufounísi 149
  Móchlos 148
  Nísos Soúda 251
  Pándes 149
  Paximádha 149
  Paximádia 224
  Petálida 225
  Pseíra 149
  Spinalógka 136–7
  White Islands 225
  Yaidouronísi (Chrýsi/Donkey Island) 149
Óhi (No Day) 17
Oloús 122
Omalós plain 239
opening times 270
Oríno 156
Ornó Mountains 156
Orthodox Academy of Crete 226
Orthodox Church 13, 16, 140
Óssia María 249

P

Pachiá Ámmos 163
Palaikastro 276, 281
Palaiókapas, Konstantínos 226
Palaiochóra 242–3
  accommodation 278
  eating out 283
Panagía Akrotirianí 155
Panagía (Anisaráki) 222
Panagía (Epáno Episkopí) 143
Panagía (Kapetanianá) 89, 106
Panagía Kerá 128
Panagía (Méronas) 169
Panagía Rouméli 223
Panagía (Savvathanon Monastery) 189
Panagía (Sklavopoúla) 250
Panagía (Thrónos) 168
Pándes 149
Pánormo 277
Papadakis, Manassis 181
Papadogiánnis 101
Paraspóri 156
passports and visas 257
Paterákis, Antoni 39

Paterákis, Costis 39
Paterákis, Manólis 39, 193, 238, 239
Paximádha 149
Paximádia 224
people and culture
  Cretan character 10, 18–19, 22
  Cretan heroes 56–7
  etiquette and local customs 269–70
  festivals and celebrations 16–17
  hospitality 22
  mourning rituals 124
  music and dance 160–1
  Orthodox Church 13, 16, 140
  Sfakiots 219, 223, 236, 237
  town life 14
  traditional dress 41, 110, 146, 161, 198
  village life 15, 40–1, 135
Pérama 14, 186–7
Perkins, Sgt Dudley (Captain Vasilí) 235
Petálidha 225
Petrás 150
Petrés 241
pharmacies 267
Phílargos, Pétros 134
philoxénia (hospitality) 22
Phokás, Nikephóros 57
photography 270
Piskokéfalo 156
Píso Préveli 181
píthoi 104
Piyaidhákia 100
places of worship 270
Pláka 134
  eating out 281
Plakiás 277
Plátanias 186
Platanías 209
  eating out 283
Plátanos 243, 252
Plateía Perámata 100
Pláton, Nikólaos 158
Ploutí 88
Poikilássos 237
police 266
Polirrínia 244
politics 18, 19
Pómbia 100
post offices 264–5, 270
potteries 104, 178
Praisós 148
Preveläkis, Pandelís 182
Préveli Monastery 180–1, 246
Prodrómi 237
Profítas Ilías 176
Psiloreítis 10, 166–7, 192–3
Pseíra 149
Psychoundákis, George 38, 40, 170, 239
Psychró 125
public transport
  buses and coaches 261–2
  domestic flights 262
  ferry services 254, 256–7, 263
  taxis 263

R

religious festivals 16–17
Renault, Mary 25
Rendel, Sandy 235
Réthymno 14, 166, 182–3
  accommodation 277
  Archaeological Museum 184
  eating out 282
  Ethníkos Antistáseos 185
  Fortétza 184
  history 182–3
  Kostís Giampoudákis statue 185
  Loggia 184
  Mosque of Kara Pasha 185
  Mosque of Nerantziés 185
  Museum of History and Folk Art 184
  Plateía Petiháki 184
  public gardens 185
  Rimondi fountain 184
  Venetian harbour 184
  walk 184–5
  Wine Festival 183
River Anapodáris 126
River Geropótamos 187
road system 11
roadside shrines 102
Rodákino 188
Rodiá 188–9
Rodopoú 245
Rodopoú Peninsula 218, 245

S

sailing to Crete 256–7
St John 221
St Paul 32, 100, 235
St Titus 32, 58, 86
Samariá 249
Samariá Gorge 219, 248–9
San Rocco 204
Sarakíniko 224
Savvathanon Monastery 189
self-catering holidays 268
Selínou 218–19, 232
Selliá 167
Sfáka 163
Sfakiá 219, 228, 229
  accommodation 278
Sfakiots 219, 223, 236, 237
Sfinári 252
shepherds' gates 110
shepherds' sticks 237
shops (opening hours) 270
Síderos Peninsula 141, 154
Sítanos 156
Siteía 140, 150–1
  accommodation 276
  Archaeological Museum 151
  eating out 281
  fort 151
  graveyard 151
  Old Sitiá 151
  Plateía Venizélou 151
  Sultana Festival 17
  walk 151
  waterfront 151
Siteía Mountains 10, 141, 156
Schinokápsala 156
Sklavopoúla 250
Skotinó cave 177
Skoúlas, Alkibíades 169
Smith-Hughes, Jack 235
solo travellers 271
Sotíros Khristós (Loutró) 235
Sotíros Khristós (Sklavopoúla) 250
Soúda Bay 225, 250
Soúgia 236, 251
  accommodation 278
Souré 177
Spíli 190
  accommodation 277
Spinalógka Island 136–7
Spinalógka Peninsula 122, 136
Stavrochóri 156
Stávros 209, 220
Stróumboulas 187
Strovlés 253
student and youth travel 263

T

taxímata (votive plaques) 143
taxis 263
telephone offices 270
telephones 265
television and radio 264
Tértsa 134
  eating out 281
Theotokópoulos, Doménico *see* El Greco
Thrapsanó 104
Thrónos 168
Thryptí 152
  eating out 281
Thryptís Mountains 10, 140–1, 152, 156
Tigáni Bay 227
time differences 259
Tímios Stavrós 193
tipping 270
toilets 270–1
topless sunbathing 20, 271
Tóplou Monastery 143, 154–5, 246
tourism 20–1
tourist information offices 10, 270, 272
Tourlotí 163
town life 14
travel insurance 257
travelling to Crete
  by air 256
  by car 257
  by sea 256–7
  by train and coach 257
Tripití 224
Tsoútsouros 104–5
  accommodation 275
Tympáki 99
  eating out 280
Tzermiádo 125, 130
  accommodation 276
  eating out 281

V

vaccinations 267
Vagioniá 106
Vái 141, 155
Valley of the Dead 153, 159
Varsamónero Monastery 190–1
Vasilikí 101
Vathýpetro 105
Vatsianá 224
Venizélos, Elefthérios 56–7, 199, 209, 220
Vidhianís 247
village life 15, 40–1, 135
Voilá 147
volta (evening perambulation) 69, 213
Voríza 167, 190
Vóroi 280
Voukoliés 253
Voutás 250
Vrontísiou Monastery 191, 246
Vrýses 169, 241, 283

W

walking 71
walks
  Ampeloúsos to Zarós 88
  Episkopí to Thryptí and back 152
  Ímpros Gorge 231
  Kamáres cave 174–5
  Kapetanianá to Mount Kófinas 106–7
  Lasíthiou Plateau 125
  Rodopoú Peninsula 245
  Samariá Gorge 248–9
  Valley of the Dead (Áno Zákros to Káto Zákros) 153
  see also towns and cities
Waugh, Evelyn 229
waymarks 111
White Islands 225
White Mountains 10, 219, 236–7
windmills 130, 154
women travellers 271
worry beads 147

Xerókampos 141, 155
  accommodation 276
  eating out 282

Yaidouronísi 149
Yeoryióupoli *see* Georgióupoli
Yerondoyiánnis 156
Yiampoudákis, Kostis 171, 172, 185
Yiánnaris, Khátzi Mihális 239
youth hostels 263, 268

Z

Zákros 26, 158–9
  accommodation 277
Zarós 88
  accommodation 275
Zíros 141, 156
Zorba the Greek 220

Acknowledgements

The Automobile Association would like to thank Cháris Kakoulákis for his assistance in the preparation of this book.

Picture credits

The Automobile Association would like to thank the following photographers, libraries and associations for their assistance in the preparation of this book.
MARY EVANS PICTURE LIBRARY 24a Icarus, 27 Palace of Knosós, Queen's Megaron,
33c Constantine the Great
T HARRIS 16b preparing lamb
HISTORY MUSEUM CRETE 36b Turkish attack on Candia, 60 *Deposition*
GETTY IMAGES 229a German invasion of Crete, 229b Battle of Crete
MUSEUM OF IRAKLEÍO 26a goddess with a sacred knot (*La Parisienne*) fresco from Knosós,
26b snake goddess from Knosós, 30/1 mosaic, 48 the dolphin fresco from Knosós, 81b harvester vase, 93 ladies in blue fresco from Knosós, 82 the Faistós disc, 133a Mália gold ornaments
NATURE PHOTOGRAPHERS LTD 96b golden eagle (W S Paton), 227a flowery meadow, Kanenós
(E A Jones), 227b eastern yellow bee orchid (P Sterry)
M REBANE 17 decorated church
SPECTRUM COLOUR LIBRARY 29 vase, Irakleío Museum, 73 Knosós, 151 Sitiá
TIME & LIFE PICTURES/GETTY IMAGES 24b Theseus and the Minotaur, 25 Daedalus and Icarus

The remaining photographs are held in the Association's own photo library (AA PHOTO LIBRARY) and were taken by KEN PATERSON with the exception of the photographs on pages 5a, 8, 9, 23, 56a and 265, which were taken by P ENTICKNAP, 239t which was taken by N HICKS, and those on pages 40/1, 41, 56b, 74, 108/9, 114, 122, 130, 166b, 167, 184a, 184b, 197b, 199, 201b, 207a, which were taken by W VOYSEY.

Contributors

Revision edit and design: Bookwork Creative Associates **Original copy editor**: Hilary Hughes
Revision verifier: Lindsay Bennett